WEST ACADEMIC PUBLISHING'S EMERITUS ADVISORY BOARD

JESSE H. CHOPER
Professor of Law and Dean Emeritus
University of California, Berkeley

YALE KAMISAR
Professor of Law Emeritus, University of San Diego
Professor of Law Emeritus, University of Michigan

MARY KAY KANE
Late Professor of Law, Chancellor and Dean Emeritus
University of California, Hastings College of the Law

LARRY D. KRAMER
President, William and Flora Hewlett Foundation

JAMES J. WHITE
Robert A. Sullivan Emeritus Professor of Law
University of Michigan

AF732354

WEST ACADEMIC PUBLISHING'S LAW SCHOOL ADVISORY BOARD

MARK C. ALEXANDER
Arthur J. Kania Dean and Professor of Law
Villanova University Charles Widger School of Law

JOSHUA DRESSLER
Distinguished University Professor Emeritus
Michael E. Moritz College of Law, The Ohio State University

MEREDITH J. DUNCAN
Professor of Law
University of Houston Law Center

RENÉE McDONALD HUTCHINS
Dean and Joseph L. Rauh, Jr. Chair of Public Interest Law
University of the District of Columbia David A. Clarke School of Law

RENEE KNAKE JEFFERSON
Joanne and Larry Doherty Chair in Legal Ethics &
Professor of Law, University of Houston Law Center

ORIN S. KERR
William G. Simon Professor of Law
University of California, Berkeley

JONATHAN R. MACEY
Professor of Law,
Yale Law School

DEBORAH JONES MERRITT
Distinguished University Professor,
John Deaver Drinko/Baker & Hostetler Chair in Law Emerita
Michael E. Moritz College of Law, The Ohio State University

ARTHUR R. MILLER
University Professor and Chief Justice Warren E. Burger Professor of
Constitutional Law and the Courts, New York University

GRANT S. NELSON
Professor of Law Emeritus, Pepperdine University
Professor of Law Emeritus, University of California, Los Angeles

A. BENJAMIN SPENCER
Dean & Chancellor Professor of Law
William & Mary Law School

MARIJUANA LAW
IN A NUTSHELL®

SECOND EDITION

MARK K. OSBECK
Clinical Professor of Law
The University of Michigan Law School

HOWARD BROMBERG
Clinical Professor of Law
The University of Michigan Law School

WEST
ACADEMIC
PUBLISHING

The publisher is not engaged in rendering legal or other professional advice, and this publication is not a substitute for the advice of an attorney. If you require legal or other expert advice, you should seek the services of a competent attorney or other professional.

Nutshell Series, In a Nutshell and the Nutshell Logo are trademarks registered in the U.S. Patent and Trademark Office.

© 2017 LEG, Inc. d/b/a West Academic
© 2022 LEG, Inc. d/b/a West Academic
444 Cedar Street, Suite 700
St. Paul, MN 55101
1-877-888-1330

West, West Academic Publishing, and West Academic are trademarks of West Publishing Corporation, used under license.

Printed in the United States of America

ISBN: 978-1-64708-259-8

To Andy and Franklin, for their support.

—*Howard*

To my father, Ken, for leading the way.

—*Mark*

PREFACE

This is the Second Edition of our Nutshell on marijuana law in the United States. Given the rapid changes in marijuana law since publication of the First Edition in 2017, we have updated every chapter and expanded most. Reflecting the federal legalization of hemp in 2018, and the increasing popularity of Cannabidiol (CBD), we added a chapter to cover these topics. Given that criminal prosecution of marijuana remains ongoing in most states, we expanded the chapter dealing with criminal law. Specifically, the chapter goes into greater depth in the role marijuana activity plays in developing doctrine in search and seizure, constructive possession, and sentencing. We also expanded the chapters dealing with civil law issues, including the chapter on miscellaneous civil issues, which now includes a section on marijuana and trademark law.

Our public policy chapters incorporate empirical evidence gleaned from the recent experience of legalizing states. The medical pro and con arguments chapter benefits from the 2017 publication of the National Academies of Sciences, Engineering, and Medicine meta-report, *The Health Effects of Cannabis and Cannabinoids: The Current State of Evidence and Recommendations for Research*. The international law chapters are updated with the quickening changes in marijuana law throughout the world, including the U.N. Commission on Narcotic Drugs vote to reclassify cannabis in 2020. And the chapter on marijuana and other drugs has been expanded to consider the recent movement toward decriminalization of certain hallucinogenic drugs such as Mescaline and Psilocybin.

We have also increased coverage of the topic of social justice and marijuana law to reflect that a number of states are not only legalizing marijuana but compensating for the harsh treatment accorded marijuana users for decades. And in the Looking Forward chapter, we assess the numerous bills being proposed to align federal laws with the fact of marijuana legalization in the states.

Finally, we have added for this edition an appendix, "Legality of Marijuana by United States Jurisdiction," which charts medical, adult recreational, and CBD legality by federal and state jurisdiction.

Since 1996, when California became the first state to legalize marijuana for medical use, the marijuana legalization movement has increasingly gained momentum. More than two thirds of the states in the United States, as well as the District of Columbia, now have legal medical marijuana. Eighteen states, plus the District of Columbia, comprising more than a third of the U.S. population, now have recreational marijuana. These states have pioneered laws to regulate, monitor, and tax marijuana consumption, and they have done so against a framework of federal laws that classify marijuana activity as illegal and subject to criminal sanctions. Congress, the executive branch, and federal and state courts continue to wrestle with the practical complexities of this evolving area of law, while legal scholars and students wrestle with the nuanced theoretical questions that are raised.

Across the 50 states the status of marijuana varies from strictly prohibited, to authorized for medical purposes, to fully legal, subject only to the kinds of restrictions imposed on substances like tobacco and alcohol. Meanwhile, Congress is giving serious consideration to making marijuana legal at the federal level, even as federal law-enforcement agencies continue to treat it as a dangerous illegal substance. Given such disparate treatment, it is not surprising that marijuana law has unique and fascinating legal characteristics.

This Nutshell covers the wide range of U.S. laws affecting marijuana. There is no creative re-packaging of marijuana issues. We organize our topics according to the basic divisions of marijuana law. This involves primarily accounting for the differences between federal and state law, and for the diversity among the 50 states themselves. The federal law of marijuana is largely shaped by its inclusion in the most restrictive schedule (Schedule I) of the 1970 Controlled Substances Act (abbreviated throughout the book as the "CSA"). For the states, we focus on issues raised by its legalization for medical and recreational purposes, noting peculiarities of one or other state where necessary.

U.S. marijuana law is also shaped at a global and local level. The United States is signatory to international treaties that curtail marijuana use. The United Nations estimates 192 million persons use marijuana worldwide; thus we review the experience of foreign nations as well. And municipalities are shaping their own marijuana law, raising questions as to how far local ordinances can conflict with state law. The law of marijuana as it relates to Native Americans is also of importance, both for the sovereign status of Indian tribes and because of initial forays into cultivation of marijuana and hemp on Indian reservations.

In addition to these jurisdictional questions that divide marijuana law, the subject is also organized around its illegal or legal status. Where marijuana is illegal, marijuana law is primarily a subset of criminal law and procedure. Accordingly, we focus on the criminal law of marijuana in two ways: first, by examining the range of its prohibitions and penalties, and second, by looking at how the unique characteristics of marijuana law shape our criminal jurisprudence in such areas as Fourth Amendment search and seizure. Where marijuana is legal, marijuana law is largely a subset of the law of regulated substances, but with special characteristics. For example, marijuana businesses must account for federal regulations affecting their dealings with banks, bankruptcy courts, the Internal Revenue Service, and employees. States must calibrate new rules to cover issues such as excise and sales taxes on marijuana, parental custody for medical marijuana users, and driving while marijuana-impaired. Lawyers must take into account canons of professional responsibility against advising illegal businesses.

Given this wide range of issues, marijuana law is an ideal topic for understanding the unique characteristics of American law and legal institutions. All branches of government make their presence felt in marijuana law, often at odds with each other. We include for further investigation citations to the important marijuana-related constitutional provisions, court cases, statutes, amendments, and regulations promulgated by federal and state agencies.

In preparing the Second Edition of this Nutshell, we feel a certain kinship with the legendary painters of the Golden Gate Bridge, who no sooner reaching the end of the bridge, return to the beginning to start a new coat of paint. When we finish updating our final chapters, we have to return to our first chapters to start the process over again in this rapidly evolving area of U.S. law. Nevertheless we endeavored to make this Second Edition current as of late 2021.

We would like to acknowledge the assistance of our former students and now colleagues in the legal profession—Reid Murdoch and Elizabeth Bundy—who provided invaluable assistance with the First Edition. For this Second Edition, we would like to acknowledge the excellent research assistance of Hannah Paton, Elizabeth McElvein, Keith Ketola, and Bogyung Lim.

HOWARD BROMBERG
MARK K. OSBECK

November 2021

OUTLINE

TABLE OF CASES

References are to Pages

MARIJUANA LAW
IN A NUTSHELL®
SECOND EDITION

PART 1

BACKGROUND

CHAPTER 1

OVERVIEW—MARIJUANA REGULATION IN THE UNITED STATES

§ 1-1 INTRODUCTION

We believe that marijuana law is one of the most interesting, diverse, and dynamic areas of legal study. Yet as a legal discipline, marijuana law is a quite recent phenomenon. Only in the past five to ten years have legal scholars begun to think of it as an independent field of law, worthy of study in its own right. Prior to that, marijuana law was principally associated with criminal law, and grouped within the category of drug crimes generally.

To look at marijuana law in this narrow way, however, is to ignore a host of interesting and important legal issues that arise with respect to marijuana regulation. These issues arise primarily as a result of the discrepancy between federal law, which has long outlawed the possession and use of marijuana, and state laws (beginning with California in 1996) that authorize its use for medical and/or adult "recreational" purposes. This discrepancy, and related discrepancies between states and localities, and between U.S. law and international law, give rise to several significant theoretical and constitutional issues, as well as a number of practical issues confronting individuals and businesses in legalization states that seek to exercise their rights under state law.

In this chapter, we discuss the parameters of marijuana law and provide an overview of the various issues that arise under it. Accordingly, § 1–2 provides a brief description of what "marijuana law" includes and discusses why it is an important area of law. And § 1–3 provides a bird's-eye view of the types of legal issues that are currently being worked out by Congress, state legislatures, and the courts in connection with marijuana regulation.

§ 1–2 WHAT IS MARIJUANA LAW AND WHY DOES IT MATTER?

When people think of "marijuana law," they tend to think of criminal laws regulating the use, possession, and distribution of cannabis.[1] And those laws certainly raise a number of important and interesting issues. But there is actually much more to marijuana law than just those criminal issues. In fact, marijuana law is one of the more far-reaching of legal topics because it necessarily implicates a variety of different areas of law.

One of the principal reasons for this is that legal controversies have arisen between the various levels

---

[1] There are traditionally some subtle differences between the meanings of the terms "marijuana" and "cannabis" (*see* Chapter 2), although, for the most part, people have tended to use the two terms interchangeably in the past. We are aware that some people now consider "marijuana" to be an offensive term, given its racially charged historical use, and we are sympathetic to that position. Nevertheless, we generally continue to use the word "marijuana" in this book when discussing the law because that is the word (sometimes spelled "marihuana") that legal sources in the United States have consistently used, and we wish to track those sources for the sake of clarity.

of government in the United States, and these controversies raise difficult theoretical as well as practical issues. The most important of these controversies is the divergence between the federal Controlled Substances Act, which criminalizes marijuana across the board, and the laws of more than half of the individual states, which legalize marijuana for medical use, and sometimes also for recreational use. (As of the publication date, 36 states have legalized marijuana for medical use, and 18 of these states have also legalized it for adult recreational use.) This divergence, in particular, generates the lion's share of legal issues that have now come under the umbrella of marijuana law. But conflicts have also arisen between the laws of certain states and the laws of certain local governments within those states. And there is a growing concern internationally about the conflict between state laws legalizing marijuana and certain international treaty obligations of the United States that require it to criminalize marijuana possession and use. Each of these conflicts generates its own set of interesting issues.

At the theoretical/constitutional level, these issues include: (1) whether the federal government has a constitutional right to enforce federal laws within states with respect to the mere possession of marijuana, even if such possession results from an individual's own cultivation of marijuana plants; (2) whether federal law preempts state laws regulating marijuana, and if not, whether and to what extent state laws directly conflict with federal law; (3) whether the federal government has a right to force states to enforce federal laws regulating marijuana; and (4) whether the executive branch has an obligation to enforce federal criminal laws vigorously, versus taking a more hands-off approach and allowing the states to operate independently.

Related to these theoretical questions are a number of more practical issues concerning the competing legal demands that are placed on marijuana-related businesses, and to some extent, on individuals, in states that have legalized marijuana. Because of the conflict between federal and state law, marijuana-related business owners, such as dispensaries, have had to operate under a cloud of uncertainty regarding the law, which hinders their ability to operate under state laws legalizing marijuana use. For marijuana-related businesses, this uncertainty means that they cannot take advantage of many of the legal benefits ordinary businesses take for granted, and it also creates uncertainty with respect to certain employer/employee issues.

Marijuana law also includes practical administrative issues that states have had to deal with when they decide to legalize, in whole or in part, marijuana possession and use, such as how to reign in impaired driving caused by marijuana use, how to keep legal marijuana out of the hands of minors, and how best to regulate the number and location of marijuana-related businesses. Thus, the marijuana-law practitioner must be conversant with a variety of statutes, regulations, and ordinances that pertain to these types of matters, as well as administrative matters such as licensing requirements, taxes, reporting and recordkeeping requirements, etc.

Finally, marijuana regulation raises a number of important scientific, medical, and policy related issues, and a proper understanding of marijuana law must account for these considerations as well. A long-standing debate among those who favor liberalization of marijuana regulation, for example, has been whether it is better to decriminalize marijuana possession and use without actually legalizing it (e.g., by imposing a civil fine instead of a criminal sanction), or whether it is better to legalize and regulate marijuana. And if legalization is preferred, that raises another important issue as to the proper scope of such legalization. Should possession and use be allowed to all persons, or only to those who use marijuana for medical purposes pursuant to the authorization of a physician? Related to these types of debates are scientific questions such as whether marijuana is harmful, whether it is habit-forming, whether it is a "gateway" to more dangerous drugs, whether it has legitimate medical uses, etc. These issues, too, fall within the broad umbrella of marijuana law. And it is the interdependent nature of all of these different types of issues that creates the complex fabric of marijuana law as a legal discipline.

Over the past few years, marijuana law has become an important legal subject for several reasons. First, marijuana users are prevalent, estimated to comprise about 30 million Americans. The laws regulating its use in the United States, moreover, are diverse, complex, and often, as noted above, contradictory. Second, the law of marijuana touches many major areas of American law. It has important implications for criminal law, of course, but also for the law of federalism, criminal procedure, the constitutional structure of government, civil liberties, local law, federal Indian and tribal law, interstate commerce, international treaties, federal taxation, federal banking law, and so on. Third, it is currently the subject of an important political debate in the United States as to its consequences for criminal justice, social justice, public health, public policy, and public revenues. For all of these reasons, marijuana law has become an important legal discipline. And while many of the individual strands of marijuana law can certainly be studied piecemeal as parts of other legal disciplines, together they create an organic whole that can be fully appreciated only when they are studied together.

§ 1–3 A BIRD'S-EYE VIEW OF MARIJUANA LAW

Although, as discussed in Chapter 3, the history of marijuana regulation in the United States goes back about 150 years, the starting point for understanding contemporary marijuana law is 1970. For it was in 1970 that Congress enacted the Controlled Substances Act, or "CSA" which still governs federal law to this day. As discussed further in Chapter 5, the CSA categorized a wide variety of drugs into five "schedules" that correspond to various levels of regulation. It included marijuana on Schedule I, which applied to the most strictly regulated drugs—

those that were not allowed to be used legally, even for medical purposes.

It is against this background of largely unchanged federal law that marijuana law has arisen over the past several decades through the actions of various states and municipalities that have set out on their own paths. (The only significant change to the federal treatment of marijuana under the CSA took place in 2018, when Congress excluded hemp—defined as derivatives of the cannabis plant with 0.3% or less THC—from the CSA's definition of marijuana, thereby essentially legalizing hemp at the federal level, subject to various regulatory and licensing requirements.)

Early on, this involved the *decriminalization* of marijuana possession and use, meaning that possession and use were no longer regarded as criminal acts in certain states and municipalities, but were instead treated as mere civil violations, or, at worst, mere petty offenses with no possibility of jail time. Later, certain states began to go further, starting with California in 1996, by legalizing marijuana for medical use under certain circumstances. And still later, in 2012, some states began to legalize marijuana generally, allowing for so-called recreational use by adults. (Notwithstanding these legalization efforts, the unique characteristics of marijuana have continued to make an impact on criminal law—for example in the areas of search and seizure, and in the constructive possession of narcotics.)

This discrepancy between the approach of the federal government and the approaches of many state and local governments has created numerous challenging theoretical and practical issues related to marijuana regulation. On the theoretical side, the most immediate question that arose when the states began to branch out on their own was whether the federal government had the constitutional power to enforce federal law with respect to the private actions of citizens within the states and localities that had adopted more lenient laws. The Supreme Court answered that question in the affirmative in *Gonzales v. Raich*, 545 U.S. 1 (2005), where the Court held that the federal government's power under the Commerce Clause extended even to seemingly purely local conduct that could not enter into a legal stream of interstate commerce, such as growing marijuana plants for personal use.

The next, related question that arose was whether state and local governments were prohibited from legalization and decriminalization efforts altogether, either because federal law preempted the field under the Supremacy Clause of the Constitution, or because laws decriminalizing or legalizing marijuana directly conflicted with federal law. The Supreme Court has not yet spoken authoritatively on this topic, but the lower courts that have considered the issue tend to find that federal law does not preempt the field, and that decriminalizing marijuana, or even legalizing it, does not cause a direct conflict with federal law, because such laws do not require individuals to do that which is prohibited by federal law. Simply put, if state laws *required* or *facilitated* the use of marijuana, in violation of the Controlled Substances Act, they would be unconstitutional, but since they merely *allow* individuals to do so, they are not.

The third important theoretical question is whether the federal government can force the states to enact provisions similar to federal law or require them to enforce the federal Controlled Substances Act itself. Again, the Supreme Court has not ruled directly on this topic, but there are several related Supreme Court cases, referred to as the "anti-commandeering cases," that seem to establish quite clearly that the federal government does not have this type of power.

Finally, the question has arisen as to the duty of the executive branch to enforce the Controlled Substances Act vigorously, since the President and executive branch are charged with the enforcement of federal law. This question arose when the Obama administration basically took a hands-off approach to state legalization efforts, whereby the administration let the states know that it did not intend to shut down state medical or even recreational legalization schemes, so long as certain conditions were met. (Although the Trump administration technically rejected this hands-off approach to state legalization efforts, as a practical matter the administration essentially followed it, as has the Biden administration to date.) These conditions included such things as making sure marijuana-related businesses are in full compliance with state law, making sure that minors do not have access to marijuana, making sure that legal marijuana does not come from illegal sources, and so on. Whether this type of hands-off approach could theoretically constitute an abrogation of the executive branch's duty to enforce federal law is still an unresolved question.

Similar issues to these arise at the state/local level as well. Many municipalities, for example, have enacted laws decriminalizing marijuana possession and use, in states where such possession and use is still a significant crime under state law. This has created a variety of theoretical issues similar to those that arise in the federal/state context: e.g., (1) whether state law preempts the field, and whether local laws are in direct conflict with state law if they decriminalize possession and use; (2) whether local municipalities can refuse to allow marijuana use within their jurisdictions; and (3) whether municipalities have a right to require police officers and prosecutors within their jurisdictions to prosecute violators only under local laws decriminalizing possession and use, and not under harsher state laws.

At the other end of the spectrum, certain international treaty obligations of the United States arguably conflict with state legalization efforts. The United States is a signatory to several multinational agreements that require the criminalization of various drugs, including marijuana. To the extent the majority of states now legalize marijuana, at least with respect to medical use, there is a growing concern on the part of some commentators that the

United States is no longer in compliance with these treaty obligations.

In addition to these important theoretical issues that arise by virtue of the conflict between federal law, international, and state/local law, there are a number of more practical legal issues arising from the legalization efforts of the states. For example, the federal bankruptcy courts have thus far not allowed marijuana-related businesses in legalization states to avail themselves of the protections provided by the United States Bankruptcy Code. Likewise, the federal courts and the Internal Revenue Service have not allowed marijuana-related businesses to take federal tax deductions for business expenses, which makes operating a marijuana-related business an expensive endeavor. And the United States Patent and Trademark Office (USPTO) routinely rejects federal registration of trademarks for marijuana products due to their illegal status under federal law, thereby denying marijuana-related businesses the ability to protect their brands on a nationwide basis.

The difficulty in obtaining banking services is another area in which marijuana-related businesses have been disadvantaged. Traditionally, banks in legalization states have been very reluctant to deal with marijuana-related businesses because they fear they will be found liable under federal law for assisting criminal behavior. This has meant that marijuana-related businesses have generally had to operate on an all-cash basis, which makes such businesses more expensive to operate, and it also makes them more dangerous for employees and customers, due to the very real possibility of armed robberies. The Treasury Department has issued guidelines for banks to follow in dealing with marijuana-related businesses, indicating that it would not prosecute banks that complied with the guidelines. However, the reporting requirements imposed by the guidelines are stringent, and the expenses banks incur in their compliance efforts are passed on to the marijuana-related businesses, adding to the expense of running such businesses.

Similar types of problems also arise with respect to landlord-tenant issues and insurance issues, where, for various reasons, landlords and insurers have been reluctant to deal with marijuana-related businesses. Again, this adds to the expense and burden of operating marijuana-related businesses, making them less lucrative than one might expect.

State legalization efforts have also caused significant concern about the precise legal rights that may be created as a result of marijuana legalization. In particular, employers are concerned as to whether they continue to have the right to terminate employees who violate their drug policies and test positively for marijuana, which is still illegal under federal law. Likewise, in the child custody context, there are questions whether and to what extent medical and recreational marijuana laws affect custody determinations. Illegal drug use is traditionally a consideration affecting negatively the best-interests-of-the-child determination, but at the same time, medical marijuana statutes arguably give licensed users the right to use medical marijuana, even if they are parents.

Other practical issues have arisen as well in legalization states. For example, state legislatures in legalization states have been grappling with how to regulate impaired driving. Unlike alcohol, THC levels in the blood are not easily correlated with levels of impairment, meaning that the ability of police officers to test for impaired driving caused by marijuana is more difficult. As a result, different states have taken different approaches to testing, ranging from strict *per se* blood tests to purely observational determinations made by specially trained police personnel. Another issue that state and local authorities have been grappling with is zoning. They must decide where and how many marijuana-related businesses should be allowed to operate in a given area, and under what restrictions (e.g., not allowing such businesses within a certain distance of schools). They must also decide whether individual municipalities should be allowed to preclude marijuana-related businesses from operating within their jurisdictions if they so choose.

These are the types of issues that are discussed in the following chapters of this book. Marijuana law is a complicated subject area, and is also a rapidly changing area, adding to the challenge of mastering the field. It is, nevertheless, an important area of law because it directly affects the lives of millions of Americans. It is also, we think, a fascinating area of law because of the interrelated mix of theoretical and practical issues it generates. We hope that you will enjoy your journey into these issues as you work your way through the book.

CHAPTER 2

MARIJUANA

§ 2–1 INTRODUCTION

This chapter provides a basic primer on marijuana for those who are not especially conversant with the substance. Section 2–2 provides an overview and defines basic terms, § 2–3 discusses the psychogenic properties of marijuana, and the remaining two sections discuss the use of marijuana as both an intoxicant (§ 2–4) and a medicine (§ 2–5).

§ 2–2 BACKGROUND AND TERMINOLOGY

The word "marijuana" (sometimes spelled "marihuana") refers to an herbal substance made from the crushed leaves and flower buds of the *Cannabis sativa* plant. It is the world's most widely used illegal drug. The word "cannabis" is generally used as a synonym of marijuana, but is also used in a somewhat broader sense to refer to the whole cannabis plant. (There is some debate in the scientific community about whether there are actually three related *Cannabis* species, or whether these are just varieties of the same species.) The flower buds on a cannabis plant contain trichomes, which are tiny crystal-like glands that produce a sticky resin, which captures pollen to fertilize the plant. That resin contains the greatest concentration of tetrahydrocannabinol (or "THC") of any part of the cannabis plant. THC is the psychoactive compound in cannabis that is primarily responsible for its intoxicating effect.

The term "cannabinoids" refers to the various psychoactive compounds (the most important being THC) that are found in the *Cannabis* plant. Different cannabinoids have different effects, and they interact with each other in complex ways to alter the intoxicating effect of marijuana.

The term "marijuana" is principally used in North America. It was coined in Mexico, and Americans later adopted it from Mexican immigrants in the 19th century. In Europe and many other parts of the world, marijuana is referred to as "herbal cannabis." Of course, marijuana is also known by numerous slang terms in various parts of the world.

"Hemp" refers both to a low-THC variety of the cannabis plant itself, as well as to the fibers derived from its stalks and stems. These fibers have a long history of commercial use. Prior to the invention of nylon, hemp fiber was the principal source for rope. In addition, its fibers could be woven into a sturdy fabric, which was used for a variety of purposes, including sails for ships, tents, clothes, etc. Hemp fibers were also used to make paper. And hemp seed was used extensively as birdfeed at one time. Hemp is now being used again as a food supplement, and its rich oil is being used as a cooking oil, as well as an ingredient in body lotions.

Industrial-grade hemp is made from cannabis strains that have been bred over time to be taller and sturdier than strains of the plant used to produce marijuana. These strains are also significantly lower in THC than the cannabis plants used to produce marijuana, and thus they lack their intoxicating potential. Since Congress passes the Farm Bill of 2018, "hemp" is legally defined as cannabis that contains no more than .3% THC.

Cultivation of the hemp plant appears to have originated in the area of western China several thousand years ago. It spread out from there into other parts of Asia, including the subcontinent of India, where marijuana and hashish have been used since well before the beginning of the common era. By the 10th century, it was widely cultivated throughout large parts of the Islamic world as well.

It is not clear when exactly hemp was first introduced to Europe, but we know that it was widely cultivated there for its fiber during the Renaissance. It was then brought to the new world by early European colonists (probably first by the Spanish), who used its fiber extensively for various purposes. Hemp was also grown in the earliest English colonies in America (Jamestown and Plymouth), and a bit later it was grown as a commercial crop by some of our most important founding fathers, including George Washington and Thomas Jefferson. Eventually, hemp was cultivated commercially throughout large parts of the United States. Commercial production peaked around the mid-nineteenth century, centering in the area around Kentucky and in the Great Lakes states. After that time, production began to fall off due to commercial substitutes, and the hemp industry was largely shut down by the late 1930s, in part due to legal restrictions (*see* Chapter 3 below). Production was ramped up temporarily during World War II, however, because hemp had various military uses, such as rope production.

Prior to the latter part of the 19th century, it appears that the cannabis plant was not widely used in the United States to produce marijuana herb for use as an intoxicating drug. However, by the middle of the 19th century, as discussed below in § 2–5 of this chapter, marijuana began to be cultivated for medicinal purposes and added to certain patent medicines. It was in that way that marijuana first showed up on the legal radar screen.

§ 2–3 PSYCHOACTIVE PROPERTIES OF MARIJUANA

Until the 1960s, marijuana was generally classified as a "narcotic," which encompasses a group of drugs—most notably opioids, such as morphine and heroin—that depress the central nervous system, dulling the senses and inducing sleep. And it was believed to have similar potential for addiction as those drugs. In the 1960s, however, marijuana began to develop a much wider following, particularly among young people, and proponents began espousing the drug for its "consciousness expanding" properties. At that time it was thought of as a mild hallucinogen, without the potential for addiction that the opioids had.

Subsequent research, however, has shown that neither of these descriptions is entirely accurate. Marijuana has a fairly unique psychoactive profile. It is neither a true stimulant, nor a true depressant. And while it has some hallucinogenic properties, particularly at high doses, most of its users do not use it primarily for that effect, as would users of LSD, peyote, or psilocybin. Marijuana's active ingredients, its cannabinoids, have a complex effect, interacting with nerve receptors in a way that is different from these other types of drugs. Thus, it is probably best understood as being in its own separate category. In addition, the psychoactive effects also vary significantly, depending not only on the dose received, but also on the mix of cannabinoids within any particular sample of marijuana. And marijuana is in fact addicting (approximately 10% of regular users develop a physical dependence on the drug), though the withdrawal effects are relatively mild compared to the opioids.

As noted above, the principle psychoactive component in marijuana is the cannabinoid tetrahydrocannabinol, or THC. It is the chemical primarily responsible for marijuana's intoxicating effect. But there are dozens of other cannabinoids found in marijuana, and the mix of these compounds varies among different genetic strains of marijuana. The growing conditions can also affect the mix of cannabinoids within a particular plant. The other cannabinoids do not by themselves produce a drug "high," but they do interact with THC to produce its varying psychoactive effects. Thus, different batches of marijuana can affect the user differently, depending on the mix of cannabinoids. This has enabled commercial growers to tinker with the cannabinoid mix in order to produce marijuana strains with varying effects, thus catering to the varying tastes of consumers. Dispensaries in legalization states now carry dozens of such strains.

The most plentiful cannabinoid in marijuana other than THC is cannabidiol, or CBD, which balances out some of the effects of THC. Many users claim that marijuana with more CBD and less THC makes them less anxious than marijuana with a high THC content and low CBD content. In addition, CBD is being studied extensively for a variety of possible medical uses, including treatment of some seizure disorders that are resistant to other treatment. CBD oil is also becoming increasingly popular as a dietary supplement and as a type of holistic medicine.

§ 2–4 USE OF MARIJUANA AS AN INTOXICANT

As discussed in § 2–2 of this chapter, marijuana has been used for many centuries in India and other parts of Asia as a mild intoxicant, as well as a medicine, and sometimes also as part of certain religious and spiritual practices. But while hemp fiber has been grown for centuries in Europe for industrial uses, the practice of using herbal marijuana as an intoxicant was not introduced into European culture in any significant way until the latter half of the 19th century, after it had begun to be used for medical purposes. Even then, Europe's interest in experimenting with the drug for purposes of intoxication was mainly limited to the cognoscenti, particularly members of the literary class, who had read about its use as an intoxicant in North Africa.

Likewise, the practice of smoking marijuana was not really known in the United States until the latter part of the 19th century. Before that, marijuana had been used for a relatively short time as an ingredient in patent medicines in the United States, which followed Europe's lead in using the herb for medicinal purposes.

As noted above in § 2–3 of this chapter, the psychogenic effects of marijuana are complex, and they vary among individuals, so there is no one reason people take the drug. Like alcohol, it is often described as a social drug, in that it brings similarly inclined individuals together. Additionally, many people claim to enjoy marijuana because it relaxes them, relieves their anxiety, or helps them sleep better. (Marijuana does not necessarily have this effect on everyone, however; in fact it causes some people anxiety, particularly when the THC content is high.) And many users report that it enhances sociability, promotes tolerance, gives users a greater appreciation of humor and music, and all-around contributes to a pleasurable experience.

Some adherents go beyond this, claiming that marijuana heightens sensory awareness and enhances creativity (a number of the early jazz musicians claimed this, for example). And still others claim that it enhances spiritual awareness, giving then a fuller understanding of the nature of reality. To date, however, there has been very little research to see whether these effects are consistent across various groups of users, so we are basically left with subjective anecdotal accounts to explain marijuana's intoxicating appeal.

As for the mechanics of marijuana use, marijuana products can be ingested in a number of different ways. The most popular of these, in the United States at least, has always involved smoking the plant, although consuming it in edible products (e.g., hashish brownies) has long been a popular option as well. In most states that have legalized recreational use of marijuana, users have a plethora of options. In addition to selling a variety of different strains of herbal marijuana, dispensaries offer various edible products, including cookies, brownies, and candies that contain single or multiple "doses" of the drug, as well as marijuana-laced beverages, tinctures, and concentrated extract oils that can be used in vaporizers. Vaporizers (i.e. "vapes") have become increasingly popular because they are discreet, portable, and allow the user to inhale the cannabinoids without the by-products of combustion. In addition, a newer, more controversial trend in recreational marijuana use is the practice of "dabbing." This involves inhaling the vapors of one of a number of highly concentrated marijuana extracts (i.e., "hash oils") that are dropped (or "dabbed") onto a small plate (the "nail") that is part of a specially designed water pipe (the "oil rig") that has been superheated with a blowtorch, or by way of a plug-in device. When the marijuana concentrate is dabbed onto the nail, it is immediately vaporized and inhaled to deliver a very potent dose of THC to the user.

Generally, recreational marijuana that is high in THC content costs more than marijuana with a lower THC content because it is the THC that creates the intoxicating effect. (Some people, however, prefer marijuana strains with lower THC and higher CBD because it makes them less anxious.) As noted in § 2–2 above, cannabis intended for use as marijuana (as opposed to industrial hemp) has been cultivated over the years to produce varieties that are high in THC. Industrial hemp, by contrast, has a THC content too low to make it suitable for intoxication. (The 2018 Farm Bill defines hemp as cannabis containing no more than .3% THC.) Cannabis that is used to make marijuana generally has a THC content of anywhere from 5–30%, depending on how it is grown, the strain, and which parts of the plant are used. The flowers of the *Cannabis* plant (especially the trichomes within the flower) contain most of the THC; the leaves contain some, and the stems and seeds very little. Thus, a batch of marijuana made exclusively from flowering buds will generally have a higher THC content than one that is comprised of buds mixed with leaves and stems.

"Sinsemilla" has long been valued for its high THC content. Sinsemilla (Spanish for "without seeds") is the name for marijuana that is made entirely from the flowering buds of female marijuana plants (marijuana plants are somewhat unusual in that they are considered gendered) that are not allowed to pollinate. Female plants naturally produce a sticky resin on their trichomes that is designed to trap grains of pollen for purposes of fertilization. If they are prevented from pollinating, the female plants produce more and more resin, and it is this resin that contains the highest amounts of THC in the plant. To help avoid pollination, sinsemilla growers have traditionally eliminated the male plants (other than those used to make seed) from their crops before they reach maturity. In addition, commercial growers these days raise the female plants in greenhouses so that they are not exposed at all to the natural pollination process.

Hashish, which is produced by drying and crushing the resinous trichomes of the flowering buds, generally has an even higher THC content than sinsemilla. And so-called "hash oil" has a higher THC content still. Hash oil is a generic term for various concentrated extracts of marijuana or hashish, made by using a solvent (e.g., butane) to strip away the cannabinoids from the plant material. Some of these are liquid, some are waxy in consistency, and some are solid. The most intoxicating way to ingest marijuana is by "dabbing" the concentrates and inhaling the resulting vapor. When ingested in this manner, marijuana concentrates can yield THC amounts as high as 90%.

Determining the scope of marijuana use in the United States is not easy, given that it relies on self-reporting, and there is evidence that users significantly under-report. Nevertheless, some statistics are available. It has been estimated that at least 30 million Americans use marijuana at least occasionally, and approximately 20 million use it at least once per month. Usage is highest among young people between the ages of 18 and 25 years. Many younger adolescents have tried marijuana as well, however. According to some sources, close to half of all high school seniors in recent years have tried the drug at least once; over 20% use the drug at least monthly, and 6% use marijuana nearly every day. Among all Americans, over 40% have tried marijuana at least once. About 5 million use it nearly every day. Marijuana use varies somewhat across different areas of the country. The states with the highest marijuana use per capita include Alaska, Colorado, Oregon, and Vermont, and the states with the lowest marijuana use per capita include Alabama, Kansas, and Louisiana.

§ 2-5 USE OF MARIJUANA AS A MEDICINE

Marijuana's medicinal value has been extolled for centuries in some areas of the world. Its medicinal value was not recognized in Western Europe or North America, however, until somewhat later—around the middle third of the 19th century. At that time, the medical community started to investigate ways in which marijuana might be valuable in treating various conditions, including convulsions and chronic pain. In 1850, marijuana was first included in the United States' Pharmacopoeia, which is the country's standard compendium of medical drugs. (It was later removed in 1942.) During this time, marijuana was available as an herb, and marijuana extracts were also frequently included in patent medicines that were sold widely in pharmacies.

As discussed in Chapter 3, however, the availability of these medicines declined as the states and the federal government began to regulate "narcotic" drugs in the early years of the 20th century. Thus, the alleged medical benefits of marijuana could no longer be studied by the medical community and were mainly relegated to the realm of anecdotes from illicit users. To a great extent, the criminalization of marijuana has prevented the medical and scientific communities from being able to adequately research the potential medical benefits (and adverse side effects) of marijuana. This was particularly the case after Congress enacted the Controlled Substances Act of 1970. Under that federal act, which is still in effect, marijuana was designated a Schedule I drug, meaning that Congress has deemed it to be a substance that lacks a demonstrated safety record, has a high potential for abuse, and has no currently recognized medical value in the United States.

This designation has significantly hampered the ability of scientists to research the alleged medical benefits of marijuana. The federal government controls all access to legal sources of marijuana for purposes of testing, and it requires would-be researchers to apply to the federal government for permission to undertake such research. This has created a quandary for proponents of medical marijuana. On the one hand, the FDA maintains that marijuana has not been adequately tested to be approved for medical use, but at the same time, the federal government severely limits access to legal marijuana that would allow such testing.

Notwithstanding this information deficit, a number of states have moved forward with efforts to legalize the medical use of marijuana, even though it remains illegal for all purposes under federal law. The first state to do so was California in 1996. Today, 36 states in addition to the District of Columbia have enacted statutes authorizing the medical use of marijuana, and most of the remaining states have enacted statutes allowing marijuana strains or extracts that are very low in THC content to be used for medicinal purposes under tightly controlled circumstances. (*See* Chapter 4 for a more detailed discussion of these medical marijuana laws.) Thus far, the federal government has not attempted to shut down these state initiatives, even though they arguably conflict with federal law.

For the most part, medical marijuana is consumed in the same way that recreational marijuana has traditionally been consumed, that is, by smoking, and, to a lesser extent, by way of edibles. But vaping, which involves vaporizing marijuana herb or a marijuana extract, has also become a popular option for both medical and recreational users. (Certain states, however, have limited the methods of consumption available to medical users, e.g., by requiring edibles instead of smoking.) In states that have legalized both medical and recreational marijuana, the medical marijuana is generally not subject to the same degree of taxation as the recreational marijuana, so it is usually available to medical users at a significantly lower cost.

Since the effects of medical marijuana have not been rigorously tested, claims of its efficacy are still somewhat speculative. Nevertheless, proponents of medical marijuana claim that there is significant evidence—both anecdotal evidence as well as evidence from studies done abroad—that indicates marijuana has therapeutic value for a variety of conditions. (Furthermore, the United States federal government actually owns the patents on several potential medical applications and products, which would seem to undermine its claim that medical marijuana has no known medical efficacy.)

The medical conditions most often cited as candidates for medical marijuana include nausea and appetite loss (e.g., among cancer patients), chronic pain, insomnia, anxiety, glaucoma, and perhaps most significantly, muscle spasms and convulsions (e.g., as a result of seizure disorders). In recent few years, for example, the use of a special strain of marijuana called "Charlotte's Web," which is high in CBD content and very low in THC content, has received a significant amount of attention for its therapeutic effect on an otherwise intractable juvenile seizure disorder.

There is also some evidence that CBD may benefit certain mental conditions. An unresolved question is whether effective drugs can be manufactured from marijuana extracts that can be standardized and put into pill form to treat such conditions. Some scientists believe that the various cannabinoids and other compounds in marijuana work synergistically (what one prominent researcher has called the "entourage effect"), and that isolating out the various compounds may reduce the therapeutic benefits of marijuana consumption.

Opponents of medical marijuana argue that marijuana has adverse side effects that make it unsuitable for medical use. For one thing, it is now generally agreed that marijuana is addictive, and that approximately 10% of people who use it regularly develop a dependence. The withdrawal symptoms associated with removal of the drug, however, are not nearly as severe as they are for the opioids or even alcohol. Second, there has long been a suspicion that marijuana may be associated with psychoses. The evidence is still somewhat inconclusive on this issue, but it appears that THC can exacerbate symptoms of schizophrenia, and that it can perhaps trigger episodes of acute psychoses in certain other susceptible individuals. Third, there has been some recent evidence that heavy marijuana use may impair the user's memory and may even cause a small decrease in IQ when consumed for a long period of time. This effect seems to be particularly pronounced in young people who use marijuana, which is one reason legalization states have limited legalization to those aged 21 and over. Finally, there is some evidence that heavy and chronic marijuana use may impair ambition in users.

Opponents of medical marijuana also argue that the alleged therapeutic benefits of marijuana are too speculative to justify legalization, and that even if the medical benefits are real, better alternatives already exist for the conditions in question. Most experts agree, for example, that opioids such as morphine are more powerful analgesics (i.e., pain killers) than marijuana. Proponents of medical marijuana, however, counter that marijuana is safer than these conventional alternatives. For example, thousands of people a year die from overdoses of opioids, whereas there are no documented cases of anyone dying from marijuana poisoning. And there is some recent evidence that the use of marijuana to relieve chronic pain allows some patients to reduce significantly their reliance on opioids such as morphine and oxycodone.

At this point, the state of medical research is still inconclusive, and it is not possible to draw too many firm conclusions about either the medical benefits or the adverse effects of marijuana. But it is important to keep in mind that medical benefits themselves do not make a conclusive case for legalization, just as the potentially adverse effects discussed above do not make a conclusive case for prohibiting all medical use of marijuana. Many legal drugs, such as the opioids, and even over-the-counter drugs such as aspirin, have some potentially very harmful side effects, and these side effects have to be balanced carefully against the medical benefits of a drug in determining under what conditions (if any) medical use is appropriate. Both the U.S. Center for Disease Control and the U.S. Food and Drug Administration have issued advisories cautioning doctors about the dangers of opiate use and recommending that their use be limited.

Ultimately, it is the medical and scientific communities that are best qualified to make a determination as to the appropriate balancing of risks and benefits of medical marijuana. But in order for them to do so, they need to be allowed the freedom to undertake the requisite research studies. Fortunately, the federal government now seems more inclined to give them that freedom than was traditionally the case in the past.

CHAPTER 3

HISTORY OF MARIJUANA LAW (PART I—THE MARCH TO TOTAL PROHIBITION)

At the end of the Civil War, marijuana was subject to less regulation in the United States than tea; a century later, the mere possession of even a small amount of marijuana could result in years of imprisonment. This chapter discusses how that dramatic change in the law transpired.

Cannabis was well-known in America from colonial times. For several centuries, it was grown as a cash crop to produce hemp, which was used for various products, including rope, clothes, paint, paper, sails for boats, and birdseed. In the middle third of the 19th century, marijuana—the "drug" made from the flowers and leaves of the *Cannabis sativa* plant—began to be studied in Western medicine for its therapeutic properties. (Marijuana had long been used as a medicine in other parts of the world.) By 1850, marijuana was included in the United States Pharmacopeia, which is the country's compendium of drug information (first published in 1820), establishing accepted standards for medicines, drugs and related products. And by the 1870s, herbal marijuana was appearing fairly frequently in patent medicines and other elixirs that were sold in drugstores to treat various medical conditions. It was then that marijuana first began to be regulated.

The impetus for this regulation, however, was not so much marijuana itself, but its association with other types of substances that had significant potential for harm, particularly opium and its derivatives, which were growing in popularity in the late 19th century and proving to be quite addictive. Thus, it is difficult to study the history of marijuana regulation in a vacuum. Instead, it is best evaluated in the context of a more comprehensive societal crackdown on psychoactive substances generally—particularly the opiates and cocaine—as well as the burgeoning (alcohol) prohibition movement that was beginning to spread across the United States by the turn of the century.

The first regulations affecting (albeit indirectly) the sale of marijuana were accordingly state-enacted "poison laws" that imposed labeling and other requirements on patent medicines sold in pharmacies. At the urging of the American Medical Society, approximately two-thirds of the states enacted such poison laws in the period between 1870 and 1900. The concern motivating these laws was a lack of consumer awareness of the types of potentially harmful substances that were often contained in the patent medicines, including strychnine, arsenic, and prussic acid, as well as psychoactive substances such as opiates, cocaine, marijuana, and alcohol. A patent medicine containing "soothing syrup" to help infants sleep better, for example, might contain, unbeknownst to the child's parents, a significant amount of alcohol, or even an opiate. Thus, the state-enacted poison laws typically required labels listing each ingredient in the patent medicine, as well as visual warnings, such as a skull-and-crossbones symbol or the word

POISON prominently displayed upon the label, if the medicine contained substances such as those listed above. Most of these state-enacted poison laws did not specifically require cannabis to be included among the list of poisons, though some did.

The federal government, however, did specifically include cannabis when it followed the lead of the states and enacted the Pure Food and Drug Act in 1906. Like the state-enacted poison laws, the Pure Food and Drug Act prohibited misleading labeling, and it required the quantity of certain substances, including the opiates, cocaine, alcohol, and cannabis, to be identified on the label. The Act also established dose and purity standards for various drugs, based upon the United States Pharmacopeia.

The state-enacted poison laws and the U.S. Pure Food and Drug Act were effective in helping to eliminate the veiled use of psychoactive drugs and other potentially harmful substances in patent medicines. But they did not strictly speaking prevent public access to such substances. And by the last decade of the 19th century, state lawmakers were becoming increasingly concerned with the nonmedicinal, "street" use of these "narcotics." Much of this concern was focused on the smoking of opium, a practice that had recently been introduced into the United States. But much of it was also focused on the ready availability of cocaine and opiates (e.g., morphine) for medical use, often obtainable without even a prescription. Worried that the unrestricted access to such drugs would create a generation of addicts (it has been estimated that as much as 1% of the population in the United States was addicted to opiates at the turn of the 20th century), state legislatures began to supplement their poison laws to prohibit the distribution of opiates and cocaine without a doctor's prescription. Accordingly, between 1890 and 1914, 29 states had adopted statutes making it illegal to sell or distribute opiates without a prescription or other authorization, and almost all states had enacted similar restrictions on the distribution and sale of cocaine. Mere possession of these drugs, however, was criminalized in only six of these states.

At the federal level, Congress passed its first major anti-drug legislation, the Harrison Narcotics Tax Act, in 1914. The impetus for the Act was not only the increasing problem with narcotic addiction, but also the pressure the federal government felt to discourage non-medical use of narcotics, given that it was playing a leading role in organizing international conferences, such as the Hague Conference of 1911, that sought to bring about international cooperation in controlling these drugs.

The Harrison Act was ostensibly a taxing measure, requiring all persons who imported, produced or distributed opium, coca leaves, and their related derivatives to register with the federal government and pay a nominal occupational tax. But it also required them to file detailed paperwork with the federal government describing all such transactions. Failure to do so was a criminal violation, subjecting the violator to fines as well as imprisonment for up to five years. The Act exempted patent medicines that contained very small amounts of opiates or cocaine. It also exempted certain authorized persons, including physicians who prescribed these drugs, so long as they maintained records of these prescriptions. However, the exemption applied with respect to prescriptions that were made "in the course of [the physician's] professional practice only." And this provision was later interpreted to mean that physicians could prescribe opiates and cocaine only for the treatment of illness, and *not* for the maintenance of addicts to ward off the suffering caused by their addiction. *See Webb v. United States*, 249 U.S. 96 (1919). The ultimate effect of this interpretation was to force many addicts underground in search of their drugs, thereby bolstering the black-market trade in narcotics.

The constitutionality of the Harrison Narcotics Tax Act was upheld by the Supreme Court in *United States v. Doremus*, 249 U.S. 86 (1919), in which a five-member majority of the Court found that the Act was a valid exercise of Congress' taxing authority. Four members of the Court, however, including the Chief Justice, voted to strike down the Act as an unconstitutional attempt by Congress to exert a power not delegated to Congress, i.e., the reserved police power of the states.

Although the Harrison Act did not directly apply to marijuana, its passage was significant with respect to marijuana regulation for two reasons. First, it served as the federal government's principal weapon against the non-medical use of opiates and cocaine prior to the passage of the Controlled Substances Act of 1970. Second, it established an important precedent for later federal regulation and control of illicit drugs, including marijuana. In fact, the constitutional authority upon which it relied, the Article I power of Congress to raise revenue through taxation, was later relied upon by Congress as the constitutional authority of the Marihuana Tax Act of 1937, which served as the federal government's principal weapon against marijuana possession prior to the enactment of the Controlled Substances Act in 1970.

The apparent reason for Congress' reliance on its taxing authority as the constitutional basis for the Harrison Narcotics Tax Act was a widely shared view at the time that the federal government did not otherwise have the constitutional authority to regulate medical and pharmaceutical practices within the various states. *See Linder v. United States*, 268 U.S. 5, 18 (1925). The Controlled Substances Act of 1970 would later rely upon the commerce clause for its constitutional authority, but in 1914, the courts had not yet given the commerce clause the expansive reading it was to receive later in the century. Thus, Congress chose to rely instead upon its uncontroverted authority to raise revenue through taxation.

The Harrison Act was clever, moreover, insofar as it not only imposed an administrative burden on would-be dealers in narcotics who wished to avoid violating the Act; it also created a catch-22 of sorts for illicit dealers of these drugs. Specifically, section 5 of the Act provided that the federal government must make available to state law enforcement officials upon their request copies of the forms that registered distributors had filed with the IRS. And as noted above, most of the states by this time had prohibited the non-medical use of opiates, and nearly all the states had prohibited the non-medical use of cocaine. Thus, illicit distributors of opiates and cocaine faced a serious dilemma. If they complied with federal law, registering, filing the proper forms, and paying the associated tax, but they were not authorized distributors under state law, then they had essentially admitted in writing to the commission of felonies under state law. On the other hand, if they failed to comply with the requirements of the Harrison Act, they faced under the Act itself penalties that included imprisonment for up to five years. Thus, the Act had the effect of criminalizing the non-medical sale and possession of opiates and cocaine, even if, on its face, it was merely a taxing provision.

Following enactment of the Harrison Narcotics Tax Act in 1914, the state legislators began to ramp up their criminalization efforts with respect to opiates and cocaine. Prior to this time, only a handful of states had made simple possession of these drugs illegal, concentrating instead on illegal sales and distribution. By 1931, however, 35 states had criminalized the possession of opiates, and 36 had criminalized the possession of cocaine. In addition, penalties for the sale and distribution of non-medical opiates and cocaine were significantly increased.

It was also during this time that a majority of the states enacted laws prohibiting the non-medical use of marijuana. By 1929, 24 states had prohibited the non-medical use of marijuana (i.e., they required a prescription for its use), and by 1933, another 9 states had followed suit. The impetus for outlawing the non-medical use of marijuana during this time was a perception in many state legislatures that burgeoning marijuana use was causing significant increases in crime and other social problems. While cannabis had been grown in the United States for centuries, the practice of smoking marijuana here was quite recent, having been introduced by immigrants and workers from Mexico (and, to a lesser extent, by immigrants from the Caribbean), where the practice was fairly well established. Newspaper accounts of the time reflect quite racist accounts of crazed men, under the influence of this new drug, committing all sorts of violent and depraved acts. It was also widely believed that marijuana was highly addictive, and that regular use led frequently to madness. As a result, many states legislatures saw fit to enact prohibitions on the non-medical use of the "killer weed."

In 1930, Congress created the Federal Bureau of Narcotics under the auspices of the Treasury Department in order to consolidate enforcement of federal drug laws. Harry J. Anslinger was appointed as its first commissioner, having previously served in the Treasury Department's Bureau of Prohibition. Anslinger is an important figure in the history of drug regulation in the United States. A strident anti-drug crusader, he served as Commissioner of the

Bureau for 32 years, spanning five different administrations. In that role, he was instrumental in helping to formulate the first federal statute regulating marijuana use: the Marihuana Tax Act of 1937. His first main agenda as Commissioner of the Bureau, however, was to push for the adoption of the Uniform Narcotic Drug Act, which was drafted by a commission appointed by Congress. The Uniform Narcotic Drug Act was a model statute designed to bring uniformity to state narcotic laws, and to encourage greater enforcement of such laws at the state level. The Commission approved the Act in 1932, and by 1937, after fairly intensive lobbying on the part of the Bureau, most of the states had enacted it.

Commissioner Anslinger had initially pushed for the inclusion of marijuana within the coverage of the Uniform Narcotic Drug Act, describing the drug as a "national menace." And the issue was hotly debated through the five drafts of the Act. Ultimately, however, the Commission decided to include a marijuana prohibition as a separate, optional provision. Thus, states adopting the Act could choose for themselves whether to include marijuana within the Act's prohibition on non-medical use of narcotics, along with the opiates and cocaine. Approximately two-thirds of the states that adopted the Act ultimately decided to do so. In addition, several other states that had not previously prohibited marijuana possession had declined to include marijuana within their version of the Model Act, nevertheless enacted separate provisions criminalizing non-medical marijuana use. By 1937, therefore, nearly every state had criminalized non-medical marijuana sales and possession in one way or another. (And since medical use had declined significantly by this time, the net effect was to prohibit almost all marijuana use.)

This nearly universal prohibition on marijuana use at the state level, however, did not prevent the federal government from getting involved. In 1937, Congress enacted the Marihuana Tax Act, over the testimonial objection of Dr. Woodward, the spokesman for the American Medical Association, who believed that the purported dangers of marijuana were exaggerated. The impetus for the Act is not entirely clear; however, there appears to have been an increasing marijuana hysteria among the public in the 1930s. This was probably fueled by the popular press, which published numerous political cartoons illustrating the evils of marijuana and narcotics generally, as well as lurid accounts of crime sprees and madness caused by the street use of the allegedly dangerous drug. In addition, it appears that local law enforcement agencies were pushing the Bureau of Narcotics for federal legislation during this time.

Modeled after the Harrison Narcotics Tax Act, the Marihuana Tax Act of 1937 was ostensibly a revenue-generating statute, passed under Congress' constitutional taxing authority. Like the Harrison Act, it imposed a registration requirement on non-exempt producers and distributors of marijuana (the main exemptions being for physicians and pharmacists). And like the Harrison Act, it also required these non-exempt users to file a form and pay a tax ($1 per ounce) for each transaction to a registered person. However, unlike the Harrison Act, it also imposed a prohibitive $100 per ounce tax on transactions made to non-registered persons. And violators of these provisions faced fines of up to $2000 and imprisonment of up to five years.

The Marihuana Tax Act also contained a provision, similar to the one in the Harrison Act, which provided that the federal government must make available to state law enforcement officials, for a nominal fee, copies of the forms that registered distributors had filed. Thus, the Act created a dilemma for non-exempt distributors. If they complied with the Act, registering, filing the proper forms, and paying the associated tax, but they were not authorized distributors under state law (e.g., they were street dealers), then they essentially admitted in writing to the commission of felonies under state law. On the other hand, if they failed to comply with the requirements of the Act in order to avoid such admissions, then they faced under the Act itself penalties that included imprisonment for up to five years. Thus, the Marihuana Tax Act had the effect of criminalizing non-medical sales and possession of marijuana, even if, on its face, it was merely a taxing provision—particularly since, under § 8 of the Act, mere possession of marijuana without being able to produce the appropriate paperwork was presumptive evidence of guilt.

The Marihuana Tax Act of 1937 remained the federal government's principal tool for combating marijuana trafficking until the United States

Supreme Court struck the statute down as unconstitutional in 1969. Between 1937 and 1969, there were no dramatic changes in marijuana law, except, except, as discussed below, for Congress' passing increased penalties and mandatory sentencing laws in the 1950s. During the World War II years, the federal government actually encouraged the restricted cultivation of (hemp) cannabis in order to make up for a military shortage of rope.

In the 1950s, however, societal fear of the "marijuana menace" once again reared its head. Congress enacted the Boggs Act in 1951, in response to a widespread perception that narcotic drug use was spreading in society, particularly among America's youth. Predictably, the response of Congress to this perceived problem was to further ramp up penalties for possession and use of these drugs. Whereas the Marihuana Tax Act had provided for imprisonment of "not more than five years," the Boggs Act imposed mandatory minimum sentences of two years for a first offense of simple possession, five years for second offense, and ten years for subsequent offenses. Five years later, Congress increased the penalties for certain possession offenses even higher when it enacted the Narcotics Control Act of 1956. Under this Act, the mandatory minimum prison sentence for possession of marijuana known to have been brought into the United States illegally was set at five years. In addition, the Act eliminated the possibility of probation, suspension, and parole for most importation-related offenses.

Similar legislative changes took place at the state level. By 1956, the majority of the states had either modelled their narcotics laws after the Boggs Act, or had otherwise increased criminal penalties for the purchase and sale of marijuana. And by 1961, a majority had also imposed mandatory minimum penalties for these crimes. Accordingly, in some states, illegally selling marijuana could now result in a decades-long prison sentence.

As the 1960s progressed, however, societal attitudes toward marijuana began to change fairly quickly. The practice of smoking marijuana became increasingly popular with America's youth, particularly on college campuses, and by the late 1960s approximately half of the nation's college students had at least tried marijuana. Many were regular users. In addition, various scientific and medical groups began to cast doubt on the long-accepted narrative that marijuana was a highly addictive drug that led its victims to insanity and lives of crime.

As a result of this shift in societal attitudes, various groups pushed for reforming the criminal laws regulating marijuana use. And by the late 1960s, the states began to consider decreasing their penalties for marijuana possession.

The tipping point for legal reform came in May 1969 with the United States Supreme Court's decision in *Leary v. United States*, 395 U.S. 6 (1969). There the Court struck down the Marihuana Tax Act of 1937 as unconstitutional. It also struck down an important section of another federal drug statute, the

Narcotic Drugs Import and Export Act of 1954, which imposed a legal presumption that persons in possession of marijuana knew that the drug had been illegally imported into the U.S. in violation of the Act.

The *Leary* case involved Timothy Leary, a former Harvard psychology instructor who in the early 1960s experimented with using hallucinogenic drugs as a form of psychotherapy. Leary later became a leading figure in the counterculture movement of the late 1960s, best known for advocating the use of LSD and other psychedelic drugs to expand consciousness. In the case before the Supreme Court, Leary was arrested at the Mexican border in 1965 for possession of marijuana. He was convicted of transporting and concealing marijuana without paying the appropriate transfer tax imposed by the Marihuana Tax Act, and of knowingly transporting and concealing marijuana that had been illegally brought into the United States in violation of the Narcotic Drugs Import and Export Act. He was tentatively sentenced to the maximum prison terms under both statutes, pending a sentencing review.

On appeal, the Supreme Court reversed his conviction. First, it held that the legal presumption imposed by the Import and Export Act (which presumed as a matter of law that defendants found to be in possession of marijuana had knowledge that it was illegally imported under the Act) violated Leary's due process rights under the Fifth Amendment. It further held that the registration and transfer tax requirements of the Marihuana Tax Act violated his Fifth Amendment right against self-incrimination. With respect to the latter, the Court essentially held that the "clever" catch-22 the Act created for illicit users through its mandatory registration and tax-form requirements also rendered it unconstitutional. This is because the Marihuana Tax Act essentially required illicit users to identify themselves as such when they filled out the required forms under the Act—forms that were expressly made available to state law enforcement officials for inspection. Thus, by complying with the Act, non-exempt users were required to admit to violations of state criminal laws, since marijuana was illegal in every state. Accordingly, the Supreme Court held, "we think the conclusion inescapable that the statute was aimed at bringing to light transgressions of the [state] marihuana laws," and therefore it violated the defendant's Fifth-Amendment right against self-incrimination. 395 U.S. at 27.

Around the same time *Leary* was decided, Congress began extensive hearings on the issue of drug regulation, in hopes of rationalizing the patchwork system of statutes that governed the federal government's control of illegal drugs. One of the main objectives of the hearings was to revisit the rationale for the harsh minimum sentences for marijuana possession imposed by the Boggs Act and the Narcotics Control Act in the 1950s. The *Leary* decision provided an additional strong incentive for reform, since it basically gutted the federal government's main tools for controlling marijuana trafficking.

Congress responded by enacting the Controlled Substances Act of 1970 (*see* Chapter 5 for a detailed discussion of the Act)—a comprehensive scheme that has remained the cornerstone of federal drug-control policy to this day. In doing so, it ushered in a new paradigm for marijuana regulation in the United States, one in which federal law would basically remain fixed, while state and local laws increasingly diverged from the rigid federal standards for marijuana control, moving more and more toward full legalization. The story of that divergence is the subject of Chapter 4.

CHAPTER 4

HISTORY OF MARIJUANA LAW (PART II—THE SLOW AND HALTING RETURN TOWARD LEGALIZATION)

The year 1970 marked an important milestone in the history of marijuana law in the United States. As discussed in the previous chapter, the United States Supreme Court had struck down the Marihuana Tax Act of 1937 the previous year, leaving a void in the federal criminal law with respect to marijuana. Also in 1969, Congress had commenced hearings on the topic of drug enforcement and control, hoping to modernize and rationalize a diverse group of federal statutes regulating potentially harmful drugs. In large part this was due to changing societal values regarding illegal drug use and its regulation (e.g., shifting the focus away from punishing possession and more toward punishing drug trafficking), as well as an improved scientific understanding of the actual effects of drugs such as marijuana. Meanwhile, the new President of the United States, Richard Nixon, who described drug abuse as "Enemy Number One," was beginning a so-called "War on Drugs," reflecting the deep divisions within society on the issue. As President Nixon's rhetoric reflects, clearly not everyone agreed that a more liberal policy toward marijuana use was such a good idea.

In the midst of this societal division, Congress enacted the Controlled Substances Act of 1970, which itself reflected America's conflicted views on marijuana at this time. On the one hand, the

Controlled Substances Act took a more lenient approach toward mere possession or use of marijuana (and illegal drugs generally), eliminating the harsh mandatory minimum sentences first imposed by the Boggs Act in 1951. On the other hand, Congress elected to include marijuana within the list of the Act's most highly regulated "Schedule I" drugs. The Act designated five different schedules of drugs, classified on the bases of their safety profile, their potential for abuse, and their accepted medical value, if any. Schedule I, which included drugs such as heroin, LSD, and, notably, marijuana, was for drugs that were deemed to have no accepted medical use, in addition to having a high potential for abuse, and a lack of a proven safety record. (Curiously, cocaine received a Schedule II designation, along with drugs such as morphine, because Congress believed it, unlike marijuana, had some medical value.) Accordingly, marijuana retained its status as a strictly outlaw drug under the Controlled Substances Act. (*See* Chapter 5 for a more detailed discussion of the Controlled Substances Act.)

Thus, the year 1970 marked a new, divergent path for marijuana law in the United States. No longer, after this point, was there a state and federal consensus on marijuana policy. The federal government's policy toward marijuana possession became fixed, adopting a more lenient attitude toward punishing possession of small amounts of marijuana, while rigidly opposing any kind of legalization, even for medical purposes. The states, meanwhile, followed somewhat divergent paths. Most followed the lead of the federal government, enacting state statutes that continued to punish simple possession as a felony or high misdemeanor. But other states moved instead in the direction of adopting a more lenient approach toward the personal possession of small amounts of marijuana. And by the mid-1990s, beginning with California, states began to adopt measures (usually as a result of ballot initiatives) legalizing marijuana for medical use. In 2012, two states, Colorado and Washington, pushed the envelope even further, legalizing marijuana for "recreational" use as well.

A poignant example of how some states adopted a more lenient attitude toward marijuana use in the early 1970s is found in the case of John Sinclair. Sinclair, a poet and political activist whose was actively involved in the burgeoning counterculture movement in Ann Arbor, Michigan, during the mid-late 1960s. He also managed the proto punk-rock Detroit band MC5.

Ann Arbor was a hotbed of political activism during that time, and it was home to several important countercultural political organizations, including Tom Hayden's Students for a Democratic Society, as well as its more radical offshoot, the Weather Underground, led by Bill Ayers. (Hayden would later marry actress Jane Fonda and become a member of Congress; Ayers ultimately became a professor at the University of Illinois and was active in mainstream Chicago politics.) Sinclair himself co-founded the White Panthers, a group whose stated objective was to lend support to the Black Panthers, who were based in Oakland, California.

As a result of his political activities and associations, Sinclair was well known to law enforcement officials, both local and federal. In 1967, the Detroit Police Department set up a sting operation and attempted to infiltrate a Detroit establishment called the Artists' Workshop, which Sinclair ran, and where he also was living at the time. After several weeks of this activity, an undercover police officer managed to persuade Sinclair to give her two marijuana joints. Sinclair was subsequently arrested and charged with possession of marijuana in violation of state law. He remained on bail for two years until his trial, at which he was convicted, and sentenced by the judge to 9 ½ to 10 years in prison. Subsequent to the verdict, the judge denied a further bail bond, and Sinclair was taken immediately from the trial to prison.

Sinclair's imprisonment caused a national outcry among sympathizers, particularly within the college community and the counterculture movement. During the famous Woodstock Music Festival in the summer of 1969, for example, noted political activist Abbie Hoffman, co-founder of the Youth International Party (i.e., the "Yippies"), ran onstage while the rock band The Who was performing and grabbed Pete Townshend's microphone while Townshend had his back turned. Hoffman managed to get out a few sentences about the folly of listening to music "while John Sinclair rots in prison" before a less-than-amused Townshend berated Hoffman and reportedly tried to whack him with the neck of his guitar, inducing Hoffman to hastily exit stage center into the crowd below.

Meanwhile, Sinclair continued to serve his time in prison until December of 1971, when a "John Sinclair Freedom Rally" concert was held in Ann Arbor for his benefit. The concert was headlined by John Lennon (still at the height of his fame following the dissolution of the Beatles the previous year) and his wife, Yoko Ono, as well as a number of other well-known musicians (including Stevie Wonder, Commander Cody, and Bob Seger), poet Allen Ginsberg, and political activists such as Jerry Rubin and Bobby Seale. Lennon even wrote a special song for the event, called "John Sinclair," with the refrain: "They gave him ten for two, what else could Judge Colombo do?"

The concert was a huge success, and remarkably, within a few days, the Michigan Supreme Court issued an order freeing Sinclair from prison. Three months later, in March 1972, the court issued its opinion on the matter, formally dismissing Sinclair's conviction. The justices concurring in this dismissal issued several opinions that relied upon different theories, including: (1) a violation of the equal protection clauses of the United States and Michigan constitutions; (2) entrapment on the part of the police in soliciting the sale of the two joints; and (3) a violation of the cruel and unusual punishment clauses of the U.S. and Michigan constitutions due to the excessive sentence Sinclair received.

The Michigan Supreme Court's decision reflects the shift in many states toward more lenient policies with respect to marijuana use in the early 1970s. It was, however, one of the few state courts that actually struck down a state statute as unconstitutional. More commonly, state legislatures took the initiative and began easing the penalties for simple marijuana possession, making it a minor misdemeanor rather than a high misdemeanor or felony. In fact, by 1973, all but 6 of the states had reduced the crime of possessing small amounts of marijuana for personal use to minor misdemeanor status.

During this time, there was also a movement toward decriminalizing marijuana, that is, to making possession a mere civil infraction rather than a criminal violation. When the Marihuana Commission, which Congress had created when it enacted the Controlled Substances Act of 1970, issued its report in 1972, it recommended the elimination of criminal penalties for the possession of small amounts of marijuana for personal use. Not surprisingly, that recommendation spurred a lot of opposition, even though it had received the support of the American Bar Association. President Nixon, for one, made it clear that he was adamantly opposed to the Commission's recommendation, even though he had appointed 9 of its 13 members (Congress appointed the other 4). And the former Bureau of Narcotics Commissioner, Harry Anslinger, also weighed in, warning that decriminalization would likely result in "about a million lunatics" that would require institutionalization, as well "just plain slaughter" on the nation's highways. In the face of such opposition, Congress never acted upon the

Commission's proposal to decriminalize marijuana possession.

Decriminalization received a somewhat more favorable reception at the state and local level, however. The Oregon legislature took this approach in 1973, passing legislation that made marijuana possession for personal use merely a civil infraction, with a $100 fine. And by 1979, the legislatures of 10 additional states effectively decriminalized personal possession of small amounts of marijuana, either by making it a civil infraction, or by eliminating the possibility of imprisonment for a violation. In Alaska, the state's supreme court effectively decriminalized possession of marijuana for personal use in *Ravin v. State*, 537 P.2d 494 (Alaska 1975). There the court held that the Alaska Constitution contains an implicit right to privacy that protects possession of small amounts of marijuana kept in the home for personal use.

A few municipalities also got in on the decriminalization movement, beginning with Ann Arbor, Michigan. After he was released from prison, John Sinclair helped to rally support for marijuana decriminalization, and in 1972, voters elected two young members of the pro-marijuana Human Rights Party to the city council, where they joined with the Democrats on the council to enact an ordinance reducing marijuana possession to a civil infraction and making its violation a mere $5 fine. While that initial ordinance was subsequently struck down by a state trial court as an improper exercise of local authority, a similar city charter amendment was passed by the voters in 1974, and upheld (though the fine was later increased to $25).

In addition to Ann Arbor, several other municipalities passed decriminalization measures in the late 1970s, including Madison, Wisconsin (1977), which reduced the penalty for simple possession to a $100 fine, and Berkeley, California (1979), which passed an ordinance explicitly making enforcement of marijuana prohibitions the lowest police priority.

Thus, it looked by the end of the 1970s that the liberalization of marijuana laws was picking up steam. Marijuana use was at record levels among the younger set, and it appeared to be only a matter of time until decriminalization would become the norm.

But that vision proved to be a chimera after Ronald Reagan was elected as the 40th President of the United States. The Reagan administration ushered in a new era of political conservatism, and the country's attitudes toward drug policy followed suit. This was reflected in the First Lady's "Just Say No" campaign beginning in the early 1980s. That campaign sought to combat drug abuse among America's youth, and it received widespread publicity. It even led to the creation of "Just Say No" clubs within thousands of schools and youth organizations across the country.

In addition, Congress enacted several significant acts that had the effect of tightening marijuana policy in the 1980s during the Reagan administration. The two most significant were the Comprehensive Crime Control Act of 1984 and the

Anti-Drug Abuse Act of 1986. The former created the United States Sentencing Commission, which then formulated mandatory sentencing guidelines for federal judges. This had the effect of significantly reducing judicial discretion in sentencing. The Act also increased the penalties for transfer and possession of large quantities of marijuana. The 1986 Act further targeted narcotic trafficking, imposing stiff mandatory minimum sentences for various offenses. With respect to marijuana, possession of 100 or more kilograms of marijuana subjected the defendant to imprisonment for a minimum of five years, along with a fine of up to $2 million. And possession of 1000 or more kilograms of marijuana subjected the defendant to imprisonment for a minimum of 10 years, along with a fine of up to $4 million. These mandatory minimum sentences helped set in motion the trend toward a dramatically expanding prison population in the United States over the next several decades.

At the state level, marijuana law mostly marked time during the 1980s, though some states imposed additional restrictions on marijuana trafficking. For example, in the wake of a perceived crack cocaine epidemic, a number of states, following the federal lead, imposed drug-free zones around schools, and imposed harsh penalties for illegal drug possession in those zones. Furthermore, no additional states decriminalized marijuana during this time, tracking the nation's increasing impatience with drug abuse.

By the beginning of the 1990s, therefore, marijuana reformers were becoming somewhat discouraged, since the advances they had made toward decriminalization in the 1970s seemed to be reversing course. Additionally, marijuana use declined significantly, at least among young people, during the 1980s. According to a study by the Institute for Social Research at the University of Michigan, for example, marijuana use among high school seniors dropped from 50% in 1978 to 12% in 1991.

In fact, however, the 1990s turned out to be an important decade for the push toward legalization. First, it was during this decade that an American President (Bill Clinton) admitted for the first time to having smoked marijuana in his youth (though he qualified this admission by claiming that he did not actually inhale). More significantly, it was during this decade that many states and municipalities began passing laws legalizing the use of marijuana for medical purposes. The first of these was the result of a ballot initiative in San Francisco in 1991. Subsequently, various other municipalities began to follow suit. In 1996, California became the first state to legalize marijuana for medical use; two years later several other states passed such measures.

By 2021, 36 states and the District of Columbia had enacted laws to legalize the medical use of marijuana. Some of these laws were passed by state legislatures, but most enacted by ballot measures.

These medical marijuana laws vary significantly among the various states, both as to the amount that the medical marijuana user can possess, as well as the manner in which the marijuana can be obtained and consumed. Most states, for example, allow medical marijuana dispensaries, though some allow merely the private growing of medical marijuana for personal use or by caregivers, and some are silent as to how marijuana used for medical purposes can be obtained. State laws also vary significantly with respect to the types of medical conditions that come within the scope of the law. Some states limited the ability to obtain a medical license to persons with just a few serious conditions, while other states are less restrictive. California is among the least restrictive, allowing doctors to recommend marijuana for any conditions they think it will help, including such common conditions as anxiety, chronic pain, and insomnia.

In addition to these 36 states that have enacted medical marijuana laws, most of the other states in the past several years have passed legislation that permits the use of either low-THC cannabis or a cannabis extract like CBD for the treatment of certain limited conditions, such as seizure disorder or cancer. Thus, only a few states still prohibit marijuana altogether.

The biggest obstacle to the enactment of state and local medical marijuana laws, of course, has been the conflict they create with federal laws, particularly the Controlled Substances Act. As discussed further in Chapter 8, federal law allows no exception to the Controlled Substances Act's prohibition on marijuana for medical use. Thus, a strong argument can be made that the Supremacy Clause of the United States Constitution empowers the federal government to shut down medical marijuana programs within the states, notwithstanding the fact that individual states have chosen to legalize marijuana use for medical purposes. That issue reached the United States Supreme Court in the 2005 case *Gonzales v. Raich*, 545 U.S. 1 (2005). In *Raich*, the court ruled in favor of the federal government, stressing that Congress had the power under the Commerce Clause to regulate activities that are purely intrastate, if those activities have a substantial effect on interstate commerce. The Court found that intrastate production of medical marijuana would have such an interstate effect, and thus it fell within Congress' power to regulate. Since the *Reich* decision, however, the federal government has, for the most part, chosen not to exercise this authority, leaving it to the individual states to decide whether they want to allow medical marijuana use, subject to certain conditions. (For a more detailed discussion of these federalism considerations, *see* Chapter 8.)

In the year 2000, a conservative Republican president, George W. Bush, was elected to the White House. Based on the aggressive policies previous Republican administrations had adopted with respect to illegal drugs, it was reasonable to expect that the new millennium would see a retrenchment in the continuing movement toward liberalization of marijuana laws in the states. In fact, however, that did not take place. As discussed above, the first decade of the new millennium witnessed a number of states adopting medical marijuana statutes. And while the federal government made some arrests in connection with abuses of these laws, it did not shut the programs down.

In addition, decriminalization efforts were renewed. In 2001, Nevada became the first state in 23 years to decriminalize possession of small amounts of marijuana for personal use. And by 2020, 27 states plus the District of Columbia had enacted laws decriminalizing possession of small amounts of marijuana for personal use (including states that had fully legalized it), and a handful of other states were expected to consider such legislation in the near future. In some of these states, possession of small amounts of marijuana for personal use is reduced to a civil infraction with a fine; in the remainder, such possession is still technically a crime, but only a minor misdemeanor, with no possibility of imprisonment for a violation, at least for a first offense.

Decriminalization also picked up steam at the local level. In a number of states that had not yet decriminalized marijuana, voters in marijuana-friendly pockets of the states championed local initiatives that make possession of small amounts of marijuana for personal use merely civil infractions. By 2016, in Michigan and Wisconsin alone, approximately 2 dozen municipalities had passed laws decriminalizing simple possession. (Michigan has since legalized recreational marijuana on a state-wide basis.) It is likely that this trend will continue in the states that have not legalized or decriminalized marijuana possession statewide.

The final frontier for marijuana liberalization, it would seem, is full legalization, and in 2012, Colorado and Washington, crossed this historic divide by enacting ballot initiatives that made "recreational" marijuana legal, within certain parameters.. Of these two, Colorado was the first to implement its ballot initiative, enacting a regulatory scheme in 2013, and opening the first recreational-use marijuana dispensaries (which are rather similar to liquor stores) in January 2014. In doing so, Colorado in effect became the first government in the world to fully legalize and regulate marijuana use. (Many people mistakenly assume that Amsterdam had done this earlier; in fact, however, there were still prohibitions on the sale of marijuana in Amsterdam, they were just not actively enforced.)

Under Colorado law, as is true in many legalization states, local municipalities are not *required* to allow marijuana dispensaries within their jurisdiction; rather it is optional with the municipality. Interestingly, the majority of the municipalities in Colorado chose not to allow dispensaries; most of the larger cities do allow them, however, so the majority of citizens of the state live in or near a municipality that has recreational marijuana dispensaries, and they can therefore obtain recreational marijuana without much difficulty.

The State of Washington lagged behind Colorado a bit in terms of implementing regulations, but in July 2014, it too began opening licensed dispensaries. Later that same year, two additional states, Oregon and Alaska, along with the District of Columbia, adopted measures legalizing recreational marijuana use. And November 2016, four additional states legalized recreational marijuana use, including the nation's most populous state, California. Since then, 10 more states (for a total of 18) have enacted legalization schemes, and the move toward legalization at the state level shows no signs of abating.

The federal response to state-enacted recreational marijuana laws has largely been restrained. The Obama administration took the position that states should be able to decide for themselves on the issue of legalization, subject to certain broad restrictions. Accordingly, the Justice Department issued a series of memoranda in 2012 (the most important of which is often referred to as the "Cole Memo"), outlining the conditions under which the federal government would agree not to interfere with state marijuana laws. (For a more detailed discussion of the Obama administration's approach, *see* Chapters 6 and 8.) To date, the recreational marijuana states, like the medical marijuana states, have largely complied with the federal government's conditions. Thus, the potential conflict between state and local law has not created an insuperable problem for the marijuana industry in the states that have chosen to legalize it (although it has led to a number of practical problems that are discussed further in Part III below).

That situation looked like it might change under the Trump administration, after Attorney General Sessions retracted the Obama administration's Cole

Memo and empowered the individual U.S. attorneys to prosecute federal marijuana crimes at their discretion. But by the end of President Trump's term, nothing had really changed in terms of the federal response, and it appears that the Biden administration will continue to follow the Obama administration's hands-off approach to enforcement.

Thus, the slow and halting march toward full legalization in the United States seems to be picking up the pace. However, the future of legalization efforts will depend in large part on how the federal government resolves the conflict between state laws legalizing marijuana use and federal laws prohibiting it. Democrats in Congress have introduced several legalization bills over the past few years that would either allow the individual states to decide the matter for themselves, or would legalize marijuana by removing it from the Controlled Substances Act altogether. And since Democrats now have control of both chambers, the next year could usher in a very interesting new chapter in the history of marijuana law in the United States.

PART 2
FEDERAL LAW

CHAPTER 5

THE CONTROLLED SUBSTANCES ACT OF 1970

§ 5-1 INTRODUCTION

Marijuana is illegal under federal law for most purposes. Cultivating, possessing, distributing, and consuming marijuana are prohibited under the Controlled Substances Act of 1970 (CSA). The major exception was enacted in 2018 to legalize hemp.

The CSA is the most significant legislation regulating drug and marijuana use in the United States. It establishes a closed registration system for all substances it controls, regulating categories of drugs and punishing use not in accordance with the Act. Because marijuana is controlled in Schedule I, the CSA does not so much regulate as prohibit marijuana. Although states have enacted laws allowing marijuana use for medical and recreational purposes, and although the federal government has been willing to accommodate such laws, marijuana activity remains no less a serious federal crime.

This chapter summarizes the CSA, especially as it governs marijuana use. Section 5–2 discusses the enactment of the CSA. Section 5–3 details its provisions, including scheduling definitions and penalties. Section 5–4 explains the dissemination of the CSA into state law through the Uniform Controlled Substances Act. And § 5–5 explores the rescheduling of marijuana. Section 5–6 gives examples of pending marijuana reform bills. The legalization of hemp, the most significant change to the CSA treatment of marijuana since its inception, is treated in Chapter Eleven.

§ 5-2 HISTORY OF THE CSA

At the turn of the twentieth century, regulation of marijuana, like most other drugs, was left largely to the states. The Progressive era saw strong pressure to regulate drugs, but Congress was limited in how it could respond. According to constitutional theory of the time, the federal government lacked direct authority to enact general measures for the health, welfare, morals, and safety of the nation. Such legislation, included in the so-called "police powers" of sovereign governments, was reserved to the states under the federal structure and Tenth Amendment to the U.S. Constitution. Under this theory, the federal government could only exercise powers granted to it under the Constitution, which did not include the authority to make general health or criminal laws for the nation.

The states began regulating marijuana under various health provisions towards the end of the nineteenth and early twentieth century. The federal government enacted its first major health and consumer laws during the administration of President Theodore Roosevelt: the Pure Food and Drug Act and the Federal Meat Inspection Act. Passed in 1906, both acts were essentially truth-in-labeling laws of products moving in interstate commerce. The Pure Food and Drug Act did not outlaw but required correct labeling of medicinal drugs, including cannabis, and prohibited manufacture and shipment of adulterated or misbranded drugs. Pure Food and Drugs Act of 1906, ch. 3915, 34 Stat. 768, *repealed by* Federal Food, Drug, and Cosmetic Act of 1938, ch. 675, 52 Stat. 1040, 1059A.

The Pure Food and Drug Act was upheld as a constitutional exercise of congressional authority under the Commerce Clause. *United States v. Johnson*, 221 U.S. 488, 498–99 (1911). The Harrison Narcotics Tax Act, enacted in 1914, under the Taxing and Spending Clause, Art. I, § 8, cl. 1., did not prohibit narcotics but required registration and payment of an occupational tax (an excise tax imposed on those involved in an occupation or industry) by purchasers, sellers, and producers of marijuana and other drugs.

Demand for the federal government to act against narcotics continued to grow, but the outcry against alcohol was greater. As with drugs, the federal government was seen as lacking constitutional authority to prohibit alcohol. Therefore, in 1919, the Eighteenth Amendment was added to the Constitution, prohibiting the "manufacture, sale, or transportation of intoxicating liquors." Under this authority, Congress passed the Volstead Act in 1920, ushering in the era of prohibition.

Because there was no similar constitutional amendment to ban drugs, Congress continued to act on narcotics obliquely through such express constitutional powers as taxation. In 1934, the Uniform State Narcotic Drug Act indicated guidelines to the states in fashioning their anti-drug laws. The Marihuana Tax Act of 1937 imposed heavy taxes on marijuana, burdensome registration processes for medical restrictions, and strict penalties for noncompliance in an effort to curb marijuana use. Pub. L. No. 75–238, 50 Stat. 551, *invalidated by Leary v. United States*, 395 U.S. 6 (1969). The Federal Bureau of Narcotics enforced the Tax Act.

With increased global cooperation in the post-World War II era, international treaties were enacted against drug use. The two most significant were the 1961 Single Convention on Narcotic Drugs and the 1971 Convention on Psychotropic Substances. The hallmark of these treaties was to require signatory nations, including the United States, to control the use, production, and trafficking of drugs, including marijuana. *See* Chapter Ten for a discussion of the international drug treaties.

The end of the 1960s was fertile for federal drug legislation. The United States had led the effort to implement an international anti-narcotics regime that prohibited marijuana. The growth of the counterculture and use of drugs among youth led the Johnson and Nixon administrations to look to strengthen U.S. drug laws however possible, in a so-called "War on Drugs."

Furthermore, the central piece of federal legislation curbing marijuana use—the Marihuana Tax Act of 1937—was declared unconstitutional in 1969. *Leary v. United States*, 395 U.S. 6 (1969). This left a significant void in federal drug law, as marijuana was now largely unregulated at the federal level.

The Nixon administration was elected in 1968 on a campaign of law and order. Marijuana use was the very symbol of the counterculture. Perhaps most importantly, sweeping federal legislation against drug use now seemed feasible. The reach of federal powers under the Commerce Clause, Art. 1, § 8, cl, 3, had extended greatly in the New Deal and Civil Rights eras. President Nixon assigned Attorney General John Mitchell to draft a comprehensive federal statute, consolidating existing federal drug legislation and expanding federal reach over regulation of prescribed drugs and trafficking in illegal drugs. The framework was to combine both public health and law enforcement measures. To make increased federal intervention more palatable, and in accord with the administration's rhetoric on states' rights, the legislation was drafted to spur federal cooperation rather than displacement of state anti-drug efforts. Congress explicitly based its power to regulate drug use on its Commerce Clause powers.

The CSA was passed by the House on September 24, 1970 by an overwhelming vote of 342 to 7 (82 not voting), and in the Senate on October 7, 1970 without a dissenting vote, 54 to 0 (46 not voting). On October 27, 1970, President Nixon signed the CSA into law as Title II of the Comprehensive Drug Abuse Prevention and Control Act of 1970, Pub. L. No. 91–513, § 1101(b)(30)(A), 84 Stat. 1236 (codified as amended at 21 U.S.C. §§ 801–971 (2012)). Since 1970, the CSA has been the dominant federal framework for controlling lawful and unlawful drugs.

§ 5–3 PROVISIONS OF THE CSA

The CSA is a comprehensive and complex statute, consolidating and extending 65 years of federal legislation in the field of drug regulation. Reflecting its hybrid status as both a public health measure and a criminal statute, the CSA is codified in U.S.C. Title 21: Food and Drug Acts, and many of the criminal provisions necessary for its enforcement are codified in U.S.C. Title 18: Crimes and Criminal Procedure. In sum, it establishes a tightly controlled regime to administer medicinal drugs. It criminalizes diversion of such drugs, and bans drugs of high abuse of no medical efficacy. As such, it prohibits the marijuana plant, its parts, seeds, resins, compounds, and derivatives, and the cannabinoid THC (delta-9-tetrahydrocannabinol).

The CSA was drafted with several goals in mind. It represented compliance of the United States with the 1961 Single Convention on Narcotic Drugs, which itself had classified narcotics into four schedules. It was enacted in 1970 as the major plank in the Nixon administration's "War on Drugs." The federal government had previously attempted to regulate drugs and marijuana at the margins so to speak, leaving most criminal enforcement to the states. The federal government enacted over 200 diverse laws that sought to discourage narcotics use through labeling laws, excise taxes, revenue measures, model legislation, and health care provisions, but had not yet established a centralized regulatory regime for drugs. The CSA gathered this plethora of legislation into one overarching framework. The central aim was to create a regime where tight controls could be exercised over drugs for medicinal and pharmaceutical purposes and their diversion for unlawful use prevented. Nevertheless, the CSA was not to obliterate traditional divisions of powers between state and federal criminal enforcement. The federal government would focus on large-scale trafficking; the states, on street-level use. Likewise, the CSA is constructed so that many of its provisions can be referred to or adopted by the states. Its meticulous classification of drugs according to schedules relieved states of the onerous task of classifying hundreds of drugs.

A "controlled" substance is a drug with potential for abuse that is regulated by comprehensive legislation. Possession, manufacture, and dispensing of a controlled substance are illegal except as allowed for in the CSA. 21 U.S.C. § 841(a)(1) (2018). The CSA schedules substances according to their danger, known medical benefit, and potential for abuse. Controlled substances include drugs such as narcotics, hallucinogens, opiates and opium derivatives, stimulants, depressives, and anabolic steroids. The CSA does not classify alcohol, nicotine, or caffeine as controlled substances. In the initial statute, 42 opiates, 22 opium derivatives, and 17 hallucinogenic substances, including marijuana, were classified under Schedule I, the most restrictive schedule, as having no recognized medical value.

The CSA closely regulates physicians and pharmacies in prescribing medicinal drugs. Every person who manufactures, dispenses, imports, or exports any controlled substance is required to register with the DEA and record inventories and transactions. The CSA also regulates scientific research regarding drug use.

Marijuana is classified as a hallucinogenic substance and is controlled under Schedule I. 21 U.S.C. § 812(c), Sched. I(c)(10); 21 C.F.R. § 1308.11(d)(23), (58) (2018).

The definition of marijuana under the CSA is broad, encompassing all marijuana plants containing a tetrahydrocannabinol (THC) concentration of more than 0.3 percent and any mixture, derivative, or compound from these plants, including their seeds or resin. Notably, the definition explicitly excludes hemp—defined as a marijuana plant with a THC concentration below 0.3 percent—as well as mature plants that are incapable of germination. 21 U.S.C. § 802 (16); 7 U.S.C. § 1639*o*(1).

The CSA defines marijuana as

> all parts of the plant Cannabis sativa L., whether growing or not; the seeds thereof; the resin extracted from any part of such plant; and every compound, manufacture, salt, derivative, mixture, or preparation of such plant, its seeds or resin [. . .] The term "marihuana" does not include—(i) hemp, as defined in section 1639*o* of Title 7; or (ii) the mature stalks of such plant, fiber produced from such stalks, oil or cake made

> from the seeds of such plant, any other compound, manufacture, salt, derivative, mixture, or preparation of such mature stalks (except the resin extracted therefrom), fiber, oil, or cake, or the sterilized seed of such plant which is incapable of germination.

21 U.S.C. § 802(16). Although this definition specifically refers to Cannabis sativa L., it includes all types of the cannabis plant, including *Cannabis indica, Cannabis ruderalis, Cannabis gigantea*, and other cannabis plants not yet named. *United States v. Walton*, 514 F.2d 201, 202 (D.C. Cir. 1975); *United States v. Gagnon*, 635 F.2d 766, 770 (10th Cir. 1980), *cert. denied*, 451 U.S. 1018 (1981).

Likewise, any cannabinoid found in the plant is automatically controlled in Schedule I, except for hemp, which was excluded from the regulations of the CSA by the Agricultural Improvement Act of 2018.

Schedule I also includes Tetrahydrocannabinol (THC), the psychoactive agent in marijuana, encompassing "any material, compound, mixture, or preparation, which contains any quantity of . . . Tetrahydrocannabinols. . . ." 21 U.S.C. § 812(c), Schedule I(c)(17); *Hemp Indus. Ass'n v. DEA*, 357 F.3d 1012, 1014–17 (9th Cir. 2004).

The definition of THC for Schedule I is detailed in 21 C.F.R. (*Code of Federal Regulations*) § 1308.11(d)(31):

> naturally contained in a plant of the genus Cannabis (cannabis plant), as well as synthetic

> equivalents of the substances contained in the cannabis plant, or in the resinous extractives of such plant, and/or synthetic substances, derivatives, and their isomers with similar chemical structure and pharmacological activity to those substances contained in the plant. . . tetrahydrocannabinols does not include any material, compound, mixture, or preparation that falls within the definition of hemp set forth in 7 U.S.C. 1639*o*.

Therefore tetrahydrocannabinols contained in hemp—"the plant Cannabis sativa L. and any part of that plant . . . with a delta-9 tetrahydrocannabinol concentration of not more than 0.3 percent on a dry weight basis"—are excluded from the CSA definition in 21 U.S.C. § 812(c), Schedule I(c)(17). However, substances similar to marijuana, intended for human consumption, are included in Schedule I under the Analogue Act. 21 U.S.C. §§ 802(32)(a), 813. "Cannabimimetic agents" were explicitly added to Schedule I under the Synthetic Drug Abuse Prevention Act of 2012, Food and Drug Administration Safety and Innovation Act, Pub. L. No. 112–144, § 1152, 126 Stat. 993, 1130–31 (2012); 21 U.S.C. § 821(c), Schedule I(d). Thus, the CSA also includes in Schedule I what is known as "synthetic marijuana"—synthetic cannabinoids and analogues such as "Spice" and "K2." 21 C.F.R. § 1308.11(g).

The Controlled Substances Import and Export Act was also enacted as part of the Comprehensive Drug Abuse Prevention and Control Act of 1970. It imposes substantial penalties for illicitly importing or exporting Schedule I and II controlled substances into the United States. 21 U.S.C. §§ 951–971.

§ 5–3.1 SCHEDULES

The CSA classifies drugs into five schedules based on three criteria: 1) the currently accepted medical use of the drug in the United States; 2) the safety of the drug; and 3) the potential for abuse or addiction. Schedule I drugs are deemed to have no medicinal value and present the greatest danger. Schedules II through V contain drugs with accepted medical use and ascend in level of presumed safety from Schedule II, still subject to significant controls, to Schedule V, the least restricted of the schedules.

The current list of the hundreds of scheduled substances is contained in 21 C.F.R. § 1308. The better-known controlled drugs are listed below (with examples of trademark drugs given in parentheses). Most opiates, opium derivatives, and hallucinogens are listed in Schedule I. Depressants and stimulants are spread among all five schedules. Substances listed in Schedules II–V require a prescription.

Schedule I drugs are those with "a high potential for abuse," which have "no currently accepted medical use in treatment in the United States," and which lack "accepted safety for use . . . under medical supervision. . . ." 21 U.S.C. § 812(b)(1)(A)–(C). Marijuana and THC are classified as Schedule I drugs, along with opium derivatives such as heroin, and hallucinogens such as LSD, ecstasy, mescaline, and peyote.

Hence, under the CSA, marijuana cannot be prescribed by a physician for any purpose, and no state law authorizes physicians to do so. (Instead, state medical marijuana laws require a "physician recommendation".)

Schedule II drugs have a high potential for abuse which may lead to severe psychological or physical dependence. They include cocaine, morphine, opium, codeine, PCP, amphetamines (Dexedrine, Adderall), methamphetamine (Desoxyn), methylphenidate (Ritalin), hydromorphone (Dilaudid), methadone (Dolophine), meperidine (Demerol), oxycodone (OxyContin, Percocet), and fentanyl (Sublimaze, Duragesic).

Schedule III drugs have less potential for abuse but may still lead to moderate or low physical dependence and high psychological dependence, including stimulants, depressants, and anabolic steroids (Depo-Testosterone), ketamine, benzphetamine (Didrex), and Tylenol with Codeine.

Schedule IV drugs have low potential for abuse, which may lead to limited dependence (including Ambien, Xanax, Valium, Halcion, Soma, Darvocet, Ativan).

Schedule V drugs have lowest potential for abuse and dependence. They contain very limited if any quantities of narcotics. They include cough suppressants with codeine (Robitussin AC) and pregabalin (Lyrica).

§ 5–3.2 PENALTIES

Criminal sanctions follow the scheduling classification but also depend on the specific drug and quantity involved. The CSA imposes heavy penalties for drug use. For example, first possession of any amount of a Schedule I drug, including marijuana, is punished by as much as a year in prison. Penalties mostly increase one year for subsequent possessions. A sale is punished more harshly. Sale of any amount of a Schedule I drug, including marijuana, is subject to 5 years in prison and a $250,000 fine. Sales of amounts greater than 50 kilograms increase exponentially, even to life sentences.

The Anti-Drug Abuse Acts of 1986 and 1988, enacted as planks of President Reagan's renewed "War on Drugs," increased drug offense penalties, for example by setting mandatory minimum and "three strikes" sentences for marijuana. A second offense marijuana possession has a statutory minimum of 15 days' incarceration, and a subsequent offense, a 90-day minimum; maximum penalties range much higher.

The penalties for some of the most common crimes of marijuana (including those relating to hashish and hashish oil) are as follows.

Marijuana Possession (21 U.S.C. § 844)

A first offense possession of marijuana in any amount is punishable by up to a one-year imprisonment and a minimum fine of $1,000. A second offense is punishable by a sentence of 15 days to two years' imprisonment and a minimum fine of

$2,500. A third or subsequent possession offense is punishable by a sentence of 90 days to three years' imprisonment, and a minimum $5,000 fine.

Mixtures containing marijuana are measured by total weight, including adulterant. (21 U.S.C. § 841(b); U.S. Sent'g Guidelines Manual § 2D1.1(A) and (26) (U.S. Sent'g Comm'n 2018). Some state controlled substances acts also aggregate total weight of mixtures containing marijuana, including adulterants, thereby significantly increasing exposure to prison time. *See, e.g.*, Tex. Health & Safety Code Ann. § 481.112 (2019).

In addition to criminal penalties, individuals may also be subject to civil penalties for possession of small amounts of marijuana. 21 U.S.C. § 844a. Fines for possession of these "personal use" amounts cannot exceed $10,000, and a civil penalty may not be assessed more than two separate times. The Attorney General may only make assessments after giving notice and an opportunity for a hearing. The Attorney General may pursue a civil action to recover the amount of the penalty.

<u>Marijuana Trafficking (§ 841)</u>

Marijuana trafficking offenses—manufacture (which includes cultivation), distribution, dispensation, or possession with the intent to commit such offenses—are felonies under the CSA. Most of the sentences imposed are without eligibility for parole. Sentences are roughly doubled for second offenses. Fines are substantially increased for defendants other than "individuals."

Trafficking of less than 50 kilograms of marijuana (or 10 kilograms of hashish, 1 kilogram of hashish oil, or 1 to 49 plants) is punishable by up to 5 years' imprisonment and a maximum $250,000 fine. Trafficking of 50 to 99 kilograms (or 50–99 plants) is punishable by up to 20 years' imprisonment and a maximum $1 million fine. Trafficking of 100 to 999 kilograms (or 100–999 plants) is punishable by 5 years to 40 years' imprisonment, with a maximum fine of $5 million. Trafficking of 1000 kilograms or more (or 1,000 or more plants) is punishable by a mandatory minimum of 10 years to a life sentence of imprisonment, with a maximum fine of $10 million. Trafficking of over 5 grams to minors (defined as persons under 21) or within 1000 feet of a school, university, public housing project, youth center, video arcade, public swimming pool, or playground automatically doubles the prescribed punishments. 21 U.S.C. §§ 859–60. In addition, trafficking of marijuana that results in death or serious bodily injury results in substantially increased penalties.

Marijuana Paraphernalia (§ 863)

Possession of marijuana paraphernalia is a felony punishable by up to 3 years' imprisonment. Paraphernalia encompasses items "primarily intended or designed for use in ingesting, inhaling, or otherwise introducing marijuana . . . hashish, hashish oil . . . into the human body. . . ." 21 U.S.C. § 863(d).

The CSA specifically includes as paraphernalia such instruments as pipes, bowls, carburetion devices, bongs, roach clips, and cigarette papers. 21 U.S.C. § 863(d)(1)–(15).

Additional Charges and Penalties

Hundreds of additional charges and penalties that apply to drug offenses, including marijuana, are spread throughout the CSA and the criminal code. They include trafficking at truck stops, 21 U.S.C. § 849; distributing to pregnant women, § 861(f); using firearms in connection to drug trafficking, 18 U.S.C. § 924(c)(2) [§ 924(c)(3)(B) was found unconstitutionally vague as to a "crime of violence" in *United States v. Davis*, 139 S. Ct. 2319 (2019); however, the drug trafficking provision remained unaltered]; committing robberies and burglaries involving drugs, 18 U.S.C. § 2118; cultivating marijuana on federal property, 21 U.S.C. § 841(b)(5); environmental damage from illegal manufacturing, § 841(b)(6); and various tax and money laundering offenses. Broadcast and written or internet advertisements are prohibited. § 843(b)–(c). A person involved in drug crimes forfeits to the U.S. the drugs and money involved in the transaction, as well as real and personal property substantially connected to the illegal transaction. §§ 853, 881.

Although the CSA technically allows for capital punishment for drug "kingpins" whose trafficking or revenues surpass thresholds established on weight or gross drug receipts respectively, 18 U.S.C. § 3591(b), such a penalty is of doubtful constitutionality. *See Kennedy v. Louisiana*, 554 U.S. 407, 437, 467 (2008).

§ 5–3.3 RESTRICTIONS

The CSA prohibition of marijuana reaches far beyond criminal law. Because so much of the modern economy is intertwined with federal government, the illegality of marijuana affects various sectors tied to federal law. Marijuana-related businesses, even though licensed by a state, cannot obtain basic banking services, as most banks are federally chartered. Similarly, these businesses are disallowed from deducting ordinary business expense and losses on their federal tax forms. Patent protection for inventions and trademark protection for brands are hard to come by and uncertain. Contracts for marijuana sales may not be enforced in federal court. Interaction with the immigration system presents hazards. Individuals and entities engaged in marijuana commerce are not eligible for Small Business Administration loans. Likewise, they were not eligible for relief provided by the federal government to businesses hurt by the SARS-CoV-2 pandemic. For more on the civil law repercussions of the CSA prohibition of marijuana, *see* Chapters Sixteen through Twenty-one.

§ 5–4 THE UNIFORM STATE CONTROLLED SUBSTANCES ACT

The passage of the CSA was also significant in spawning similar statutes in the 50 states, which are modeled after its provisions. Most states enacted a version of the CSA as their governing law in the early 1970s. (Two states retained the Uniform State Narcotic Drug Act.) Thus, the CSA replicated itself at the state level, imposing a fairly uniform nationwide regime prohibiting and penalizing marijuana. Although this uniform scheme has changed with states decriminalizing marijuana possession, and later legalizing medicinal and recreational marijuana, state controlled substance acts remain the underlying framework for laws controlling marijuana.

Closely modeled on the CSA, the Uniform Controlled Substances Act (UCSA) was promulgated by the Uniform Law Commission (ULC) in 1970 at the urging of the Nixon administration. (The ULC proposes model legislation for the 50 states so as to disseminate effective legislation and harmonize federal and state laws.) This effort was largely successful, and by 1979, 44 states as well as the District of Columbia, Puerto Rico, and the Virgin Islands had enacted modified versions of the UCSA. As the CSA has been amended, revisions to the UCSA have been promulgated in 1990 and 1994.

The UCSA allows for quick translation of any federal rescheduling of drugs into state law. Although many states have adopted a controlled substances schedule identical to that at the federal level, states have the autonomy to create independent schedules. Processes for rescheduling vary by state. Some states—such as Texas, Illinois, and New Jersey—have an automatic rescheduling system in which the scheduling procedure is automatically triggered by a federal scheduling determination. However, several state courts have invalidated this "short-form" automatic insertion of federal scheduling into state law as an unconstitutional delegation of state legislative power to a federal agency and Congress. *Louisiana v. Rodriguez*, 379 So. 2d 1084, 1087 (La. 1980). In other states—such as Pennsylvania, New York, and California—there is no formal linkage between the federal process and the state process. In those states, rescheduling decision are made either by a state regulatory agency or the state legislature.

Although the UCSA closely follows the definitions and scheduling regime of the CSA, it provides more flexibility for states to set penalties for violations of drug laws. Nevertheless, most states enacted penalties similar to those set out in the CSA. Since 1996, many states have amended their controlled substances acts so as to account for their legalization of medicinal and recreational marijuana.

Contrary to claims that are often made, the federal prohibition of marijuana activity does not by itself add an additional ban on interstate commerce in marijuana. In fact, the commonly imposed state restrictions on interstate commerce in marijuana, may themselves violate the dormant commerce clause doctrine.

§ 5–5 RESCHEDULING OF MARIJUANA UNDER THE CSA

To administer the new drug regime created by the CSA, the Drug Enforcement Administration (DEA) was established in 1973 as a unit of the Justice Department. In addition to replacing the Bureau of Narcotics and Dangerous Drugs, the DEA represented a reorganization and consolidation of scattered federal authority as to narcotics into one agency. To better achieve its enforcement mandate, the DEA is tasked with both public health administration and criminal law enforcement of the CSA. With the nuanced approach to federalism that is a hallmark of the CSA, the DEA is meant to work in conjunction with state law enforcement in implementing drug prohibition. Many law enforcement actions against marijuana are combined efforts of the DEA and local law enforcement.

The DEA has issued extensive regulations as to the administration of the CSA. Registration must be obtained from the DEA to manufacture, distribute, and dispense controlled substances. 21 U.S.C. §§ 822–23. These requirements include registration, 21 C.F.R. § 1301.11; payment, § 1301.13; quotas, § 1303; storage and security, § 1301.72–76; inventories, § 1304.04; record-keeping and reporting, § 1304.03; and disposal, § 1317. Scientific and medical research on Schedule I drugs is not per se legal. Medical researchers are classified as practitioners and undergo extensive requirements to conduct research. 21 C.F.R. §§ 1301.18, 1301.32.

The role of the DEA in regulating and enforcing the CSA is discussed further in Chapters 6 and 7. However, because marijuana is not a prescribed drug, registration regulations are less important than regulations regarding the possible rescheduling of marijuana under the CSA.

The CSA provides procedures for modifying the listing of drugs in its schedules. 21 U.S.C. § 811(a)–

(c). One of the methods of schedules of the CSA was to enable drugs to be reclassified without overturning the framework of the entire law. The DOJ is authorized to initiate proceedings to reschedule drugs, but so far has rebuffed any attempts to do so as to marijuana.

The U.S. Attorney General may remove any drug from the CSA schedules or transfer between schedules upon finding, in consultation with the Secretary of the Department of Health and Human Services (HHS), the Food and Drug Administration (FDA), and National Institute on Drug Abuse (NIDA), that it no longer fits the classification. The criteria for rescheduling a controlled substance include:

> (1) Its actual or relative potential for abuse; (2) Scientific evidence of its pharmacological effect, if known; (3) The state of current scientific knowledge regarding the drug or other substance; (4) Its history and current pattern of abuse; (5) The scope, duration, and significance of abuse; (6) What, if any, risk there is to the public health; (7) Its psychic or physiological dependence liability; (8) Whether the substance is an immediate precursor of a substance already controlled under this subchapter.

§ 811(b)–(c). Proceedings into rescheduling can be initiated by the Attorney General, Secretary of the Department of Health and Human Services, or petition of an interested party. The Attorney General has delegated decisions about rescheduling to the DEA. 28 C.F.R. § 0.100. HHS, the FDA, and NIDA provide a scientific assessment of the drug to the DEA, which must take the recommendations "and all other relevant data" into account. However, the CSA also states that the Attorney General is required to schedule drugs according to international treaty obligations, regardless of the § 811(b)–(c) findings. The DEA has consistently argued that the extensive controls required for cannabis under the treaties compel the scheduling of marijuana in either Schedules I or II. But even if transferred from Schedule I to a less restrictive schedule, marijuana would have to be approved by the FDA as a safe and effective drug before it could be marketed.

Because the CSA is a hybrid of public health measures and criminal law enforcement, scheduling of marijuana is somewhat anomalous. The crucial factor in classifying marijuana is whether it has currently accepted medical use. If a controlled substance has no currently accepted medical use, it must be placed in Schedule I, regardless of any other factor.

"Currently accepted medical use" is indicated if the drug's chemistry is known and reproducible; if there are adequate and well-controlled safety studies proving efficacy; and if the scientific evidence showing efficacy is widely available and accepted by qualified experts. The DEA has denied the presence of all of these factors as to marijuana.

The DEA has stated that it classifies a substance as having "a high potential for abuse" if evidence indicates that individuals are taking the drug in sufficient amounts to create a hazard to themselves or the community; that the drug is widely diverted from legal use; or that individuals are taking it without medical supervision.

Although the National Commission on Marihuana and Drug Abuse, in its March 22, 1972 Report, "Marihuana: A Signal of Misunderstanding," established by the CSA at inception, recommended decriminalizing marijuana, it remained on Schedule I. The DEA subsequently denied five petitions to reschedule marijuana. In 1972, the newly formed National Organization for the Reform of Marijuana Laws (NORML) launched a high-profile petition to reschedule marijuana. Although the petition was summarily dismissed by the DEA, federal courts ordered the DEA to begin a medical and scientific inquiry as provided for in the CSA. In 1988, DEA Chief Administrative Law Judge Francis Young concluded that marijuana was safe for therapeutic purposes and should be reclassified as a Schedule II substance. However, the DEA refused to adopt this finding and again denied the petition, *In re Matter of Marijuana Rescheduling Petition*, 54 Fed. Reg. 53,767, 53,783 (Dec. 29, 1989), a decision upheld by the Court of Appeals, *Alliance for Cannabis Therapeutics v. DEA,* 15 F. 3d 1131, 1133 (D.C. Cir. 1994). Similar highly publicized petitions were filed by Carl Olsen in 1983 and 1992, and *High Times* Magazine and Dr. Jon Gettman in 1995, and Petitioners Americans for Safe Access et al. in 2002. All these petitions were rebuffed by the DEA; the DEA rulings were upheld in *Gettman v. Drug Enforcement Admin.*, 290 F.3d 430 (D.C. Cir. 2002) and *Americans for Safe Access v. DEA*, 706 F.3d 438 (D.C. Cir. 2013).

In August 2016, the DEA denied a 2009 petition by nurse petitioner Bryan Krumm and a 2011 petition by Washington State Governor Christine Gregoire and Rhode Island Governor Lincoln Chafee to reschedule marijuana. 81 *Federal Register* 53,687. The DEA received a lengthy scientific and medical evaluation from the Department of Health and Human Services and the FDA, concluding again that marijuana has a high potential for abuse, has no currently accepted medical use in treatment in the United States, and lacks accepted safety for use under medical supervision. However, the DEA for the first time relaxed its marijuana strictures. For example, it announced that it intends to register growers of research-grade marijuana, in addition to the NIDA-funded program at the University of Mississippi. Furthermore, researchers are no longer required to submit a proposed study of marijuana to the U.S. Public Health Service for review, a requirement not imposed for any other Schedule I substance.

After motions for rehearing were denied, Krumm appealed to the Court of Appeals for the D.C. Circuit in 2018, which ultimately denied the appeal. *Krumm v. Drug Enforcement Admin.*, 739 F. App'x 655 (D.C. Cir. 2018) (mem.). Krumm also petitioned for a writ of certiorari to the Supreme Court but was denied in 2019.

In 2017, another lawsuit, *Washington v. Barr,* 925 F.3d 109 (2d Cir. 2017), challenged the constitutionality of the CSA and called for rescheduling of marijuana. The District Court dismissed on procedural grounds, holding that the Plaintiffs had not exhausted their administrative remedies with the DEA. On appeal, the Second Circuit rebuked the DEA's history of handling rescheduling petitions. While the Second Circuit agreed that Plaintiffs should have first petitioned the DEA, the court also maintained jurisdiction over the case if the DEA does not "act promptly." In its opinion, the court wrote that:

> Plaintiffs document that the average delay in deciding petitions to reclassify drugs under the CSA is approximately nine years. . . . where agencies have a history of dilatory proceedings, federal courts have sometimes retained jurisdiction of related cases to facilitate swift review.

Washington v. Barr, 925 F.3d 109, 120–21 (2d Cir. 2019); *accord Sisley v. DEA*, No. 20-71433 (9th Cir. June 10, 2021). One of the reasons for the DEA's refusal to consider rescheduling is that it has already rescheduled the drug Marinol. Marinol is the trade name for dronabinol, which is synthesized from delta-9-tetrahydrocannabinol (THC) and is formulated in sesame oil. It is taken orally as a gelatin capsule and is available in 2.5mg, 5mg or 10mg dosages. Marinol was originally placed in 1985 in Schedule II. A rescheduling petition was filed by Unimed Pharmaceutical, which owned the Marinol patent. In 1992, Marinol was rescheduled to Schedule III so that it could more easily be prescribed to patients. Therefore, the DEA argues that rescheduling marijuana is unnecessary, as a synthetic cannabinoid has already been made available as a Schedule III drug. The FDA has also approved the drugs Syndros and Cesamet, which are also synthetically derived from cannabis.

In June 2018, the FDA approved the drug, Epidiolex, containing a purified marijuana extract, the first-such approval of a marijuana derivative, as opposed to a synthetic cannabinoid. Epidiolex is an oral-based treatment for Lennox-Gastaut syndrome and Dravet syndrome, two rare forms of pediatric epilepsy. Its active ingredient is cannabidiol (CBD), a non-intoxicating marijuana cannabinoid. In September 2018, DEA classified Epidiolex in Schedule V, the first marijuana extract of the cannabis plant to be placed in a less stringent schedule than Schedule I. 83 Fed. Reg. 48950. (In April 2020, DEA approved Epidiolex for tuberous sclerosis complex and also descheduled it, removing it from control. 85 Fed. Reg. 51,639.)

As the DEA is the administrative agency authorized to make rescheduling decisions, the standard of review by the courts is not whether there is persuasive evidence of medical efficacy for marijuana, or its high potential for abuse, but whether decisions by the DEA are arbitrary and capricious. Under this standard, it is unlikely that a court challenge to the DEA's discretion as to rescheduling will be successful in the foreseeable future.

§ 5-6 PENDING MARIJUANA REFORM

With 36 states and the District of Columbia legalizing marijuana for medical use and 18 states and the District of Columbia legalizing marijuana for recreational use, the public attitude towards marijuana is shifting. Similarly, a number of recent bills, though largely unsuccessful to date, indicate that momentum for marijuana may be shifting at the federal level, as well.

The bills take several tacks. Perhaps the most common is to simply reclassify marijuana to a less restrictive schedule than Schedule 1, most commonly to Schedule 3, as in Marijuana 1-to-3 Act of 2021, H.R.365, 117th Congress. This legislation would make marijuana legal by medical prescription with FDA approval but would not allow for recreational use. Removing marijuana from the CSA altogether would allow for recreational use. Another method would be to exempt marijuana activity from the strictures of the CSA if used in compliance with state law or tribal law. Specific bills have been introduced to ameliorate the adverse impact the CSA exerts on banks dealing with marijuana businesses and to allow for marijuana businesses to deduct ordinary business expenses. Some federal bills would remove the many collateral consequences, including deportation, that can follow in the wake of a marijuana conviction. Various provisions would allow veterans with post-traumatic stress disorder access to medical marijuana options in the Veterans Administration health system. Bills have been introduced at both the federal and state level to mitigate the effect of the decades old war on marijuana by providing revenue for business opportunities in disadvantaged areas, creating community reinvestment funds, and by expunging criminal marijuana records.

For more on the specific legislation proposed in Congress *see* 16–4 and 27–3.2. These efforts highlight the increasing momentum for marijuana reform at the federal level.

CHAPTER 6

ENFORCEMENT OF THE CONTROLLED SUBSTANCES ACT

§ 6–1 INTRODUCTION

The Department of Justice (DOJ) is the law enforcement arm of the federal government. The Drug Enforcement Administration (DEA) is an agency of the Department of Justice created specifically to administer the CSA and enforce the nation's drug laws. In the decades after passage of the CSA in 1970, the DOJ and DEA—which were granted wide discretion in enforcing and administering the CSA—insisted on their obligation to enforce the federal prohibitions of marijuana to their maximum capacity. The DEA has continued to resist liberalization of marijuana laws, even in states that have legalized medical and recreational marijuana. However, recent presidential administrations have shifted in their stated policies as to enforcement of marijuana law. During the Obama administration, the DOJ, which has supervisory authority over the DEA, stated that it would not intervene in the legalization regimes of states so long as federal enforcement priorities are maintained. This policy was rescinded during the Trump Administration, in word but not in effect. The DOJ under the Biden Administration is seemingly continuing this approach of accommodating state laws, with a Democratic Party-controlled House of Representative introducing a rash of legalization measures. Recent congressional legislation has further restrained DOJ and DEA enforcement of marijuana prohibitions in legalizing states.

This chapter summarizes federal enforcement of the marijuana provisions of the CSA by both the DOJ and the DEA. Section 6–2 describes various policies the DOJ has adopted in overseeing federal marijuana laws. Section 6–3 describes enforcement mechanisms the DEA has waged in its war against marijuana. Section 6–4 describes the consequences of marijuana violations under the CSA. Finally, § 6–5 summarizes recent changes in the response of the DOJ and the DEA to state legalization of marijuana.

§ 6–2 DOJ ENFORCEMENT OF THE CSA

The DOJ is the department of the federal government with lead authority to enforce federal criminal law. It is headed by the U.S. Attorney General, a cabinet level position. 93 U.S. Attorneys prosecute federal crimes in the 94 federal court districts. As with any law enforcement agency, the DOJ has a large amount of discretion in enforcing the law based on resources, needs, and urgency. Although the DOJ is obliged not to run afoul of equal protection and disparate treatment—common complaints in the criminal justice system—it had long asserted prosecution of marijuana crimes as a high priority. The DOJ has focused on higher level trafficking of marijuana and has relied on states to enforce street-level marijuana crimes with the same vigor. The enforcement capabilities of the federal government are limited, however, in terms of both manpower and constitutional reach due to the states' police powers. Historically, the states, with many more law enforcement officials, make over 100 marijuana arrests for every one marijuana arrest by federal agents. Thus, federal enforcement focuses on high-level traffickers, high publicity cases, and cases in which the DOJ seeks to send a message.

The CSA explicitly makes the enforcement of drug laws a cooperative venture between the DOJ and state, local and Indian tribal authorities. It directs the Attorney General to cooperate with these authorities as well as other federal agencies. 21 U.S.C. § 873. The Attorney General is authorized to exchange information with other agencies, cooperate in prosecutions, conduct joint training programs, maintain databases, and engage in joint eradication of marijuana plants. In addition, the Attorney General assesses the capability of local governments to fight drug abuse, offers them assistance, establishes cooperative investigative and enforcement efforts, and makes grants to assist drug suppression efforts.

Prosecutorial discretion is an important consideration in all criminal enforcement, but especially so in drug cases. Prosecutors have wide discretion in what criminal cases to bring, what offenses to charge, what pleas to bargain, and what sentences to propose. Because drug laws set a wide range of penalties, discretion comes into play in almost every drug case.

There has been concern about the discretionary power of federal prosecutors, especially given the so-called "federalization" of crime. Under the U.S.

Constitution, the federal government lacks inherent police power. In contrast, the states have plenary powers over criminal legislation, allowing them to enact all criminal laws not prohibited by constitutions or other superior legal authority. Federalization refers to making crimes that were traditionally just state crimes federal crimes as well, mostly as a result of increased federal powers under the Commerce Clause and the Necessary and Proper Clause of the Constitution. Such federalization places enormous discretionary power in the hands of U.S. Attorneys. The CSA is a textbook example of federalization of criminal offenses, given that the powers of the DOJ, U.S. Attorneys, and the DEA are now exercised in areas formerly left to state control. Because of the severe penalties and collateral consequences for drug offenses embedded throughout the federal criminal code, federalization itself configures a harsher treatment of marijuana law.

Prosecutors in their discretion must observe the strictures of the Equal Protection Clause of the Fourteenth Amendment. Categories of persons cannot be favored or disfavored over one another. Questions of equal protection and disparate impact have arisen from studies that show that prosecutors favor harsher penalties for drug offenders who are male over female. Likewise, critics have contended that enforcement of marijuana crimes has traditionally oppressed poor and minority communities. Studies have also shown the disproportionate impact of marijuana prosecutions under the CSA on minority populations. For example, in its latest study examining the intersection of marijuana prosecutions and race, the American Civil Liberties Union (ACLU) found that African Americans are 3.64 times more likely to be arrested for marijuana crimes, even though the incidence of marijuana use by Caucasian and African American populations is approximately equal. ACLU, *A Tale of Two Countries: Racially Targeted Arrests in the Era of Marijuana Reform* (2018), p. 29. In 2010, African Americans accounted for 58% of marijuana arrests, despite being only 15% of the population.

A 2010 study of California arrests found that Hispanic Americans were arrested and prosecuted at two to three times the rate of whites, despite the fact that Hispanics have lower rates of marijuana use.

While national arrest rates for marijuana possession were lower in 2018 than in 2010, racial disparities in arrests persist. In every state, African Americans are arrested for marijuana possession at higher rates regardless of whether states have legalized or decriminalized marijuana. In 31 states, racial disparities were actually larger in 2018 than in 2010.

§ 6–3 DRUG ENFORCEMENT ADMINISTRATION AND THE CSA

The Drug Enforcement Administration (DEA) is the drug law enforcement agency of the United States government, operating under the aegis of the DOJ. It was created in 1973 as the chief federal drug enforcement unit. Reflecting the nature of the CSA itself, the DEA combines law enforcement and public health functions. First, it enforces the criminal provisions of the Controlled Substances Act (CSA) through intelligence gathering, investigation, education, arrests, drug eradication, assistance to other law enforcement branches, asset forfeiture, and assistance in DOJ prosecutions. DEA enforcement includes both civil and criminal sanctions. Second, it administers the complex civil rules that govern the provision of controlled medicines in the nation's health system. The DEA publishes the implementing regulations for the CSA in 21 C.F.R. §§ 1300–1321.

The DEA considers enforcement of federal laws against marijuana, as a Schedule I drug, as among its core priorities, effectuating the intent of Congress as demonstrated through its classification of marijuana as a Schedule I drug and its ratification of international treaties imposing such obligations. As intended by the CSA, the DEA works in cooperation with state and local drug enforcement, as well as with other federal agencies and foreign countries.

Just as the CSA consolidated previous drug laws, the DEA consolidated several federal agencies into one centralized enforcement agency with extensive resources to combat drug abuse. The DEA is headed by an Administrator of Drug Enforcement, who reports to the Attorney General, under the supervision of the Deputy Attorney General. One of the nation's largest criminal enforcement agencies, it has 293 domestic offices in 23 field divisions in the United States and 91 offices in 68 foreign countries as of 2021. In addition, the DEA has 4,924 Special Agents and boasts a budget of over $3 billion as of 2019. As the chief federal agency in defining an overall strategy against drug abuse, the DEA is considered the lynchpin in both law and practice in the federal government's efforts at combatting illegal drugs, and works in cooperation with other law enforcement agencies such as the Federal Bureau of Investigation (FBI), the Bureau of Alcohol, Tobacco, Firearms and Explosives (ATF), the U.S. Coast Guard (USCG), the U.S. Department of Homeland Security (which now includes U.S. Customs and Border Protection (CBP)), the U.S. Postal Inspection Service, and the U.S. Immigration and Customs Enforcement (ICE).

The DEA has resisted drawing a distinction between marijuana and other Schedule I drugs, as indeed the CSA makes no such distinction. The agency has a complete arsenal of programs in its enforcement campaign against marijuana. These include domestic and international investigations by its law enforcement agents; arrests of marijuana users, manufacturers, and distributors; cannabis plant eradication; and marijuana, paraphernalia, and asset seizure. As the administrative agency entrusted with enforcing the CSA, the DEA also registers controlled substances for medical use and scientific study and prevents diversion of legally prescribed controlled substances into illegal channels.

The DEA also coordinates the nationwide prohibition against domestic manufacture, distribution, and use of marijuana. It makes its resources available to state and local drug enforcement agencies. Internationally, it works with foreign governments to suppress cannabis cultivation and distribution.

DEA agents are elite law enforcement officers, trained in firearm use, investigative techniques, and other skills essential to combating the drug trade. They gather intelligence, investigate drug activity, make strategic decisions about resources and arrests. They also assist U.S. Attorneys and other officials in prosecution of marijuana crimes through every stage including trial, appeals, incarceration, and probation.

The DEA has state and local task forces to assist in state anti-drug efforts. Because of the extent of their resources, these task forces often take a leadership role in working with local law enforcement. Although most DEA programs are designed to combat the entire range of illicit drugs, operations against marijuana activity have been a major component. The DEA, local task forces, and state enforcement agencies are still active in combatting large-scale marijuana operations, even in legalizing states. For example, one of the largest marijuana raids and arrests took place on June 8, 2021, when the DEA and other federal and state agencies seized 16 tons of marijuana, worth an estimated $1.19 billion, from illegal large-scale marijuana farms near Los Angeles.

§ 6–3.1 INVESTIGATION AND INTELLIGENCE GATHERING

The Intelligence Division of the DEA is a multifaceted division that collects, analyzes and disseminates drug-related intelligence information to coordinate with enforcement mechanisms at the federal, state, and local level. In this role, the DEA takes on a range of responsibilities with teams ranging from special operations, mobile enforcement, and organized crimes, amongst others. This section analyzes some of these roles in turn.

The Intelligence Division of the DEA collects, analyzes, and disseminates drug-related intelligence. It coordinates this intelligence with other federal, state, local and international law enforcement organizations. Its aviation division conducts airplane surveillance of suspected marijuana growing and trafficking sites. The DEA's Special Operations Division (SOD) came under scrutiny for its mass collection of U.S. overseas call records as part of its investigation program. This practice has since been terminated after a 2013 leak of U.S. National Security Agency (NSA) records.

As a feature of the cooperative efforts against drug use, the DEA Mobile Enforcement Teams (MET) are a support staff for state and local crime investigation. METs are quick-deployment teams that, at the request of local law enforcement, deploy with local police when marijuana activity linked to violence is suspected. From 1995 to 2002, Mobile Enforcement Teams seized 6,656 pounds of marijuana in their deployments.

The Organized Crime Drug Enforcement Task Force Program (OCDETF) targets major drug trafficking and money laundering operations. It combines the efforts of federal, state, and local law enforcement agencies through its creation of Strike Forces. Strike Forces are intelligence-driven teams of various law enforcement agencies situated in key cities across the United States. As of July 2020, there were 19 OCDETF Strike Forces located throughout the country. (Strike Forces are currently located in Atlanta, Baltimore, Boston, Chicago, Cleveland, Dallas, Denver, Detroit, El Paso, Houston, Kansas City, Los Angeles, New York, Phoenix, Sacramento, San Diego, San Juan, St. Louis, and Tampa.)

The DEA cooperates closely with the Office of National Drug Control Policy (led by the "Drug Czar"), an executive office tasked with coordination of antidrug policies. It actively opposes marijuana legalization and educates youth against marijuana use by, for example, providing anti-marijuana advertising on a national basis. It also oversees the High Intensity Drug Trafficking Areas (HIDTA) program. The HIDTA program assists federal, state, local and tribal law enforcement in combating drugs in 33 geographical regions designated as high trafficking zones. With more than 1,500 DEA special agents and a 2021 budget of $290 million, HIDTA funds numerous projects that aim to promote coordination and intelligence sharing among drug fighting agencies in these zones.

The DEA is also authorized to police drug activity outside the United States. In foreign enforcement, the DEA works under the guidance of the Secretary of State and U.S. ambassadors in cooperating with foreign governments.

Just as the legal focus of the DEA's domestic operations is the CSA, internationally the DEA acts according to the 1961 Single Convention Treaty on Narcotic Drugs. In addition to foreign governments, the DEA cooperates with Interpol and United Nations officials.

The DEA has been involved in high publicity anti-drug campaigns overseas. For example, it helped prosecute Panamanian dictator Manuel Noriega on drug trafficking charges. The killing of DEA agent Enrique Camarena by a Mexican drug cartel in 1985, in retaliation for raids on marijuana plantations, resulted in the largest homicide investigation ever undertaken by the DEA and strained relations with Mexican police authorities.

The Border Enforcement Security Task Force headed by the Department of Homeland Security protects against drug importation, for example, marijuana smuggled in underground tunnels from Mexico.

For a discussion of DEA enforcement and international law, *see* § 10–3.2.

§ 6–3.2 ERADICATION AND DIVERSION CONTROL

The DEA marijuana eradication program began in 1979. The DEA describes marijuana as the only drug of abuse grown within U.S. borders. Its Domestic Cannabis Eradication/Suppression Program (DCE/SP) engages in efforts to eradicate cultivated marijuana throughout the nation and provides resources to 128 state and local eradication programs. In 2019, the DCE/SP eradicated 3,232,722 cultivated outdoor cannabis plants and 770,472 cultivated indoor plants for a total of 4,003,194 marijuana plants. In the course of these operations, the DEA made 4,718 arrests, and seized over $29 million in marijuana cultivator assets and 3,210 weapons from marijuana cultivators. Although the DEA has in previous decades eradicated billions of non-cultivated, "feral" cannabis plants, such efforts have largely ceased. Instead, the DEA now primarily targets sophisticated cultivators.

The DEA Office of Diversion Control seeks to prevent diversion of legally prescribed drugs into illegal channels. In doing so, the DEA has brought numerous civil and criminal cases against physicians and other registrants under the CSA. As the CSA allows for no legally prescribed use of Schedule I drugs such as marijuana, the Office of Diversion Control has been less involved in marijuana operations. This may well change with marijuana legalization efforts, when the DEA may seek to confine marijuana use to legally regulated streams.

§ 6–3.3 ADMINISTRATION OF SCIENTIFIC AND MEDICAL RESEARCH

The DEA and NIDA

In addition to enforcing the criminal violations of the CSA, the DEA also administers its public health provisions. As the administrator of the CSA, the DEA classifies controlled substances under the five Schedules, registers manufacturers, distributors, and dispensers of controlled medicines, administers denial, revocation, or suspension of registration, compiles records and reports of registrants, enacts rules as to labeling, packaging, and prescriptions of controlled medicines, and sets their production quotas and rules for security.

Most of these duties involve controlled substances on Schedules II through V, which the CSA allows for medical use. As medical use of marijuana is prohibited on Schedule I, the chief administrative task the DEA carries out in regard to marijuana is authorizing and supervising research into marijuana.

The DEA imposes strict requirements that it claims are necessary to ensure that research marijuana does not fall into the wrong hands, or that scientific research is not used as a pretext for marijuana trafficking. In addition, the DEA takes the position that no test with rigorous criteria has indicated medical benefits to marijuana. However, the DEA is loosening the stringent research restrictions imposed since 1970. As of 2020, the DEA has registered 595 individuals to conduct research on marijuana, marking a dramatic increase in the number of approved researchers from DEA historic averages.

The National Institute on Drug Abuse (NIDA) funds scientific research on marijuana. Until 2020, the DEA designated the National Center for Natural Products Research at the University of Mississippi as the exclusive source of marijuana growing research. However, in December 2020 the DEA promulgated a final rule that allows other sources of marijuana growers for research under certain conditions. 21 C.F.R. §§ 1301.18, 1318.04. This ruling is intended to remedy some of the obstacles to research mentioned in this chapter. On May 14, 2021, the DEA provided a Memorandum of Agreement (MOA) to several manufacturers to allow them to cultivate marijuana for research needs in the United States.

The DEA and FDA

In addition, the Food and Drug Administration (FDA) plays an active role in marijuana regulation through research and marketing under both the Controlled Substances Act (CSA) and the Food, Drug and Cosmetic Act (FDCA). Under the FDCA and the CSA, the FDA is tasked with approving marketable drugs ensuring that consumers have adequate information on the risks and benefits of such substances. To date, the FDA has approved only one marketing application for cannabis (Epidiolex) for the treatment of a disease or condition. Epidiolex is a marijuana derivative used to treat seizures. Moreover, only a handful of synthetic cannabinoid drugs have been approved by the FDA. These drugs are Marinol, Syndros, and Cesamet, which the FDA has approved for therapeutic uses related to extreme weight loss.

The Agriculture Improvement Act of 2018 (also called the "Farm Bill") removed hemp from the CSA, meaning that cannabis plants and derivatives that contain no more than 0.3% Tetrahydrocannabinols (THC) are no longer considered controlled substances. However, this change in the definition of marijuana has not affected the FDA's authority to regulate products containing cannabis or cannabis-derived substances, even if these substances are classified as "hemp."

Although the FDA has only approved only one substance containing cannabis or cannabis derivatives, the FDA is not hostile to the idea of increased clinical research on marijuana. The FDA relies on clinical trials and medical research to inform its decisions to approve application for drug marketability. Most recently, the agency's July 2020 draft guidance, *Cannabis and Cannabis-Derived Compounds: Quality Considerations for Clinical Research Guidance for Industry*, provides information and consideration for research in the field, By and large the FDA evaluation of the therapeutic efficacy of marijuana, its derivatives, and its synthetic cannabinoids determines DEA's placement of the substance on CSA schedules.

§ 6–3.4 ANTI-MARIJUANA EDUCATION

A major component of the DEA anti-marijuana campaign is its efforts in the field of education. This campaign is carried out by the DEA Demand Reduction Section, established in 1986. The Demand Reduction Section produces a voluminous amount of anti-marijuana literature, including "Fact Sheets," booklets, pamphlets, and an annual, lengthy report on The DEA Position on Marijuana. Additionally, the DEA has created numerous resources for parents, caregivers, and educators through the "Get Smart About Drugs" education and prevention program.

Perhaps reacting to the tide of state legalization and the increasing prevalence of the opioid crisis, the DEA titled its 2020 annual report as *Drugs of Abuse: a DEA Resource Guide.*

Every DEA field division participates in the local Drug Abuse Resistance Education (D.A.R.E.) program that educates young people on the dangers of narcotics abuse. The DEA also speaks out against efforts to decriminalize or legalize marijuana.

§ 6–4 CONSEQUENCES OF CSA VIOLATIONS

The legal consequences of a marijuana conviction are both direct—the penal sentence and fine imposed, and assets that are forfeited—and indirect, including the collateral consequences of a conviction, which are far reaching.

§ 6–4.1 ARRESTS AND CONVICTIONS

Relying on state law enforcement for arrest of non-major marijuana users, growers, and sellers, the DEA focuses on arrests of large-scale marijuana growers and sellers linked to organized crime, both in the United States and abroad. In 2019, the DEA performed 4,718 arrests, marking a dramatic decrease from averages between 5,000 and 8,000 yearly arrests in prior decades. (Arrests by all law enforcement for marijuana crimes totaled 545,602 in 2019, also a decrease from peak of about 800,000 in 2008.) In this same year, the DEA seized 363,098 pounds of bulk processed marijuana, accounting for over $29 million dollars in assets.

As the DEA undertakes these operations against large-scale enterprises, it often makes arrests in heavily armed deployments. In response to criticism for its "military-style" arrests, the DEA defends such efforts as necessary against marijuana growers and traffickers who themselves may be heavily manned and armed. Certainly, the DEA is more open to criticism for excessive use of force in arresting less organized marijuana users.

For example, on July 30, 2013 the DEA paid a $4.1 million settlement to marijuana user Daniel Chong. Chong was a student at the University of California San Diego when he was arrested for marijuana possession. He was left in a DEA holding cell for five days, without food, hydration, or access to a bathroom.

§ 6–4.2 ASSET SEIZURES

The DEA and other law enforcement agencies are authorized to seize property used in marijuana activities and assets derived from marijuana sales. The CSA authorizes both criminal and civil seizure of drug assets. Criminal forfeiture is a sentencing proceeding against the person (in personem), the defendant in the case, who must be proved guilty beyond a reasonable doubt. 21 U.S.C. § 853. However, criminal forfeiture of assets is not part of the charge that must be proved beyond a reasonable doubt, but only a part of the sentence that must be proved by a preponderance of the evidence.

In contrast, DEA seizures under civil asset forfeiture are proceedings against the property (in rem). 21 U.S.C. § 881. No charges even have to be brought against the property owner, only evidence that links the property to drug crimes. In 1990, the standard for civil asset forfeiture was amended from "beyond a reasonable doubt," to a "preponderance of the evidence" that the property was used or derived from drug activity. In 2000, the burden of proof was further amended to place the burden on the government rather than the owner. 18 U.S.C. § 981. The "preponderance of the evidence" standard is now the same for both criminal and civil forfeiture. 18 U.S.C. §§ 982–983. The result of the differing standards is that property of the accused can be seized by the government without the litany of protections afforded criminal defendants.

All 50 states have enacted similar asset forfeiture provisions for drug activity. Because of the nature of their operations, the FBI, U.S. Customs Service, U.S. Border Patrol, and the U.S. Coast Guard also seize assets connected to marijuana activity, as well as marijuana itself that is transported into the country. 19 U.S.C. § 1607. Although asset seizure connected to criminal activity dates back to the beginning of law enforcement in the United States, it remains controversial, especially given the less stringent requirements of proof in civil forfeiture.

§ 6–4.3 SENTENCING

The CSA imposes minimum and maximum sentences of imprisonment for a federal marijuana conviction, as well as a maximum fine. The United States Sentencing Commission, an independent judicial agency, sets detailed guidelines for imposing these sentences for federal marijuana offenses. U.S. Sentencing Guidelines Manual § 2D1.1 (U.S. Sentencing Commission 2018). These guidelines, which are advisory, are intended to foster uniformity in federal sentencing and are widely followed by federal judges.

The sentence levels are determined by the identity and quantity of the controlled substance, with the quantity measured by the weight of the mixture rather than that of the pure controlled substance. The guidelines include a "Drug Quantity Table," and a "Drug Conversion Table." The Drug Quantity Table provides for 17 different base levels of drug offenses, with Level 6 being the lowest and Level 38 being the highest. Each level specifies the weight of marijuana necessary to constitute an offense. For example, a quantity of 90,000 KG or more of marijuana constitutes a Level 38 offense, whereas less than 1 KG of marijuana constitutes a Level 6 offense. If a mixture or substance contains more than one controlled substance, the weight of the entire mixture or substance is assigned to the controlled substance that results in the greater offense level. The Drug Conversion Table, on the other hand, can be used for drugs not directly listed in the Drug Quantity Table, or can be used to provide a means to combine different controlled substances to obtain a single offense level. USSG § 2D1.1(c).

Sentencing levels can be enhanced by "special offense characteristics," such as joint criminal activity resulting in death or serious bodily injury, use of a dangerous weapon, bribery, pollution, trafficking in prison, misuse by a licensed professional, and cultivation on state, federal, or tribal land. United States Sentencing Commission USSG §§ 3B1.1; 2D1.1(b).

Especially because marijuana serves as the basic measure for equivalent quantities of Schedule I and II controlled substances, the Sentencing Guidelines define marijuana with greater precision than the CSA. For purposes of the Guidelines, a marijuana plant is defined as an "organism having leaves and a readily observable root formation (e.g., a marihuana cutting having roots, a rootball, or root hairs is a marihuana plant)." USSG § 2D1.1(c) cmt. n.2. Hashish is defined as "a resinous substance of cannabis" that includes THC or a combination of other listed cannabinoids. Likewise, hashish oil is "a preparation of the soluble cannabinoids derived from cannabis" that includes THC or a combination of other listed cannabinoids. USSG § 2D1.1(c) n.(H)–(I).

Under the sentencing tables, one marijuana plant, regardless of sex, is equivalent to 100 grams of marijuana, although the actual weight of the plant, if greater, is used for sentencing. USSG § 2D1.1(c) n.(E).

Measuring the quantity of marijuana for sentencing can present complications. Are the number of marijuana plants counted according to the scientific and botanical definition of "plant," which would disqualify cuttings from marijuana plants that lack a fully developed root system? Or should the everyday definition of plant prevail which count such cuttings as separate marijuana plants for aggregating the quantity? *See, e.g.*, *United States v. Eves*, 932 F.2d 856 (1991) ("We conclude that the word 'plant' under the Sentencing Guidelines is to be given its plain and ordinary meaning and that the district court did not err in counting cuttings with roots as plants.").

§ 6–4.4 COLLATERAL CONSEQUENCES

The collateral consequences of a conviction for illicit drug use, including marijuana, are extensive. Collateral consequences of a conviction are considered civil sanctions, and the rules of criminal procedure do not apply. The far-reaching consequences of drug violations, often unknown by criminal defendants, including those who accept plea bargains, have received national attention.

A criminal conviction, especially a felony, brings collateral consequences. For example, a conviction can affect the right to vote, to hold public office, to serve on a jury, to serve in the military, and to receive federal benefits. It can also affect employment, professional licensing, and immigration status.

However, drug convictions are singled out for especially severe consequences, and are embedded in thousands of federal statutes. These include denial of federal benefits such as grants, contracts, and licenses. Drug convictions on a person's record have become even more consequential given the availability of public records on the Internet. Such offenses are now easily discovered by employers, government agencies, schools, colleges, and the like.

Some examples that may be applied to persons convicted of marijuana and other drug-related offenses are the following:

Public Housing—Denial or eviction from federally assisted housing. 42 U.S.C. §§ 13661–13662; *Dep't of Housing v. Rucker*, 535 U.S. 125 (2002).

Federal Benefits Program—Denial of federal benefits such as grants, contracts, and licenses.

Federal Assistance—Denial of cash assistance and food stamps through the Supplemental Nutrition Assistance Program (SNAP). As of 2019, 25 states have ended the ban on SNAP assistance for convicted felons, 24 have a modified ban, and only South Carolina provides a lifetime ban.

Social Security—Denial of SSI and SSDI for a person whose primary disability is drug dependence.

Aid Elimination Penalty—Denial of federal assistance to university students. Approximately 1,000 students a year have lose their student aid due to drug violations, but estimates indicate that the number of students denied is likely even higher, since many students with drug convictions are deterred from applying for federal student aid in the first place. However the FAFSA Simplification Act, signed into law on December 27, 2020, removes many of the negative consequences associated with a drug conviction in obtaining financial aid for college.

American Opportunity Tax Credit, formerly the Hope Scholarship Credit—Exclusion of this tax credit.

Firearms—Prohibited from obtaining or using firearms. 18 U.S.C. §§ 922(g)(3), 929(a)(2); 27 C.F.R. § 478.11 (2016). Alcohol, Tobacco, and Firearms Form 4473, Question 11e asks if the applicant is "an unlawful user of, or addicted to, marijuana." A false answer on this form is a federal crime with a 5-year maximum jail term. (For more on this topic, *see* Chapter 7).

State Driving Licenses—Pursuant to the 1992 Solomon-Lautenberg Amendment, many states originally suspended driving licenses for six months for any drug conviction, including marijuana. As of 2020, only four states—Alabama, Arkansas, Florida, and Texas—continue to suspend driving licenses under the amendment.

Felony Disenfranchisement—Exclusion from voting for a felony conviction is one of the most important collateral consequences of the widespread arrests and convictions for marijuana activity. The Supreme Court has held that the disenfranchisement of felons is authorized under § 2 of the Fourteenth Amendment and does not violate the Equal Protection Clause. However, in *Hunter v. Underwood*, 471 U.S. 222 (1985), the Court held that Alabama Code § 182, which denied the vote to those convicted of crimes involving "moral turpitude," was unconstitutional because it intentionally discriminated against African Americans. While an earlier statute had limited disenfranchisement to felonies, the new statute included a much broader category of "immoral" crimes, which the Alabama legislature believed were committed more frequently by black citizens and which included many misdemeanors. Felony disenfranchisement laws in other states, however, were allowed to stand. Given the disproportionate arrest and conviction of minority populations for marijuana crimes, it can be argued that, intentionally or not, the effect is to disenfranchise minority voters in greater proportion to white voters. At a collective level, felony disenfranchisement for marijuana and other convictions may alter the outcome of elections in certain states.

Immigration—Immigration hearings, among the most common cases in federal courts, are significantly affected by drug convictions. Drug offenses can render non-citizens, including those with permanent residence, deportable, 8 U.S.C. § 1227(a)(2)(B)(i)–(ii), and can bar their reentry into the United States, 8 U.S.C. § 1182(a)(2)(A)(i)(II), (a)(2)(C)(i). A 2015 Human Rights Watch report found that from 2007 to 2012, 33,337 people were deported for marijuana possession convictions and 18,151 for marijuana sale convictions. As of 2019, simple marijuana possession was the fourth most common cause of deportation for any offense and the most common cause of deportation for drug offenses. Ironically, the lessening of marijuana penalties can lead to more adverse immigration consequences, as defendants who do not face actual imprisonment do not have a Sixth Amendment right to assistance of counsel. Without such a right, they may not be counseled that a plea to a minor marijuana offense can result in deportation.

On the other hand, INS rules make a deportability exception for a "single offense involving possession for one's own use of 30 grams or less of marijuana." § 1227(a)(2)(B)(i). Likewise, the U.S. Supreme Court in three recent decisions ameliorated application of the deportation rules to non-citizens with marijuana convictions under certain cases, in part because of the lack of proportionality between the relatively minor marijuana violations in those cases and the severe consequences of deportation. *Padilla v. Commonwealth of Kentucky*, 559 U.S. 356 (2010); *Carachuri-Rosendo v. Holder*, 560 U.S. 563 (2010); *Moncrieffe v. Holder*, 569 U.S. 184 (2013).

The most famous marijuana deportation litigation, that of Beatle John Lennon from 1972 to 1975, was recounted in *John Lennon vs. the USA: The Inside Story of the Most Bitterly Contested and Influential Deportation* (2016), written by Lennon's lawyer during the four years of court battles, Leon Wildes. This case is discussed in further detail in Chapter 26, § 3–1.

§ 6–5 DOJ, DEA AND RECENT FEDERAL MARIJUANA POLICY

The DEA justifies its aggressive position against marijuana activity according to the CSA, which classifies marijuana in its most dangerous category. Under the Supremacy Clause of the U.S. Constitution, federal law takes precedence over conflicting state laws. This concept was explicitly extended into the realm of medical marijuana in *Gonzales v. Raich*, 545 U.S. 1 (2005). Therefore, when a state legalizes marijuana, the practical effect is that it is no longer prohibited under state law but still violates federal law and the CSA. For example, Gerald Lee Duval Jr. and his son, Jeremy Duval, were patients and caregivers under Michigan's Medical Marihuana Act. When their Michigan farm was raided in 2011, they were not permitted to challenge the search warrants on the grounds that their compliance with state law was not dispositive for purposes of evaluating a possible CSA violation. Gerald Lee Duval Jr. received a ten-year federal sentence and Jeremy, five years. *United States v. Duval*, 742 F.3d 246 (6th Cir. 2014). The Duvals post-conviction relief was denied by the Eastern District of Michigan in 2019. *Duval v. United States*, 372 F.Supp.3d 544 (E.D. Mich. 2019).

However, the DEA's unrelenting stance has been made more precarious by recent federal changes in marijuana policy. The DOJ has issued a series of memoranda that have allowed certain acquiescence in state legalization of medicinal and recreational use of marijuana. The first such document, the "Ogden" memorandum of October 19, 2009, encouraged U.S. Attorneys to focus on large-scale marijuana traffickers and not on individuals in compliance with state medical marijuana laws.

The subsequent memo, the first "Cole memorandum," emphasized enforcement against large-scale marijuana cultivators and distributors. Indeed, the DEA pursued several highly publicized arrests of large-scale marijuana cultivators and distributors who claimed to be operating according to state law. For example, in 2011, the DEA launched a major raid against two large central California medical marijuana dispensaries. One owner, Matthew Davies, was sentenced to 60 months in jail and faced a $100,000 fine; his partner, Lynn Smith, was similarly sentenced to 42 months' imprisonment. In 2012, Chris Williams, owner of a medical dispensary in Montana, was arrested by the DEA. He received a sentence of 85 years, eventually reduced to a five-year prison sentence. Perhaps the most publicized case was the arrest of the "Kettle Falls Five" in 2012, who organized a cannabis growing collective that technically exceeded maximum amounts allowed per grower under Washington's medical marijuana law. In 2015, the final three defendants in the case were sentenced to multi-year prison terms for conduct that could now be considered legal under Washington law.

Subsequent DOJ memos, however, made explicit that mere size of a marijuana operation did not implicate a federal law enforcement priority absent other evidence of illegality. In particular, the DOJ would not enforce the CSA prohibition against marijuana use in states and on Indian reservations that legalized marijuana, or against federally chartered banks in those states, so long as federal enforcement priorities are respected.

Thus, the long-term focus of the DEA on large-scale marijuana operations may not prevail against dispensaries and growers that meticulously comply with state law and avoid violating the federal priorities. However, DOJ memoranda represent the policy of the current presidential administration and can be revoked at any time by the DOJ or as a result of a change in the Presidency.

For example, DOJ guidance de-prioritizing prosecution of activities involving medical marijuana that comply with state law was revoked by the Trump administration. Despite this recission, federal marijuana prosecutions continued to decline in both 2018 and 2019, even as drug convictions at large increased. However, the Biden administration and Attorney General Merrick Garland have indicated that the DOJ will respect state-level legalization, and instead will prioritize prosecution of large-scale criminal marijuana enterprises.

In addition, Congress has also weighed in on DEA anti-marijuana efforts. Since 2015 through 2021, the House of Representatives, which has budgetary authority under the U.S. Constitution, has voted in favor of reducing the DEA's budget in relation to marijuana enforcement, e.g., with respect to funding for the DEA's cannabis eradication program. It has also defunded the DOJ from acting against marijuana activity that otherwise complies with state medical legalization. The Ninth Circuit held that this legislation prohibits federal prosecution of individuals acting in compliance with such laws. *United States v. McIntosh*, 833 F.3d 1163 (9th Cir. 2016).

In its April 2013 publication, the DEA emphasized its adherence to its long-standing positions on marijuana enforcement, at least as to recreational marijuana. It stated that marijuana is "properly categorized under Schedule I of the (CSA)" and it would continue to "vigorously enforce the CSA against those individuals and organizations that possess, manufacture, or distribute marijuana for recreational use, even if such activities are permitted under state law." However, it also conceded, perhaps in contradiction to the above statement, that the "DEA will continue to conduct its mission to enforce the CSA and other actions as so directed by the Attorney General." The DEA has consistently denied petitions to transfer marijuana from Schedule I.

Despite numerous recent efforts—including proposed bills and recent lawsuits—to remove marijuana from Schedule I, the DEA has not indicated willingness to remove marijuana from Schedule I.

CHAPTER 7

CHALLENGES, DEFENSES, AND EXEMPTIONS TO THE CSA

§ 7-1 INTRODUCTION

The CSA as it has been applied to marijuana activity has been the subject of many legal challenges, constitutional and otherwise. The chief defense related to its status as a drug offense has been that of medical necessity. Few of these challenges and defenses have succeeded and the CSA continues to operate in full force, subject to DOJ discretion in applying it to states that have legalized marijuana. However, certain exceptions to the CSA have been allowed.

As courts have sustained the CSA as a constitutional exercise of federal power pursuant to the Commerce Clause, other grounds have been sought to ameliorate its harsh provisions. These efforts at amelioration took several paths. Petitions to transfer marijuana to a less restrictive CSA schedule to recognize limited medical use of marijuana were addressed in Chapter 5. All such petitions have been denied. The FDA instituted a Compassionate Investigational New Drug Study program to allow medical use by a limited number of patients. The program was closed to new patients in 1992.

Several court challenges have been made to enforcement of the CSA on constitutional grounds. The most important were the lack of basis for the

CSA in the Commerce Clause, the fundamental right of ill patients to use medical marijuana to protect their life and liberty, free speech, religious liberty, and the right to bear arms. Although such claims were supported in several instances by lower federal courts, they were for the most part denied by the U.S. Supreme Court.

This chapter explains challenges that have been made to the CSA and certain defenses that have been brought by individuals against its provisions. Section 7–2 summarizes the major constitutional challenges to the CSA, especially the landmark case of *Gonzales v. Raich*, 545 U.S. 1 (2005). Section 7–3 describes the medical necessity defense. And § 7–4 relates the partial exemptions to the CSA of the Compassionate Investigational New Drug Program and of imported hemp, which were brought about by court challenges.

§ 7–2 CONSTITUTIONAL CHALLENGES TO THE CSA

§ 7–2.1 COMMERCE CLAUSE CHALLENGE

The CSA has withstood challenges to the constitutionality of its enactment under the Commerce Clause. Art. 1, § 8, cl. 3. Congress has acted under the Commerce Clause to accomplish national legislation beyond the traditional means of "regulating the channels, and instrumentalities of interstate commerce." In the 1930s, the Supreme Court held that in addition to regulating goods moving in interstate commerce, Congress had the power to regulate activities that substantially affect interstate commerce—a much more extensive power. Most of the New Deal landmark regulation of industry and labor was enacted under the authority of the Commerce Clause. Likewise, civil rights legislation of the 1960s, such as the Civil Rights Act of 1964 and sections of the Fair Housing Act of 1968, as well as subsequent civil rights laws, were enacted under the Commerce Clause. In upholding the constitutionality of the Civil Rights Act of 1964 under the Commerce Clause in *Heart of Atlanta Motel Inc. v. United States*, 379 U.S. 241, 252–253 (1964), for example, the Supreme Court held that "Congress was not restricted by the fact that the particular obstruction to interstate commerce with which it was dealing was also deemed a moral and social wrong."

Given the "new era" of Commerce Clause jurisprudence over the course of the twentieth century, there was little doubt as to the federal government's authority to enact the CSA. Congress was careful to ground its authority to enact the CSA in the Commerce Clause:

> (3) A major portion of the traffic in controlled substances flows through interstate and foreign commerce. Incidents of the traffic which are not an integral part of the interstate or foreign flow, such as manufacture, local distribution, and possession, nonetheless have a substantial and direct effect upon interstate commerce because—
>
> > (A) after manufacture, many controlled substances are transported in interstate commerce,

(B) controlled substances distributed locally usually have been transported in interstate commerce immediately before their distribution, and

(C) controlled substances possessed commonly flow through interstate commerce immediately prior to such possession.

(4) Local distribution and possession of controlled substances contribute to swelling the interstate traffic in such substances.

(5) Controlled substances manufactured and distributed intrastate cannot be differentiated from controlled substances manufactured and distributed interstate. Thus, it is not feasible to distinguish, in terms of controls, between controlled substances manufactured and distributed interstate and controlled substances manufactured and distributed intrastate.

(6) Federal control of the intrastate incidents of the traffic in controlled substances is essential to the effective control of the interstate incidents of such traffic.

21 U.S.C. § 801(3)–(6).

However, the CSA was challenged in a specific application to marijuana law in the case of *Gonzales v. Raich*, 545 U.S. 1 (2005). Accepting the general constitutionality of federal regulation of drugs under the Commerce Clause, the plaintiffs contended that applying the CSA to categorically prohibit intrastate cultivation and possession of marijuana for medical purposes, pursuant to California law, exceeded Congressional authority under the Commerce Clause.

In 1996, California became the first state to legalize the medical use of marijuana. Plaintiffs Angel Raich and Diane Monson were California residents who had been consuming marijuana for several years to alleviate serious medical afflictions. Their use was permitted by California law, as it was recommended by physicians. Indeed, one of their physicians testified that conventional medicine had proven ineffective, that marijuana alleviated their symptoms such that they could function on a daily basis, and that without marijuana, their condition would deteriorate and perhaps prove fatal. One plaintiff grew her own marijuana; the other was supplied with locally grown marijuana at no charge. The DEA seized and destroyed the plaintiffs' marijuana plants. The plaintiffs claimed that their personal use of marijuana for medical reasons was in compliance with California law because it was purely *intrastate* and non-commercial activity that was beyond the powers of Congress granted in the Commerce Clause. The Ninth Circuit enjoined the federal government's actions against the plaintiffs, finding a strong likelihood of success on their claim that, as applied to them, the CSA was an unconstitutional exercise of Congress's Commerce Clause authority. *Raich v. Ashcroft*, 352 F.3d 1222, 1234 (9th Cir. 2003).

The 6–3 decision of the U.S. Supreme Court in *Gonzales v. Raich*, 545 U.S. 1 (2005), overturning the decision of the Ninth Circuit, authored by Justice Stevens, upheld the authority of Congress to regulate even local cultivation and personal, medical use of marijuana. The majority in *Raich* considered the conduct at issue in *Raich* an economic conduct by defining economic activity to include distribution, production, and consumption. Therefore, the court considered growing and consumption of marijuana, even for personal use as economic activity which substantially affects interstate commerce (although an illegal drug market) in aggregate. The New Deal case of *Wickard v. Filburn*, 317 U.S. 111 (1942), had established the authority of Congress to regulate even *intrastate* activity, not itself commercial, if that class of activity in the aggregate could affect *interstate* commerce. Because home-consumed marijuana could have a substantial effect on supply and demand in the national marijuana marketplace, even the most minimal amount of marijuana, grown and consumed at home, without ever leaving the confines of one's property, could be regulated by Congress as commerce. Although *Raich* is different from *Wickard* in that there was no legal interstate commerce in marijuana, the Court did not consider the legality vs. illegality distinction significant. Nor did the Court seemed troubled that in 1919, Congress needed the Eighteenth Amendment to obtain authority to prohibit sale of alcohol nationwide, but in 1970, Congress was able to enact a more comprehensive ban on sale, manufacture, possession, and use of marijuana, without amendment of the Constitution.

In a concurring opinion, Justice Antonin Scalia classified the conduct at issue in *Raich* as non-economic one. He reasoned that Congress could regulate non-economic activity using the Necessary and Proper Clause of the Constitution, which gives Congress power to make "all Laws which shall be necessary and proper for carrying into Execution" other federal powers. Thus the CSA prohibition of all forms of marijuana activity was necessary to carry out the congressional policy of eradicating illegal drugs.

In a dissenting opinion, joined in part by Chief Justice William Rehnquist and Justice Clarence Thomas, Justice Sandra Day O'Connor wrote that the unlimited reach of Congress to make use of homegrown medical marijuana a federal crime threatened federalism in the form of California's experiment with legalizing medical marijuana. Even "Wickard did not hold or imply that small- scale production of commodities is always economic, and automatically within Congress' reach."

In a separate dissenting opinion, Justice Thomas wrote that "if the Federal Government can regulate growing a half-dozen cannabis plants for personal consumption . . . then Congress' Article 1 powers—as expanded by the Necessary and Proper Clause—have no meaningful limits." Under the reasoning of the majority, Thomas added, "the Federal Government may now regulate quilting bees, clothes drives, and potluck suppers throughout the 50 States." Thomas concluded: "Congress is authorized to regulate 'Commerce,' and respondents' conduct does not qualify under any definition of that term. . . . The majority is not interpreting the Commerce Clause, but rewriting it."

Several commentators consider *Gonzales v. Raich* to represent the furthest extension of federal power under the Commerce Clause, in allowing Congress to prohibit personal, non-commercial conduct. Employing a *Wickard v. Filburn* rationale that the marijuana use of plaintiffs could affect interstate commerce seems tenuous when there was no legal interstate commerce in marijuana. Because it came in the wake of two Supreme Court decisions that invalidated Congressional intrusion into state law under the Commerce Clause, *see United States v. Lopez*, 514 U.S. 549 (1995) and *United States v. Morrison*, 529 U.S. 598 (2000), some commentators suggest that the Court was only able to achieve a majority in *Gonzales v. Raich* because it involved drug use—what some have labeled the "drug exception" to the Bill of Rights. As a result it would seem that Congressional authority to extend regulation of drugs and marijuana under the Commerce Clause is now beyond constitutional attack.

§ 7–2.2 SUBSTANTIVE DUE PROCESS CHALLENGE

Criminal enforcement of the CSA against ill patients has also been challenged on substantive due process grounds. The claim is that persons are protected under the due process clauses of the Fifth and Fourteenth Amendments from government infringement of fundamental rights and interests in life and liberty. *See Washington v. Glucksberg*, 521 U.S. 702 (1997). For those with serious illnesses which can be ameliorated, the argument goes, enforcement of an absolute ban on marijuana use denies these patients their interest in being free of physical pain, debilitating conditions, and deteriorating conditions that can lead to death. This interest applies both to patients for whom medical cannabis is the preferred treatment and to patients for whom medical cannabis is the only effective treatment. Patients for whom medical cannabis is the preferred treatment have the right to seek such treatment without irrational or arbitrary government restrictions. Patients for whom medical cannabis is the only effective treatment have a right to such medicine, even if the government has a compelling interest in applying some restrictions.

So far, substantive due process claims for use of medical marijuana have not found favor in federal court, as *Glucksberg* requires that the fundamental interest be "deeply rooted in the nation's history." In contrast, medical treatments have a long history of being regulated for public safety. *Pearson v. McCaffrey*, 139 F. Supp. 2d 113, 121 (D.C. 2001). In *Raich v. Ashcroft*, 248 F. Supp. 2d 918 (N.D. Cal. 2003), the court found it unlikely that cultivation and use of marijuana for medicinal purposes represented a fundamental right, a holding left undisturbed on appeal by the U.S. Supreme Court in *Gonzales v. Raich*, 545 U.S. 1 (2005). However, in subsequent litigation by the *Raich* plaintiffs, the Ninth Circuit allowed some possibility that substantive due process claims for use of medical marijuana could succeed in the future. Although acknowledging that "federal law does not recognize a fundamental right to use medical marijuana prescribed by a licensed physician to alleviate excruciating pain and human suffering," *Raich v. Gonzales*, 500 F.3d 850, 866 (9th Cir. 2007), the court added that as numerous states have legalized medical marijuana, the day might come for federal law to accept that "the right to use medical marijuana to alleviate excruciating pain may be deemed fundamental."

§ 7–2.3 FREE SPEECH (FIRST AMENDMENT) CHALLENGE

Courts have found some free speech protections for physicians in the area of marijuana. The courts have decided that there is no free speech right for a physician to actually *prescribe* marijuana in contravention of the CSA. However, there is also an issue as to whether physicians advising patients that they will benefit from use of marijuana constitutes incitement of criminal activity that is outside of First Amendment protection. The distinction has generally been drawn between expressing opinions about the benefits or even necessity of consuming marijuana, and providing actual means for patients to do so. (In some ways, this resembles the distinction between a physician's "recommendation," allowed in state legalization regimes, and a physician's "prescription," which is not provided for.) In the most prominent case, *Conant v. Walters*, 309 F.3d 629, 637 (9th Cir. 2002), the Ninth Circuit Court of Appeals found that physicians have a First Amendment right to tell their patients that they would benefit from use of marijuana. *See also Wollschlaeger v. Governor, Fla.*, 848 F.3d 1293, 1310 (11th Cir. 2017). However, if the recommendation is made as a means and method for the patient to actually obtain marijuana, the physician would not be shielded from a charge of aiding and abetting violation of the CSA.

Free speech issues may also arise in the context of the CSA criminalizing marijuana paraphernalia. In determining what is paraphernalia, the CSA allows that:

"The following may be considered:

(1) instructions, oral or written, provided with the item concerning its use;

(2) descriptive materials accompanying the item which explain or depict its use;

(3) national and local advertising concerning its use;

(4) the manner in which the item is displayed for sale . . ."

§ 863(e). Such provisions necessarily invoke some manner of free speech, as whether paraphernalia is contraband is determined in part by speech associated with its dissemination, description, and sale. Nevertheless, this has not been a bar to multiple convictions for possessing paraphernalia capable of other uses besides consuming marijuana. For example, in *Hoffman Estates, Inc. v. The Flipside*, 455 U.S. 489 (1982), the U.S. Supreme Court held that ordinances that criminalize the selling of marijuana paraphernalia are not unconstitutionally vague and overbroad. Even though such statutes are by their very nature ambiguous, they legitimately target commercial activity promoting illegal marijuana use. The monthly magazine *High Times*, which promotes the legalization of marijuana, has been the subject of federal investigations, which, according to some commentators, have had a chilling effect on free speech, despite the fact that there have been no successful prosecutions against such media outlets.

Marijuana-related speech may be restricted in public schools, despite students' First Amendment rights. *Morse v. Frederick*, 551 U.S. 393 (2007). In general, public school students cannot be censored for political and socially oriented speech at school. For example, the U.S. Supreme Court held that a high school violated the First Amendment rights of students when it prohibited them from wearing black armbands to protest the Vietnam War. *Tinker v. Des Moines Independent Community School District*, 393 U.S. 503 (1969). However, in *Morse*, 551 U.S. at 401–402, decided almost 40 years later, an Alaskan high school student was told by his school to remove a banner that he displayed at a school event emblazoned with the phrase, "BONG HITS 4 JESUS." Because the banner promoted illegal marijuana use, the school could forbid its display without violating the student's First Amendment rights. Justices Alito and Kennedy concurred with the understanding that speech that commented on drugs as a social issue, such as legalizing marijuana for medical use, was protected under the First

Amendment. A dissent by Justice John Paul Stevens, joined by Justices Souter and Ginsburg, argued that it constituted censorship in violation of the First Amendment for the school principal to ban the display because she disagreed with what she believed to be a pro-marijuana message. The dissent urged that high school students be allowed to engage in unfettered debate over the legalizing of marijuana for medicinal use or the wisdom of the war on drugs.

Several commentators have described *Morse v. Frederick*, 551 U.S. 393 (2007) as "a drug exception to the First Amendment." Whether an exception or not, in the most recent school speech case, *Mahanoy Area Sch. Dist. v. B. L. by & through Levy*, 141 S. Ct. 2038 (2021), involving vulgar and profanity-laden speech, but not connected to drug-use, the Supreme Court allowed an expanded view of student speech.

§ 7–2.4 RELIGIOUS LIBERTY (FIRST AMENDMENT) CHALLENGE

As with other constitutional defenses, claims that there is a free exercise of religion claim under the First Amendment to consume marijuana have not proved successful, in contrast with sacramental peyote used in religious rituals by Native Americans. In fact, the peyote exemption is not grounded in a First Amendment right, a claim which was rejected by the Supreme Court, *see Employment Division v. Smith*, 494 U.S. 872 (1990), but by federal statute, 42 U.S.C. § 1996(a)(4) and (b)(10) (1994). Under the Religious Freedom Restoration Act of 1993 (RFRA), 42 U.S.C. §§ 2000bb–2000bb–4c, users of prohibited controlled substances for religious purposes can be exempted from the CSA. *Gonzales v. O Centro Espirita Beneficente Uniao do Vegetal*, 546 U.S. 418 (2006). The user must show that he or she practices a "sincere exercise of religion" and that the CSA restrictions on marijuana burden this sincerely held religious belief. The marijuana use can still be prohibited if accommodating the use is outweighed by a substantial government interest. This statutory standard creates an even higher burden for the government to overcome a religious claim to drug use than under the First Amendment free exercise clause. Nevertheless, religious claims to use marijuana have almost uniformly failed. Marijuana consumers have failed in court, sometimes for lack of a sincerely held belief, but more often because courts have held that the harms of marijuana justify the government prohibiting even its religious use.

For example, in *The First Church of Cannabis v. State of Indiana*, 49–C01, slip op. at ¶ 30 (Marion Cir. Ct. Ind. July 6, 2018), the court denied a RFRA claim for sacramental use of marijuana because both the federal government and Indiana have a "compelling interest in preventing marijuana use and its concomitant problems." In *Olsen v. DEA*, 878 F.2d 1458, 1459 (D.C. Cir. 1989), the Ethiopian Zion Coptic Church was refused an exemption for the CSA on religious grounds, even though the church used marijuana in its religious rituals. Likewise, in *Religion of Jesus Church THC v. Ashcroft*, No. 04–CV–200 (D. Haw. 2004), the court rejected the possibility of a religious defense for the use of marijuana. In *United States v. Quaintance*, 608 F.3d

717, 722–23 (10th Cir. 2010), the court similarly held that the plaintiff's belief in using only marijuana as a sacrament was not a "sincerely held" religious belief. Although the Ethiopian Zion Coptic Church uses marijuana in its religious rites, membership in the church is not sufficient to gain an exemption. *Olsen v. Iowa*, 808 F.2d 652 (S.D.Iowa 1986). In an older case, *United States v. Rush*, 738 F.2d 497 (1st Cir. 1984), the court declared that "every federal court that has considered the matter . . . has accepted the congressional determination that marijuana in fact poses a real threat to individual health and social welfare, and has upheld the criminal sanctions for possession and distribution of marijuana even where such sanctions infringe on the free exercise of religion."); *See also United States v. Meyers*, 906 F. Supp. 1494 (D. Wyo. 1995).

Because Rastafarianism is an established religion with marijuana as a sacrament, Rastafarians have had some success in allowing for personal use, but not in cases involving commercial transactions. For example, in *United States v. Valrey*, No. CR96–549Z, 2000 U.S. Dist. LEXIS 22390 (W.D. Wash. Feb. 22, 2000), the parties stipulated Rastafarianism as a religion, of which defendant was a sincere adherent, using cannabis as a sacrament. The court allowed a very limited personal use and possession of cannabis exclusively in connection with his practice of his religion. *Id.* at 10–11. However in *Guam v. Guerrero*, 290 F.3d 1210 (9th Cir. 2002), the court drew a distinction between a possible RFRA right to simple possession of marijuana for a religious practitioner and no RFRA right to possession with intent to distribute. *Id.* at 1222–23. Thus the court affirmed defendant's conviction for importing marijuana seeds because Rastafarianism does not require violating laws against importing cannabis. *See also Multi-Denominational Ministry of Cannabis & Rastafari, Inc. v. Holder*, 365 Fed. Appx. 817, 820 (9th Cir. 2010) ("RFRA does not permit the unlimited production or distribution of marijuana.")

Marijuana users have been no more successful in basing a religious right to use marijuana under state law. For example, in *Arizona v. Hardesty*, 214 P.3d 1004 (Ariz. 2009), the defendant claimed his use of marijuana was a sacrament of the Church of Cognizance and protected by Arizona's Free Exercise of Religion Act ("FERA"). The court did not dispute Defendant's sincere belief in a true religion, and that the law prohibiting possession of marijuana substantially burdened his exercise of religion. It found, however, that Arizona's compelling interest in preventing the deleterious health effects of marijuana and in combating the danger to public safety and welfare from marijuana trafficking, overcame Defendant's free exercise right. It also held that a ban on marijuana use was the least restrictive means of furthering those compelling governmental interests.

§ 7–2.5 RIGHT TO BEAR ARMS (SECOND AMENDMENT) CHALLENGE

Persons who use marijuana are forbidden by federal law from possessing firearms or ammunition. 18 U.S.C. §§ 922(g)(3), 929(a)(1)–(2); 27 C.F.R.

§ 478.11 (2016). The Bureau of Alcohol, Tobacco, Firearms and Explosives (ATF) enforces this rule, in part by asking in Question 11e on the Firearms Transaction Record Form 4473, which determines eligibility to purchase a firearm, if the potential purchaser is "an unlawful user of, or addicted to, marijuana. . . ." A false answer on this form is a federal crime with a five-year maximum jail term. The ATF further enforces this rule by sending an open letter to all firearms sellers that

> [A]ny person who uses or is addicted to marijuana, regardless of whether his or her State has passed legislation authorizing marijuana use for medicinal purposes, is an unlawful user of or addicted to a controlled substance, and is prohibited by Federal law from possessing firearms or ammunition.

In *United States v. Dugan*, 657 F.3d 998 (9th Cir. 2011), the Ninth Circuit held that the Second Amendment does not protect the rights of unlawful drug users, which would include marijuana users, to bear arms. Likewise in *Wilson v. Lynch*, 835 F.3d 1083 (9th Cir. 2016), the court found that a medical marijuana card holder's Second Amendment rights had not been burdened, even though she did not actually consume marijuana. In that case, a possessor of a Nevada medical marijuana registry card claimed that ATF was denying her right to buy a gun although she did not in fact consume marijuana, even though Nevada authorized her to do so. She held the card largely to make a political statement. Nevertheless, the ATF instructs firearms sellers that they cannot sell firearms to persons "in possession of a card authorizing the possession and use of marijuana under State law." The court held that "there may be some small population of individuals who—although obtaining a marijuana registry card for medicinal purposes—instead hold marijuana registry cards only for expressive purposes. But it is eminently reasonable for federal regulators to assume that a registry cardholder is much more likely to be a marijuana user than an individual who does not hold a registry card." Therefore, ATF's rule denying the plaintiff a right to purchase a firearm was reasonable.

Perhaps emboldened by this decision, the ATF has since added a boldface warning to Question 21e of the revised Form 4473, which became mandatory on November 1, 2020, that the "use or possession of marijuana remains unlawful under Federal law regardless of whether it has been legalized or decriminalized for medicinal or recreational purposes in the state where you reside."

§ 7–2.6 CRUEL AND UNUSUAL PUNISHMENT (EIGHTH AMENDMENT) CHALLENGE

Finally, the heavy penalties applied to marijuana offenses under the CSA have been challenged as violating the Eighth Amendment's prohibition against cruel and unusual punishment. Again, these kinds of challenges rarely succeed, as courts have found that Congress had a rational basis for setting lengthy penalties against marijuana activity, however imprudent such sentences might be, and despite claims that marijuana consumption is a "victimless crime." So, for example, in *United States v. Angelos*, 433 F.3d 738, 747 (10th Cir. 2011), the Court of Appeals affirmed a 55-year prison sentence, without the possibility of parole, for a defendant with no prior criminal record but in possession of a handgun, for selling 1 pound of marijuana for a total of $700 to a government informant in Utah. The court held that such a sentence for a marijuana sale by someone possessing firearms was a momentous enough crime given the scourge of drug-related violence to justify what amounts to a lifetime prison sentence for a 24-year-old. After serving 13 years in prison, the defendant was released on May 31, 2016, due in part to a high-profile campaign by celebrities and politicians.

§ 7–3 MEDICAL NECESSITY DEFENSE TO PROSECUTION UNDER THE CSA

A medical necessity defense has been advanced in numerous CSA cases, although it was ultimately rejected by the Supreme Court in *United States v. Oakland Cannabis Buyers' Cooperative*, 532 U.S. 483 (2001). Nevertheless, it is still advocated in pro-legalization literature as a defense that may succeed with jury nullification, another controversial concept.

The necessity defense is a venerable concept in Anglo-American law. The necessity defense is a defense to a crime on the basis that one's actions constituted the lesser of two unavoidable evils. The concept began in English common law as early as the sixteenth century and was prevalent in American criminal justice as well. It has been codified in over 35 states. Although no federal statute codifies a common law defense of necessity, the U.S. Supreme Court allowed for its possibility in federal cases in *United States v. Bailey*, 444 U.S. 394, 415–16 (1980).

A medical necessity defense asserts that the defendant was obligated to take marijuana to avoid loss of life or debilitating impairment. As such, it constitutes an affirmative defense, in that the defendant does not deny the elements of the crime but asserts a reason justifying violation of the statute. Such affirmative defenses are implicitly available for most crimes, but the U.S. Supreme Court in *United States v. Oakland Cannabis Buyers' Cooperative*, 532 U.S. 483 (2001), denied the availability of the medical necessity defense case in marijuana prosecutions under the CSA. After California legalized medical marijuana in 1996, the Oakland Cannabis Buyers' Cooperative (OCBC) became one of the largest marijuana dispensaries in the state. Several lower federal courts enjoined federal prosecution of the OCBC, accepting its medical necessity defense. The OCBC, a non-profit member cooperative, asserted that its distribution of marijuana was medically necessary for the health of its members who were suffering severe pain and other debilitating conditions. Thus, its activities were entitled to an affirmative defense to the CSA.

The Supreme Court rejected this defense in a 8–0 opinion (Justice Stephen Breyer had recused himself because his brother Charles Breyer was the Northern District Court judge who had granted the injunction).

The five-justice majority opinion was authored by Justice Clarence Thomas. Without negating the possibility of a medical necessity case in other federal prosecutions, the Court denied its possible use with respect to the CSA. In the CSA, Congress had determined that Schedule I drugs, including marijuana, had no currently accepted medical use. Thus, to find an implicit medical necessity defense would contradict the explicit terms of the statute. The three-justice concurrence authored by Justice Stevens accepted that there is no medical necessity defense to the *manufacturing and distribution* of marijuana, but stated that the Court should not foreclose the possibility of a medical necessity defense to the *possession* of marijuana for a seriously ill patient for whom no alternative treatment is available.

State courts have also rejected medical necessity defenses to marijuana prosecutions as either not available under their state controlled substances act, for similar reasons as the federal rejection, or because state medical acts supersede any common law necessity defense. *See, e.g.*, *Kauffman v. State*, 620 So. 2d 90, 92–93 (Ala. Crim. App. 1992); *State v. Cramer*, 851 P.2d 147, 149 (Ariz. Ct. App. 1992); *People v. Galambos*, 128 Cal. Rptr. 2d 844, 853–55 (Cal. Ct. App. 2002); *Spillers v. State*, 245 S.E.2d 54, 55 (Ga. Ct. App. 1978); *State v. Hanson*, 468 N.W.2d 77, 78 (Minn. Ct. App. 1991); *State v. Ownbey*, 996 P.2d 510, 512 (Or. Ct. App. 2000); *S. Dakota v. Ducheneaux*, 671 N.W.2d 841, 845–46 (S.D. 2003); *Murphy v. Commonwealth*, 521 S.E.2d 301, 302–03 (Va. Ct. App. 1999); *State v. Tate*, 505 A.2d 941, 946

(N.J. 1986); *State v. Poling*, 531 S.E.2d 678, 685 (W. Va. 2000); *State v. Butler*, 109 P.3d 493 (Wn. App. 2005). On the other hand, five state courts have recognized the possibility of the defense without definitively allowing it. *See Jenks v. State*, 582 So. 2d 676, 678–79 (Fla. Dist. Ct. App. 1991), *review denied*, 589 So. 2d 292 (1991); *State v. Bachman*, 595 P.2d 287, 288 (Haw. 1979); *State v. Hastings*, 801 P.2d 563, 565 (Idaho 1990); *State v. Christen*, 704 A.2d 335, 337 (Me. 1997); *State v. Kurtz*, 309 P.3d 472, 475–78 (Wash. 2013).

Although the medical necessity defense to marijuana prosecution has been rejected by federal courts and by most state courts, it continues to feature prominently in pro-marijuana literature. In this advocacy literature, the medical necessity defense is usually linked to a strategy of jury nullification. In jury nullification, the defense attempts to make known to the jurors that they are the ultimate deciders of justice in the case. Therefore, the jurors would be permitted to acquit a defendant on medical necessity grounds regardless of any statute or judicial opinion to the contrary. No recent federal court has upheld the legitimacy of advising jurors of the possibility of jury nullification. Nevertheless, it seems somewhat common for it to be suggested to jurors indirectly.

§ 7-4 EXEMPTIONS TO THE CSA

§ 7-4.1 COMPASSIONATE INVESTIGATIONAL NEW DRUG PROGRAM

Although the medical necessity defense has been rejected since passage of the CSA, its early assertion led to a pilot program allowing certain patients to consume cannabis, which effectively acts as a very limited exemption under the CSA.

The Compassionate Investigational New Drug Program (IND) commenced in 1978. It was implemented under the authority of the FDA and supplied cannabis cigarettes to a limited number of patients with medical needs. It began as a result of a federal lawsuit. Robert Randall, afflicted with glaucoma, was arrested in 1976 for cultivation and consumption of marijuana. D.C. Superior Court Judge James Washington dismissed the charges, finding that smoking marijuana presented no harm to Randall and might bring medical benefits. Although the U.S. Supreme Court would eventually reject such a medical necessity defense, the DOJ and other federal agencies reached a settlement with Randall in 1978. As a result of these "Randall lawsuits," the FDA created the IND program, administered by the National Institute on Drug Abuse (NIDA). It allowed a limited number of patients like Randall, victims of disorders which they claimed could be alleviated by marijuana, to obtain FDA-approved marijuana. The marijuana was supplied monthly from the only federally approved site for growing marijuana, in a University of

Mississippi laboratory. Fewer than 100 patients were approved for the program, with illnesses ranging from glaucoma, chemotherapy-induced nausea and emesis, to obesity. In the 1980s, certain patients with HIV were approved for the program. In 1992, the administration of President George H. W. Bush, elected on a campaign to crack down on drugs, stopped accepting new patients for the program, although existing patients were grandfathered in. There are still three known living patients from the original program who continue to receive government-backed marijuana each month.

Given the rapid movement of state decriminalization of medical marijuana, it is unlikely that there will be a federal program similar to IND in the future.

§ 7–4.2 IMPORTED HEMP

The major exception to the CSA's ban on marijuana for almost 50 years was imported hemp. Although production of hemp was banned in the CSA, it could be imported into the U.S. under strict conditions. With the legalization of hemp in 2018 the distinction between imported hemp and domestic hemp has become less significant. In fact, it is likely that imported hemp will go from being accorded favorable treatment under the CSA to being a less viable commercial product.

Hemp is a valuable agricultural commodity derived from the cannabis plant. Hemp is non-psychoactive and non-intoxicating, containing only trace THC. Its cultivation was nevertheless rejected as an exception or defense to the CSA, making the United States the only industrialized nation to prohibit the cultivation of hemp from 1970 to 2018. Although the DEA could permit hemp cultivation without violating international drug treaties, it did not do so, claiming that would weaken marijuana prohibitions.

The definition of marijuana under the CSA encompassed industrial hemp, as hemp is derived from the marijuana plant. Although hemp cultivation has been regulated since 1937, it was encouraged during World War Two, reaching its zenith of 150 million pounds in 1943. However, as the definition of marijuana includes the parts of the plant necessary to produce hemp, cultivation of hemp had been strictly prohibited since passage of the CSA, without DEA registration. Several cases brought by farmers and agricultural interests challenged the CSA for irrationally sweeping hemp into its ban on marijuana. *See, e.g.*, *Monson v. DEA*, 522 F. Supp. 2d 1188, 1202 (D.N.D. 2007); *United States v. White Plume*, 447 F.3d 1067 (8th Cir. 2006). Although courts agreed that hemp is a valuable commodity and the amount of THC in hemp is too small to render it a psychoactive agent, they upheld its prohibition under the CSA as being within the discretion of Congress.

However, after labyrinthine litigation, the DEA allowed hemp products to be imported under strict conditions, while retaining the ban on domestic cultivation. In 2001, the DEA promulgated a rule that would constitute an absolute ban on hemp products. In two cases, *Hemp Industries Association v. DEA*, 333 F.3d 1082 (9th Cir. 2003) (*Hemp I*) and *Hemp Industries Association v. DEA*, 357 F.3d 1012 (9th Cir. 2004) (*Hemp II*), the Ninth Circuit held that the DEA's proposed rule to ban all naturally-occurring THC violated the court's ruling that the Controlled Substances Act encompassed only synthetic THC. The Ninth Circuit held that the DEA could not regulate naturally-occurring THC which was "not contained within or derived from marijuana." Furthermore, the DEA's proposed definition of THC—including both naturally-occurring and synthetic THC—directly contradicted the statutory definition in the Controlled Substances Act: products made from the parts of the plant such as "mature stalks and oil or cake made from the seeds" fall outside the CSA. The court then permanently enjoined the DEA from enforcing its rules prohibiting naturally occurring THC in parts of the cannabis plant excluded from control.

As a result of the *Hemp I* and *Hemp II* cases, a wide range of hemp products could be imported, if certified as made outside of the United States from the seeds or stalk and not from psychoactive flowers or leaves. Hemp products such as sterilized hemp seeds not intended for human consumption, paper, rope, and clothing (which contain fiber made from the cannabis plant) and animal feed mixtures, soaps, and shampoos (which contain sterilized cannabis seeds or oils extracted from the seeds), could be imported into the United States. 21 C.F.R. § 1308.35(a)(1)–(2).

Congress did exercise its discretion in 2014 to allow some domestic hemp cultivation. The Agricultural Act of 2014 ("farm bill," P.L. 113–79, § 7606) allows states to run "pilot programs" cultivating hemp in conjunction with state departments of agriculture and universities. To constitute hemp under the bill, cannabis plants can contain no more than 0.3% of THC on a dry weight basis. 7 U.S.C. § 5940. Numerous states took advantage of this bill to launch pilot hemp growing programs, competing to some extent with imported hemp.

Cannabidiol (CBD) is a non-psychoactive chemical compound derived from the cannabis plant that has been of great current interest for its medical properties, such as the CBD-rich *Charlotte's Web* strain of cannabis. However, like hemp, CBD could not be produced in the United States under the CSA, unless it was produced from hemp pursuant to an approved pilot program. Like hemp, CBD derived from non-THC processed hemp (not from marijuana containing intoxicating amounts of THC), imported from outside the U.S. was permitted. Nevertheless, the FDA prohibited CBD products as medicine and from being sold as such.

For legalization of hemp in 2018, *see* Chapter Eleven.

CHAPTER 8

FEDERALISM AND PREEMPTION

§ 8-1 INTRODUCTION

Perhaps the most significant issue in marijuana law is the bifurcation between federal law and state law. The federal Controlled Substances Act prohibits marijuana activity, subjecting it to significant penalties. Although all of the states initially enacted similar statutes, more than half of the states have legalized marijuana for medical use, and for eighteen of those states, recreational purposes are legal as well.

Although this bifurcated legal regime is in flux, and its constitutional dimensions not resolved, certain legal facts must be emphasized. First, federal law is the supreme law of the land, and thus the Controlled Substances Act has universal application in the United States; hence, in a real sense, all marijuana activity constitutes a federal crime, regardless of any state legalization efforts. Second, the CSA was designed to implement federal-state cooperation in law enforcement, with state criminalization of drugs reinforcing federal law. In fact, federal law enforcement officials have primarily targeted distributors and wholesalers, leaving states to act against street-level users, constituting the vast majority of arrests over recent decades. With states now legalizing marijuana, the question arises as to what extent federal law prohibiting marijuana preempts more permissive state law, that is, renders it without effect.

Third, the federal executive branch, with the responsibility to enforce criminal laws, has signaled that it will acquiesce to a large extent in the legalization of marijuana in those states by not fully enforcing the CSA—although this is a matter of prosecutorial discretion and does not alter the letter of federal laws against marijuana. In some ways the current arrangement can be best thought of as a detente between federal and state legal systems—but like any detente, it is of a temporary nature that can evolve into lasting peace or erupt into war.

This chapter explores marijuana law as a component of federalism and the extent to which federal law preempts the legalization efforts of the states. Section 8–2 reviews federal marijuana law as the supreme law of the land. Sections 8–3 and 8–4 review the complex questions of federalism and preemption in marijuana law. And § 8–5 describes the latest enforcement policy of the Department of Justice (DOJ) as expressed in official memoranda. Finally, § 8–6 addresses congressional deference to state law.

§ 8–2 THE SUPREMACY CLAUSE AND MARIJUANA LAW

A central question of marijuana law is the relation between federal and state drug law. Marijuana law today is largely shaped by an understanding of federalism—that is, the interaction between federal and state law, and the extent to which state law is preempted by federal law.

The CSA strictly prohibits marijuana consumption in all of its forms. Theoretically, this law governs every person in the U.S. and makes all marijuana activity, including medical marijuana, a federal crime, regardless of state law. The Supremacy Clause of Article VI, Clause 2, of the U.S. Constitution declares:

> This Constitution, and the Laws of the United States which shall be made in Pursuance thereof; and all Treaties made, or which shall be made, under the Authority of the United States, shall be the supreme Law of the Land; and the Judges in every State shall be bound thereby, any Thing in the Constitution or Laws of any State to the Contrary notwithstanding.

Thus under traditional constitutional jurisprudence, marijuana would be prohibited in every state in the nation. However, the Justice Department has stated that it will allow states to enact regimes legalizing marijuana for medicinal or recreational purposes, so long as certain federal priorities are met. This policy has received congressional support in riders that have been attached to spending bills every year since 2015 prohibiting the Justice Department from interfering with medical marijuana programs in the states. As a result, the current status of marijuana law in the United States is rather paradoxical. Marijuana is strictly prohibited by federal law, the supreme law of the land, and yet it is tolerated by the Justice Department, which enforces federal law. In less than half of the states, marijuana remains illicit; in thirty-six it is legal to use marijuana for medicinal purposes, and in eighteen states, for recreational purposes as well.

Making sense of such a regime presses the boundaries of constitutional law. And it is likely that this regime will shift in the near future, both as a matter of constitutional framing and de facto application.

§ 8-3 FEDERALISM AND STATE MARIJUANA LAWS

Federalism is inherent in the structure of American law. It creates two systems of law, federal and state, both sovereign within their own sphere. States have general police powers and the power to enact legislation concerning health, safety, welfare, and morals; the federal government only has legal authority as delegated to it under the Constitution. However, over the course of the twentieth century the scope of these federal powers has received broad interpretation. When federal and state laws conflict, federal law is supreme.

The modern era of federalism is often termed "cooperative federalism." In the beginning of this nation's history, federalism chiefly concerned the relationship between powers allotted to the federal government and state governments. However, as the jurisdiction of the federal government has expanded, the federal government and state governments increasingly have concurrent jurisdiction. In such cases the federal government may be able to exercise exclusive powers in what is called competitive federalism, but usually federal laws and state laws coexist in cooperative federalism. This is especially common in the area of criminal law. With the increasing scope of federal authority, many state crimes have been made federal crimes as well. This phenomenon has been called the "federalization of criminal law."

The CSA is an exercise in cooperative federalism. It was carefully crafted to create a shared regulatory scheme of controlled substances between federal and state law, but always under the lead of the federal government. The CSA explicitly contemplates this concurrent structure.

> No provision of this title shall be construed as indicating an intent on the part of the Congress to occupy the field in which that provision operates, including criminal penalties, to the exclusion of any State law on the same subject matter which would otherwise be within the authority of the State, unless there is a positive conflict between that provision of this subchapter and that State law so that the two cannot consistently stand together.
>
> 21 U.S.C. § 903.

The CSA accomplished this cooperative arrangement in three ways. First, the CSA created and defined controlled substances, but it created schedules that the states could adapt to their own purposes. Second, most states adopted some version of the Uniform Controlled Substances Act (UCSA). Modeled on the CSA, the UCSA allows states to retain flexibility in setting penalties, whether harsher or more permissive. Third, the enforcement mechanisms set up under the CSA were carried out in tandem with federal and state law enforcement officers. Federal law enforcement concentrated on organized trafficking, often spanning several states, and large-scale supply and distribution. State law enforcement focused on street level possession and every day marijuana activity. In fact, state enforcement is responsible for approximately 99% of marijuana arrests in the country.

§ 8–4 FEDERALISM AND PREEMPTION OF STATE MARIJUANA LAWS

Although the CSA is the supreme law of the land in regards to marijuana, whether and to what extent it preempts state legalization law is debated by legal scholars and courts. This is a complex theoretical question, which draws on a century of constitutional law jurisprudence.

Preemption refers to the doctrine that any state laws in conflict with federal law are "preempted," that is, they are without effect, because federal law is supreme. However, the Supreme Court has often held that the states "have the principal responsibility for defining and prosecuting crimes." In this area of law, which lies at the heart of states' sovereign powers, courts are reluctant to find that state law is preempted by federal law.

Preemption is determined by the intent of Congress in enacting federal law: whether Congress intended that state law be preempted by federal law or that it would take effect concurrent with federal law. Constitutional law allows for express or implied preemption. In express preemption, a federal statute explicitly states the degree to which state law is preempted. Preemption may be implied in two ways: field preemption and conflict preemption. Field preemption is implied when the scheme of federal regulation is so pervasive that it is evident that Congress left no room for states to operate concurrently in that field of law. Conflict preemption can be implied either when compliance with both federal law and state law is a physical impossibility, or when state law is an obstacle to the intent and objectives of federal legislation.

Applying constitutional theory to the CSA is not a simple matter, even though it expressly disavows field preemption, since it denies "an intent on the part of the Congress to occupy the field in which that provision [of the CSA] operates, including criminal penalties, to the exclusion of any State law on the same subject matter." 21 U.S.C § 903. In fact the CSA is intended to work with a vigorous regime of state enforcement, as reflected in the Uniform Controlled Substances Act.

However, this raises the question of whether state laws that contradict the CSA are preempted as representing a conflict with federal law. The first form of conflict preemption—impossibility—is explicitly mentioned in § 903 of the CSA: state marijuana law is preempted if there is "a positive conflict between that provision of this subchapter [CSA] and that State law so that the two cannot consistently stand together." Most courts have found that state legalization of marijuana does not constitute impossibility preemption because it does not prevent the federal government from enforcing federal prohibition of marijuana if it so chooses—the states do not force anyone to violate federal law, or act to hinder federal enforcement. In other words, it is not impossible to comply with both federal and state law as to marijuana so long as an actor refrains from marijuana activity. Thus, federal and state marijuana law "can stand together," because state medical and recreational marijuana laws only permit marijuana activity, but do not require it.

As to the second form of conflict preemption—obstacle preemption—some courts have held that Congress disavowed obstacle preemption because § 903 of the CSA refers only to "a positive conflict." Other courts have taken the opposite position: that obstacle preemption can be implied. By referring to "a positive conflict" between state and federal law, Congress did not mean to exclude the possibility that state law could be preempted for creating an obstacle to federal law. However, even these courts have found that although obstacle preemption is not excluded, state legalization of marijuana does not present an obstacle to the CSA. The most common reason given by these courts is that legalizing marijuana at the state level does not legalize it at the federal level, thereby presenting an obstacle to federal enforcement. None of the legalizing states have included language that would shield their residents from federal enforcement of the CSA, and courts have already rejected any medical state necessity defense to the CSA.

In addition, some courts have held that a state law legalizing marijuana is not an obstacle to federal law enforcement because of the non-commandeering doctrine. This doctrine derives from both the federal structure of the U.S. Constitution and the Tenth Amendment thereto: "The powers not delegated to the United States by the Constitution, nor prohibited by it to the states, are reserved to the states respectively, or to the people." This doctrine has its judicial origin in a much earlier case, *Prigg v. Pennsylvania*, 41 U.S. 539 (1842), a case involving slavery. In this case, which also tried to reconcile conflicts among states and with the federal government, but in the more egregious context of the Fugitive Slave Law of 1793, the Supreme Court pronounced the anti-commandeering principle that the federal government could not compel states to enforce fugitive slave laws: "It might well be deemed an unconstitutional exercise of the power of interpretation, to insist that the states are bound to provide means to carry into effect the duties of the national government, nowhere delegated or entrusted to them by the Constitution." In the years since, this doctrine was solidified: the federal government cannot commandeer the sovereign powers of the states. States cannot be compelled to enact a federal regulatory scheme, *New York v. United States*, 505 U.S. 144, 188 (1992), and state law enforcement officials cannot be compelled to enforce federal legislation, *Printz v. United States*, 521 U.S. 898, 935 (1997). Therefore, state legalization of marijuana cannot be preempted merely because it does not advance the federal regulatory scheme prohibiting marijuana. Likewise, in *Nat'l Fed'n of Indep. Bus. (NFIB) v. Sebelius*, 567 U.S. 519 (2012), the Court held that the federal government could not employ its spending clause authority, Article I, Section 8, Clause 1, to compel states to expand Medicaid by threatening to withhold funding for Medicaid programs already in place. *See also Murphy v. National Collegiate Athletic Association*, 138 S. Ct. 1461 (2018) (states allowed to legalize gambling despite a federal prohibition). Thus there are clear limits on use of federal authority to command action by states.

A few courts have found that states expressly authorizing marijuana activity may pose an obstacle to the objectives of Congress. In *Emerald Steel Fabricators, Inc. v. Bureau of Labor and Industries*, 230 P.3d 518, 520–521 (Or. 2010), an employer terminated an employee for consuming medical marijuana. Rejecting the employee's claim that he was protected under Oregon's medical marijuana law, the Oregon Supreme Court held that Oregon's issuing a registry identification card to medical patients "affirmatively" authorized the use of marijuana and thus was preempted by the CSA. *See id* at 525. However in *Willis v. Winters*, 350 Or. 299, 253 P.3d 1058 (Or. 2011)(en banc), the same court held that because marijuana use is a federal crime, an employer in Oregon does not have to accommodate an employee's medical use. The Court thus limited the holding of *Emerald*, rejecting the rule that "any state law that can be viewed as 'affirmatively authorizing' what federal law prohibits is preempted." *Id.* at 310 n.6.

The prevailing jurisprudence, that state law permitting marijuana activity does not conflict with the CSA, suggests that positive actions by the state to facilitate marijuana use could conflict with federal anti-marijuana regulation and thus be preempted. Commentators have suggested that some state actions might go beyond merely permissive activity and thus create a positive conflict: state laws that immunize citizens from federal prosecution or from federal consequences of marijuana use such as disqualification from federally subsidized public housing; state laws that protect medical users from employment discrimination; state cultivation and distribution of marijuana to qualified residents, such as those for whom physicians have recommended marijuana use; and authorizing state officials to assist individuals in gaining access to marijuana. In the most extreme interpretation, persons who facilitate a violation of the CSA could be liable for aiding and abetting a federal crime.

A question of a positive conflict between federal and state law arises in the context of police confiscating marijuana. Courts have disagreed over whether state police can return marijuana improperly seized from a person as that person's lawful property without themselves violating the CSA. Under the CSA, distribution of drugs means transfer—there is no required element of buy or sale. Section 885(d) of the CSA grants immunity from civil or criminal liability to "any duly authorized officer of any State . . . who shall be lawfully engaged in the enforcement of any law or municipal ordinance relating to controlled substances." Although this provision would seem to refer primarily to undercover police officers, several courts have relied on this provision to uphold state laws requiring police to return marijuana to owners. *See, e.g.*, *People v. Crouse*, 412 P.3d 599 (Colo. App. 2013) (CSA carved out an exception for federal liability distribution of controlled substances by law enforcement officers). Other courts have invalidated laws requiring return of confiscated marijuana. *See, e.g.*, *State v. Ehrensing*, 296 P.3d 1279, 1286 (Or. Ct. App. 2013) (return of property only permitted if lawfully possessed; marijuana cannot be lawfully possessed under federal law).

Another conflict between state and federal law arises in the context of probation for criminal offenders. Although terms of probation imposed by courts generally forbid use of illegal substances and sometimes such legal substances as alcohol, courts have held that terms of probation cannot restrict a person's right to possess and use medical marijuana under state law. *See, e.g.*, *Reed-Kaliher v. Hoggatt*, 347 P.3d 136, 141 (Ariz. 2015). By permitting a person under probation to possess and use medical marijuana, the Arizona Supreme Court reasoned, a court does not "authoriz[e] or sanctio[n] a violation of federal law, but rather . . . recognize[s] that the court's authority to impose probation conditions is limited by [state] statute." Appellate courts in Michigan, Pennsylvania, and Oregon, and Pennsylvania have held similarly. *See, e.g.*, *People v.*

Thue, No. 353978, 2021 WL 519716, at *4 (Mich. Ct. App. 2021); *Gass v. 52nd Judicial District*, 232 A.3d 706, 715 (Pa. 2020); *State v. Miller*, 450 P.3d 578, 579–80 (Or. Ct. App. 2019); *State v. Rhamy*, 431 P.3d 103, 103 (Or. Ct. App. 2018); *State v. Bowden*, 425 P.3d 475, 478 (Or. Ct. App. 2018).

Even where one state sued another state to stop marijuana legalization, the DOJ has been permissive of state laws authorizing the sale and distribution of marijuana. In December 2014, Nebraska and Oklahoma petitioned the Supreme Court to file a complaint against Colorado. Petitioner alleged that Colorado's decision to decriminalize marijuana increased the flow of marijuana from Colorado into their territories, burdened state resources and harmed the welfare of their citizens. The Court invited the Solicitor General to "express the views of the United States" on the matter. *Brief for the United States as Amicus Curiae* at 1, *Nebraska v. Colorado*, 577 U.S. 1211 (2016) (No. 144).

The Solicitor General sided with Colorado, arguing that "[Nebraska's] motion for leave to file a bill of complaint should be denied because this is not an appropriate case for the exercise of this Court's original jurisdiction. Entertaining the type of dispute at issue here—essentially that one State's laws make it more likely that third parties will violate federal and state law in another State—would represent a substantial and unwarranted expansion of this Court's original jurisdiction." *Id.* at 8. The brief goes on to say that the injuries allegedly suffered by Nebraska and Oklahoma are not "direct [injuries] to their sovereign interests warranting an exercise of original jurisdiction. At most, they have alleged that third-party lawbreakers are inflicting those injuries, and that Colorado's legal regime makes it easier for them to do so." *Id.* at 14.

The Solicitor General distinguished this case from previous cases where the Supreme Court ruled on disputes between states. In contrast to cases in which states grappled with each other over cross-border pollution, for example, Colorado permitted but did not approve or direct its marijuana commercial activity to impact, affect, or injure the Plaintiff states. Consequently, Nebraska and Oklahoma cannot show that they have suffered a *direct injury* to their sovereign interests and their case cannot be reviewed by the Supreme Court. *See id.* For more on this significant case, *see* Chapter 14.

Oklahoma has since shown itself to be more amenable to non-preemption of state marijuana laws. In 2020, the Oklahoma Supreme Court ruled that a proposed amendment to the state constitution legalizing recreational marijuana possession and use was not preempted by the CSA. *Tay v. Kiesel, In re: State Question No. 807, Initiative Petition No. 423*, 468 P.3d 383 (Okla. 2020).

Perhaps the best way to make sense of this difficult area of the law is that states are certainly allowed to *legalize* marijuana in the sense of removing criminal penalties, leaving federal law to stand on its own. On the other extreme, states are not allowed to affirmatively *facilitate* violating federal law, for example by operating a state-owned marijuana dispensary. The difficult question then is at what point does a state regulatory and taxing framework cross the line into affirmatively facilitating a violation of the CSA.

§ 8–5 DOJ DISCRETIONARY MEMORANDA CONCERNING STATE LEGALIZATION

The Department of Justice has not pressed for a judicial declaration that state legalization of marijuana is preempted by federal law. However, it did continue raiding medical marijuana dispensaries, about 200 raids annually from 2000 to 2008, and about 100 annually from 2009 to 2011, during the first three years of the Obama administration. The DOJ eventually announced that it would acquiesce in state legalization schemes, so long as traditional federal priorities in marijuana law enforcement are upheld.

In this respect, the Obama Administration's DOJ reached a compromise that closely approximates cooperative federalism. The federal government traditionally enforces laws against large-scale marijuana trafficking operations that involve drug cartels, result in violence, or transgress state lines. In contrast, the states enforced prohibitions against small-scale marijuana activity and everyday street use. The Obama Administration's DOJ enforcement policy can be seen as maintaining this shared marijuana law enforcement, while permitting states to decide that non-dangerous marijuana use for medical, or even recreational, purposes will not be prosecuted.

Under President Trump, the DOJ announced a theoretical change in policy, that the Department, while not prioritizing interference with state legalization schemes, was leaving its options open with regard to sale or distribution of marijuana that violates federal law. And yet, the recission memo seems to have made no practical difference. Rather the DOJ seems to be operating under the guidelines set out in the Obama Administration memoranda, which basically recognizes the legality of marijuana according to state law.

The question remains, therefore, whether the DOJ's actions—or its inactions—violate the constitutional obligation of the executive branch to enforce laws enacted by Congress. While law enforcement agencies retain a certain level of flexibility in the form of prosecutorial discretion, it might violate the separation of powers for the executive branch to decide that a law passed by Congress should not be enforced in its entirety. However, the DOJ has not made such a declaration. In fact, it has maintained that the CSA retains full force, even though it will only be employed for certain federal priorities. The consensus among legal experts seems to be that the DOJ focusing on certain goals and instructing federal prosecutors to use their discretion in furtherance of these goals, fulfills the executive branches responsibility to enforce laws, while respecting state sovereignty as to laws traditionally within state domain. No court so far has held that the DOJ decision not to enforce every aspect of the CSA prohibition of marijuana activity violates the duty of the executive branch to "take care that the laws be faithfully executed." U.S. Const. Art. II, § 3.

§ 8–5.1 DOJ MEMORANDA

In a series of memoranda, dated October 19, 2009; June 29, 2011; August 29, 2013; February 14, 2014; and October 28, 2014, President Obama's DOJ announced that it would not enforce the CSA prohibition against marijuana in states that decriminalized marijuana use, so long as the states do not allow marijuana use that violates federal priorities. The memoranda list eight federal enforcement priorities to guide the states: 1) preventing distribution of marijuana to minors; 2) preventing revenue from sale of marijuana going to criminal enterprises; 3) preventing diversion of marijuana from states where it is legal to other states; 4) preventing marijuana activity from being used as a cover for trafficking of illegal drugs; 5) preventing violence and the use of firearms in marijuana activity; 6) preventing marijuana-impaired driving and other adverse public health consequences; 7) preventing growing of marijuana on public lands; and 8) preventing marijuana possession and use on federal property. As long as states have adequate measures to prevent these eight outcomes, the federal government will not interfere with state legalization of marijuana.

These memoranda illustrate the Obama Administration's slow and incremental approach to accepting medical and recreational use of marijuana by the states, first by limiting non-enforcement to patients with serious illnesses and their individual caregivers and then by expanding non-enforcement to medical and recreational users and businesses in compliance with a robust state regulatory scheme. The memos are not codified or legislated, however; they create no substantive rights and do not estop the DOJ from enforcing the CSA. *See, e.g., United States v. Washington*, 887 F.Supp.2d. 1077 (D. Mont 2012).

In January 2018, President Trump's DOJ announced that it would reverse the Obama administration policy on marijuana and direct U.S. Attorneys to "reduce violent crime, stem the tide of the drug crisis, and dismantle criminal gangs." *See* Press Release, Office of Pub. Affairs, Dep't of Just., Justice Department Issues Memo on Marijuana Enforcement (Jan. 4, 2018), https://www.justice.gov/opa/pr/justice-department-issues-memo-marijuana-enforcement. *See also* Sessions: Memorandum from Jefferson B. Sessions, Att'y Gen., U.S. Dep't of Justice, to All U.S. Att'ys, Marijuana Enforcement (Jan. 4, 2018). Like the memoranda issued before it, this memo is not codified or legislated and thus can be changed by the next presidential administration, with or without notice. Although the Obama Administration memoranda were technically revoked, they are worth reviewing in depth, because to all intents and purposes they seem to guide the Justice Department—certainly in the Obama era, but during the four years of the Trump presidency, and the first year of the Biden presidency as well. This is especially true as the Sessions memorandum did not replace the rescinded memoranda with new guidance. Moreover, Sessions did not urge U.S., attorneys to prosecute marijuana crimes. In fact, the Sessions memorandum indicated that prosecutorial discretion in this matter would remain with U.S. Attorneys, and several U.S. Attorneys stated that they would follow the Obama Administration memoranda as guiding principles. William Barr, who succeeded Sessions as U.S. Attorney General from 2019 to 2020, pledged in writing to the Senate that he "[did] not intend to go after parties who have complied with state law in reliance on the Cole Memorandum," a policy that the DOJ has since maintained.

Ogden Memorandum, 10/19/09

The "Ogden" memorandum was the first issued by the Department of Justice on enforcement in states authorizing marijuana use. Ogden: Memorandum from David W. Ogden, Deputy Att'y Gen., U.S. Dep't of Justice, to All U.S. Att'ys, Investigations and Prosecutions in States Authorizing the Medical Use of Marijuana (Oct. 19, 2009).

The Ogden memo provided guidance to federal prosecutors from Attorney General Eric Holder and represented the first major indication of the marijuana policy of the new Obama administration. While acknowledging that the DOJ was committed to enforcing the CSA, it also stated that U.S. Attorneys are vested with broad discretion in exercising their authority. In light of the rapid increase of medical marijuana states, it advised prosecutors not to focus on individual patients and caregivers who were in compliance with state regulations allowing medical marijuana. Instead, it urged enforcement against commercial enterprises that were selling marijuana to minors, engaging in money laundering, using violence or connected to organized crime, or failing to comply with state law.

The Ogden memorandum was the first official statement by the DOJ that it would not enforce federal prohibitions against marijuana to the fullest extent allowed by law. In that regard it generated wide publicity.

Cole Memorandum, 6/29/11

"Cole Memo I" was issued by Deputy Attorney General James M. Cole, David Ogden's successor, on June 29, 2011. Cole I: Memorandum from James M. Cole, Deputy Att'y Gen., U.S. Dep't of Justice, to All U.S. Att'ys, Guidance Regarding the Ogden Memo in Jurisdictions Seeking to Authorize Marijuana for Medical Use (June 29, 2011). The memo intended to tamp down the expectations of those who took the Ogden memorandum as stating that the DOJ would not intervene in state marijuana regimes. The Cole memorandum drew a distinction as to non-enforcement of individual caregivers, and enforcement against large scale marijuana cultivators and distributors, expressing concern that "within the past 12 months, several jurisdictions have considered or enacted legislation to authorize multiple large-scale, privately-operated industrial marijuana cultivation centers." Furthermore, the memorandum clarified that compliance with state law or local ordinances did not constitute a defense in the event of civil or criminal enforcement of federal law.

The memorandum had immediate effects. First, it was followed by a wave of prosecutions of marijuana dispensaries. Second, its statement that banks associated with such businesses might be in violation of anti-money laundering statutes generated concern in the financial industry, resulting in many banks closing accounts with dispensaries.

Cole Memorandum, 8/29/13

"Cole Memo II" was issued on August 29, 2013. Cole II: Memorandum from James M. Cole, Deputy Att'y Gen., U.S. Dep't of Justice, to All U.S. Att'ys, Guidance Regarding Marijuana Enforcement (Aug. 29, 2013). It was the most important of the series of memoranda indicating the guidance of the Obama Administration's DOJ. In reaction to an outcry against Cole Memo I, and in light of the impending legalization of recreational marijuana by several states, it established three important points. First, it retreated from Cole Memo I's assault on large-scale marijuana cultivators and distributors. Large-scale commercial enterprises would not be targeted so long as they complied with federal directives. In other words, size was not to be a proxy for illegality; and a large-scale California dispensary would not be treated like a drug cartel, even though the dispensary was receiving revenues in the tens of millions of dollars.

Second, it stated the eight federal priorities that states had to respect so as to avoid federal intervention in their legalization regimes. These eight federal enforcement priorities are discussed in § 8–5.2. Finally Cole II indicated that the DOJ was changing its long-standing policy that acquiescence in states that legalized medical marijuana does not include acquiescence to recreational marijuana. Cole II seemed to erase this distinction so long as the eight priorities were respected.

Banking Memorandum, 2/14/2014

On February 14, 2014, the DOJ issued a memorandum which gave guidance as to the behavior of banks in marijuana commerce. Banking Memo: Memorandum from James M. Cole, Deputy Att'y Gen., U.S. Dep't of Justice, to All U.S. Att'ys, Guidance Regarding Marijuana Related Financial Crimes (Feb. 14, 2014). The DOJ sought to indicate the same non-enforcement policy towards banks that it had towards dispensaries. Although banking transactions involving money generated from marijuana sales could violate money laundering statutes and the Bank Secrecy Act, prosecution "may" not be appropriate for banks serving marijuana-related businesses whose conduct complies with the federal priorities.

Accompanying the banking memorandum, the U.S. Department of Treasury's Financial Crimes Enforcement Network ("FinCEN") released a guidance memorandum the same day. FinCen (Rule 14.2(d)): Fin. Crimes Enforcement Network, Fin-2014-G001, Guidance: BSA Expectations Regarding Marijuana-Related Business (2014). In essence, banks were required to file reports on the marijuana-related businesses they serviced, assessing whether they were in compliance with the federal priorities and state law.

The DOJ's preservation of prosecution as an available option, even for banks complying with federal standards, contributed to the uncertain relationship between the banking and marijuana industries. (*See* Chapter 16.)

Indian Country Memorandum, 10/28/14

On October 28, 2014, the DOJ issued a memorandum giving guidance as to marijuana activities in Indian country, over which the federal government exercises direct responsibility. Indian Country: Memorandum from Monty Wilkinson, Director, Exec. Office for U.S. Att'ys, to All U.S. Att'ys, Policy Statement Regarding Marijuana Issues in Indian Country (Oct. 28, 2014). In essence the memorandum extends to Indian country the same eight enforcement priorities that Cole Memo II extends to the states, while insisting that tribal governments play an equal role in establishing marijuana policy for reservations. (*See* Chapters 9 and 14.)

Sessions Memoranda, 1/4/2018

As noted above, on January 4, 2018, Attorney General Jeff Sessions issued a memorandum reversing the policies of the Obama administration. Sessions: Memorandum from Jefferson B. Sessions, Att'y Gen., U.S. Dep't of Justice, to All U.S. Att'ys, Marijuana Enforcement (Jan. 4, 2018). The memorandum states that Congress has determined that marijuana is a "dangerous drug" and thus prohibited the "cultivation, distribution, and possession of marijuana." As such, the DOJ would return to the Department's "well-established general principles" and rescind immediately all "previous [DOJ] nationwide guidance specific to marijuana enforcement." Despite its strongly worded language, the recission memo seems to have had little practical effect.

§ 8–5.2 EIGHT AREAS OF FEDERAL CONCERN

As noted, even though the Sessions Memoranda technically supplanted its predecessors, the DOJ under President Trump largely abided by the Obama-era position: the DOJ will not intervene in state legalization of marijuana so long as eight federal priorities are respected. It is likely that this policy will govern the Biden Administration as well. Two important aspects must be noted. The first is that these priorities are an unusual form of discretion as they do not revolve around individual cases. Rather, they give guidance as to what aspects of a law will be and will not be enforced. Second, they are stated in general categories and as framed by the DOJ do not limit the power of federal enforcement or provide any substantive rights to defendants. Although the DOJ only lists and does not explain these priorities, the reasons for their emphasis by the DOJ can be extracted from other federal policies.

(1) <u>Preventing Distribution of Marijuana to Minors</u>

One federal priority is that marijuana not be distributed to minors, nor trafficked in areas adjacent to places where minors populate, such as schools, movie theaters, and shopping centers.

Likewise marijuana and marijuana-infused products cannot be marketed in ways appealing to minors and cannot be diverted, directly or indirectly, to minors.

(2) Preventing Revenue from Sale of Marijuana Going to Criminal Enterprises

The DOJ and federal enforcement agencies have traditionally focused on large-scale marijuana enterprises, especially those linked to criminal organizations in the United States or international drug cartels. The DOJ has urged that criminal enterprises not gain a foothold in the operations of medical and recreational marijuana states. However the DOJ had to clarify that size alone does not indicate a criminal enterprise. Thus, large-scale dispensaries and cultivators in California and other states do not run afoul of the law as long as they are not engaged in illegal and racketeering activities in furtherance of their operations.

(3) Preventing Diversion of Marijuana from States Where It Is Legal to Other States

States that have not legalized marijuana have asserted a strong interest in excluding marijuana from entering their borders. This concern has even reached the Supreme Court in the lawsuit brought by Nebraska and Oklahoma against Colorado. (*See* Chapter 14.) The DOJ has asserted, as a federal priority, the protection of non-legalizing states from an increase in interstate trafficking.

(4) Preventing Marijuana Activity from Being Used as a Cover for Trafficking of Illegal Drugs

The legalization of medical and recreational marijuana in recent years has not been extended to other categories of illicit drugs. In this way marijuana has been viewed as a unique Schedule I substance, and the laws of a majority of the states of the United States now reflect that perspective. Thus, the DOJ asserts its concern that marijuana activity in legalizing states in no way contributes to trafficking of drugs that remain strictly illegal under Schedule I.

(5) Preventing Violence and the Use of Firearms in Marijuana Activity

Drug trafficking is often linked to violence and use of firearms. Outbreaks of violence and violation of gun laws are likely to spur federal concern. Two important points should be noted here. First, this concern is inherently linked to regulation of firearms as well as the current controversy over the Second Amendment and the right to bear arms. Secondly, this federal priority has a certain irony to it, as in some ways the bifurcated approach of the federal government seems likely to lead to rather than restrain violence. For example, the refusal of banks to accept proceeds from marijuana-related businesses due to federal anti-money laundering laws (18 U.S.C. §§ 1956–1957) has led to a largely cash-only industry, an obvious invitation to theft, robbery and violence.

(6) Preventing Adverse Public Health Consequences

The Department of Justice and federal agencies have emphasized highway safety and laws against drunk driving for several decades now. The same attention will be given to impaired driving due to marijuana intoxication, even with the more difficult questions raised in detecting the presence of marijuana in drivers. (*See* Chapter 18.) Although the DOJ has not disclosed its criteria of other public health consequences, the federal government's educational campaigns usually stress the danger of dependency on marijuana, long-term health risks, and visits to the emergency room due to adverse effects. Increases in the potency of marijuana strains, the proliferation of synthetic marijuana, or the use of marijuana as a gateway drug by young people might trigger federal concerns under this priority.

(7) Preventing Growing of Marijuana on Public Lands

Public lands have long been a favorite site for growing marijuana. This is not only because of their size, extent, convenience and difficulty of detection, but also because a chief concern of drug growers is that their property will be seized under asset forfeiture laws. Obviously, if they cultivate marijuana on federal lands, there is no property to be seized even in the case of discovery and arrest.

(8) Preventing Marijuana Possession and Use on Federal Property

Federal property is interspersed in every state. This federal property includes government offices, parks, military bases, post offices, prisons, embassies and consulates, international crossings and borders, TSA checkpoints, airways, seaways, and the like. (*See* Chapter 9.) Legalization of marijuana in states surrounding these federal properties in no way legalizes marijuana activity on federal property. This priority is somewhat difficult to enforce, however, as many residents may be unaware of the boundaries dividing state-owned property from that falling under federal jurisdiction. This is a priority which can be enforced by arrests on federal property without necessarily disturbing the state legalization regime. Nevertheless, it will be in the interests of the state to clearly demarcate federal property within its borders so that state residents do not inadvertently engage in marijuana activity in federal jurisdictions.

§ 8–6 CONGRESSIONAL DEFERENCE TO STATE LAW

Congress has repeatedly shown ambivalence as to robust federal enforcement of the CSA. In each budget cycle since December 2014, Congress has renewed the Rohrabacher-Farr Amendment to the yearly budget. Consolidated Appropriations Act, 2018, Pub. L. No. 116–260 (December 27, 2020). Under these amendments (also called the Hinchey-Rohrabacher, Rohrabacher-Blumenauer, and Joyce Amendments), the DOJ is barred from using taxpayer funds to prevent states from passing laws that "authorize the use, distribution, possession, or cultivation of medical marijuana."

In June 2019, the House of Representatives passed the Blumenauer-McClintock Amendment, Amendment No. 17 to House Report 116–119, which would also prohibit the Justice Department from using federal funds to interfere with state adult recreational marijuana regimes. It states: "None of the funds made available by this Act to the Department of Justice may be used, with respect to any of the [states and territories] to prevent any of them from implementing their own laws that authorize the use, distribution, possession, or cultivation of marijuana." HR 3055. Although the Amendment did not become law, it passed the House on a bipartisan basis, demonstrating considerable support for extending the Rohrabacher-Farr Amendment to state recreational marijuana.

CHAPTER 9
SPECIAL FEDERAL JURISDICTIONS

§ 9-1 INTRODUCTION

The United States is a nation of multiple legal jurisdictions—federal, state, municipal, territorial, military, Indian Country, the District of Columbia and the like. This book mostly concerns itself with marijuana activity in federal law and in the 50 states. This chapter, however, discusses other U.S. jurisdictions, which we call "special federal jurisdictions." By and large, special federal jurisdictions are governed directly by the federal government, under plenary powers granted by the U.S. Constitution. This has meant that the CSA constitutes the fundamental law of marijuana in these jurisdictions. However, Congress has also delegated a great deal of local autonomy and self-government to these jurisdictions, some of which have enacted laws decriminalizing and legalizing marijuana, to which the federal government has to a large extent acquiesced.

Federal law has effect throughout the nation, but the government exercises exclusive control over three types of reserved federal lands: Indian Country, military, and public, which together comprise about 30 percent of the land area of the United States. Although Indian Country is held in trust by the United States, Indian reservations enjoy shared dual governance in recognition of the local sovereignty of tribal nations. The federal government also has oversight of airspace: according to FAA and other federal regulations, transportation of marijuana is basically prohibited in airports and on planes from the TSA security checkpoint on. Additionally, the District of Columbia has legalized marijuana for medical and recreational purposes, though marijuana remains prohibited in the numerous federal properties in the nation's capital. Federal law also governs interstate commerce and border checkpoints.

Section 9–2 looks at marijuana law in Indian Country; § 9–3, at federal properties and lands; § 9–4, at airports; § 9–5, at the District of Columbia; § 9–6, at military installations; and § 9–7, at federal territories and insular possessions.

§ 9–2 INDIAN COUNTRY

"Indian Country" refers to lands designated for American Indians that have a special status under U.S. law. (The federal code employs the term American Indian and Alaska Native for peoples commonly called Native Americans or indigenous peoples. Accordingly in this *Nutshell* we tend to the term "Indian law" when referring to federal and state laws affecting tribes and "tribal law" when referring to law within tribes. Where possible we limit our terms to the particular tribe,) Indian Country encompasses Indian reservations and federal lands held in trust for Indians or supervised for the benefit of Indians, including approximately 56.2 million acres. Federal law is enforced in Indian Country. Under the doctrine of federal Indian trust responsibility, the United States is obliged to protect

Indian rights and resources, and implement federal law in regards to American Indian and Alaska Native tribes and villages. However, as domestic dependent nations, Indian tribes are also self-governing, with their own legal regime, under the authority of Congress. Unless delegated by Congress, states do not have legal jurisdiction over Indian Country, even when located within geographical borders of a state.

In the context of marijuana law, this makes the dominant actors in Indian Country, the federal government and the Indian tribes themselves. Drug and alcohol abuse have been an endemic social problem in the 574 federally recognized American Indian and Alaska Native tribes and villages; use of marijuana is widespread. Approaches to marijuana have varied among different tribes, but the controlling law is the CSA.

On October 28, 2014, the DOJ issued "Policy Statement Regarding Enforcement of Marijuana Laws in Indian Country," (Indian Country Memorandum) signed by the Director of the Executive Office for U.S. Attorneys, Monty Wilkinson. As explained in Chapter Eight, § 8–5.1, this memorandum was technically revoked by the Memorandum from Jefferson B. Sessions, Att'y Gen., U.S. Dep't of Justice, to All U.S. Att'ys, Marijuana Enforcement (Jan. 4, 2018). However, it seems that the memorandum was very much the expression of the will of one person—Jefferson Sessions—and since he was preoccupied during his term in office, before being fired by President Trump, the recission of the Indian Country memorandum, as with the recission of other Obama-era marijuana memoranda—had no real effect. Thus, it can be assumed that the Indian County Memorandum remains DOJ policy and is reviewed here.

The Indian Country Memorandum was based on Cole Memo II, which gave guidance to U.S. Attorneys as to enforcement of marijuana law. Despite the national scope of the CSA, which prohibits marijuana activity for all purposes, Cole Memo II acquiesces to a large extent to states legalizing marijuana for medicinal or recreational purposes. The Indian Country Memorandum also acquiesces in Indian Country marijuana legalization, so long as the same eight federal priorities are ensured:

> 1) preventing distribution of marijuana to minors; 2) preventing revenue from sale of marijuana going to criminal enterprises; 3) preventing diversion of marijuana from states where it is legal to other states; 4) preventing marijuana activity from being used as a cover for trafficking of illegal drugs; 5) preventing violence and the use of firearms in marijuana activity; 6) preventing marijuana-impaired driving and other adverse public health consequences; 7) preventing growing of marijuana on public lands; and 8) preventing marijuana possession and use on federal property.

In addition, the Indian Country Memorandum, respecting the sovereignty which Indian tribes possess, requires U.S. Attorneys to consult with Indian tribes on a government-to-government basis in evaluating marijuana law enforcement in Indian Country. When a U.S. Attorney makes a significant enforcement decision as to marijuana law, that U.S. Attorney is instructed to apprise the Executive Office for United States Attorneys, the Office of the Deputy Attorney General, and the Office of Tribal Justice (the office within the Department of Justice which is the principal point of contact with Indian tribes).

The Indian Country Memorandum is significant in that it signals that the federal government will allow Indian tribes to enact their own marijuana policy. In addition, it requires U.S. Attorneys to pay respect to the sovereign claims of Indian tribes in enforcing marijuana law, a concern that the Department of Justice did not explicitly extend to any of the 50 states. Thus, whereas the memoranda addressed to the states represent a measure of deference to state law, the Indian Country Memorandum envisions an affirmative partnership between federal agencies and Indian tribes in fashioning marijuana law on Indian reservations and Alaska Native villages. In 2015, the Suquamish and Squaxin Island Tribes formed tribal-state compacts with Washington governing legal marijuana on their reservations and opened retail marijuana shops. The Puyallup Tribe signed a compact with the Washington State Liquor and Cannabis Board to open a marijuana testing laboratory.

Of course, like the DOJ marijuana memoranda to the states, the Indian Country Memorandum does not enact formal changes in the law, but rather emphasizes the enforcement priorities of the current administration, which create no substantive rights and can be changed at any time, and probably with no notice requirement.

The DOJ marijuana memoranda raise questions specific to Indian Country. For example, the third priority enumerated by the DOJ is preventing diversion of marijuana from states where it is legal to other states that have not legalized. However, Indian and Alaska Native tribes are concentrated within states that have legalized marijuana—for example, more than half of the approximately 326 federal Indian reservations are located in Alaska, Colorado, Oregon, Washington, and California, which have legalized recreational marijuana. It would seem nearly impossible, especially given the often amorphous boundaries of Indian reservations, for these states or the tribes to prevent diversion of marijuana into Indian Country. Likewise, for Indian tribes that legalize marijuana and are located within states that have not legalized marijuana, it would seem similarly difficult to prevent diversion of marijuana from Indian Country to the surrounding state that has not legalized it.

Despite the October 28, 2014 Indian Country Memorandum, DEA raids on marijuana activity in Indian Country continued, reflecting the unsettled state of marijuana law and Indian tribes. In July 2016, DEA and Bureau of Indian Affairs (BIA) agents raided cannabis cultivation operations on the Alturas and Pit River Indian rancherias in Modoc County, California. In October 2016, the DEA raided the Menominee Tribe in Wisconsin, eradicating 30,000 marijuana plants. In July 2016, the Flandreau Santee Sioux tribe of South Dakota burned a million dollar grow of cannabis in light of threatened government raids.

A further complication is that Congress under Public Law 83–280 has delegated law enforcement authority to state jurisdiction in six states (California, Minnesota, Nebraska, Oregon, Wisconsin and Alaska, known as "mandatory" PL 280 states), and to some degree to twelve other states ("optional" PL 280 states). On both types of PL 280 reservations, state law enforcement of criminal justice to a large extent replaces federal law enforcement. If a state with criminal law jurisdiction over the PL 280 reservation has legalized marijuana, it would seem both hypocritical and logistically difficult for state law officers to arrest marijuana users on the reservation for the same activity. Likewise, if a state with criminal law jurisdiction over a PL 280 reservation has not legalized marijuana, it would seem to have the authority to enforce its prohibition on Indian reservations, even if the tribe has legalized marijuana.

Priority number eight of the Department of Justice memoranda is "preventing marijuana possession and use on federal property." However, according to the traditional legal framework, tribal lands are in a certain respect federal land. It would be contradictory to grant tribes autonomy to make marijuana law on reservations, while considering reservation land to be federal land from which marijuana activity must be excluded. This contradiction reflects the difficulty of translating the complicated federal-state dichotomy that currently constitutes the marijuana regime of the United States to the equally complex, 250-year-old legal landscape of American Indian law.

§ 9–3 FEDERAL PROPERTY, LANDS, AND EMPLOYMENT

Federal property and lands can be thought of as the geographical entities which the United States government governs directly with plenary authority (under the Enclave Clause of the U.S. Constitution, Art. I, § 8, cl. 17), as opposed to concurrent jurisdiction which is shared with the sovereign entities known as states. With plenary powers, the federal government has the exclusive authority to pass legislation regarding so-called police powers—that is, health, safety, and morals legislation—in these geographical regions. (As to states, the federal government cannot exercise "police powers," but only those powers granted to it under the Constitution.) Hence federal drug laws have always been enforced on U.S. property.

Marijuana activity is prohibited on all federal property. 41 C.F.R. § 102–74.400. These properties include federal office buildings, federal agencies, federal courthouses, post offices, military installations, service academies, territorial waters, border crossings, National Park Service land, national forests and monuments, federal airports, airspace, TSA checkpoints, and federally funded public housing projects.

In addition, Executive Order 12564 (51 Fed. Reg. 32889, Sept. 17, 1986) forbids any use by federal employees of marijuana in the public workplace, as well as off-duty. The Order's specification that "[p]ersons who use illegal drugs are not suitable for Federal employment" remains applicable to users of medical/recreational marijuana in states where such use has been legalized. The order was reaffirmed in May 2015 in reaction to D.C.'s legalization of recreational marijuana.

Covered federal contractors and all federal grant recipients must maintain a drug-free workplace or lose federal funds. 41 U.S.C. §§ 8101–8106.

U.S. Customs and Border Protection warns travelers crossing the border that possession of any amount of marijuana remains a violation under Federal law. Border agents can confiscate marijuana and can bar entry to foreign nationals who admit to having smoked marijuana. A lawsuit against U.S. Border Patrol for asking a New Mexico medical patient at a Border Patrol checkpoint whether he was in possession of illegal drugs was dismissed. *Marrufo v. U.S. Border Patrol*, No. CV 15–01086 WJ/SMV, 2016 U.S. Dist. LEXIS 49109 (D.N.M. Apr. 11, 2016). The court held that the Border Patrol is not restrained in its enforcement procedures by the Rohrabacher-Farr Amendment, which prohibits the Department of Justice from acting against state medical marijuana legalization, as the Border Patrol is under the Department of Homeland Security.

Marijuana cannot be sent through U.S. mail under several federal laws. Under the Administrative Non-

Mailability Protocol (ANP) program, U.S. postal inspectors detain, document, and process mail packages that are reasonably suspected of containing marijuana from the mail stream. In 2019, the Postal Inspection Service processed 54,877 packages suspected of containing marijuana. The postal service provides "Proper Handling of Suspected Marijuana Parcels Mandatory Stand-Up Talk" to guide postal employees on how to handle mail suspected of containing illicit drugs. Marijuana and hemp vaping products cannot be mailed, 86 Fed. Reg. 58398 (10/21/2021).

In 2015, U.S. postal inspectors seized 7,783 parcels containing marijuana, collectively weighing 34,305 pounds, resulting in 1,932 arrests; in 2016, U.S. postal inspectors seized approximately 36,000 pounds of marijuana. By 2019, the quantity seized had increased to 93,652 pounds.

Marijuana advertisements are nonmailable. 21 U.S.C. § 843(c). Because of federal control over interstate commerce, marijuana cannot be shipped across state lines, even by private carriers such as Federal Express or the United Parcel Service (UPS). However, interstate highways are not federal property; although paid for largely with federal funds, they are owned by the states they traverse. Private individuals traveling on highways might be allowed to possess marijuana based on the state in which they are traveling, subject to motor vehicle laws. The Department of Transportation's drug testing program for a commercial driver's license and for safety-sensitive transportation employees does not permit medical or recreational use of marijuana. 49 CFR Part 40, at 40.151(e).

Obviously it is not always clear to persons whether they are on federal property and lands, or in areas under the concurrent jurisdiction of one of the 50 states. For example, some national monuments in urban areas consist of a single building in a city block—not what most people think of as a national park. Federally subsidized public housing constitutes federal property for purposes of marijuana law; both residents and visitors may be unaware of this prohibition, when neighboring housing is subject to state laws and not directly to federal law.

Some ski resorts and slopes in legalizing states can nevertheless be subject to federal marijuana law, if those slopes are located on land leased from the federal government. For example, it has been reported that 22 of Colorado's 25 major ski slopes are located wholly or in large part on federal land.

Because of the nuances of these regulations, it is not always clear to users when they are crossing the line into a federally regulated area.

§ 9-4 AIRPORTS AND AVIATION

Most airports are not federal property, but are subject to FAA regulation and federal law as to transportation of drugs.

FAA regulations ban the carriage of narcotic drugs, marijuana, and depressant or stimulant drugs or substances in a civil aircraft. 14 C.F.R § 121.15. Travelers cannot bring marijuana past the

Transportation Security Administration (TSA) screening stations or onto airplanes, or check marijuana onto luggage. The TSA, which itself is not a law enforcement agency, is required to report to airport law enforcement any passenger carrying marijuana, regardless of state law or medical marijuana registration.

According to the TSA website:

> Marijuana and certain cannabis infused products, including some Cannabidiol (CBD) oil, remain illegal under federal law except for products that contain no more than 0.3 percent THC on a dry weight basis or that are approved by FDA. (See the Agriculture Improvement Act of 2018, Pub. L. 115–334.) TSA officers are required to report any suspected violations of law to local, state or federal authorities.
>
> TSA's screening procedures are focused on security and are designed to detect potential threats to aviation and passengers. Accordingly, TSA security officers do not search for marijuana or other illegal drugs, but if any illegal substance is discovered during security screening, TSA will refer the matter to a law enforcement officer.

https://www.tsa.gov/travel/security-screening/whatcanibring/items/medical-marijuana.

All employees working in airports and aviation are prohibited from using marijuana and are subject to drug testing. 14 C.F.R § 120.33(b).

State airports are required to grant "assurances" to the FAA that they will comply with FAA regulations. 49 U.S.C. § 47107. FAA regulations forbid operating a civil aircraft with knowledge that marijuana is carried inside the aircraft but do not apply if the carriage of marijuana is "authorized by or under any Federal or State statute or by any Federal or State agency." 14 C.F.R. § 91.19. Legality of marijuana in a state does not necessarily carry over to the airport. Even in the first states that have legalized adult use marijuana, Denver International Airport, McCarran International Airport in Las Vegas, and Colorado Springs Airport prohibit marijuana possession. Likewise, Washington's Spokane International Airport confiscates marijuana found at checkpoints. In contrast, Los Angeles Airport and New York airports have disclaimed jurisdiction to arrest marijuana possessors who are in compliance with state law. Portland International Airport allows passengers to carry marijuana on in-state flights. San Francisco International Airport (SFO) allows medical marijuana patients to carry up to 8 ounces of marijuana. The Canadian Air Transport Security Authority allows passengers to fly domestically, but not internationally, with limited amounts of medical marijuana and proper documentation.

In addition, many airlines including Delta Air Lines, Alaska Airlines and American Airlines, ban marijuana, including medical marijuana, even if the passenger possesses a valid medical marijuana card.

§ 9–5 DISTRICT OF COLUMBIA

As to marijuana law, the District of Columbia is in a unique situation. Under the Enclave Clause, Art. I, § 8, cl. 17, Congress exercises exclusive jurisdiction over the District of Columbia. Under the District of Columbia Home Rule Act, Congress has delegated authority as to local D.C. law to a thirteen-member District Council and a mayoral office, although Congress retains ultimate authority. 1973 District of Columbia Home Rule Act, Pub. L. No. 93–198, 87 Stat. 774. Importantly, although the District of Columbia is explicitly included in most national legislation that is applied to the 50 states, it is not mentioned in the DOJ memoranda that acquiesce to state legalization efforts.

Nevertheless, in February 2015, the District Council legalized marijuana for both medicinal and recreational purposes as a result of Ballot Initiative 71. Congress had previously resisted such efforts. For example, District of Columbia voters had voted to legalize medicinal marijuana in 1998, but Congress prevented it from taking effect until 2009. Several Congressmen threatened the District if it went ahead with legalizing recreational marijuana, but Congress has taken no punitive action since legalization. And so for now at least it seems that the federal government will apply the same criteria to the District that it applies to legalizing states in the DOJ memoranda.

As a result of this back-and-forth, the District of Columbia legalization scheme is somewhat limited. Adults are permitted to possess up to two ounces of marijuana and cultivate within their residence up to six marijuana plants, no more than three of which are mature. Marijuana can be consumed on private property, but not in public places or in public view. Small amounts of marijuana can be transferred gratuitously, but no amount of marijuana can be sold. District of Columbia Uniform Controlled Substances Act (D.C. Code §§ 48–904.01 et seq.; D.C. Law 20–153). Marijuana paraphernalia is legalized. Drug Paraphernalia Act of 1982 (D.C. Code §§ 7–1671.01 et seq.). Although the District Council voted to allow marijuana use in privately owned businesses and cannabis clubs, under pressure from Congress, it reversed its vote. Congress also defunded the efforts to legalize dispensaries.

In terms of criminal procedure, the District of Columbia staked out new ground by limiting the presence of marijuana as grounds for police action. For example, odor of marijuana, which traditionally gave rise to suspicion that a crime is being committed, can no longer count as such. Other previously recognized grounds that no longer constitute a reasonable suspicion of a crime include possession of marijuana, or of multiple containers of marijuana, or in proximity to any amount of cash or currency, without evidence of quantity in excess of two ounces. D.C. Code § 48–921.02a (2015).

The unique jurisdiction of the nation's capital creates unusual situations. Approximately 29% of the land in the District of Columbia is directly controlled by the federal government and thus is not affected by the legalization of marijuana. Marijuana activity is not allowed on the Capitol grounds, on the National Mall, in Rock Creek Park, or any other National Park Service land. Numerous federal law enforcement agencies have jurisdiction in the District of Columbia. For example U.S. Park police have jurisdiction throughout the city. However, law enforcement in the District of Columbia have followed arrangements that federal officers will enforce federal marijuana law only on federal property, and District of Columbia police regulate marijuana in the rest of the District.

The United States is in the odd position that, with one of the most stringent national anti-marijuana laws—the CSA—its capital, under the direct and exclusive authority of Congress, is now one of the few jurisdictions in the world that has formally legalized marijuana.

§ 9–6 MILITARY PERSONNEL AND INSTALLATIONS

Marijuana usage is strictly prohibited for any members of the Armed Forces and anywhere on a military base. In addition to the CSA, which applies to the military, the military has its own legal code, the Uniform Code of Military Justice (UCMJ), which prohibits any use of marijuana by any military personnel at any time, and subjects any offending members of the armed services to court-martial. UCMJ article 112a, U.S.C. § 912(a). Thus, despite legalization efforts in much of the Country, marijuana activity is strictly prohibited for all military personnel, active or reserve, and at any military installation, by military and civilian personnel alike. No distinction is made for medical marijuana.

All military personnel are subject to the UCMJ. The military ban on illicit drugs includes marijuana. According to 10 U.S. Code § 912a, article 112a:

> (a) Any person subject to this chapter who wrongfully uses, possesses, manufactures, distributes, imports into the customs territory of the United States, exports from the United States, or introduces into an installation, vessel, vehicle, or aircraft used by or under the control of the armed forces a substance described in subsection (b) shall be punished as a court-martial may direct.

Subject to this prohibition are almost all military personnel, at any stage of duty, including: Active-duty service members in the Army, Marine Corps, Navy, Air Force, members of service academies, and for the most part, the Coast Guard; Reserve members of these forces; and National Guard activated in a federal capacity. Although National Guard service members not activated in a federal capacity are exempt from the Uniform Code of Military Justice, they are subject to their individual state codes of military justice which prohibit marijuana activity, even in legalizing states.

Department of Defense employees are also forbidden from using marijuana. DoD Directive 1010.9 (2012). Employees are subject to random drug testing; applicants for several categories of

Department of Defense employment are subject to mandatory testing.

As with the CSA, under the Military Code of Justice marijuana is classified in Schedule I with the most dangerous drugs. Marijuana activity is subject to court-martial, dishonorable discharge, forfeiture of pay and allowances, and the following maximum terms of confinement:

2 years:	Possession or use of less than 30 grams of marijuana.
5 years:	Possession or use of more than 30 grams of marijuana; Manufacture of marijuana.
15 years:	Possession with intent to distribute; Manufacture of marijuana with intent to distribute; Wrongful exportation or importation of marijuana.

(Manufacture of marijuana here, as with many drug laws pertaining to marijuana, refers primarily to cultivation.)

Military installations are under the exclusive authority of Congress under the Enclave Clause. Marijuana is strictly forbidden on all military installations, extending to civilians as well, including spouses, family members, and visitors. Therefore even a spouse living on a military installation authorized under state law to take medical marijuana is prohibited from doing so.

Additionally, Department of Defense Directive (DoDD) 1010.1, calls for extensive drug testing of military personnel. Military personnel on bases are frequently tested, perhaps more so in states that have legalized marijuana. For example in 2014, 75% of the 41,000 soldiers assigned to Camp McCord in Washington were tested for marijuana use. In the same year, 100% of the 26,000 soldiers at Fort Carson in Colorado were tested for marijuana. These statistics highlight the stark contrast in the treatment of marijuana in military and civilian contexts.

§ 9–7 U.S. TERRITORIES AND INSULAR POSSESSIONS

More than four million U.S. citizens and nationals live in territorial areas of the United States—the five most populous being Puerto Rico, the Virgin Islands, the Northern Mariana Islands, American Samoa, and Guam. Congress has plenary authority over U.S. territories, maritime water, and insular possessions. U.S. Const. Art. I, § 8, cl. 17; *id.* Art. IV, § 3, cl. 2. Congress has delegated local law making authority to these territories, and designated a territorial court system. As federal law extends to these territories, the CSA applies.

In American Samoa, marijuana remains strictly illegal. In the Virgin Islands and Puerto Rico, marijuana has been legalized for medical use. In Guam and the Northern Mariana Islands, both medical and adult use marijuana are legal. Although U.S. territories and insular possessions are not explicitly mentioned in the Department of Justice marijuana memoranda, it is reasonable to assume that the Department of Justice is acquiescing in legalization of marijuana in U.S. territories as well.

As is evident from the discussion in this chapter, the status of marijuana law varies dramatically, even in jurisdictions where Congress has exclusive or primary legal authority. These complexities make for a somewhat confusing pattern in federal domestic and overseas lands and creates potential dangers for the unsuspecting user of marijuana.

CHAPTER 10

INTERNATIONAL TREATY OBLIGATIONS OF THE UNITED STATES

§ 10–1 INTRODUCTION

Marijuana law in the United States cannot be considered without regard to international obligations. The United States is a signatory to treaties, protocols, and conventions which require member nations to prohibit the cultivation, possession, consumption, and sale of marijuana. Three major international agreements frame the global drug regime and oblige the United States. Almost all nations have ratified these treaties, but the United States attracts special attention. Ironically, although it was the prime mover in enacting an international drug regime and insisting that cannabis prohibition be central to that regime, the United States has now been criticized by the United Nations for violating its obligations.

The fundamental drug control treaty is the 1961 Single Convention on Narcotic Drugs as Amended by the 1972 Protocol ("the Single Convention"), which prohibits cannabis cultivation, possession, consumption, and sale except for limited scientific and medical reasons. The United States was a major advocate of this treaty and insisted that marijuana be included as a dangerous drug. The second treaty is the 1971 Convention on Psychotropic Substances ("Psychotropic Convention"), which added synthetic drugs to the list of illicit substances. The third, the 1988 United Nations Convention against Illicit Traffic in Narcotic Drugs and Psychotropic Substances, takes measures against the rise of international drug cartels. The 1961 Single Convention classified the cannabis plant, as well as cannabis resin, in Schedule IV—the most restrictive category of the Single Convention, in addition to the already restrictive Schedule I. In a significant development, the United Nations in December 2020 voted to delete cannabis and cannabis resin from Schedule IV.

According to both international and domestic law, changes in U.S. law as to marijuana have to take into account these treaty obligations. Because the United States has sovereign powers vested in both the national and state governments, two questions arise. The first is whether the federal government can mitigate its sanctions against marijuana, for example by transferring marijuana in the Controlled Substances Act to Schedule III, or an even less restrictive Schedule, without violating international law. The second question is whether individual American states can legalize marijuana without causing the United States to fall into violation.

Section 10–2 describes the 1961 Single Convention, and the subsequent treaties—the 1971 Convention on Psychotropic Substances and the 1988 Convention against Illicit Traffic in Narcotic Drugs and Psychotropic Substances. Section 10–3 addresses the two questions posed above, as shaped by CSA mandates. And § 10–4 reviews the reaction of the

U.N. monitoring committees to the evolving marijuana law of the United States.

§ 10–2 1961 SINGLE CONVENTION ON NARCOTIC DRUGS AS AMENDED BY THE 1972 PROTOCOL

The first international drug treaty was the 1912 International Opium Convention, convened by the United States and ratified by the United States and four other countries. It obtained global reach when it was incorporated into the Treaty of Versailles in 1919, which made ratification of the Opium Convention mandatory for signatory nations. An important step towards international oversight took place when the League of Nations, created the same year, assumed duties for overseeing compliance with the treaty, although enforcement was hampered by the profits some countries made from the drug trade. At the time, trade was largely unregulated; the 1912 Convention relied on export restrictions rather than criminal sanctions.

Marijuana was first made the subject of international agreement in the 1925 Geneva Opium Convention. The agreement, taking effect on September 25, 1928, made only sparse mention of cannabis. It required signatories to "prevent the illicit international traffic in Indian hemp and especially in the resin." Art. 11, § 2. Indian hemp received a somewhat limited definition, referring only to the tops of female (pistillate) cannabis plants (male cannabis plants contain lower levels of THC): "the dried flowering or fruiting tops of the pistillate plant *Cannabis sativa* L. from which the resin has not been extracted, under whatever name they may be designated in commerce." Art. 1. The scope of prohibition was also limited, imposing only minimal restrictions on domestic production or consumption, and allowing for licit international trade in cannabis with statistical reporting. However, "export of the resin obtained from Indian hemp and the ordinary preparations of which the resin forms the base" was prohibited to countries in which cannabis was illegal; countries in which cannabis was legal had to certify that they had a legitimate use for imported cannabis and that it would not be re-exported. Art. 11 § 1. A League of Nations subcommittee was established in 1935 to study Indian hemp from a medical and scientific viewpoint, as well its relation to crime.

After World War II, the United Nations assumed oversight of international drug agreements from the League of Nations. The United Nations Economic and Social Council (ECOSOC) established the Commission on Narcotic Drugs (CND) in 1946 to assist the ECOSOC in applying the international drug control treaties. Economic and Social Council Res. 9(I) (Feb. 16, 1946). In 1954, the ECOSOC adopted the judgment of the World Health Organization (WHO) that "there is no justification for the medical use of cannabis preparations," which is "practically obsolete." Economic and Social Council Res. 548 FI (XVIII) (July 12, 1954). In 1955, a WHO study, requested by the CND, emphasized the danger of cannabis "from every point of view, whether physical, mental, social or criminological." For these reasons, subsequent sessions of the CND requested governments to take measures to suppress domestic cannabis consumption, except for scientific purposes, and except for medical purposes on the Indian subcontinent, where cannabis was used as traditional medicine.

The international efforts at drug control were ultimately consolidated in the most important drug treaty: the 1961 Single Convention on Narcotic Drugs, *opened for signature* Mar. 30, 1961, 18 U.S.T. 1407, 30 T.I.A.S. No. 6298, 520 U.N.T.S. 151, 14 I.L.M 302 (entered into force Dec. 13, 1964). As the dominant post-World War II power, the United States worked to create a worldwide drug regime, which would also prohibit marijuana. The Single Convention limits "exclusively to medical and scientific purposes the production, manufacture, export, import, distribution of, trade in, use and possession of drugs." The Convention represented a shift in the method of international control. Prior agreements were largely administrative, in that they relied on nations to provide statistics as to manufacture and consumption of drugs and information about medical uses, which were filtered through expert committees. While the Single Convention kept and made more rigorous these administrative requirements, it also added a prohibitive element, defining controlled drugs and chemicals, and specifying which activities were illicit.

The Single Convention consolidated all previous international law on narcotic drugs. It created four schedules for classifying drugs, according to potential for abuse, medical use, and safety. Schedule I is the standard regime for drugs, strictly regulated for medical and scientific purposes. Schedule II drugs are regulated somewhat less rigorously than Schedule I drugs, and Schedule III drugs, considered the safest, are minimally regulated. Schedule IV consists of a subset of Schedule I drugs deemed to be the most addictive and abused, with no offsetting medical benefits that cannot be obtained by safer drugs. Heroin and cannabis were listed in Schedule IV, for example, but not cocaine. States have flexibility to adopt more (but not less) restrictive measures for Schedule IV drugs.

Cannabis was classified in both Schedule I and Schedule IV of the Single Convention, the first systematic prohibition of marijuana and hashish on an international level. Nevertheless, in allowing medical use, although strictly controlled, the Single Convention is to some extent less restrictive than earlier CND and WHO pronouncements, which rejected therapeutic use of cannabis. Whereas cannabis and cannabis resin were also listed in Schedule IV, extracts and tinctures of marijuana are listed only in the less restrictive Schedule I, which presupposes "potential therapeutic uses." In January 2019, the World Health Organization (WHO) recommended removing the cannabis plant, as well as cannabis resin, from Schedule IV—the most restrictive category of the Single Convention based on WHO's comprehensive study of the health effects of cannabis, *The Health and Social Effects of Nonmedical Cannabis Use*. In December 2020, the UN Commission for Narcotic Drugs (IND) voted by narrow majority to reclassify cannabis and cannabis resin, removing them from Schedule IV of the Single Convention while retaining them in Schedule I. It is not clear what will be the impact of the UN vote as nations remain free to classify cannabis under the most stringent laws.

Nations can decide whether, per Schedule I, to limit marijuana to medical and scientific purposes, or to impose even greater restrictions. The Controlled Substances Act of 1970 (CSA) is the national legislation by which the United States complies with the Single Convention. According to notes of the Convention Committee, the United States insisted that marijuana be classified among the most serious drugs. Unlike the CSA, however, the Single Convention does not restrict industrial hemp. "This Convention shall not apply to the cultivation of the cannabis plant exclusively for industrial purposes (fibre and seed) or horticultural purposes." Art. 28(2). Also, unlike the Single Convention, the CSA places all cannabis only under its most restrictive schedule.

The Single Convention definition of cannabis is broader than the 1925 Opium Convention definition of Indian hemp, including, for example, both male and female plants, and including all species, not just *Cannabis sativa* L., but it is still less extensive than the botanical definition of the plant.

> (b) "Cannabis" means the flowering or fruiting tops of the cannabis plant (excluding the seeds and leaves when not accompanied by the tops) from which the resin has not been extracted, by whatever name they may be designated.

> (c) "Cannabis plant" means any plant of the genus cannabis.
>
> (d) "Cannabis resin" means the separated resin, whether crude or purified, obtained from the cannabis plant.

Art. 1, § 1(b)–(d).

Thus, certain parts of the cannabis plant—for example the seeds and leaves of the plant when separated from the tops, and the tops of the plant from which the resin has been extracted—are not covered by the treaty definition, as they were thought to contain little psychoactive capacity. Restrictions as to trade in cannabis are broader than the definition of the drug, requiring for example, signatories to prevent "illicit traffic in the leaves of the cannabis plant." Art. 28(3).

Scheduling is flexible, so that drugs can be added, deleted, or modified without requiring amendment of the treaty, but only with the formal decision of the WHO or the International Narcotics Control Board (INCB), created to implement the Single Convention. Medical and scientific purposes are not strictly defined under the treaty. According to the official commentary on the Single Convention, the "term 'medical purposes' does not necessarily have exactly the same meaning at all times and under all circumstances. Its interpretation must depend on the stage of medical science at the particular time in question."

However, if drug use is allowed by a nation for medical purposes, such use must be subject to strict controls. The Single Convention requires each signatory nation to create a government agency to control cultivation and handling of cannabis for research purposes; the U.S. complies through the National Institute on Drug Abuse (NIDA) Drug Supply Program, in which the Drug Enforcement Administration registers applicants to conduct research and supplies cannabis.

The Single Convention took effect with 40 signatory nations. As of 2021, the Single Convention had 186 signatory nations. The United States ratified the Single Convention in 1967.

The Single Convention established the International Narcotics Control Board (INCB) to monitor treaty compliance. The INCB has enforcement powers but relies more on negotiation and publicity to convince signatory nations to adhere to treaty terms. The Commission on Narcotic Drugs (CND) is the United Nations governing body that guides the policies and scope of international drug treaties. The U.N. Office on Drugs and Crimes (UNODC) implements policies enacted by the CND.

The international drug regime was supplemented by amendments to the Single Convention and additional treaties. In 1971, the Convention on Psychotropic Substances added over 100 newly available prescription, synthetic, and hallucinogenic drugs to the list of controlled substances. 32 U.S.T. 543, 1019 U.N.T.S. 175 (entered into force Aug. 16, 1976). As to cannabis, it added tetrahydrocannabinol (THC) to Schedule I (later transferred in part to Schedule II). It also provided for the destruction of illegally cultivated marijuana. The 1972 Protocol amended the Single Convention so as to correlate with the 1971 Convention on Psychotropic Substances. In reaction to a worldwide increase in drug manufacturing, the 1988 United Nations Convention Against Illicit Traffic in Narcotic Drugs and Psychotropic Substances provided for international cooperation to combat organized drug trafficking and drug money laundering. S. Treaty Doc. No. 101–4, 1582 U.N.T.S. 95, 28 I.L.M. 493 (entered into force Nov. 11, 1990). Whereas the Single Convention in Article 36 requires drug use to be "punishable offenses," which could conceivably be satisfied by civil sanctions, the 1988 Convention Against Illicit Traffic in Narcotic Drugs and Psychotropic Substances required signatories to make personal consumption of drugs—ostensibly including marijuana—"specifically a criminal offense." Art. 3. These changes reflect the shift from the more administrative approach of earlier treaties, focusing on drug manufactures, to a punitive approach more compatible with the war on drug consumption and trafficking.

§ 10–3 LEGALIZATION IN THE U.S. AND TREATY OBLIGATIONS

Most of the debate over legalization of marijuana in the United States revolves around questions of domestic policy. But international law obliges as well, a point that is often made by the DOJ and federal drug enforcement agencies. Under Article VI, clause 2 of the U.S. Constitution, "all Treaties made, or which shall be made, under the Authority of the

United States, shall be the supreme Law of the Land." Thus, the Single Convention is binding to the same extent as federal law. However, unlike certain treaties that contain specific rules that translate directly into domestic law, the Single Convention is not self-executing law. *See Medellin v. Texas*, 552 U.S. 491, 505 (2008). It contains no specific offenses or penalties that automatically take effect. Rather, it indicates a general regime for controlling drugs and relies on the signatory nations to enact implementing statutes. Signatory nations are prohibited from enacting domestic laws contrary to the Single Convention. Although several countries made reservations to certain provisions of the international drug treaties, allowing them increased flexibility, the U.S. made none.

§ 10–3.1 INTERNATIONAL DRUG TREATIES AND THE CSA

The United States complied with the Single Convention by enacting the Controlled Substances Act of 1970 (CSA). The DEA is the administrative agency tasked under the CSA as the government entity that decides the scheduling of marijuana.

The Single Convention was the model for the U.S. Controlled Substances Act of 1970. Various provisions of the CSA directly reference the Single Convention. One such provision is 21 U.S.C. 811(d)(1), which relates to scheduling of controlled substances.

Because the CSA was enacted in large part to satisfy United States obligations under the Single

Convention, many of the CSA's provisions directly implement the treaty requirements. None of the foregoing obligations of the United States could be satisfied for a prohibited drug if that drug were removed entirely from the CSA schedules. At least one of the foregoing requirements (quotas) can only be satisfied if the drug that is listed in Schedule I of the Single Convention is also listed in schedule I or II of the CSA. 21 U.S.C. 826.

Neither the Single Convention nor CSA adopt a pharmacological definition of cannabis, but a legal definition. The Single Convention defines cannabis as:

> the flowering or fruiting tops of the cannabis plant (excluding the seeds and leaves when not accompanied by the tops) from which the resin has not been extracted, by whatever name they may be designated.

Art. 1(b). It defines "Cannabis resin" as the "separated resin, whether crude or purified, obtained from the cannabis plant." Art. 1(d).

The CSA definition of "marihuana," includes all parts of the cannabis plant except for the mature stalks, sterilized seeds, oil from the seeds, and certain derivatives and extracts thereof. 21 U.S.C. 802(16) (58). Currently, the CSA's definition includes all parts of the plant, limited by its exceptions. The Convention's definition, on the other hand, limits itself to the flowering tops of the plant only. (In other words, the Single Convention and CSA define the prohibited substance from different angles: the CSA bans the marijuana plant and then excepts certain parts; while the Single Convention bans only parts of the plant.)

The 1961 Single Convention and the 1971 Psychotropic Convention provide for the international control of marihuana constituents. Many of the CSA's provisions were drafted to comply with these Conventions. The CSA includes schemes of drug scheduling and procedures for adding, removing, and transferring drugs among the schedules that are similar, in some ways, to those in the Single Convention. With respect to those drugs that are subject to control under the Single Convention, the CSA mandates that DEA control such drugs in a manner that will ensure the United States meets its obligations under the Single Convention. 21 U.S.C. 811(d)(1).

Drug codes are an administrative mechanism by which the CSA complies with the Single Convention. As provided in 21 CFR 1308.03, controlled substances are assigned four-digit Administration Controlled Substance Code Numbers employed to tabulate quantities of controlled substance imported and exported to and from the United States. Code numbers are also used to denote aggregate production quotas as required by 21 U.S.C. § 826 for substances controlled in Schedules I and II.

Somewhat like the CSA, the Single Convention lists substances in four schedules. However, under the Single Convention, the drugs that are subject to the most stringent controls are in Schedule IV. Another difference between the CSA and the Single

Convention is that, under the latter, a drug can be listed in more than one schedule. Cannabis and cannabis resin were listed in both Schedule IV and Schedule I of the Single Convention until reclassified in 2020.

Although the United States was a major advocate for classifying cannabis in Schedule IV in the original 1961 Single Convention treaty, it voted in 2020 to delete cannabis and cannabis resin from Schedule IV of the Convention. The United States delegation explained that its vote to remove cannabis and cannabis resin from Schedule IV of the Single Convention, while retaining them in Schedule I, was motivated by development of identified therapeutic uses for certain isolated cannabinoids, for example, Epidiolex, but "cannabis itself continues to pose significant risks to public health and should continue to be controlled under the international drug control conventions." Epidiolex, contains highly purified cannabidiol extracted from the cannabis plant and was approved by the U.S. Food and Drug Administration in 2018 for the treatment of two rare seizure disorders in children.

§ 10–3.2 DEA ENFORCEMENT ACCORDING TO INTERNATIONAL DRUG LAW

The DEA takes the position that its strict enforcement of the marijuana prohibition in the United States is dictated in large part by adherence to the international drug conventions—The 1961 Single Convention on Narcotic Drugs, the 1971 Convention on Psychotropic Substances, and the

1988 United Nations Convention against Illicit Traffic in Narcotic Drugs and Psychotropic Substances. Thus it is worthwhile to review some of the major points of the international drug conventions that the DEA has stated bind U.S. law.

The DEA has argued that marijuana can only be rescheduled under the CSA if the WHO or the INCB first reschedules marijuana under the Single Convention. For example, *NORML v. DEA*, 559 F.2d 735 (D.C. Cir. 1977), revolved around a petition to reschedule marijuana under the CSA. The DEA opposed rescheduling, in part because the Single Convention classifies marijuana as a Schedule IV dangerous drug with uncertain therapeutic benefits. The court, by and large ruling for the DEA against rescheduling, cited the deference that the CSA itself pays to international obligations, overriding procedures that could otherwise be taken to reschedule. "If control is required by United States obligations under international treaties, conventions, or protocols in effect on October 27, 1970, the Attorney General shall issue an order controlling such drug under the schedule he deems most appropriate to carry out such obligations." CSA, § 811(d)(1). This provision is consistent with the Supremacy Clause of the U.S. Constitution (art. VI, sec. 2), which provides that all treaties made under the authority of the United States "shall be the supreme Law of the Land." In accordance with this constitutional mandate, under section 811(d)(1), Congress directed the Attorney General (and the Administrator of DEA, by delegation) to ensure that compliance by the United States with the nation's obligations under the Single Convention is given top consideration when it comes to scheduling determinations. In other words, the Attorney General is to place cannabis in the minimum schedule to satisfy international law, regardless of other mandated findings and procedures of the CSA.

When control of a drug is required by the Single Convention, the DEA Administrator "shall issue an order controlling such drug under the schedule he deems most appropriate to carry out such obligations, without regard to the findings required by [21 U.S.C. 811 (a) or 812(b)] and without regard to the procedures prescribed by [21 U.S.C. 811 (a) or (b)]." 21 U.S.C. 811(d)(1). Thus, in such circumstances, the Administrator is not obligated to request a medical and scientific evaluation or scheduling recommendation from the Department of Health and Human Services (HHS) (as is normally done pursuant to section 811(b)).

DEA insists that marijuana be scheduled in either CSA Schedule I or II to satisfy Single Convention controls such as import and export permits, licensing of manufacturers and/distributors, annual statistical reporting, and quota recordkeeping. The National Institute on Drug Abuse (NIDA) fulfills the requirement of a government agency to enforce the controls mandated by the Single Convention. The DEA claimed it need not hold any hearings before an administrative law judge to maintain marijuana in these schedules, thus short-circuiting the rescheduling procedures. This claim was rejected by the court in *NORML v. DEA*, 559 F.2d 735 (D.C. Cir.

1977), and the DEA was compelled to at least consider whether there is latitude to reschedule consistent with treaty obligations, and to receive expert testimony on this treaty issue.

The controls mandated by the Single Convention for Schedule I drugs include

- Authorization for imports and exports
- Licensing of manufacturers/distributors
- Recordkeeping
- Prescriptions required for medical use
- Annual estimate of needs
- Quotas
- No accumulation of stocks
- Security and inspection
- Annual statistical reporting.

The DEA also maintained that international treaties required it to license only one marijuana supplier; that license was granted to the University of Mississippi under contract with NIDA. However, this interpretation was rejected by the State Department in August 2016, stating that the treaty allows multiple licenses to be issued. In fact, on December 18, 2020, the DEA finalized new regulations pertaining to applications for entities seeking to grow marijuana, and in May 2021 announced that it had almost completed its review of grower applications.

As DEA explained in 81 Fed. Reg. 90194, 90195 (2016): While "cannabis resin" is extracted from "cannabis," the Single Convention specifically controls "extracts" separately. Extracts of cannabis are controlled only under Schedule I of the Convention, which is a lower level of control than "cannabis resin." The DEA decided to define the term "marihuana extract" so as to exclude material referenced as "cannabis resin" under the Single Convention on Narcotics. "Cannabis resin" (regulated under the CSA as a resin of marihuana) contains a variety of "cannabinoids" and would continue to be regulated as marihuana under drug code 7360. The new drug code for marihuana extracts under 21 CFR 1308.11(d)(58) excludes the resin. Cannabis resin and marihuana resin remain covered under the drug code for marihuana (drug code 7360), thus differentiating this material from marihuana extracts (new drug code 7350). This maintains compliance with the Single Convention.

Accordingly, after notice and comment, the DEA amended 21 CFR 1308.11(d) in 2016 to include a new subparagraph (58) which creates a new code number in Schedule I as follows (updated to exclude hemp):

(58) Marihuana Extract—7350

"Meaning an extract containing one or more cannabinoids that has been derived from any plant of the genus Cannabis, containing greater than 0.3% delta-9-tetrahydrocannabinol on a dry weight basis, other than the separated resin (whether crude or purified) obtained from the plant."

DEA defines extracts as concentrates of chemicals obtained by a physical or chemical process. As the Final Rule indicates, the "United Nations Conventions on international drug control treats extracts from the cannabis plant somewhat differently than marihuana or tetrahydrocannabinols." Bottom Line: with two codes, DEA can also control marijuana extracts differently from marijuana and marijuana resin.

There has been opposition from U.S. and DEA officials to marijuana legalization due to treaty obligations. On March 4, 2013, eight former heads of the DEA, four former heads of the Office of National Drug Control Policy, and 32 concerned organizations addressed a letter to senators and other federal officials expressing their concern that the legalization of marijuana by Colorado and Washington violates international law:

> Keeping marijuana illegal is a treaty obligation under the 1961 International Convention on Narcotic Drugs and supported by the two other Conventions: the 1971 Convention on Psychotropic Drugs and the 1988 Anti-Trafficking Convention. The United States was a prime mover of these multilateral treaties and largely responsible for signature ratification by virtually every other country in the world. The President of the International Narcotics Control Board (INCB) has already protested the initiatives in Colorado and Washington.

Letter from Save Our Soc'y from Drugs to Senators Patrick Leahy and Chuck Grassley (Mar. 4, 2013).

Because the DEA has allied its enforcement policies so closely to the international drug conventions, any loosening of the international cannabis prohibition may represent a major challenge to DEA's historically strict enforcement of the CSA as applied to marijuana.

§ 10–3.3 CHANGES IN U.S. MARIJUANA LAW AND COMPLIANCE WITH DRUG TREATIES

For the United States, noncompliance with the international drug treaties, even if permitted by interpretation of domestic law, would have a dramatic effect. Although the international treaties contain sanctions for parties that violate its obligations, e.g., Article 14 of the Single Convention and Article 19 of the Psychotropic Convention, these sanctions are unlikely to be applied to the United States. Afghanistan is currently the only nation under sanction, because of widespread cultivation of opium poppy. However, the U.S. is widely perceived as the prime mover in the international treaties, and has been vocal in keeping cannabis center stage. If the U.S. were to abrogate its international treaty obligations as to marijuana, either in law or by example, the international anti-marijuana regime would lose much of its force. For example, Mexico's former President, Felipe Calderon, declared that the United States has "no moral authority" to insist that other countries enforce drug laws if it allows states to legalize marijuana.

As to state law, the international treaties have relevance as well. Certainly treaties are addressed primarily at the national level because most nations have a unitary legal system—that is, a system of centralized, national laws, in contrast to the U.S. system of multi-sovereignty. The international drug treaties are binding on American states under the Supremacy Clause, as is the CSA. In fact, an argument can be made that international treaties are even more restrictive in the sense that while § 903 of the CSA disclaims intent to preempt the field of marijuana except for a positive conflict, the treaties obviously do not mention similar flexibility as to the law of the 50 states. If the majority of states were to legalize marijuana for recreational purposes—a purpose not allowed for in any of the international agreements—it would seem difficult to say that the United States is in compliance, simply because it has a federal drug law on its books, although not enforced.

The official commentary of the United Nations Secretary-General to the Single Convention allows for an open-ended definition of medical purposes, and so it can be argued that state legalization of medical marijuana does not violate the treaty obligations. However, both the DEA and the INCB have stated that a lax state medical marijuana scheme that did not employ the strict controls mandated by the Single Convention would violate the international treaties. As marijuana is allowed under the international treaties only for medical and scientific purposes, legalization of recreational marijuana appears to contravene the terms of the treaties.

Beginning with California medical legalization in 1996, many states have not felt so constrained. A question remains as to whether state legalization violates international law, even if federal prohibitions stay in place. In light of the federal government's own partial relaxation of federal enforcement of the CSA, and its forbearance of state legalization, the United States can maintain that it is in compliance with the Single Convention only with strained interpretations.

§ 10–4 ASSESSMENT BY THE UNITED NATIONS COMMITTEES

As already noted, the United Nations agencies tasked with monitoring the international drug treaties have declared that legalization of marijuana by the United States, and by other countries as well, violates international drug treaties. Their position finds support in the 1969 Vienna Convention on the Law of Treaties (VCLT). May 23, 1969, 1115 U.N.T.S. 331.

The United Nations seems on firm ground in claiming that the United States is required to enforce its federal law in every state. The VCLT states that "a party may not invoke the provisions of its internal law as justification for its failure to perform a treaty." Art. 27. Likewise, Article 29 states "a treaty is binding upon each party in respect of its entire territory." As Colorado and Washington prepared to legalize marijuana, INCB President Raymond Yans wrote on March 13, 2013 that state legalization would constitute "a violation of international law," and that the "INCB urges the Government of the United States to ensure that the treaties are fully implemented on the entirety of its territory.... Those treaty obligations are applicable with respect to the entire territory of each State party, including its federated states and/or provinces." The INCB has retained this position. As recently as 2019, in the wake of the INCB's Annual Report, INCB President Viroj Sumyai said, "legalization of cannabis for recreational purposes, as seen in a small number of countries, represents not only a challenge to the universal implementation of the treaties and the signatories to the treaties, but also a significant challenge to health and wellbeing, particularly among young people."

However, there is some debate as to what constitutes a violation. International law does not rigidly control the marijuana regime of the United States or of any other nation. The treaties have built in a good deal of flexibility; each nation has to enact the treaties with specific provisions. In addition, the Single Convention allows each country to take into account its own "constitutional principles and basic concepts of its legal system," and article 36 of the 1988 United Nations Convention against Illicit Traffic in Narcotic Drugs and Psychotropic Substances allows a nation to take into account "provisions of its domestic law and its extradition treaties." For example, the Netherlands ratified the 1988 Convention accepting the imposition of criminal penalties, but only in accord with Dutch criminal law and policy. Uruguay justified its legalization of marijuana on its commitment to human rights. In

2015 the Mexican Supreme Court issued a ruling, upholding a right to grow marijuana for individual use in language similar to the "free development of personality," in Article 22 of the Universal Declaration of Human Rights. The Court went on to hold that a law prohibiting marijuana was unconstitutional in 2019 and in 2021 ordered the government to issue permits for the personal use and growing of marijuana.

However, the United States has made no such reservations to any of the treaties or justified state legalization on principles of human rights. Rather, it has stated that the CSA remains in full force while permitting certain autonomy as to medical and everyday recreational use, and state legalization creates no substantive rights against enforcement. Likewise, courts so far have not found a positive conflict between state legalization and the purposes of the CSA. Still, it is unlikely that international bodies will be persuaded by what may seem to them a strained and anomalous reading of American federalism.

As to compliance with the international marijuana agreements treaties, the United States seems to be tied in a knot of its own making. The United States brought its cultural experiences and legal tradition to international law when it began to advocate regulating the worldwide trade, supply, and consumption of cannabis. As a result, the approach that the United States would emphasize in drug regulation through the course of the twentieth century was a combination of legal agreements and prohibitions. The United States played the major role in convening the Single Drug Convention and in creating its provisions. It insisted on applying stringent prohibitions of the Single Convention to cannabis, for example by including it in the strictest category, Schedule IV, in addition to its inclusion in Schedule I, already a stringent category. As to its own cannabis laws, the DEA has opposed any relaxation of marijuana laws in the United States that would violate the treaty provisions.

However, a seeming contradiction seems to have arisen in maintaining adherence to marijuana laws. Some of the strongest U.S. voices in favor of supporting the United Nations and international law are drawn from the political spectrum inclined to support cannabis legalization. In contrast, portions of the political order that might see themselves as protective of "law and order" and opposed to legalization, have in the last few decades often been opposed to the international order. For example, during the Trump Administration, the United States took steps to withdraw from such international agreements as Treaty of Amity, Economic Relations, and Consular Rights with Iran, Optional Protocol to the 1961 Vienna Convention on Diplomatic Relations (VCDR), Universal Postal Union (UPU), the Intermediate-Range Nuclear Forces (INF) Treaty, the 2015 Paris Agreement on climate change mitigation, the Trans-Pacific Partnership, and the Open Skies Treaty.

In a sentence then, the commitment of the American political constituency to maintaining the international drug order seems to have little support, as the American polity is either progressive in favor of cannabis legalization or conservative in not supporting the international institutions entrusted with maintaining the prohibitions against cannabis legalization. Neither side then is inclined to support adhering to the international drug treaties prohibitions of cannabis.

CHAPTER 11

HEMP AND CBD

§ 11-1 INTRODUCTION

Hemp is generally legal under American law. Hemp is a cultivar of the Cannabis sativa L. plant bred as an agricultural product with only trace amounts of delta-9-tetrahydrocannabinol (THC). Hence it is non-intoxicating. Its legalization is the most significant amendment to the marijuana provisions of the Controlled Substances Act (CSA) since enactment.

The 2018 Farm Bill deleted from the CSA definition of marijuana derivatives of cannabis with low THC content, under 0.3%. As a result, hemp, and cannabidiol (CBD) products produced in compliance with the Farm Bill, are not prohibited under federal law. Almost all states have legalized hemp as well.

States, American Indian tribes, and U.S. territories now have primary responsibility to oversee and control production of hemp upon obtaining federal approval of their regulations. Hemp is also the cannabis substance that historically is most intertwined with Indian Country. The United States Food and Drug Administration (FDA) retains substantial jurisdiction over both hemp and CBD products.

Hemp is cultivated easily and can be used in the production of textiles, fibers, paper, construction materials, and in FDA-regulated products such as foods, nutritional supplements, and cosmetics. Hemp has large economic potential, without the opprobrium of being a mind-altering drug. CBD and THC are the most abundant cannabinoids in the cannabis plant, but unlike THC, CBD has minimal psychoactive effect. CBD products have become popular due to alleged medicinal and relaxing properties, although its uses are regulated by many states, and the FDA has warned of adverse side effects.

Section 11–2 defines hemp. Section 11–3 narrates how hemp cultivation in the United States traveled from prohibition to legal status. Section 11–4 updates the ongoing establishment of federal and state regulatory plans for hemp. Section 11–5 examines CBD, both as derived from hemp and otherwise.

§ 11–2 HEMP DEFINED

Hemp is an industrial product of wide utility, different from what is commonly thought of as marijuana, in that hemp is not intoxicating. Hemp has two uses in common parlance and in most U.S. law as well: as the cannabis plant bred for industrial uses and as derivatives and extracts of such plant. Hemp is also the marijuana variety that has been most changed under federal law, essentially converting from illegal to legal status, although much regulated. It is defined under federal law, and under the laws of most states, as the cannabis plant, or any part thereof, including its extracts and cannabinoids, containing 0.3% or less THC content by dry weight. Hemp is cultivated and manufactured by major industrial nations, as it is allowed by the 1961 Single

Convention on Narcotic Drugs, and was only prohibited by one such nation—the United States—from 1970 to 2018. Prior to 1970, hemp was legal under federal law, even if taxed. The CSA outlawed hemp cultivation, as it declared all marijuana illegal, although certain finished hemp products and raw hemp fibers could be imported under strict certification. *See* § 7–4.2 for an account of legally imported hemp products.

Hemp plays a significant role in the world economy for several reasons, many of which are shared with other varieties and cultivars of the cannabis plant. First, like all marijuana, it is relatively easy to grow ("weed"), thriving in a wide variety of climates and conditions. Second, hemp is largely resistant to insects and pests. Finally, hemp fibers are sturdy and high in tensile strength; they can be both silky and strong. As a result, hemp has many uses. As food, its seeds, oils, and cakes are used in world cuisines and in animal feed. The woody core of the hemp stalk is used for furniture, mulch, and building materials. Hemp oil is used in cosmetics and detergents. Most of all, hemp fibers are used for textiles, clothing, sails, canvas, carpet, and paper. (However, the common claim that the U.S. Declaration of Independence or the U.S. Constitution was written on hemp paper is apparently false). With the advent of cotton and synthetic materials in recent centuries, the importance of hemp declined. During World War II, when the United States was deprived of resources from Asia, hemp again became essential. For example, in 1943 the United States produced more than 150 million pounds of hemp on 146,200 harvested acres. Nevertheless, hemp remains a significant commodity. For that reason, its cultivation and distribution are explicitly allowed in Article 28(3) of the 1961 United Nations Single Convention on Narcotic Drugs. As such, it is the major exception to the prohibition of the cannabis plant under international law.

§ 11-3 HEMP: FROM PROHIBITION TO REGULATION

Although the 1961 United Nations Single Convention on Narcotic Drugs permits hemp production, the United States banned the cultivation of hemp under the CSA, the only major industrial country in the world to do so, collateral damage from the war on drugs. Although the United States is the largest consumer of hemp products, the definition of marijuana under the CSA encompassed hemp, as it did all marijuana plants, derivatives, and extracts. In contrast, about 30 other countries grow hemp, of which China is the largest producer. The CSA ban on marijuana plants was a blanket prohibition, regardless of the plant's psychoactive capability, quantity of THC contained therein, or intended use—industrial, medical, recreational or otherwise. Indeed, the word "hemp" does not appear in the original CSA, much less any differential based on THC concentrations of marijuana.

There is an argument that the inclusion of low-THC cannabis in the CSA was a historical accident. This argument was made in various courts but never successfully from a legal perspective, although from the political perspective, this argument contributed to removal of hemp as a controlled substance by Congress in 2018. As such, it is worth reviewing.

The definition of "marijuana" in the CSA is identical to that used in the federal Marihuana Tax Act of 1937 (declared unconstitutional in 1968). (*See* Chapter Three for a fuller account of this Tax Act.) The 1937 Tax Act allowed hemp by not taxing transfers of the mature stalk of the plant, which is useful only for industrial use, and applying only small taxes to registered producers of marijuana, but applying a high tax of $100 per ounce to each transfer of other intoxicating parts of the plant to anyone who had not registered with the government and paid an occupational tax. The intention and result of this legislation were to permit makers of hemp, as their product was legal under most state laws. Producers of marijuana for uses illegal under state law—in other words high-THC marijuana for intoxication—were discouraged by high taxes and the fear of prosecution under state law if they registered under the Marihuana Tax Act of 1937, even though failure to pay the tax was itself a federal crime.

When Congress enacted the CSA, it adopted the 1937 Tax Act's definition of marijuana word for word—thus grouping all marijuana plants under the same prohibition. The 1937 Tax Act's complicated tax hierarchy that differentiated hemp producers was no longer relevant, as categories of taxation were no longer a means of control. Rather the CSA prohibited cultivation of all marijuana regardless of whether bred for use as a narcotic or as a low-THC commercial product. Historical research presented to several courts, *see, e.g., Monson v. DEA*, 522 F. Supp. 2d 1188, 1202 (D.N.D. 2007); *United States v. White Plume*, 447 F.3d 1067 (8th Cir. 2006), indicated that while Congress in the 1937 Tax Act allowed marijuana for industrial uses with a complex scheme of differential tax rates and other requirements for transfers, Congress did not consider how a broad criminal prohibition would affect hemp production. Two possible reasons for this indifference come to mind. First, as noted at several places in this *Nutshell*, the CSA was the product of a newfound power of Congress. To enact alcohol prohibition earlier in the twentieth century, Congress required a constitutional amendment to obtain authority. However, to prohibit marijuana (and other narcotics) in 1970, Congress found authority in new interpretations of the Interstate Commerce Clause. It is possible that Congress had not fully refined the application of its newfound powers in the fields of healthcare and narcotics, and neglected the impact of outlawing criminal acts formerly left to the states, for example, in prohibiting hemp (subject to federal licensing). Another possible explanation is simply that Congress allowed the prohibition of hemp to support the Nixon Administration war on drugs. Indeed, the DEA insisted for many years that prohibiting hemp was necessary to fight visually undistinguishable but intoxicating marijuana plants.

Whatever the reason for the criminalization of hemp in 1970, courts agreed that it was beyond judicial authority to revise legislative text that unambiguously banned the growing of all cannabis.

Problems of detection and enforcement raised by hemp's similarity to marijuana, requiring laboratory analysis, justified a ban broader than the psychoactive variety of the plant. The possibility that Congress would not have adopted the blanket prohibition on cannabis plants if it had been aware of the effect on cultivation of non-psychogenic plants for industrial uses, was irrelevant. Nevertheless, the ban on hemp was never popular. It was opposed by industry as an unnecessary restraint on business and opposed by many individuals as a senseless federal excision of a harmless plant, contrary to the preference of most states. Although hemp could not be cultivated, low-THC cannabis materials derived from parts of the marijuana plant excluded from the CSA definition, and certified as such, could be imported. *See* § 7–4.

In 2001, the DEA attempted to ban all products containing hemp, even if made from parts of the marijuana hemp plant legally exempted from the CSA definition of "marijuana," such as sterilized seeds and cannabis fiber separated from the plant. The CSA definition of marijuana includes all its derivatives and compounds, thus including all cannabinoids of the cannabis plant in Schedule I. However THC is the one cannabinoid separately listed in the CSA as a Schedule I substance. The rule proposed by the DEA in 2001, 21 C.F.R. § 1308.35, argued that any parts of the cannabis plant, even those excluded from the CSA definition of marijuana, were illegal if they contained trace amounts of THC, given the inclusion of THC on Schedule I. If followed, this rule would have prohibited all hemp products, even low-THC hemp products produced from cannabis plants grown overseas and imported into the United States. Companies that manufactured and sold food and cosmetic products made from imported hemp seed and oil brought suit. In *Hemp Industries Association v. DEA*, 333 F.3d 1082 (9th Cir. 2003) (*Hemp I*) and *Hemp Industries Association v. DEA*, 357 F.3d 1012 (9th Cir. 2004) (*Hemp II*), the Ninth Circuit enjoined enforcement of this rule, finding that the DEA could not regulate naturally-occurring THC which was "not contained within or derived from marijuana." The court held that Congress intended to regulate only materials containing synthetic THC, and not natural THC; if naturally-occurring THC were covered under the THC ban, there would be no need for a separate category for marijuana, which contains naturally-occurring THC. After these court rulings, the DEA suspended enforcement of its proposed rule banning the importation of hemp products, although it did not formally acquiesce to the Ninth Circuit's interpretation until 2018.

In 2014, Congress finally allowed expansion of hemp cultivation. The Agricultural Act of 2014 ("farm bill," P.L. 113–79, § 7606, codified at 7 U.S.C. § 5940) allows states to conduct pilot programs cultivating hemp in cooperation with state departments of agriculture and research universities. 7 U.S.C. § 5940. Under this legislation, a majority of states initiated these pilot programs, which increased the supply of domestic marijuana that could be legally used for hemp products. A 2016 joint "Statement of Principles on Industrial Hemp" issued by DEA, the

United States Department of Agriculture (USDA), and FDA clarified that under Section 7606 of the Agricultural Act of 2014, the importation of viable hemp seeds still requires DEA registration according to the Controlled Substances Import and Export Act (21 U.S.C. §§ 951–971). It also reiterated that the Federal Food, Drug, and Cosmetic Act (FD&C Act) approval process for new drug applications applied to any products derived from hemp cultivated under Section 7606 pilot programs. In *United States v. Mallory*, 372 F. Supp. 3d 377 (S.D.W. Va. 2019), the court ruled that hemp grown under Section 7606 could be transported across state lines.

In 2016, Congress took another step in relaxing prohibitions against hemp. Similar to the Rohrabacher-Farr amendments prohibiting the U.S. Justice Department from spending funds to interfere with implementation of state level medical cannabis laws, Congress's August 12, 2016 budget prohibited the DEA from expending funds to close down hemp programs that comply with state law.

Finally in 2018, Congress legalized hemp and hemp seeds by amending the CSA to remove hemp as a controlled substance. Agriculture Improvement Act of 2018, Pub. L. 115–334, § 10113, amending 21 USC §§ 802(16), 812(c). Hemp is defined as

> the plant Cannabis sativa L. and any part of that plant, including the seeds thereof and all derivatives, extracts, cannabinoids, isomers, acids, salts, and salts of isomers, whether growing or not, with a delta-9

tetrahydrocannabinol concentration of not more than 0.3 percent on a dry weight basis.

As a result, hemp can be cultivated, processed, marketed, and sold under federal law. Also legalized are cannabinoids derived from hemp (such as CBD). Likewise, THC in hemp is deleted from the definition of THC in Schedule I. The USDA enacts regulations to monitor compliance and production, and the FDA retains substantial jurisdiction of hemp products. By and large, the FDA has not approved hemp products to be marketed for therapeutic or medical uses or as a dietary supplement, or to be introduced into interstate commerce as food (or animal feed), except for hulled hemp seed, hemp seed protein powder, and hemp seed oil.

§ 11–4 REGULATION OF HEMP

Although hemp was legalized under federal law in 2018, it is heavily regulated. Basically, there is shared regulatory oversight over hemp manufacture and products between the federal government and the 50 states and American Indian tribes. The 2018 farm bill defines "a State" as a state, the District of Columbia, the Commonwealth of Puerto Rico, and any other territory or possession of the United States. Therefore all provisions applying to states described below also apply to these jurisdictions. State departments of agriculture, governors, and chief law enforcement officers, and tribal governments, establish regulations to license and regulate hemp for their jurisdictions. The USDA must approve of these plans. States and tribes are not required to establish their own regulatory plan, but if they do not enact a plan, they must abide by USDA default regulations.

§ 11–4.1 STATE REGULATION

In essence, each state is entrusted to develop its own guidelines as to hemp production but under the oversight of the USDA. The USDA published a final rule on January 19, 2021, that provides regulations for the production of hemp in the United States and became effective on March 22, 2021. This final rule builds on a 2019 interim rule establishing the U.S. Domestic Hemp Production Program, as required by the 2018 Farm Bill, to create consistent regulations for hemp production throughout the nation.

Modeled on the methodology of the CSA, state plans are required to exercise extensive control over hemp activity. These controls include tracking the production of hemp throughout the state. Hemp must be tested for levels of THC, so that it remains at 0.3% or less. If plants exceed that level, a plan is required for effective disposal so that the plants cannot be accessed. The state plan must include random inspection of hemp sites and enforcement of these measures, including sharing aspects of this enforcement with federal officials. Importantly, enforcement of the state plan is largely removed from criminal sanctions. Hemp growers are eligible for Federal Crop Insurance.

On July 22, 2020, the FDA published "Cannabis and Cannabis-Derived Compounds: Quality Considerations for Clinical Research," 85 Fed. Reg.

44305–44307. These guidelines intend to remedy obstacles to marijuana and hemp research. For example, the federal government now allows hemp to serve as a source of cannabis and cannabis-derived compounds for drug development. (The only marijuana previously available to researchers was grown by the University of Mississippi at the National Center for Natural Products Research under contract with the National Institute on Drug Abuse Drug Supply Program.)

States can also choose to forego a hemp plan of their own. In that case, the state must follow federal regulations as to hemp, which exhibit similar controls as above. At least 47 states, as well as Puerto Rico and the U.S. Virgin Islands, have enacted legislation to establish hemp production programs or allow for hemp cultivation research. In 2018, growers cultivated 78,176 acres of hemp. Total sales for hemp-based products in the United States were about $1.1 billion in 2018, and are expected to more than double by 2022 to $2.6 billion.

§ 11–4.2 INDIAN TRIBE REGULATION

As with states, Indian tribes create their own regulations overseeing hemp activity, subject to USDA certification. All the requirements applied to states listed above, apply to Indian tribes as well. Whereas for states, regulatory authority to license and regulate hemp is entrusted to state departments of agriculture, governors, and chief law enforcement officers, for Indian tribes, regulatory authority is entrusted to tribal governments. Through 2021, approximately 50 Indian tribes have plans approved for hemp cultivation.

Indian tribes have a long history of cultivating hemp which creates additional issues as to oversight. American Indian tribes have traditionally employed hemp as material for nets, bags, clothing and ceremonial calendars. Bast fibers of hemp are used for string, thread, rope, baskets, snares, netting, straps, belts, hairnets and ceremonial regalia such as capes, skirts, and head-dresses. In addition, Indian tribes cultivated hemp for products sold in the stream of commerce. The prohibition of hemp thus had a particularly adverse effect on Indian farming and traditions.

Hemp cultivation on Indian lands may involve interaction with Indian treaties. Based on the Treaty of Fort Laramie of 1868 providing that the U.S. government would support the Sioux nations of South Dakota in farming their land, Alexander White Plume, a Lakota Sioux farmer, argued that since the Tribe cultivated hemp in 1868, cultivating hemp was guaranteed to the Tribe, regardless of other federal law. The court ruled in *U.S. v. White Plume*, 447 F.3d 1067 (8th Cir. 2006) that because the treaty did not specifically mention farming hemp, it did not reserve any such right, and White Plume could not cultivate hemp without a DEA registration. The court reached this conclusion despite judicial policy to interpret treaties liberally in favor of Indians, and to resolve ambiguities in their favor. Likewise, a federal court, despite proclaiming the same policy of judicial interpretation in favor of Indians, ruled against the

Menominee Indian Tribe in relying on a 1854 treaty to cultivate hemp. *Menominee Indian Tribe of Wisconsin v. Drug Enforcement Administration*, 190 F. Supp. 3d 843 (E.D. Wis. 2016). This derogation of Indian treaty rights was criticized by commentators for allowing the Controlled Substances Act to abrogate the historic right of the Sioux nation to cultivate hemp. Reservation lands are inhospitable to many agricultural products, but hemp cultivation thrives. Thus Congress should be required to provide compensation for the income lost to these farmers for farming rights preserved under various treaties.

Section 7–2 explores the marijuana prohibitions of the CSA as one of the furthest extensions of federal power under the commerce clause. To this can be added the CSA's contentious reach to a commercial and non-intoxicating plant, and one woven into the traditional agricultural and ceremonial practices of American indigenous tribes.

As outlined above, hemp is now legal in Indian country subject to federal regulations. These regulations are further complicated by the complex and often disputatious relations between tribes and the states in which they are located. For example, many tribes are located in Public Law 280 states, which gives the state increased jurisdiction over Indian affairs.

§ 11–5 CBD

Cannabidiol (CBD) is a non-intoxicating cannabinoid contained in the cannabis plant. Of the over 120 cannabinoids in the cannabis plant, studies have found THC and CBD to be the most prevalent. A fundamental question for the legality of CBD is its source. If derived from the marijuana plant as defined by the CSA, it is illegal under federal law. However if derived from the hemp plant, CBD is legal under federal law and most state law. Likewise CBD products containing a substantial amount of the euphoriating compound THC are federally illegal. Low-THC, high-CBD products are legal under federal law but may be subject to approval under the FD&C Act. 21 U.S.C. § 355.

The vast majority of states allow high-CBD, low-THC products, although some states impose limits which might include allowing only for medical use; prohibiting smokable CBD flower or the ingestion of low THC oil through vapor; and prohibiting sale of food or beverage infused with low THC oil, or as dietary supplements. In states that allow CBD products with high THC for medical purposes, these products can be obtained through recommendation of a physician. Like marijuana, physicians cannot prescribe marijuana-derived CBD, as only FDA-approved drugs are available by prescription.

CBD is contained mostly in oil, tincture, liquid vape, and edible (including pill and capsule) form. In general terminology, CBD isolate is a pure form of CBD containing no other cannabis compounds. Broad-spectrum CBD contains all cannabis compounds, including terpenes, flavonoids, and cannabinoids, except THC. Full-spectrum CBD contains all cannabis compounds, including up to 0.3% THC. The FDA retains jurisdiction of CBD products marketed with a claim of therapeutic benefit, or added to foods, under the FD&C Act and section 351 of the Public Health Service Act. The only FDA-approved medicine containing CBD is Epidiolex, to inhibit seizures associated with two rare, intractable forms of childhood-onset epilepsy; Epidiolex, a plant-derived, purified CBD derivative, is controlled in Schedule V. (In April 2020, DEA approved Epidiolex for a third disease and also descheduled it, removing it as a controlled substance.) The FDA also prohibits sale of CBD products as dietary supplements or any food (including animal feed) or beverage to which CBD has been added.

With the popularity of CBD, other cannabinoids are being examined for commercial potential including Cannabinol (CBN), Cannabichromene (CBC), Cannabigerol (CBG), Cannabidiolic acid (CBDA), Cannabigerolic acid (CBGA), and Delta-8 tetrahydrocannabinol (delta-8 THC).

Although hemp-derived CBD was marketed for many years labeled as a legal substance, this labeling was often incorrect. Cannabinoids are mostly concentrated in the flowers and upper leaves of the cannabis plant, included in the CSA definition of marijuana. Likewise CBD is found in the resin of the cannabis plant, prohibited under the CSA even if derived from a part of the plant, such as stalks and seeds, excluded from the CSA definition. This was again asserted by the DEA in a rule which purported to establish a new drug code specifically for marijuana extract. Fed Reg, 81(240): 90194–96

(12/14/2016). This rule defined illegal marijuana extract as any containing one or more cannabinoids derived from the cannabis plant, explicitly including CBD. This created alarm among hemp industries that even CBD derived from hemp legal under Section 7606 of the Agricultural Act of 2014, from the parts of the plant excluded from control, and from lawfully imported hemp, was now illegal. In *Hemp Industries Association v. U.S. Drug Enforcement Administration*, 720 F. App'x 886, 887 (9th Cir. 2018) (*Hemp III*), the Ninth Circuit denied a petition to review the rule. Nevertheless in a 2018 clarification of the rule, the DEA conceded that cannabinoids, such as CBD, are controlled only to the extent that they are found in parts of the cannabis plant included in the definition of marijuana. Confusion as to CBD's status was resolved in the 2018 Farm Bill (§ 10113) legalizing hemp, which includes derivatives, extracts, and cannabinoids thereof, such as CBD.

CBD is alleged to have therapeutic benefits, including anti-inflammatory, anti-anxiety, analgesic, and seizure-suppressant properties. The U.S. Department of Health and Human Services (HHS) itself holds U.S. Patent No. 6,630,507, "Cannabinoids as antioxidants and neuroprotectants." This 2003 patent, giving HHS the right to use some non-intoxicating cannabinoids in treating neurological diseases, includes CBD. A November 2017 report by the World Health organization concluded that CBD "does not appear to have abuse potential or cause harm," and recommended that CBD not be scheduled as a controlled substance. However the FDA has issued warnings about the potential of CBD use to cause liver and gastrointestinal disorders, interfere with the metabolism of prescription drugs, and cause somnolence or affect mood. Research as to the therapeutic benefits and adverse effects of CBD are in the early stages with mixed results. In 2019, over one thousand people contacted poison control centers about CBD-induced illnesses; 46 people were admitted to a hospital intensive care unit, due to complications of CBD use, perhaps combined with other drugs. Nevertheless conclusive evidence of CBD's dangers has not been found. But CBD products can present other risks. FDA studies from 2014 through 2019 revealed that a majority of CBD products were mislabeled as to the quantity of CBD they contain. Many of these products also had higher THC concentrations than indicated or allowed.

Despite these difficulties, sales of CBD products are expected to grow to $1.3 billion in 2022 from the $390 million expended in 2018.

PART 3

STATE AND LOCAL LAW

CHAPTER 12
STATE LAW

§ 12–1 INTRODUCTION

Prior to the 1970s, the states generally followed the federal government's lead when it came to criminalizing marijuana. Beginning with the adoption of the Uniform Narcotic Drug Act in 1932, and continuing through the federal government's adoption of the Boggs Act and other federal legislation in the 1950s, the states had imposed increasingly harsh penalties for marijuana-related offenses, just as the federal government had called for them to do. And following the passage of the Controlled Substances Act in 1970, most states enacted their own versions of the CSA. In doing so, they adopted the scheduling scheme imposed by the CSA, including the inclusion of marijuana among the Schedule I prohibited drugs.

Beginning in the early-mid 1970s, however, the law in many states began to diverge from federal law—a trend that continues to the present time. This divergence has manifested itself in several distinct ways. Thus, while no two states are exactly the same in terms of their treatment of marijuana, there are certain trends that are apparent when examining state marijuana laws that have put a number of states in conflict with federal law. The first of these is decriminalization. Beginning in the early 1970s, certain states, as well as a few municipalities, began to decriminalize simple (i.e., personal use) marijuana possession, making it a mere civil offense, or, in some jurisdictions, a petty criminal offense with no possibility of jail time. At the present time, over half of the states have taken this approach. In addition, beginning in the mid-1990s, certain states began to allow the medical use of marijuana, thereby breaking down the blanket prohibition (whether civil or criminal) on marijuana use that had existed almost universally among the states since the early part of the 20th century. Later still, beginning in 2012, some states began to break down the barriers even further, legalizing marijuana for recreational (also known as "adult-use") purposes as well. Similarly, a number of states diverged from federal law in legalizing related cannabis products, including hemp and CBD oil.

This chapter examines these four trends among state laws regulating marijuana. It is important to keep in mind, however, that these trends are not mutually exclusive. Several states have deviated from federal law thoroughly, legalizing both medical and recreational marijuana, as well as related marijuana products. Most states, however, have adopted certain provisions, such as legalizing medical marijuana or CBD oil, but not others, such as legalizing recreational marijuana. And a few states have not followed any of these trends, remaining in lockstep with the federal government. Those states in the latter category, however, are becoming increasingly isolated as more and more states adopt one or more of these provisions.

Section 12–2 of this chapter discusses traditional criminalization states, that is, states that continue to follow the federal government in criminalizing all marijuana use. Section 12–3 looks at states that have decriminalized the personal use and possession of marijuana. Section 12–4 examines the law in states that have enacted medical marijuana schemes. Section 12–5 looks at the law in states that have legalized the recreational use of marijuana. And § 12–6 discusses how various states treat related cannabis products, such as hemp, CBD oil, and paraphernalia.

§ 12–2 TRADITIONAL CRIMINALIZATION STATES

In 1970 Congress enacted the Controlled Substances Act (i.e., the "CSA"). The CSA designated five different schedules of drugs, classified on the bases of their demonstrated safety profile (or lack thereof), their potential for abuse, and their acceptance for efficacious medical use. (*See* Chapter 5 for more on the CSA.) Schedule I, which included drugs such as heroin and LSD, was for drugs that were deemed to have no accepted medical use, in addition to having a high potential for abuse, and a lack of a proven safety record. Congress elected to include marijuana within the list of Schedule I drugs; thus, possession of marijuana was strictly outlawed under the Controlled Substances Act.

At the same time, however, Congress provided in the Controlled Substances Act for the appointment by the President of a blue-ribbon panel, called the National Commission on Marihuana and Drug Abuse (also known as the "Shafer Commission") to study the marijuana issue further and issue recommendations to Congress.

The states generally followed the lead of the federal government in the years immediately following 1970, enacting their own versions of the CSA. Accordingly, they adopted, with some minor individual modification, the scheduling scheme that the CSA had imposed at the federal level. This included including marijuana on Schedule I, along with other drugs deemed to have no accepted medical use, an uncertain safety profile, and a high potential for abuse. Thus, personal possession of marijuana remained a serious criminal offense under state laws, subjecting the defendant to possible prison time.

In 1972, however, the Shafer Commission issued its recommendations, calling for the decriminalization of marijuana possession for personal use. The Commission concluded that marijuana did not constitute a health risk, was not a gateway drug, and did not constitute a danger to public safety. But the federal government did not heed the Commission's advice. President Nixon soundly rejected the conclusions of the Shafer Commission, and Congress never acted on its recommendations.

Nevertheless, a few states struck out on a more lenient path in response to the Commission's recommendations, reducing the penalties for the personal possession of small quantities of marijuana to fines and other minor, non-detention remedies. Oregon led the way in this regard, passing legislation in 1973 that made marijuana possession for personal use merely a civil infraction, subject to a $100 fine. Over the next several years, the legislatures of 10 additional states followed suit, decriminalizing personal marijuana use. And in Alaska, the state's supreme court effectively decriminalized possession of marijuana for personal use in *Ravin v. State,* 537 P.2d 494 (Alaska 1975). There the court held that the Alaska Constitution contains an implicit right to privacy that protects possession of small amounts of marijuana kept in the home for personal use. Among states that did not decriminalize marijuana, the majority nevertheless reduced the penalty for possessing small amounts of marijuana for personal use to minor misdemeanor status, though still allowing for the possibility of jail time.

At the present time, 23 states remain traditional criminalization states, meaning that they leave open the possibility of jail time for possession of even small amounts of illegal marijuana intended for personal use. Almost all of these states allow low-THC marijuana (or at least CBD products) for licensed medical use, however, for certain limited conditions, so they are no longer traditional criminalization states in the strict 1970's sense. Only 3 states still impose significant criminal sanctions across the board for marijuana and its derivatives.

Furthermore, the amount of jail time a defendant can face in traditional criminalization states varies significantly by state. One state, Arizona, still makes the possession of any amount of marijuana a felony, punishable by four months to two years incarceration, and a fine up to $150,000. On the other hand, some of the traditional criminalization states, such as North Dakota and Virginia, limit the amount of possible jail time to as little as 30 days for a first offense. For many of the traditional criminalization states, the maximum penalty for possession of small amounts of marijuana is one year in jail. But criminal penalties are higher where possession involves larger amounts of marijuana, or is sold to a minor or within the vicinity of a school. Some of these penalties can be quite harsh. In Tennessee, for example, possession of more than 300 pounds of marijuana is a felony punishable by 15 to 60 years in prison and a fine of up to $200,000. In Texas, possession of more than 2000 pounds of marijuana is punishable as a felony by incarceration of 5 to 99 years (including a mandatory minimum sentence of five years), and a fine of up to $100,000.

Within some of the traditional criminalization states, individual municipalities have elected to decriminalize marijuana on their own. The City of Milwaukee, for example, has decriminalized possession of small amounts of marijuana for personal use, even though the state of Wisconsin makes first-offense possession of any amount of marijuana a misdemeanor punishable by up to six months in jail and a $1000 fine. (For further reading on municipal decriminalization efforts, *see* Chapter 13.)

§ 12–3 DECRIMINALIZATION STATES

After the Shafer Commission report was released in 1972, some states legislatures began to think further about the wisdom of criminalizing marijuana possession for personal use. In 1973 Oregon became the first state to decriminalize marijuana, eliminating criminal penalties simple possession and substituting a $100 civil fine. Between 1973 and 1979, 10 other states followed suit, reducing the penalties for the personal possession of small quantities of marijuana to fines or other non-detention-oriented remedies. (Technically, "decriminalization" refers to the complete elimination of criminal penalties, generally with the substitution of a civil fine; however, states that designate marijuana possession as a minor misdemeanor but eliminate the possibility of jail time are also frequently referred to as decriminalization states). And as noted above, the Alaska Supreme Court effectively decriminalized possession of marijuana for personal use by recognizing a right under the Alaska Constitution to possession of small amounts of marijuana kept in the home for personal use.

In the 1980s, the move toward decriminalization among states came to a halt with the election of Ronald Reagan as President of the United States. President Reagan re-ignited the so-called War on Drugs that President Nixon had begun, and the nation generally took a more conservative approach to marijuana use once again. But while many states ramped up penalties for illegal drug possession during this time, no state that had decriminalized marijuana possession in the 1970s repealed its decriminalization laws.

By the late 1990s, interest in decriminalization among state legislatures was beginning to pick up again, and in 2001, Nevada became the first state in 23 years to decriminalize possession of marijuana for personal use. So began the second wave of state decriminalization. At present, 27 states plus the District of Columbia have enacted laws decriminalizing possession of small amounts of marijuana for personal use (including the 18 states that have legalized it for recreational use), and a number of other states are expected to consider such legislation in the near future. In most of the decriminalization states, possession of small amounts of marijuana for personal use is reduced to a civil infraction with a fine; in a few of them, such possession is still technically a crime, but only a minor misdemeanor, with no possibility of imprisonment for a violation. In states that impose merely a civil fine, the amount of the fine ranges from a maximum of $100 (Maryland and California) to a maximum of $1000 (North Dakota).

At present, state decriminalization laws apply only to possession of small amounts of marijuana for personal use. Possession of large amounts is still a crime in every state, as is the sale and distribution of marijuana outside of state legalization schemes. Thus, even in states that have legalized recreational use of marijuana, the sale and distribution of the drug outside of the state's regulatory framework is a misdemeanor or felony, depending on the amount and other factors. In Washington, for example, possession of up to 1 ounce of marijuana for personal use is legal, but the sale or distribution of marijuana by a non-licensed person is a felony, punishable by imprisonment for up to five years and a $10,000 fine.

Even among states that have not actually decriminalized personal possession of marijuana, there is a trend toward reducing penalties for marijuana-related offenses. In the past decade, more than a dozen states have passed legislation reducing adverse consequences for marijuana-related offenses, e.g., by raising the maximum amount an individual can possess before it becomes a felony, or by reducing penalties for possession of drug paraphernalia.

There is also a growing movement among the states toward expungement of criminal records for those convicted of minor marijuana-related offenses. At present, 7 states have passed expungement statutes that specifically address marijuana offenses, and most of the remaining states have general expungement statutes that can apply to minor marijuana offenses.

§ 12–4 MEDICAL MARIJUANA STATES

The enactment of California's Compassionate Use Act in November 1996 (a.k.a. Proposition 215) commenced a new era in marijuana law—an era of legalization. Of course, such legalization was confined to a limited group of individuals: namely, those who managed to obtain a doctor's recommendation to use marijuana for therapeutic purposes. But it was nevertheless a significant milestone, since it was the first time in the better part of a century that anyone could use marijuana products legally.

Naturally, the federal government did not agree with this, and it maintained its prerogative to enforce federal drug laws in California, notwithstanding the California Act. This prerogative was affirmed by the Supreme Court of the United States in *Gonzales v. Raich*, 545 U.S. 1 (2005), where the Court upheld the federal government's power to prohibit medical marijuana schemes within the individual states, even if those schemes had been enacted by the voters of the state. It held that Congress had the power under the commerce clause to regulate activities that are purely intrastate, if those activities had a substantial effect on interstate commerce, and that the production of medical marijuana within California would have such an interstate effect. (For more on these types of federalism issues, *see* Chapter 8.) Nevertheless, while the federal government did exercise its authority to shut down certain grow operations and dispensaries that were allegedly out of compliance with California law, it did not elect to shut down California's medical marijuana scheme in its entirety, and so other states were motivated to follow California's lead.

In the 25 years since California enacted the nation's first medical marijuana act, more and more states have followed suit, to the point where a substantial majority of states now allow the medical use of marijuana products. Accordingly, as of the date this book went to publication, 36 states, plus the District of Columbia and several U.S. territories, had legalized medical marijuana. In addition, another 11 states have legalized the use of low-THC marijuana or CBD extracts for limited medical use, e.g., to treat certain types of seizures. (For more on the status of CBD extracts, *see* § 12–6 below.)

Medical marijuana laws vary somewhat between the various states. For one thing, each state decides for itself the qualifying conditions for which a physician may recommend medical marijuana. The state of Maryland, for example, lists only five qualifying conditions in its medical marijuana act: anorexia (i.e., wasting syndrome), chronic pain, nausea, seizures, and severe or persistent muscle spasms. The state of Illinois, on the other hand, lists some 36 qualifying conditions, including such conditions as cancer, Crohn's disease, Parkinson's disease, and spinal cord disease. The various state laws differ in other ways as well, such as how medical marijuana can be ingested. For example, a few states prohibit the smoking of marijuana, mandating instead that patients use extracts or pills.

The various states also differ in terms of the amount of marijuana that a patient may possess. And they vary with respect to whether patients may obtain medical marijuana through dispensaries or caregivers, or whether they have to grow their own plants at home. A clear majority of states allow dispensaries to distribute medical marijuana, but some states have prohibited this. The Michigan Medical Marihuana Act of 2008, for example, which was instituted by a ballot initiative, was silent on the issue of dispensaries, and the state attorney general subsequently issued a ruling concluding that dispensaries were not legal under the Act. Nevertheless, over time, dispensaries began cropping up in various marijuana-friendly counties and municipalities, and the state did not shut them down. Eventually, in late 2016, the state legislature removed the uncertainty around dispensaries by enacting legislation to establish a licensing and regulation framework for the various entities in the medical marijuana industry, including growers, processors, and dispensaries.

Interestingly, a particular state's decision to legalize medical marijuana does not necessarily reflect a general lenience toward marijuana possession on the part of the state. In fact, some of the harshest penalties for the *illegal* use of marijuana are found in states that authorize the medical use of marijuana. Arizona, for example, allows medical marijuana patients with various qualifying conditions to possess up to 2 ½ ounces of usable marijuana for medical purposes. However, strict compliance with the state's medical marijuana act is necessary, and possession outside of the strict confines of the medical marijuana act is a felony, punishable by incarceration of four months to 45 months years, depending on the amount, as well as a fine of up to $150,000. Thus, patients, caregivers, and marijuana-related businesses in medical marijuana states need to carefully monitor their activities, as well as new developments in the law, to ensure that they are staying within the strict confines of the law; otherwise they may face severe penalties.

Medical marijuana patients also face certain obstacles to important activities that most of us take for granted. For example, as discussed further in

Chapter 18, medical marijuana patients have to be careful when driving, particularly in states such as Colorado and Washington that have *per se* limits on blood THC levels. Because they are using the drug frequently, medical marijuana users may carry enough THC in their blood to violate criminal laws prohibiting impaired driving, even if the patients are not "high" at the time they are driving.

Similarly, as discussed further in Chapter 17, medical marijuana patients face challenges in the workplace, because most states allow employers to terminate medical marijuana patients who fail random drug tests, even though the patients are not using marijuana at work and are not impaired at work. Medical marijuana patients may face other legal difficulties as well (e.g., with landlords who don't want marijuana used in the premises, with child custody evaluators who don't think parental marijuana use is in the best interests of the children, etc.). In short, state medical marijuana laws exempt medical marijuana patients from prosecution, but they do not necessarily create a recognized right to use marijuana for therapeutic purposes.

§ 12–5 RECREATIONAL MARIJUANA STATES

So-called "recreational" marijuana states allow adults in the state to use and possess limited amounts of marijuana as they see fit. The first two states to legalize marijuana generally (that is to say for personal, non-medical use) were Colorado and Washington in November 2012. In doing so, they became the first jurisdictions in the world to enact comprehensive schemes to legalize and regulate the recreational use of marijuana. (The City of Amsterdam is often thought of as a legalization pioneer, but in fact its policy is to refrain from enforcement of laws criminalizing marijuana in certain contexts, such as personal use in coffee shops.)

Colorado took the lead in terms of forging a regulatory scheme. After the voters of the state passed Amendment 64, which amended the state constitution to provide for possession of up to 1 ounce of marijuana, the governor promptly appointed a task force to make recommendations regarding regulations, and a few months later the task force issued its report. The legislature then enacted several bills implementing the task force's recommendations, and the Colorado Department of Revenue issued regulations supplementing the legislation in September 2013.

A few months later, in January 2014, the first dispensaries opened their doors for business, selling marijuana in much the same way that liquor stores sell alcoholic beverages. Thus, customers over 21 could stroll in from the street and purchase a variety of cannabis products, including not only herbal cannabis for traditional smoking, but also a variety of extracts for use in vaporizers and other devices, marijuana infused beverages, and a variety of edible products, including cookies, brownies, and gummy bears. Local municipalities were allowed to opt out of the regulatory scheme, however, insofar as they could pass ordinances that would prohibit marijuana-related businesses, such as dispensaries, from operating within their city limits.

In the state of Washington, voters passed Ballot Initiative 502, also in 2012, which legalized the personal use of marijuana in amounts of 1 ounce or less, and authorized the state liquor control board to tax and regulate sales of marijuana by licensed entities to persons 21 years of age and older. The state set up a detailed regulatory scheme, granting licenses to marijuana producers and marijuana processors, as well as marijuana retailers (i.e., dispensaries). Recreational sales of marijuana to the public began in July 2014.

Unlike Colorado, Washington does not allow individuals to grow their own marijuana for recreational use. Both states, however, prohibit the public consumption of marijuana. Both impose *per se* limits of 5 ng/ml of blood for purposes of regulating impaired driving. And both states have generated significant revenue by taxing recreational sales of marijuana.

In November 2014, voters in Alaska, Oregon, and the District of Columbia also approved legalization measures. The Alaska measure became effective in February 2015. It allowed adults 21 or older to possess up to 1 ounce of marijuana and to grow up to six plants for personal use. The state issued its first licenses for retail distributors in September 2016. The Oregon measure became effective in July 2015. It allowed adults to possess up to 1 ounce of marijuana in public places, and to grow up to 8 ounces of marijuana for personal use at home. It also set up a regulatory scheme that allows dispensaries to sell up to ¼ ounce of marijuana to adults 21 and older. Retail sales in Oregon began in October 2015. Both states prohibit the public consumption of marijuana.

Voters in the District of Columbia also approved recreational marijuana in November 2014. Initiative 71 allowed adults 21 and older to possess up to 2 ounces of marijuana and up to six marijuana plants at home for personal recreational use. However, Congress blocked the D.C. City Council's attempt to implement a regulatory scheme that would license marijuana-related businesses by prohibiting the Council from spending any federal funds in pursuit of implementation. Thus, it remains legal for adults in the District to use and grow marijuana at home, but is not legal to buy or sell it. Furthermore, it remains illegal to use marijuana on federal land, which comprises about one third of the District.

The move toward legalization of recreational marijuana continues apace. Four additional states passed legalization via voter approval in the November 2016 elections, including California, the largest state in the U.S. Since then, 10 more states have followed suit, including several that did so via legislation rather than ballot initiatives. Thus, recreational marijuana is now legal in 18 states plus the District of Columbia, and it appears that the movement toward the legalization of marijuana for recreational use is continuing to gain momentum at the state level.

§ 12-6 STATE REGULATION OF HEMP, CBD OIL, AND RELATED PRODUCTS

The previous sections have discussed the significant differences between states as to their approaches to marijuana regulation. These differences extend beyond the regulation of marijuana itself, however. The way states regulate related products such as hemp, CBD, and paraphernalia also varies from state to state, though Congress did bring a significant degree of uniformity to the regulation of hemp and CBD when it passed the 2018 Farm Bill.

Prior to the enactment of the Marijuana Tax Act in 1937, hemp (traditionally consisting of fibers derived from the stalks and stems of the cannabis plant) had been a valuable commodity, used for a variety of different products, including rope, clothes, paint, paper, sails for boats, and birdseed. After the enactment of the Marihuana Tax Act, however, the cultivation and distribution of hemp was effectively prohibited under federal law, since "marijuana" was defined under the Act to include hemp, even though hemp contains only trivial amounts of THC, and was therefore subject to the tax and reporting requirement of the Act. Similarly, the Controlled Substances Act of 1970 included hemp and its derivatives within the definition of marijuana, thereby subjecting hemp to strict Schedule 1 prohibitions.

Hemp started making a comeback, however, following Congress' decision in 2014 to loosen restrictions on hemp cultivation. Specifically, the

Agricultural Act of 2014 legalized the cultivation of industrial hemp for research purposes within states that allowed such cultivation under state law. Such cultivation, however, was limited to "pilot programs" conducted by state departments of agriculture and institutions of higher learning for purposes of research regarding the cultivation and marketing of industrial hemp. Thus, hemp products could be sold for commercial use in such states under the Act only for purposes of "marketing research." By 2016, 29 states had legalized the cultivation of hemp pursuant to the Act, but only about half of these allowed production for commercial use.

The hemp landscape changed dramatically again in 2018, when Congress passed the Farm Bill of 2018. In that legislation, Congress essentially legalized hemp cultivation, provided it complied with certain state and federal regulatory requirements. More specifically, Congress defined hemp as cannabis containing no more than .3% THC and removed it from the prohibitions of Controlled Substances Act. It also authorized the states to set up licensing schemes for growing hemp; these schemes must be approved by the U.S. Department of Agriculture. If states choose not to do so, then the hemp farmers can apply for licenses directly from the U.S.D.A. Hemp and its derivatives can legally be sold across state lines, so long as they comply with these requirements. (For more on hemp and its regulation, *see* Chapter 11.)

Another, related product that has generated significant interest (and a significant market) in the recent years is CBD, or cannabidiol, which is one of the principal chemical constituents of the cannabis plant. But unlike THC, CBD is not considered to be intoxicating (though it may have anti-anxiety properties). As a result, it has gained support as a medicine even among those who oppose medical marijuana generally, since it is not subject to recreational use and does not get the patient "high" as a side effect.

Proponents of medical CBD use tout a number of supposed therapeutic uses, including antipsychotic activity, anti-inflammatory activity and anti-tremor activity. The substance has been generating significant attention for its apparent ability to mitigate symptoms in children with severe and intractable seizure disorders. A high CBD, low THC cannabis extract called "Charlotte's Web" (named for a young girl with that name whose parents claim that her rare seizure disorder was helped greatly by CBD) was developed in 2011 in Colorado principally for this purpose.

Publicity associated with Charlotte's Web led many state legislatures that had not previously legalized medical marijuana to create an exception for CBD for use in these types of cases. By 2016, 16 states (primarily in the South) that did not have medical marijuana laws nevertheless passed legislation allowing low-THC marijuana and/or CBD oil to be used for certain therapeutic purposes, such as treatment of seizure disorders. And in 2018 the FDA approved a prescription CBD drug called

Epidiolex to treat seizures associated with two rare and severe forms of epilepsy.

With the enactment of the 2018 Farm Bill, the status of CBD became a little more complicated. Technically, CBD remains within the definition of marijuana within the Controlled Substances Act, and it is therefore subject to Schedule 1 treatment. However, the 2018 Farm Bill provides an exception for derivatives of hemp, including CBD, so long as they are derived from hemp that is produced in compliance with state and federal law. Thus, if CBD is derived from cannabis that meets the Farm Bill definition of hemp (cannabis that has less than or equal to .3% THC), and it is produced by a licensed grower in compliance with state and federal regulations, then that CBD is legal under federal law.

One other cannabis-related product (or more accurately, group of products) that receives disparate treatment among the various states is **paraphernalia**. That term is defined under federal law as "any equipment, product, or material of any kind which is primarily intended or designed for use in manufacturing, compounding, converting, concealing, producing, processing, preparing, injecting, ingesting, inhaling, or otherwise introducing into the human body a controlled substance. . . ." 21 U.S.C. § 863(d). Under § (a) of this statute, it is a crime for any person to sell or offer for sale drug paraphernalia, to transport the equipment in interstate commerce, or to import or export drug paraphernalia.

Examples of paraphernalia listed in the statute include ceramic pipes, water pipes, roach clips, bongs, and various other types of devices designed for ingesting marijuana. However, § (f) of the federal statute exempts from the legal prohibition "any item that, in the normal course of business, is imported, exported, transported, or sold through the mail or by any other means, and traditionally intended for use with tobacco products, including any pipe, paper, or accessory." Thus, so-called "head shops" continue to operate in many parts of the United States, but they are very careful to make it clear to potential customers that the products are "intended" to be used exclusively for tobacco use.

At the state level, regulation of paraphernalia varies widely. In some states, the mere possession or use of paraphernalia is a crime. In many other states, the mere possession of paraphernalia is not a crime and is punishable only by a civil fine. In Vermont, for example, possession of paraphernalia is punishable by a fine in an amount ranging from a maximum of $200 for the first offense to a maximum of $500 for the third or subsequent offense. In a number of states, criminalization is reserved solely for advertising or selling paraphernalia. In the State of Washington, for example, the advertisement of paraphernalia is a misdemeanor punishable by up to 90 days in jail, whereas the sale of paraphernalia is just a civil infraction punishable by a $250 fine, and mere possession is not penalized at all.

Of all the states, Alaska is the most lenient with respect to paraphernalia, as the state has no laws punishing the possession, sale or manufacture of paraphernalia. At the other end of the spectrum, Rhode Island makes manufacture and sale a crime punishable by imprisonment for up to two years, unless the sale was to a minor, in which case the offense is punishable by a term of up to five years. And Arkansas imposes criminal penalties that range from up to one year in jail for mere possession, to imprisonment up to six years for possession of "growing paraphernalia," to imprisonment up to 20 years for delivering paraphernalia to a minor.

In sum, the great variation between the states in terms of how they regulate drug paraphernalia reflects the divergent paths the various states have followed with respect to marijuana policy since the early 1970s.

CHAPTER 13
LOCAL LAW

§ 13-1 INTRODUCTION

As discussed in the previous chapter, almost every state followed the federal government's lead following the passage of the Controlled Substances Act in 1970. Thus, the states enacted their own versions of the CSA, adopting, with some individual modification, the five-schedule scheme that the CSA imposed at the federal level. This led certain municipalities within such states (particularly liberal college towns) to effectively opt out of state law by adopting their own decriminalization measures (or by otherwise significantly reducing the criminal penalties for marijuana possession). More recently, after a long period of dormancy, local decriminalization efforts have been revived in states that have not legalized or decriminalized marijuana possession at the state level. Thus, there have essentially been two waves of local decriminalization efforts. In addition, there are a handful of municipalities that have attempted in recent years to avoid state-mandated medical marijuana initiatives, seeking to restrict or prohibit use of medical marijuana within their jurisdictions, notwithstanding state laws allowing it.

All of these efforts involve nuanced considerations involving a state's ability to require individual municipalities to enforce state law. This analysis in many respects mirrors the nuanced federalism considerations discussed in Chapter 8, which discusses the states' right to deviate from federal law in their own legalization efforts.

Section 13–2 of this chapter discusses the early efforts on the part of some municipalities in the 1970s to decriminalize personal marijuana possession within their jurisdictions. Section 13–3 looks at more recent efforts in this regard among municipalities located in states that have not legalized or decriminalized simple marijuana possession. Section 13–4 looks at the opposite side of the coin: that is, it looks at local efforts opposing or opting out of state legalization. Some municipalities in states with medical marijuana laws have sought to enforce more restrictive laws against marijuana possession than state law provides. And some municipalities have exercised their option under state medical marijuana law to disallow marijuana-related businesses, particularly dispensaries, within their local jurisdictions. Finally, § 13–5 briefly discusses efforts on the part of local governments to regulate the possession and use of legalized marijuana within their jurisdictions through zoning, licensing, etc.

§ 13–2 LOCAL DECRIMINALIZATION—THE FIRST WAVE

As discussed in previous chapters, in 1970 Congress enacted the Controlled Substances Act, which designated five different schedules of drugs, classified on the bases of their potential for harm and abuse, as well as their potential for efficacious medical use. Schedule I, which included drugs such as heroin and LSD, was for drugs that were deemed to have no accepted medical use, in addition to having a high potential for abuse, and no demonstrated safety record. Because Congress elected to include marijuana within the CSA's Schedule I drugs, the possession of marijuana was strictly outlawed under the Controlled Substances Act.

Most states followed the lead of the federal government in the years immediately following 1970, enacting their own versions of the CSA. Thus, in most states, possession of marijuana, even for personal use, remained a serious criminal offense under state law, subjecting the defendant to possible prison time. A few states, however, struck out on a more lenient path, reducing the penalties for the simple possession of small quantities of marijuana to fines and other non-detention-oriented remedies. As discussed in Chapter 11, Oregon went the furthest in this regard, passing legislation in 1973 that made marijuana possession for personal use merely a civil infraction with a $100 fine. And in Alaska, the state's supreme court effectively decriminalized possession of marijuana for personal, at home use in *Ravin v. State,* 537 P.2d 494 (Alaska 1975).

Certain municipalities joined the decriminalization movement as well, beginning with Ann Arbor, Michigan in 1972. After he was released from prison, John Sinclair (*see* Chapter 4) helped to rally support for decriminalization efforts within Ann Arbor city limits. And in April of 1972, voters elected two members of the (pro-marijuana) Human Rights Party to the city council, where they joined with the Democrats on the council to enact in September of

1972 an ordinance reducing marijuana possession to a civil infraction, and making its violation a mere $5 fine.

While that initial ordinance was supported by local police and prosecutors (at least with regard to minor infractions), it was promptly struck down by a local District Court judge, S. J. Elden, who ruled that the measure was an improper intrusion by local government into the judicial functions of the state. And in April 1973, the city council repealed the ordinance. One year later, however, a similar provision was passed by the voters of Ann Arbor as a city charter amendment, and that charter provision remained in effect until it was effectively mooted by the State's legalization of marijuana in 2018 (although in 1990 voters amended the charter again to raise the civil fines to $25 for a first offense, $50 for a second offense, and $100 for subsequent offenses).

A few years later, however, a very similar ordinance that had been passed by the neighboring town of Ypsilanti (home of Eastern Michigan University) was challenged. There a city police officer referred a case involving possession of a large amount (about 100 pounds) of marijuana to a county prosecutor to seek prosecution under state felony laws, notwithstanding a provision in the ordinance that prohibited city police from referring matters to entities other than the city attorney, who was required to seek no more than a civil fine. The Michigan Court of Appeals upheld the prosecution under state law and stuck down the provision in the ordinance that required city police to refer all matters to the city attorney for civil prosecution. *See Joslin v. Fourteenth District Judge*, 255 N.W.2d 782, 786 (Mich. Ct. App. 1977). Thus, it appears that under this somewhat murky precedent, at least, city police officers have the authority under state law to refer matters to county prosecutors for state prosecution under state law, notwithstanding any prohibition to the contrary in a local law decriminalizing marijuana possession.

In addition to Ann Arbor and Ypsilanti, several other "college-towns" around the U.S. passed decriminalization measures in the late 1970's. For example, Madison, Wisconsin passed a measure in 1977 that reduced the penalty for simple possession to a $100 fine, and Berkeley, California passed an ordinance in 1979 that explicitly made enforcement of marijuana prohibitions the lowest police priority.

By 1973, however, all but 6 of the states had reduced the crime of possessing small amounts of marijuana for personal use to minor misdemeanor status. And by 1979, the legislatures of 11 states (including Oregon) had effectively decriminalized personal possession of small amounts of marijuana, either by making it a civil infraction, or by eliminating the possibility of imprisonment for a violation.

To some extent, this movement toward greater leniency at the state level took the wind out of the sails of decriminalization efforts at the local level, since there was now less of an incentive for municipalities to pass their own measures. In addition, the election of President Ronald Reagan in 1980 ushered in a new era of political conservatism and a renewed effort to fight the so-called "War on Drugs." Accordingly, decriminalization measures pretty much dried up at both the state and local levels for the last two decades of the 20th century.

§ 13-3 LOCAL DECRIMINALIZATION—RECENT YEARS

In 2001, Nevada became the first state in 23 years to decriminalize possession of small amounts of marijuana for personal use. By the end of 2016, 21 states plus the District of Columbia had enacted laws decriminalizing possession of small amounts of marijuana for personal use (including states that had fully legalized it), and currently 27 states plus the District have enacted such legislation. In most of these states, possession of small amounts of marijuana for personal use is reduced to a civil infraction with a fine; in a few of them, such possession is still technically a crime, but only a minor misdemeanor, with no possibility of imprisonment for a violation.

Decriminalization efforts were also renewed at the local level in states that continued to maintain criminal penalties for personal marijuana possession that included the possibility of prison time. The first large municipalities to enact such ordinances in the second wave were Seattle (2003), Denver (2004), and Oakland (2005). Since then, in a number of states that have not legalized or decriminalized marijuana, voters in marijuana-friendly pockets of the states have championed local initiatives that make possession of small amounts of marijuana for personal use merely civil infractions. For example, by 2016, in Michigan and Wisconsin alone, approximately 2 dozen municipalities had passed laws decriminalizing simple possession, including Milwaukee and Detroit, the largest municipalities in the two states. (Michigan has since gone on to legalize marijuana for recreational use.)

Other states in which multiple municipalities have decriminalized marijuana possession include Pennsylvania, Texas, and Florida. In Tampa, for example, the penalty for the first possession offense is a $75 fine, and for subsequent offenses, a fine of $450. This contrasts significantly with Florida state law, where a first offense for possession can result in imprisonment up to one year. Since 2012, nearly 100 municipalities across the U.S. have enacted decriminalization ordinances.

The individual local measures vary somewhat from municipality to municipality. In some municipalities, for example, the measures provide that local police *must* apply the civil fine rather than the state's criminal penalties, while other municipalities, such as New Orleans, provide that police use of a civil fine under the city's municipal ordinance is merely optional, and that local police have the discretion to apply state law. The reactions of state law enforcement officials to these decriminalization measures also vary from municipality to municipality. Some county and state governments say they will continue to apply state law, notwithstanding local decriminalization measures, and some have raised court challenges to such measures.

In Grand Rapids, Michigan, for example, the voters of the city approved a city charter amendment in November 2012 that made the possession, control, use, or giving away of marijuana a civil infraction. The amendment also prohibited city police officers and city attorneys from referring complaints of such conduct to the county prosecutor. The county prosecutor responded by filing a declaratory judgment action, seeking a court order that the local measure was preempted by state law. The trial court ruled for the city, and the Court of Appeals, in an unpublished opinion, *Kent County Prosecuting Attorney v. City of Grand Rapids*, affirmed the order of the trial court in January of 2015. The court held that the amendment was not preempted by state law and did not interfere with the county prosecutor's rights, powers, or duties. The court noted that a municipal ordinance creating a civil infraction for possession of marijuana would be improper under a state statute, M.C.L. 117.4, which provided that "an ordinance shall not make an act or omission a municipal civil infraction or a blight violation if that act or omission constitutes a crime under . . . [a]ny law of the state under which the act or omission is punishable by imprisonment for more than 90 days." But that statute did not apply in this instance, the court held, because M.C.L. 117.4 applied on its face only to municipal *ordinances*, and not to city *charters*.

To date, the case law is limited with respect to these types of challenges, but it is likely that courts will further elaborate on state law preemption issues as additional local decriminalization measures are challenged.

§ 13–4 LOCALITIES OPPOSING OR OPTING OUT OF STATE LEGALIZATION MEASURES

While the majority of cases in which municipalities seek to deviate from state law with respect to marijuana possession have involved local laws that are more lenient than state laws, there have also been a few municipalities that have sought to impose more restrictive local laws in response to a state's legalization of medical marijuana. The results of court challenges to these more restrictive local laws have been mixed.

In *Ter Beek v. City of Wyoming*, 846 N.W.2d 531 (Mich. 2014), for example, the city of Wyoming, Michigan, a suburb of Grand Rapids (which, as discussed above, enacted a local decriminalization measure in 2012) adopted an ordinance that amended the zoning chapter of the city code to provide that any property uses contrary to federal law, state law, or local ordinances were prohibited. Ter Beek, a medical marijuana patient, then filed a lawsuit alleging that he wished to grow and possess medical marijuana in his home pursuant to the Michigan Medical Marihuana Act, but he was prevented from doing so by the ordinance's incorporation of federal law prohibiting marijuana possession. This, he argued, impermissibly contravened the Michigan Medical Marihuana Act, which provides that registered qualifying patients shall not be subject to arrest or prosecution for medical use of marijuana in accordance with the Act.

The trial court ruled in favor of the city, but it was overruled by the Michigan Court of Appeals on the ground that the ordinance directly conflicted with the Michigan Medical Marihuana Act. The Michigan Supreme Court affirmed this ruling, holding (1) that the Michigan Medical Marihuana Act was not preempted by the federal Controlled Substances Act, and (2) that the ordinance was preempted by state law. With respect to the second point, the court held that the ordinance directly conflicted with the Act because it permitted licensed medical marijuana patients, such as the plaintiff, to be penalized by the city for engaging in the very activity that the state law authorized: medical marijuana use in conformance with the Act. The court rejected the city's argument that the measure was within its legitimate zoning authority, since that general grant of authority conflicted with and was subordinate to the Act's specific grant of authority to use marijuana for medical purposes.

In *Cannabis Action Coalition v. City of Kent*, 351 P.3d 151 (Wash. 2015), on the other hand, the Supreme Court of Washington reached a contrary conclusion, upholding a local ordinance that prohibited medical marijuana "collective gardens" within the city of Kent, even though such gardens were explicitly allowed by the state's Medical Use of Cannabis Act. The idea behind the collective gardens was to allow medical marijuana users to share responsibility for growing and producing marijuana for their individual medical use. The city ordinance prohibiting collective gardens within the City of Kent was fashioned as a zoning ordinance, since the Act also explicitly provided that local governments retained the authority to regulate medical marijuana through zoning, licensing, health and safety requirements, and taxation. Thus, the two provisions of the Act appeared to conflict.

The Cannabis Coalition argued that the ordinance was preempted by the Act by virtue of this conflict, since the state's constitution provided that ordinances are valid only to the extent they do not conflict with state law. The Washington Supreme Court rejected this argument, however, reading the Act's grant of zoning authority broadly so as to include the imposition of zoning restrictions on collective gardens, which it determined to be a permissible land use measure. Thus, the court concluded that the zoning ordinance was not in direct conflict with state law, and accordingly it was not preempted by state law. *See also DeRuiter v. Township of Byron,* 949 N.W.2d 91 (Mich. 2020) (distinguishing *Ter Beek* case discussed above, and holding that the local zoning ordinance did not conflict with the Michigan Medical Marijuana Act, where it did not prohibit use of medical marijuana, but merely limited where caregiver could grow it to the caregiver's "dwelling or attached garage.")

Finally, even where they have not directly challenged state law, many municipalities in medical-marijuana states have exercised their rights under state law to not allow dispensaries and other marijuana-related businesses to operate within their jurisdictions. Thus, in a number of states that have legalized medical and/or recreational marijuana use and have authorized dispensaries, marijuana may not be available in many municipalities. In Colorado, for example, some of the largest municipalities, such as Colorado Springs and Lakewood (a close-in suburb of Denver) chose not to allow recreational dispensaries. However, even in these municipalities that do not allow recreational sales, access to marijuana is usually not far away. For example, although Colorado Springs, the state's second-largest city, bans marijuana dispensaries, the small enclave of Manitou Springs (home of the Pikes Peak Cog Railway), which is located adjacent to it, allows dispensaries, and accordingly generates a significant amount of local tax revenue that would otherwise go to Colorado Springs. Thus, the decision whether to opt in or out of the marijuana industry can have significant economic consequences for local governments.

§ 13–5 LOCAL REGULATION OF LEGALIZED MARIJUANA USE

As discussed in the previous section, states that have legalized medical and/or recreational marijuana generally grant local municipalities certain authority to regulate marijuana possession and use within their jurisdictions with respect to matters such as zoning, licensing, health and safety, and taxation.

Zoning restrictions can be particularly vexing for prospective marijuana-related businesses, which must make sure they comply with all such restrictions before they open for business. Zoning restrictions can vary significantly between different localities, so there is no getting around the need for a thorough understanding of local ordinances.

Some municipalities create specific zones to which marijuana-related businesses are confined, and some others allow such businesses to operate broadly across the municipality, but then they create exclusionary zones in which marijuana-related businesses may not operate. Chicago, for example, allows dispensaries throughout most of the city but prohibits them in the so-called "Downtown Exclusion Zone," which encompasses a large part of the central business district adjoining Lake Michigan, including the Magnificent Mile.

Other types of zoning restrictions that municipalities may impose on marijuana-related businesses include restrictions on the number of such businesses allowed in certain parts of the city, as well as restrictions on the permissible size of such businesses. Zoning restrictions also typically include limits on how close marijuana-related businesses can be to entities such as schools, churches, and day-care centers.

An interesting local provision that the City and County of Denver adopted in 2016 was Denver Initiative 300, which created a four-year pilot program allowing businesses to apply for permits for special "designated consumption areas," where customers could consume cannabis. (Under Colorado state law, all public consumption is prohibited.) Those that were indoors could allow vaping and edibles, but not smoking; those with outdoor areas could also allow smoking. However, the initiative also provided that a business seeking a permit would need to obtain the approval of a local "eligible neighborhood organization," and these neighborhood organizations are allowed to set certain operating restrictions in exchange for their approval of the applications. Thus, in Denver, zoning restrictions on marijuana-related business were extended down to even the sub-governmental level (e.g., neighborhood associations empowered by local governments).

In keeping with the uneasy tension between state and local marijuana laws generally, the State of Colorado significantly restricted the scope of Initiative 300 just days after it was enacted. The state did so by issuing a regulation that prohibited businesses that serve alcohol from obtaining permits for designated consumption areas. This excluded many businesses one would expect to apply for such permits, such as restaurants and bars, but it left open the possibility of opening businesses that resembled bars but served cannabis instead of alcohol.

Thus, Initiative 300 was important because it created for the first time an exception to the general prohibition on public consumption of cannabis. It thus laid the foundation for more recent legislation, both in Colorado and some other legalization states, such as Nevada and California, that allows for "consumption lounges," where patrons are allowed to consume cannabis in a commercial setting, subject to certain restrictions on alcohol consumption, odor control, etc. And while the COVID pandemic has certainly slowed the development of the consumption-lounge concept, the trend is likely to resume going forward.

CHAPTER 14

STATE VS. STATE DISPUTES

§ 14–1 INTRODUCTION

Although much of this book addresses the differences between federal and state marijuana law, tensions exist between other sovereign entities in the U.S. For example, these tensions can result from geography, as jurisdictions that legalize marijuana adjoin those that prohibit marijuana. They can arise from different interpretations of the conflicting mosaic of marijuana laws. Legal actions will be the inevitable result and have already begun.

The potential for disputes is highest between states that have legalized marijuana and neighboring states that have not. Likewise, disputes may arise between states and Indian tribes, both sovereign entities. Indian tribes are domestic dependent nations that exercise inherent sovereign authority. Tribal law regarding marijuana may clash with the law of states that encompass their reservations. Added to the difficulty is that Indian reservations have to navigate federal law as well. (Local governments and municipalities are not sovereign entities, as they are creations of the states which constituted them and are not treated in this chapter.)

This chapter explores these disputes. Section 14–2 places the divisions in U.S. marijuana law in larger perspective. Section 14–3 explores state vs. state disputes, mainly in the form of the 2014 lawsuit filed by Nebraska and Oklahoma against Colorado's legalizing regime. Section 14–4 explores disputes between other sovereign entities within the United States, most notably between the states and American Indian tribes. And § 14–5 assesses the impact of these tensions on the U.S. marijuana regime.

§ 14–2 A HOUSE DIVIDED

A central question of marijuana law is the relation among various sovereign entities in U.S. law. Only a few legal issues in the United States have presented as divided a face as current marijuana law. It is certainly true that earlier conflicts between federal and state law, such as those that characterized slavery, the fugitive slave laws, and civil rights, were of far greater importance. Still, almost every question of marijuana law today is shaped to some extent by an understanding of federalism, and of the relations among various jurisdictions.

The current status of marijuana law in the United States resembles a patchwork quilt. Marijuana activity is prohibited by federal law, the supreme law of the land, yet tolerated for many purposes by the Justice Department, which is required to enforce the laws enacted by Congress. In a majority of states marijuana is legal for medicinal purposes, and in eighteen of those states, recreational purposes as well. As domestic dependent nations, Indian tribes are subject to the plenary authority of Congress, although Congress has delegated considerable authority to the states and to the tribes themselves.

Thus, marijuana law on the reservation will inevitably relate to the regulatory scheme of the surrounding state. Indian tribes have experience with this complex status of their laws in regard to such enterprises as casino gaming, alcohol, and tobacco sales. But they have not had to confront the situation where the laws outside the reservation are themselves in contradiction. Unlike other jurisdictional differences in such laws as prostitution (legal in some Nevada counties) and alcohol sales (banned by various state counties), marijuana is also subject to a national prohibition, which can make the interplay between states, Indian tribes, and the federal government bewildering. In addition, Indian tribes have begun to warn that in this complex interaction of laws, their inherent sovereignty over tribal law will be compromised.

With respect to a much more consequential tragedy in U.S. laws—slavery—and the conflicting laws of federal, state, and territorial governments, President Abraham Lincoln declared in 1858 that "A house divided cannot stand." Echoing these comments in 1972, President Richard Nixon, responding to the National Commission on Marihuana and Drug Abuse recommendation to decriminalize possession, stated: "you can[not] have effective criminal justice based on a philosophy that something is half legal and half illegal." For Nixon's War on Drugs, that meant that marijuana would be fully illegal, at a national, state, and local level. That is no longer the reality of the United States. It seems fair to say that marijuana consumption in the United States is now "half legal and half illegal." At the present time, it seems unlikely that the more than half of states that have legalized will return to strict prohibition; also unlikely, however, is that the federal government will embrace full legalization in the near future.

The existing patchwork of marijuana law is inherently unstable, and its future is hard to predict. The relations between the sovereign entities enacting those laws will be tested in national and state legislatures, in popular initiatives and referendums, and in the courthouse.

§ 14–3 STATE VS. STATE

The discrepancy between federal law and state law has implications for relations between the states as well. If State N (No) has not legalized marijuana and neighboring State Y (Yes) has legalized marijuana, can State N complain that Y's legalization will adversely impact State N's marijuana prohibitions? State Y is not actively encouraging the overflow of marijuana into State N, but surely legal accessibility to marijuana will increase consumption and trafficking across the border. The laws of neighboring states often differ one from another, but in this scenario State Y's law contrasts with federal law as well. What is more, the federal government bases its authority to enforce marijuana prohibition nationwide in the Commerce Clause, under the theory that it needs to exercise authority over both interstate and intrastate marijuana activity. Can State N bring a lawsuit against State Y demanding an end to its legalization campaign? Can State N bring a lawsuit against the federal government demanding that it enforce its laws against marijuana activity in State Y? If so, in what courts can State N bring a lawsuit, given the traditional notions that a sovereign entity must give its consent to be sued?

Such was the genesis of the lawsuit that Nebraska and Oklahoma brought against the state of Colorado in 2014. In this lawsuit, the two states complained about the consequences of Colorado's marijuana legalization for the health and safety of their citizens. Although the Supreme Court eventually decided against adjudicating this complaint, leaving the states with no other forum to litigate this matter, the lawsuit both raises the issues in conflict between legalizing and non-legalizing states and prefigures tensions among the states in years to come.

On December 18, 2014, Nebraska and Oklahoma filed a lawsuit in the U.S. Supreme Court contending that Colorado's legalization of marijuana conflicts with, and hence is preempted, by the CSA. Before reviewing this complex litigation in a detailed manner, it may help to summarize it from a non-technical perspective.

In a sense, Nebraska and Oklahoma were saying to the federal government that, given its long-standing insistence on its interstate authority to prohibit marijuana at a national level, it was vital to exercise this authority to maintain consistency in the law. Now that some states had legalized marijuana, to the detriment of states that were faithfully executing the law, Nebraska and Oklahoma wanted the Supreme Court to exercise its exclusive jurisdiction over interstate conflicts and to remedy this illegal action by a renegade state. In short, their message to the Court was to declare that the CSA preempts such legalization efforts and to enjoin Colorado's licensing scheme.

However the first obstacle that the Nebraska and Oklahoma lawsuit faced was obtaining leave from the Supreme Court to proceed with the complaint. Without such permission, the lawsuit would be quashed. Given that this was a legal action by one state against another, it could be heard only in the U.S. Supreme Court, as it falls within the Court's exclusive, original jurisdiction. While the Supreme Court usually hears cases that have originated in other courts by writ of certiorari, it has original jurisdiction in certain cases. U.S. Const. Art. III, § 2, cl. 2. The most elevated such cases are controversies between two or more states, over which "[t]he Supreme Court shall have original and exclusive jurisdiction." 28 U.S.C. § 1251(a). This means that not only does a lawsuit between two states originate in the U.S. Supreme Court, but only that Court can decide the case (unlike other original jurisdiction lawsuits which can be filed in other courts). It might be expected that "original and exclusive jurisdiction" would be granted automatically to a lawsuit by one state against another, but in fact the Supreme Court has interpreted its authority so as to have discretion to decide whether such lawsuits should be heard at all. If the Supreme Court does not grant leave to file the complaint, the state has no other judicial remedy. Therefore, Nebraska and Oklahoma had to file a motion, complaint, and a brief showing not only that they would prevail on the merits, but that the Supreme Court should take jurisdiction of the case in the first place. *See* Motion for Leave to File Complaint, Complaint, & Brief in Support, *Nebraska v. Colorado*, 577 U.S. 1211, No. 144 (2016).

The lawsuit was itself a well-documented summary of 50 years of federal authority in the area of marijuana law—now asserted on behalf of states that wanted to keep marijuana use criminal. A summary follows:

The federal government has preeminent authority to regulate interstate and foreign commerce, including commerce involving legal and illegal trafficking in drugs. Under this authority, Congress has banned marijuana by means of the Controlled Substances Act (CSA) and assigned to the Department of Justice, and its subdivision the Drug Enforcement Administration, the primary task of enforcing this ban. Nevertheless, Colorado has enacted legislation permitting use of marijuana, devoid of safeguards to prevent diversion to neighboring states, such as Nebraska and Oklahoma, straining their law enforcement, judicial, and penal systems. The CSA is the supreme law of the land, and § 903 preempts state marijuana laws which conflict with it. As Colorado marijuana legalization "affirmatively authorizes conduct prohibited by federal law," offends § 903, and violates the three major international drug treaties, which carry the force of law in the United States, it is preempted.

On February 19, 2015, an amicus brief was filed in support of the complaint of Nebraska and Oklahoma by all nine former administrators of the DEA, raising the stakes in the litigation. Brief for All Nine Former Administrators of Drug Enforcement as Amici Curiae in Support of Plaintiff States' Motion for Leave to File a Bill of Compliant, *Nebraska v. Colorado*. In response, the Supreme Court ordered the U.S. Solicitor General to submit a brief on behalf of the United States. 575 U.S. 994, No. 144 (2016). Although conceding that there existed no other forum to litigate this dispute, the United States argued that this case did not require adjudication because one state was not interfering with the territorial integrity of another state. The "licensing" scheme adopted by Colorado permitting marijuana-related conduct in no way affected the "full authority" of other states to prohibit the same conduct. It is irrelevant that third parties may illegally bring marijuana into Nebraska and Oklahoma, as such actions are not "directed or authorized" by Colorado.

In a supplemental brief, Nebraska and Oklahoma emphasized that Colorado's law was not just passively permitting marijuana use but was affirmatively encouraging it, making the conflict with federal law even more evident.

> Colorado has created a massive criminal enterprise whose sole purpose is to authorize and facilitate the manufacture, distribution, sale, and use of marijuana. It has granted a property interest in federal contraband and, like any well-run cartel, it protects its distributers' operations.

Plaintiff's Supplemental Brief on Motion for Leave to File, *Nebraska v. Colorado*.

The Supreme Court conferenced five times as to whether to hear this high level case. On March 21, 2016, the Court without opinion denied leave to file a bill of complaint. It is perhaps not surprising that the Court did not take up the case as the United States itself disclaimed the necessity of enforcing its marijuana prohibition in legalizing states.

Justice Thomas, joined by Justice Alito, wrote a dissent, 577 U.S. at 1211, arguing that the Court should grant leave for the lawsuit to proceed as "the plaintiff States have alleged significant harms to their sovereign interests caused by another State," which "this Court alone has authority to adjudicate." For more on this case from the perspective of the preemption doctrine, *see* Chapter 8.

§ 14–4 STATES VS. INDIAN TRIBES

Just as there exist tensions between conflicting state marijuana schemes, so are there between the laws of states and Indian nations, both possessing a certain sovereign status. The possibility for conflict is increased because reservations can span several states, which themselves may have contradictory marijuana laws. For example, the 17 million acre Navajo nation reservation is located in Arizona, New Mexico and Utah and shares a border with Colorado. Utah has legalized marijuana for medical purposes; Arizona, Colorado, and New Mexico have legalized marijuana for both medical and recreational purposes.

States have made accommodations with Indian tribes, but the results are in dispute. For example, when Washington legalized marijuana, it exempted the Yakama nation and other tribes that wanted to retain local laws against marijuana use. Nevertheless, the Yakama claimed that Washington-labeled marijuana was infiltrating their 1.2 million-acre reservation. In response, the Yakama sought to enforce an 1855 treaty, so as to ban marijuana over an additional 10.8 million acres of ancestral land in Washington, comprising one-fifth of Washington's land mass. The Yakama filed objections to marijuana licensing applications made from within this ceded territory, but apparently to no effect.

Other tribes, such as the Suquamish and Squaxin Island in Washington, believing the impossibility of excluding marijuana once the state has legalized it, decided to legalize marijuana on the reservation. "The state legalized this. It was brought to our doorstep by a neighboring government," a Suquamish Tribal Chairman explained. "The fact is, it's here." On September 15, 2015, the Suquamish and the state of Washington signed the first state-tribal marijuana compact, with provisions governing production, processing, purchase, and sale of marijuana on tribal land, as well as taxation and law enforcement. A Squaxin Island Tribe-Washington compact followed soon after.

Tensions between tribes and states are likely to be most exacerbated between traditional criminalization states and tribes that have legalized marijuana on their reservations. For example, in

June 2016 the Flandreau Santee Sioux tribe voted to legalize recreational marijuana on its reservation located in South Dakota and made plans to open a marijuana resort. Marijuana was illegal for all purposes in South Dakota, and federal and state officials threatened to raid the reservation. In response the Santee Sioux eradicated their marijuana crop. The consultants who advised the tribe and obtained cannabis seeds for the project were convicted of drug offenses by South Dakota.

With respect to Indian autonomy, the DOJ Indian Country Memorandum refers to the same eight federal priorities as the Cole II Memorandum. Memorandum from Monty Wilkinson, Director, Exec. Office for U.S. Att'ys, to All U.S. Att'ys, Policy Statement Regarding Marijuana Issues in Indian Country (Oct. 28, 2014). Although technically revoked, this memorandum still seems to represent current DOJ policy. *See* Chapter 8. The memorandum purports to treat Indian tribes as sovereign entities, equal partners with the states for purposes of marijuana law. However, the very framework of the law would seem to place Indian tribes at a disadvantage. For example, the third federal priority is to prevent diversion of marijuana to states where it is illegal. This would seem to be almost impossible for a tribe that legalizes marijuana but is located within a traditional criminalization state, especially as the borders of Indian reservations are often amorphous.

A recent case seems to subject an Indian tribe to state law. The Menominee Indian Tribe of Wisconsin filed a declaratory action against the United States after federal agents seized its crop of hemp in an October 2015 raid. In their November 18, 2015 Complaint for Declaratory Judgment, the Menominee sought a declaration that they were entitled to grow hemp pursuant to a 2015 tribal ordinance legalizing the cultivation of hemp and federal law that allows states to authorize cultivation of industrial hemp in conjunction with a research program of an institution of higher education. In addition, as a sovereign entity, the tribe was not subject to the laws of Wisconsin, which did not permit industrial hemp cultivation. In his May 23, 2016 decision, U.S. District Court Judge William Griesbach ruled against the Menominee. *Menominee Indian Tribe v. DEA and DOJ*, 190 F. Supp. 3d 843 (E.D. Wis. 2016). The court conceded that Indian tribes are often treated as states under U.S. law, that U.S. jurisprudence construes statutes liberally in favor of Indians, resolving all ambiguities in their favor, and that the Menominee are not subject to Wisconsin's jurisdiction under federal law. The court nevertheless found that the exemption for growing industrial hemp granted to states under § 7606 of the Agricultural Act of 2014 did not apply to Indian tribes because it did not define "state" as encompassing Indian tribes in its definitional sections. And because Wisconsin did not allow the cultivation of hemp, the tribe was likewise prohibited.

The complexity of the triangular relationship among federal, state, and Indian relations as regards marijuana legalization is also illustrated by the two-decade legal saga of farmer Alex White Plume, which is still inconclusive.

After his tribal council legalized the growing of hemp in 1998, White Plume, an elder and former tribal president of the Oglala Sioux tribe in South Dakota, began growing hemp on his farm on the Pine Ridge Reservation in 2000. However, as hemp was still banned under the CSA, federal agents raided White Plume's farm and eradicated his crop. The DEA then obtained a federal court injunction permanently prohibiting White Plume from harvesting hemp without DEA registration. The Eighth Circuit U.S. Court of Appeals affirmed the permanent injunction, holding that the CSA made no distinction between marijuana and industrial hemp. *United States v. White Plume*, 447 F.3d 1067, 1072–73 (2006).

In 2015, White Plume moved the court to lift the injunction against him for growing hemp, pursuant to § 7606. As a result, on March 28, 2016, the U.S. District Court for the District of South Dakota lifted the permanent injunction against White Plume. *United States v. Plume*, No. 02–5071–JLV, 2016 U.S. Dist. LEXIS 40138 (D.S.D. Mar. 28, 2016). However the court carefully noted that its order did not resolve the merits of whether federal law in fact authorizes cultivation of industrial hemp on the Pine Ridge Indian Reservation.

In cultivating hemp, legal to a large extent since 2018, Indian tribes may have the same commercial advantage over competitors in adjoining states that tribes enjoy in selling cigarettes and alcohol not subject to state sales tax (although sales to nonmembers of the tribe are taxable by states). On the other hand, contracts between Indian tribes and neighboring businesses present their own risks. Federally recognized tribes are domestic sovereign nations, and as such are generally immune from being sued. As a result, business ventures that enter contracts relating to marijuana with Indian tribes face three difficulties in enforcing their agreements. Firstly, federal courts may refuse to enforce marijuana-related contracts as illegal under federal law. Secondly, state courts may refuse to enforce marijuana contracts if the Indian tribe has not waived sovereign immunity, which must be done in writing and according to specific procedures. Finally, the contracts may be enforced according to tribal law.

There is an added wrinkle for indigenous natives living in Alaska, which has legalized marijuana for medical and recreational purposes. Alaskan native villages, although reserved land under the Alaska Native Claims Settlement Act, are not necessarily authorized to enact law for the village, as opposed to individual members of the tribe. The Act eliminated most of Alaska's smaller reservations, leaving tribes with jurisdiction over individual members but not over geographical entities known as "Indian Country." Although Alaska has a much higher proportion of indigenous persons in its population than any of the continental states, the state government can accordingly impose its legalization regime on an unwilling indigenous village.

§ 14–5 JURISDICTIONAL CONFLICTS

Just as questions remain as to the relationship between federal and state marijuana law, so questions remain of the relationship between other sovereign entities. If anything, these questions are only now germinating, in large part because they depend on first settling the difficult questions of contradictory federal and state laws.

Certainly laws of the various states differ, and they differ as to subjects which many consider harmful activities, such as prostitution, prize fighting, and casino gambling. However, there are two central differences between these activities and marijuana use that make jurisdictional differences as to marijuana more complex. First, these other activities are not also illegal under federal law, if confined within state borders. Second, they are by and large localized activities, unlike marijuana, which is easily transported across state lines.

Absent significant legislation, these questions will have to be settled by the judiciary. However, in the last couple of years little judicial clarity has been obtained. The U.S. Supreme Court refused to hear the suit by Nebraska and Oklahoma against Colorado, thereby quashing for now the issue of whether the federal government was abdicating its oversight over interstate marijuana commerce. Some version of this lawsuit is likely to return, brought by a state or third party, challenging state legalization regimes, and demanding that the federal government protect sovereign entities which choose to enforce marijuana prohibitions.

Although the court's decision in *United States v. Alexander White Plume* did not resolve the question of whether hemp can be legally grown on Indian reservations this question received clarification in the Farm Bill of 2018, which legalized hemp, subject to federal and state regulation. *See* Chapter 11. Nevertheless, Indian Country can also be subjected to state law in various ways, and states are making their own laws as to hemp. Further clarification of the law is needed for Indian tribes to be allowed to arrange their own marijuana laws without undue interference by states.

CHAPTER 15

SPECIAL CRIMINAL ISSUES

§ 15-1 INTRODUCTION

Despite the trend towards legalization by American states, marijuana in the United States remains in many ways forbidden. Certainly marijuana activity is a crime under federal law. Likewise, in all 50 states, marijuana cultivation, possession, consumption, and sale remain offences, subject to limited exceptions in states that have set up legalization schemes. And while a majority of states have carved out exceptions for medical use of marijuana, and a minority of states for adult recreational use, there are precise restrictions for such use, and marijuana activity outside of these limits constitutes a criminal offense. Similarly, criminal penalties remain for such offences as driving while marijuana impaired, possessing marijuana in public view, and possessing a quantity of marijuana beyond authorized amounts, even in jurisdictions that have legalized medical and recreational marijuana.

Marijuana activity is not technically criminalized in its own right, but is rather an illicit use of a controlled substance outside of restricted channels. Because according to the Controlled Substances Act (CSA), marijuana is controlled under Schedule I, for which no use is permitted (except for narrowly granted DEA registration), marijuana activity is by definition an offense against the Act.

Marijuana crimes fall under the general category of misuse of controlled substances, that is, drug crimes. Nevertheless, marijuana raises unique evidentiary issues, relating to the law of possession, search and seizure, sentencing, and asset forfeiture, and these have played a significant role in the jurisprudence of criminal law.

Section 15–2 of this chapter situates marijuana within criminal jurisprudence. Section 15–3 addresses issues of search and seizure, especially as to canine forensics, closed containers in automobiles, and surveillance technology. Section 15–4 addresses constructive possession of marijuana. Section 15–5 explores issues of distribution of marijuana. Section 15–6 addresses punishment for marijuana crimes, specifically as to sentencing and asset seizures. And § 15–7 introduces questions arising from marijuana's unique status as a substance that is controlled under Schedule I of the CSA and yet may be legal, depending on purpose and jurisdiction.

§ 15–2 MARIJUANA CRIMINAL JURISPRUDENCE

Marijuana offenses arise in three ways: 1) marijuana activity violates the federal CSA; 2) marijuana activity violates state and/or local prohibitions against marijuana use; and 3) in states where marijuana prohibitions have been repealed or overridden by legislation or constitutional amendment, so as to permit medicinal and/or recreational use, marijuana activity goes beyond permitted limits.

The so-called "War on Drugs" involves an expansion of federal powers, issues of racial and class discrimination, drug courts, prosecutorial discretion, and exponential increases in incarceration. The strategy to treat drug offenses as serious crimes rather than public health issues is controversial and widely debated. With application of the Bill of Rights to states under the Fourteenth Amendment, most drug prosecutions raise constitutional questions of criminal procedure. While the War on Drugs has implicated the criminal clauses of the Fifth, Sixth, and Eighth Amendments, it has perhaps its most significant impact on questions of probable cause for search and seizure under the Fourth Amendment. These issues include racial profiling, informants, no-knock drug raids, drug testing, plain view rules, exigent circumstances, the automobile exception, and warrantless and consensual searches.

As with all crimes, marijuana offenses consist of violating the elements listed in the statute. Although the elements may vary somewhat by jurisdiction, they tend to be similar—reflecting the common law, constitutional requirements, and the uniformity obtained in the federal and state Controlled Substances Acts.

The basic drug offenses are possession and sale. Typically the crime of possessing marijuana entails 1) knowing 2) possession of 3) the quantity of marijuana indicated by the statute. Possession can be actual or constructive. Actual possession consists of having marijuana on one's person. Constructive possession is having marijuana in near proximity and under one's control.

For the crime of selling marijuana, or of possession with intent to sell, the elements are 1) knowing 2) possession of 3) the statutory quantity of marijuana 4) with intent to sell. Sale does not have to be completed or even begun, so long as there is possession and a concrete plan to sell. This intent can be demonstrated by producing, transporting, or distributing marijuana. Possessing large amounts of marijuana may itself suffice to indicate intent to sell, as opposed to consume. And federal courts consistently exclude evidence, under Federal Rules of Evidence 402 and 403, that the defendant possessed the marijuana for personal use per state legalization schemes.

For the crime of possessing marijuana paraphernalia, the elements are 1) knowing 2) possession of items commonly used for marijuana consumption and intending such use. These items include such objects as pipes, hashish bowls or heads, roach clips, bongs, cigarette papers, and blunts. Intent to use an item as marijuana paraphernalia can be demonstrated in several ways. Typical of the wide range of what constitutes paraphernalia is 21 U.S.C. § 863(e):

> In determining what constitutes drug paraphernalia, in addition to all other logically relevant factors, the following may be considered:

(1) instructions, oral or written, provided with the item concerning its use; (2) descriptive materials accompanying the item which explain or depict its use; (3) national and local advertising concerning its use; (4) the manner in which the item is displayed for sale; (5) whether the owner, or anyone in control of the item, is a legitimate supplier of like or related items to the community, such as a licensed distributor or dealer of tobacco products; (6) direct or circumstantial evidence of the ratio of sales of the item(s) to the total sales of the business enterprise; (7) the existence and scope of legitimate uses of the item in the community; and (8) expert testimony concerning its use.

The crime of producing drugs is referred to in many statutes as "manufacturing" to encompass synthetic drugs, but also includes production of naturally occurring substances like marijuana. For marijuana, "manufacture" mostly refers to cultivating and growing plants, but can also include any activity which assists cannabis seeds in becoming full-fledged crops and thereupon a consumable substance, such as planting, propagating, watering, fertilizing, harvesting, drying, extracting, cutting, cooking, pruning, and processing cannabis.

Other drug crimes in addition to possession, selling, and manufacturing, include maintaining a drug-involved premise, using firearms in connection with drug crimes, violating drug-free school zones, using illegal drugs while pregnant, driving under the influence of drugs, transporting drugs, and conspiring to commit drug crimes and to engage in a continuing criminal drug enterprise.

Many issues relevant to establishing the elements of marijuana crimes are a subset of issues arising with drug crimes in general. For in-depth treatment of criminal law, *see Criminal Law in a Nutshell* (6th ed. 2020) by Arnold Loewy, *Advanced Criminal Procedure in a Nutshell* (3d ed. 2016) by Mark Cammack and Norman Garland, and *Criminal Procedure, Constitutional Limitations in a Nutshell* (9th ed. 2020) by Jerold Israel and Wayne LaFave.

Within the general category of drug crimes, six characteristics of marijuana account for its special significance in criminal jurisprudence. First, marijuana is by far the most used illicit drug in the U.S. (not counting alcohol). The National Survey on Drug Use and Health (NSDUH), conducted annually by the Substance Abuse and Mental Health Services Administration, reported that 48.2 million Americans used marijuana in 2019, and 49.6 million in 2020, more than all other illicit drugs combined. Second, marijuana is relatively inexpensive, easy to cultivate, and easy to buy and sell. It is shared casually, passed around among friends, and left lying about in shared domiciles. Therefore, questions of who is in possession of marijuana arise frequently.

Third, marijuana has a distinctive aroma. If the odor of burnt marijuana is detectible in a social gathering, automobile, apartment, or on one's belongings, clothing, or person, it is hard to deny knowledge of its presence—usually an element of the offense. Marijuana has a distinctive and pungent odor, even when not burnt, which can be detected by experienced police officers and trained police dogs and thereby gives probable cause for a search and seizure. The odor can also be detected on currency, which may allow for its forfeiture.

Fourth, marijuana is widely known and easily identified by sight, unlike narcotics like heroin, LSD, and methamphetamine. Marijuana in its natural flower state has a distinctive look. Thus courts can accept identification of a substance as marijuana by lay witnesses, even without expert or police witness or laboratory analysis. *See, e.g., Swain v. Oklahoma*, 805 P.2d 684 (Okla. Crim. App. 1991); *Ohio v. McKee*, 744 N.E.2d 737 (Ohio 2001).

Fifth, marijuana can be a difficult drug to quantify, which gives rise to sentencing issues based on amount and weight. It is a complex plant—and courts determine its characteristics according to either common usage or scientific classification. If the marijuana plant is in an undried state, some jurisdictions allow an offender to be sentenced based on its wet, hence heavier, weight. If the cannabis is in edible form, the substance with which it is mixed—the adulterant—may be counted in the weight for sentencing purposes.

Finally, marijuana is unique in that, on the one hand, it is a drug controlled under Schedule I, yet on the other, it is legal under the laws of many states. Traditional criminal doctrines are being modified, given marijuana's bifurcated status.

Particular criminal issues raised by the unique characteristics of marijuana are addressed in the remainder of this chapter.

§ 15–3 SEARCH AND SEIZURE

Marijuana cases have been central to U.S. Supreme Court jurisprudence as to search and seizure of contraband. In most of these cases, the justices divided sharply, often with 5–4 votes, revealing a sharp rift in the Court as to understanding the legitimacy of drug searches under the Fourth Amendment. In particular, these issues have been raised as to police dog sniffs, closed containers in automobiles, and surveillance technology. Marijuana has figured significantly in this area of law, chiefly because it has a distinctive aroma which can be detected by forensic narcotic canines, is easily and commonly transportable, and it is commonly grown in homes, greenhouses, and backyards, where it may be visible. Likewise, indoor manufacture requires large amounts of electricity, producing a significant energy fingerprint. Of course, other drugs and contraband share some of these characteristics, but marijuana is most widely consumed and more easily detected.

Although marijuana crimes can be commonly revealed by informants, undercover agents, and by suspicious activity, they are most usually detected by sight or smell. Thus, many marijuana cases revolve around whether the police had probable cause under the Fourth Amendment to seize the marijuana and arrest the defendant: "The right of the people to be secure in their persons, houses, papers, and effects, against unreasonable searches and seizures, shall not be violated, and no warrants shall issue, but upon probable cause. . . ." U.S. Const. amend. IV. Pretrial motions to suppress are common in marijuana prosecutions; without probable cause, the contraband marijuana can be excluded from evidence, which may result in dismissal of the charges or acquittal of the defendant.

§ 15–3.1 DOG SNIFFS

Police have probable cause to search a vehicle if incident to a lawful traffic stop they detect the smell of burnt or raw marijuana emanating from a car or driver. *See, e.g.*, *State v. Pena-Flores*, 965 A.2d 114, 128–29 (2009) (overruled on other grounds) (raw marijuana odor constituted probable cause); *McKenney v. State*, 165 P.3d 96 (Wyo. 2007) (raw marijuana odor same as burnt for probable cause).

However, even without any articulable suspicion of drug activity, police can bring a dog unit to the scene to smell for marijuana or other controlled substances. For example, in *Illinois v. Caballes*, 543 U.S. 405 (2005), the police pulled over a speeding motorist. Even though there was no articulable suspicion of drug activity, another officer arrived on the scene with a trained dog. The dog alerted at the trunk, which the officers then searched and found marijuana. The Supreme Court upheld the search because the canine sniff did not compromise any legitimate interest in privacy, as it alerted the officers only to the presence of illegal drugs, and not to other information. (Canine sniffs were thus deemed *sui generis*—in a "class of their own" for Fourth Amendment purposes.) Two justices dissented on the grounds that the canine sniff broadened the scope of the traffic violation-related seizure and that the frequent false positives given by forensic dogs demonstrate their lack of reliability.

Although *Caballes* found that a dog sniff conducted during a lawful traffic stop does not violate the Fourth Amendment, it does violate the Fourth Amendment when the police prolong the stop to allow a forensic dog to arrive on the scene. *Rodriguez v. United States*, 575 U.S. 348 (2015).

There is greater expectation of privacy in homes than in cars, which also extends to the "curtilage" of the home, that is the area "immediately surrounding and associated with the home." *Florida v. Jardines*, 561 U.S. 1 (2013). In *Jardines*, the police brought a trained police dog to the front door of a house where it detected the smell of drugs inside, alerting the officer. The police obtained a search warrant and found marijuana inside the house. Because the front porch of a home is curtilage, the Supreme Court held in a 5–4 decision that the police needed probable cause to bring the dog to the front door and excluded the marijuana from evidence. Although the police, like private citizens, are entitled to approach a home, knock on the door, receive a response, and leave, they are not permitted to bring a forensic narcotic dog without probable cause. In a vigorous dissent, four justices contended that the defendant had no "reasonable expectation of privacy in the odor of marijuana wafting from his house." Likewise as friends, mail carriers, deliverers, solicitors, peddlers, and police themselves are permitted to approach the front door, the legitimate police approach to the front door did not become a search merely because accompanied by a trained dog.

Likewise protected may be the front door of an apartment in a secure apartment building, at least according to one state's highest court. In *People v. Burns*, 50 N.E.3d 610 (Ill. 2016), the police brought a trained dog to the front door of an apartment dweller. The dog detected drugs, the police obtained a search warrant and found marijuana inside the apartment. Again, because the apartment landing in a locked apartment building counted as curtilage, the Illinois Supreme Court held the canine sniff to be unlawful.

§ 15–3.2 CLOSED CONTAINERS AND AUTOMOBILES

Marijuana cases have also been instrumental in developing the law of searching closed containers, especially in relation to automobiles. A traditional doctrine in Fourth Amendment Law is that a warrantless search of an automobile, based upon probable cause to believe that the vehicle contains evidence of crime or contraband, does not contravene the Warrant Clause of the Fourth Amendment. (This "automobile exception," also known as the *Carroll doctrine*, was first articulated in the context of transporting illicit liquor during Prohibition.) This doctrine was carried over to the so-called war on drugs, with several important cases involving marijuana. For example, in the landmark case of *New York v. Belton*, 453 U.S. 454, 460 (1981), a police officer stopped a speeding car and smelled burnt marijuana, and lawfully arrested the occupants of the automobile. The officer's subsequent search of a zipped jacket on the back seat was justified, as police can search, incident to an arrest, the passenger compartment of the automobile and any containers in the passenger compartment.

Nevertheless several cases involving marijuana allowed for a restriction of the automobile exception (overruled in anther marijuana case, *California v Acevedo*, see below). In *United States v. Chadwick*, 433 U.S. 1 (1977), the police suspected presence of marijuana in a traveler's footlocker, which was confirmed by a police dog trained to detect marijuana. The Court held the subsequent search of the footlocker, being loaded onto the trunk of a car, was invalid without a search warrant because of the heightened expectation of privacy in locked luggage. *Id.* at 15–16 This protection of locked containers against the automobile exception to warrantless searches was extended in another marijuana case, *Arkansas v. Sanders*, 442 U.S. 753, 766 (1979). The police, acting on a reliable tip that defendant was transporting marijuana in a suitcase, had probable cause to stop and search his car. However, without a warrant, the police were not allowed to open the unlocked suitcase containing marijuana that was being transported in the trunk of the car.

In two subsequent cases where police had reasonable suspicion of marijuana possession, the trend to minimizing the automobile exception was reversed. The automobile exception was expanded to apply to motor homes, *California v. Carney*, 471 U.S. 386, 394 (1985), and to pick-up trucks, *United States v. Johns*, 469 U.S. 478, 484 (1985), even when the search was not contemporaneous with seizure of the motor vehicle. Finally in *California v. Acevedo*, 500 U.S. 565 (1991), the exception was returned to full force. In this case, the police observed men leaving an apartment, known to have received marijuana in the mail, with paper bags roughly the size of the mailed packages. The police arrested one of the men in his automobile, removed the bag from the trunk, and opened it, finding marijuana. The Court used the opportunity to reexamine its rules as to searching closed containers in automobiles and looked to revive the *Carroll* exception in full extent. The Court announced one rule to govern all automobile searches: Police may search an automobile and the containers within, without a warrant, where they have probable cause to believe that it holds contraband or evidence. *Id.* at 579–80.

This rule prompted strong reactions on the Court. Justice Stevens bemoaned that the Court upheld searches in almost all of the 30 Fourth Amendment cases involving narcotics it had decided since 1982. He accused the Court of becoming "a loyal foot soldier in the Executive's fight against crime." *Id.* at 601. The majority responded that the overruled *Chadwick-Sanders* line of cases had failed to protect privacy and also confused police officers and impeded law enforcement. *Id.* at 576.

§ 15–3.3 SURVEILLANCE

Because marijuana is visually distinctive, and is often cultivated in fields and greenhouses, it has been central to surveillance cases. It is well-established that police can enter and search an open field for marijuana without a warrant. *Oliver v. United States,* 466 U.S. 170, 184 (1984). In the 1970s and 1980s, police undertook thousands of aerial searches for marijuana. In two important cases, the U.S. Supreme Court held that surveillance flights, even over areas that constitute curtilage, do not require search warrants if the marijuana is visible to the naked eye, that is, in "plain view," even if from airspace. In *California v. Ciralo*, 476 U.S. 207, 215 (1986), the police, flying at an altitude of 1,000 feet, observed marijuana growing in the defendant's yard. Because the marijuana was exposed to view from publicly navigable airspace, the five-justice majority held that the police were entitled to observe the marijuana without a warrant. Four justices dissented, writing that the defendant had a reasonable expectation of privacy from low-flying air surveillance, which would offer only fleeting glimpses of the private yard immediately adjacent to the house.

The *Ciralo* holding was extended in another 5–4 decision in *Florida v. Riley*, 488 U.S. 445, 447–48 (1989). A police helicopter observed marijuana growing in a greenhouse through an opening in the roof from an altitude of about 400 feet. The majority decision held that the warrantless flyover did not constitute a search requiring a warrant. The plurality opinion explained that because the flightpath was permitted under FAA regulations, and would not be uncommon for public flights, the surveillance flight did not cause undue disturbance. The dissent argued that the defendant's reasonable expectation of privacy in his backyard greenhouse should not depend on arcane calculations of FAA regulations and public flight paths.

However, when police helicopter surveillance at only 50 feet revealed marijuana growing in a backyard garden, the New Mexico Supreme Court held the flyover unlawful under the Fourth Amendment because it went beyond mere observation and constituted an unreasonable intrusion on the ground, by stirring up wind and dust, breaking objects, and causing panic. *State v. Davis*, 360 P.3d 1161 (N.M. 2015). Likewise, surveillance using advanced technology that can reveal information about one's private space other than the presence of drugs is not lawful absent probable cause. In *Kyllo v. United States*, 533 U.S. 27, 32 (2001), the police, directing a thermal imaging device at a home, detected an unusual amount of heat radiating from the roof and side walls of the garage, consistent with photosynthesizing marijuana. The police obtained a search warrant for the home and seized over 100 marijuana plants. In a 5–4 decision, the U.S. Supreme Court found that the warrantless thermal imaging was unlawful, as this device, not in general public use, could have revealed intimate details of the interior of the home, otherwise unknown without a physical intrusion. *Id.* at 40.

§ 15–4 MANUFACTURE, POSSESSION

Manufacture and *production* as elements of marijuana crimes have the broadest definition. The CSA defines manufacture as "production, preparation, propagation, compounding, or processing of a drug or other substance, either directly or indirectly or by extraction from substances of natural origin, or independently by means of chemical synthesis or by a combination of extraction and chemical synthesis. . . ." 21 U.S.C. § 802(15). State laws have similar definitions. *See e.g. North Carolina v. Childers*, 41 N.C. App. 729 (1979). Likewise, the CSA definition of production "includes the manufacture, planting, cultivation, growing, or harvesting of a controlled substance." § 802(16). Cooking marijuana to produce more potent marijuana can constitute the crime of manufacturing.

The element of actual possession of marijuana is usually a factual matter. But constructive possession also satisfies the element of a marijuana offense.

Constructive possession is mostly a legal conclusion. A person is in constructive possession of marijuana if aware of the presence of marijuana which is subject to the person's dominion and control. Two factors make constructive possession especially prominent in marijuana law: the wide availability of marijuana and its distinctive aroma. Because marijuana is widely available, inexpensive, casually bought and sold, and frequently shared by acquaintances, marijuana is often found in "common areas," such as living rooms or kitchens in apartments shared by several occupants. This differs from other Schedule I drugs, which courts have described as "commodit[es] of significant value, unlikely to be abandoned or carelessly left in an area." *Dodd v. Commonwealth*, 50 Va. App. 301, 309 (2007).

For example, in *Delgado v. United States*, 327 F.2d 641 (9th Cir. 1984), the police found marijuana cigarettes on the nightstand and loose marijuana in newspapers in the bedroom of a couple. The court concluded that at least one member of the couple was in possession of the marijuana, but without additional evidence as to which one, the couple singly or together could not be found to be in constructive possession of the marijuana. Likewise, in *Commonwealth v. Sterling*, 361 A.2d 799 (Pa. Super. Ct. 1976), customs officials detected evidence of hashish in a package addressed to a third party "in care of" the Sterlings, a married couple. After the package was delivered, the police executed a search warrant and seized the unopened package. The court held that although the Sterlings were unquestionably in possession of the package containing hashish, with no one else in the premises, because the package was not addressed directly to the Sterlings, and the package was unopened, the evidence was insufficient to show that the Sterlings intended to exercise control ("conscious dominion") over the hashish. In accord is *Oregon v. Barnthouse*, 380 P.3d 952 (2016) where the Oregon Supreme Court held that the recipient of a mail package containing marijuana had a possessory interest in the package, even though he did not have constructive possession, that was sufficient to prevent police interdiction of the package.

In contrast, in *Ervin v. Commonwealth*, 704 S.E.2d 135, 148 (Va. Ct. App. 2011) (en banc), the odor of marijuana gave rise to constructive possession. The defendant was stopped by a police officer for a traffic violation. The officer detected the odor of burnt marijuana, searched the car, and found 23 bags of marijuana in the locked glove compartment. However the defendant did not own the car and denied knowledge of the presence of marijuana. Nevertheless, the Virginia Court of Appeals found that the driver was in constructive possession of the bags of marijuana. They were within his control and because of the strong odor he could not deny knowledge of their presence. The dissent in *Ervin v. Commonwealth* relied on *Commonwealth v. Young*, 659 S.E.2d 308, 310 (Va. 2008) (defendant not in constructive possession of an odorless, unlabeled bottle of pills, without proof that she knew that the pills were morphine) to contend that the driver was not in constructive possession, as the odor of burnt marijuana would not necessarily indicate the presence of fresh marijuana in the glove compartment. Even taking a quick smoke from a marijuana pipe or cigarette, passed around and possessed by somebody else, can count as possession to the momentary smoker. *See e.g., Hawaii v. Hogue*, 52 Haw. 660 (1971).

§ 15-5 ISSUES OF DISTRIBUTION

Distribution of marijuana is a more serious crime, with heavier sentences, than mere possession. Typically, the elements of this offense include delivering marijuana to another person, usually in exchange for money, but not necessarily. In addition, actual delivery is not required; attempted or constructive transfer suffices. Intent to distribute marijuana can be demonstrated by circumstantial inference besides apprehending sellers in the midst of sale. One of the most common methods to infer intent is simply possession of a large amount of marijuana, beyond a quantity for personal use. Of course, additional presence of paraphernalia common in marijuana sales—scales for weighing marijuana, dime bags for packaging marijuana ("dime bags" sell small amounts of marijuana for $10)—further establishes the inference. *See e.g. United States v. Glenn*, 667 F.2d 1269 (9th Cir. 1982) (large amounts of marijuana divided into small bags, a scale, a box of plastic bags, cigarette papers, and handwritten pages showing anticipated business transactions were sufficient to prove intent to distribute). Selling counterfeit marijuana (plant materials passed off as cannabis) can constitute the crime of distributing counterfeit controlled substances, 21 U.S.C. § 843(5).

Buying large amounts of marijuana allows an inference of intent to subsequently distribute, under federal law and most state law. *See, e.g., United States v. Rodriguez*, 375 F. Supp. 589 (S.D. Tex. 1974). However, some courts have balked at the notion of equating a user as a distributer simply because the buyer facilitates the transaction. *See, e.g., Abuelhawa v. United States*, 556 U.S. 816 (2009) ("The traditional law is that where a statute treats one side of a bilateral transaction more leniently, adding to the penalty of the party on that side for facilitating the action by the other would upend the calibration of punishment set by the legislature.")

§ 15-6 ISSUES OF PUNISHMENT

Punishments for illegal use of marijuana vary widely among jurisdictions, from harsh penalties, relics of the war on drugs, to minimum penalties for minor possession, in what is essentially decriminalization. However, even when the punishment for use is minimal, habitual offender statutes might result in long imprisonment, even when the most recent crime involved only a small quantity of marijuana.

This section addresses the questions of punishment for marijuana activity, in terms of sentencing and seizure of assets.

§ 15–6.1 SENTENCING

When awaiting sentence, or afterwards, medical marijuana patients can be denied access to marijuana. While defendants arrested for marijuana consumption or possession are on bond awaiting trial, or on probation, parole, or other types of government supervisions, courts usually include as one of the "standard terms and conditions" of bail that the defendant not consume marijuana and be monitored for substance abuse. This condition of bail is typically applied even for medical use of marijuana in states where such use is legal. Similarly prison inmates, even in states with legal medical marijuana, are usually not allowed to possess or consume marijuana. *See, e.g.*, 410 Ill. Comp. Stat. 130/25(p) (2015).

Prison sentences for marijuana are determined by quantity of marijuana, measured by weight and/or number of plants. *See, e.g.*, United States Sentencing Guidelines § 2E1.1. Before 1995, marijuana in a wet condition would be weighed as such, increasing its weight. A 1995 amendment to the federal sentencing guidelines provided that a court should approximate the dry weight of marijuana. *See United States v. Carter*, 110 F.3d 759 (11th Cir. 1997).

Measuring the type and quantity of marijuana for sentencing can raise difficulties as the scientific and botanical definition of "plant," can differ from conventional definitions. The Supreme Court of Pennsylvania, in *Commonwealth v. Burnsworth*, 669 A.2d 883, 889 (Pa. 1995), reversed the decision of a lower court which held that the statutory term "plant" was unconstitutionally vague for sentencing because it did not specify such factors as the size, maturity, sex, or intoxicating productivity. The Pennsylvania Supreme Court held that "plant" should be interpreted according to its commonplace meaning, consisting of roots, stems, and leaves, rather than a scientific definition. Federal courts are in accord. *See, e.g.*, *United States v. Eves*, 932 F.2d 856, 860 (10th Cir. 1991) ("We conclude that the word "plant" under the Sentencing Guidelines is to be given its plain and ordinary meaning and that the district court did not err in counting cuttings with roots as plants."); *United States v. Robinson*, 35 F.3d 442 (9th Cir. 1994).

Most sentencing guidelines punish "resinous extractives of cannabis" (hash oil) more severely than the equivalent weight in marijuana buds, because of its concentration of THC. Guidelines also include "adulterants and dilutants" in calculating the weight of marijuana. Thus for marijuana edibles, the aggregate weight of the baked goods, rather than the net weight of the THC or hash oil contained therein, may constitute the sentencing weight. In 2014, first-time offender 19-year-old Jacob Lavaro, was arrested with a pound and a half of hash brownies, exceeding the 400 gram cutoff for hash concentrates under Texas law. He was initially charged under Texas felony law § 481.116, subjecting him to a possible sentence of 10 years to life, until a national outcry led to reducing the charges.

§ 15–6.2 ASSET SEIZURES

The CSA mandates both criminal forfeiture, 21 U.S.C. § 853, and civil forfeiture, 21 U.S.C. § 881, of assets related to illicit drug activity. Most states have similar statutes.

Asset seizure rules are particular to marijuana for two reasons. First, as marijuana is often grown over a large expanse, asset seizure can include homes, fields, gardens, and greenhouses as crime-related assets subject to seizure. Second, as marijuana odor is often detected on currency, asset seizure can include large amounts of cash.

Asset forfeiture statutes allow the government to seize assets that are associated with drug activity. Under the federal civil asset forfeiture statutes, 21 U.S.C. § 881; 18 U.S.C. § 981(b), property is subject to forfeiture if the government can establish a substantial connection between the property and the drug offense. In *United States v. Usery*, 518 U.S. 267 (1996), the police found marijuana growing adjacent to defendant's house and marijuana seeds, stems, and stalks inside the house. The defendant was sentenced to 63 months in prison, and the house was subject to forfeiture under 21 U.S.C. § 881(a)(7), as it had been used to facilitate marijuana transactions. The U.S. Supreme Court upheld the seizure, finding that civil forfeitures do not constitute punishment, and hence can be added to sentences of criminal imprisonment without violating the Double Jeopardy Clause of the Fifth Amendment.

Under civil asset statutes, the guilt of a property owner does not need to be established, but only that "a preponderance of the evidence" shows a "substantial connection" between assets and illegal drug transactions. *See, e.g.*, 18 U.S.C. § 983(c). Under these statutes, drugs of course have been seized, as well as drug profits, but also automobiles, houses, yachts, planes, farms, currency, and the like have been forfeited to the government as facilitating drug transactions. Law enforcement regards forfeiture as an essential tool to cripple drug rackets and eliminate the instrumentalities of crime. Critics claim that such statutes create an incentive for government agencies to seize assets to enhance their budgets. A notorious case is the death of Donald Scott, a wealthy and reclusive California rancher. In 1992, a large team of law enforcement officials entered Scott's 200 acre southern Californian ranch with a search warrant for marijuana. When a surprised Scott emerged from his bedroom carrying a gun, the officers shot him to death. In fact there was no marijuana on his ranch. An investigation by the Ventura County District Attorney concluded that the chief motive for the raid was the desire by law enforcement officials to seize Scott's valuable ranch as a forfeited asset, "District Attorney County of Ventura Report of Forfeiture Motive for Raid" (March 30, 1993), although this controversial report was itself criticized as "gratuitous" by the California Attorney General. *See Bradbury v. Superior Court*, 57 Cal. Rptr. 2d 207, 213 (1997).

The Eighth Circuit has decided a series of significant cases involving currency forfeitures, in which the odor of marijuana on large amounts of secreted currency was a primary factor in allowing § 881 forfeiture. In *United States v. U.S. Currency, in the Amount of $150,660*, 980 F.2d 1200, 1204 (8th Cir. 1992), a police officer detected a strong odor resembling dry marijuana on approximately $150,000 of currency in the luggage of a man he was searching. The Eighth Circuit upheld a proceeding for the forfeiture of the currency, finding that the smell of dry marijuana on the currency, confirmed by a trained police dog, demonstrated probable cause for substantial link to drug activity. Likewise in *United*

States v. $117,920.00 in U.S. Currency, 413 F.3d 826, 829 (8th Cir. 2005), a police officer searched defendant's car and found marijuana paraphernalia and the smell of marijuana in proximity to bags containing U.S. currency totaling $117,920. The court affirmed forfeiture of the currency under § 881(a)(6), as the marijuana paraphernalia and odor, and evidence of concealment, supported a connection between the money and drug trafficking.

In *United States v. $63,530.00 in U.S. Currency*, 781 F.3d 949 (8th Cir. 2015), the Eighth Circuit rejected a challenge to the probative value of marijuana odor. In the forfeiture hearing the defendant asserted that most American currency is tainted by the smell of marijuana or other drugs. Thus, that a police dog alerted the smell of narcotics in defendant's vehicle, and the police officer noted the smell of marijuana in a backpack containing 64 bundles of currency totaling $63,530, did not demonstrate a link to drug activity. The Eighth Circuit conceded that much of the money supply is tainted but maintained that marijuana odor on currency, even if not dispositive, could factor in calculating whether the preponderance of the evidence demonstrated a substantial connection to drug trafficking.

§ 15–7 EVOLVING MARIJUANA CRIMINAL JURISPRUDENCE

Marijuana now exists in something of a legal netherworld—traditionally criminal, now decriminalized and/or legalized in small amounts in some jurisdictions, but not in others. In jurisdictions where it is legalized, traditional doctrines as to contraband may have to be revised.

To give one example, the long-established doctrine that the aroma of marijuana gives rise to probable cause that a crime is being committed may be challenged in states that have legalized marijuana. After all, forensic narcotic dogs cannot distinguish between illegal marijuana and marijuana that is legal for medical purposes, or quantities of marijuana, also a threshold for legality.

As to these doctrines, it seems better to think of medical marijuana states not so much as legalizing marijuana, but as carving a narrow exception to a criminal law regime. For example, in *State v. Myers*, 442 N.J. Super. 287 (App. Div. 2015), the defendant argued that as New Jersey legalized medical marijuana in 2010, the police officer who detected the odor of marijuana from his car and conducted a search (turning up a small baggie of marijuana) lacked probable cause. The court held that the "plain smell" marijuana doctrine is still valid, and that given the requirements that must be satisfied to legally possess medical marijuana, a police officer is still entitled to presume from the odor of marijuana that illegal drug activity is taking place. Likewise in Michigan, the burden is on the person claiming legal use of marijuana to present a defense of immunity under Michigan Medical Marihuana Act § 4, showing a valid license or registration, or an affirmative defense under § 8, showing that a physician, in a bona-fide relationship with a patient, recommended use of a reasonable amount of marijuana to alleviate the patient's medical condition. *People v. Hartwick*, 842 N.W.2d 545 (Mich. App. 2013).

In some states where recreational marijuana remains illegal, the odor of marijuana continues to give rise to probable cause for a search. *See, e.g.*, *State v. Green*, No. 99196, 2013 Ohio App. LEXIS 3870 (8th Dist. Aug. 29, 2013); *State v. Harris*, No. 99481, 2013 Ohio App. LEXIS 3878 (8th Dist. Aug. 29, 2013) (police officer who smells marijuana emanating from a car or house has probable cause for a search). However, in states that have legalized recreational use of marijuana, there is a trend to forbidding detection of marijuana aroma to represent probable cause to believe that a crime is being committed. For example, the District of Columbia explicitly excludes the odor of marijuana (or the proximity of a limited amount of marijuana to any amount of cash) as constituting "reasonable articulable suspicion of a crime." D.C. Code § 48–921.02a (2015). New York's Marijuana Regulation and Taxation Act, § 222.05(3), enacted in 2021, prohibits probable cause to believe a crime has been committed based solely on the odor of cannabis or burnt cannabis. Likewise in 2021, Virginia enacted Va. Code Ann. § 4.1–1302(A), that "no law-enforcement officer may lawfully stop, search, or seize any person, place, or thing solely on the basis of the odor of marijuana, and no evidence discovered or obtained as a result of such unlawful search or seizure shall be admissible in any trial, hearing, or other proceeding." In contrast, the Colorado Supreme Court held that while Colorado law allows for legal possession of limited amounts of marijuana, "a substantial number of other marijuana-related activities remain unlawful," and therefore "the odor of marijuana is still suggestive of criminal activity," contributing to determination of probable cause. *People v. Zuniga*, 372 P.3d 1052 (Colo. 2016).

PART 4

PRACTICAL ISSUES ARISING FROM LEGALIZATION

CHAPTER 16

FEDERAL BANKING LAWS AND THE MARIJUANA-RELATED BUSINESS

§ 16–1 INTRODUCTION

One of the most challenging aspects of running a marijuana dispensary or other marijuana-related business has been the difficulty of obtaining banking services. The banking system in the United State is highly regulated by federal law. And pursuant to federal statutes and regulations, banks generally cannot deal with illegal businesses. Accordingly, since marijuana is illegal under federal law, banks are arguably prohibited from dealing with marijuana-related businesses under federal law.

This creates a serious problem for marijuana-related businesses. It often means that they have to run cash-only businesses, since they cannot open checking accounts or savings accounts, and even credit-card transactions are themselves subject to federal law. As a result, marijuana-related businesses have to keep large amounts of cash on the premises, which creates a significant private and public safety issue, given the potential for theft. The lack of electronic records also makes it harder for government regulators to monitor crimes such as tax fraud and money laundering. In addition, the inability of marijuana-related businesses to open checking accounts makes it cumbersome for them to pay their bills and to satisfy their payroll obligations. To pay employees, for example, the owners or managers have had to either arrange secret locations where they can meet employees and pay them in cash—putting everyone present in danger—or assume the risk of transporting large amounts of cash to non-banking entities that will issue money orders that they can then pay to the order of vendors and employees. These difficulties have created a significant amount of consternation on the part of the owners of marijuana-related businesses that has led to an increasing groundswell of support for changes to federal law to enable such businesses to have better access to traditional banking services.

Section 16–2 of this chapter provides an overview of the federal laws that regulate banking, and their impact on marijuana-related businesses. Section 16–3 examines the approach the federal government (starting with the Obama administration) has taken with respect to helping marijuana-related businesses obtain banking services within the constraints of federal banking laws. Basically, the Justice Department and the Treasury Department have issued guidelines for depository institutions that wish to deal with marijuana-related businesses. These guidelines impose certain oversight responsibilities on them, but otherwise take a hands-off approach with regard to transactions that comply with the guidelines. And § 16–4 looks at possible congressional fixes to the current conflict between federal banking laws and state legalization schemes that would allow marijuana-related businesses to access banking services.

§ 16–2 FEDERAL BANKING LAWS AND MARIJUANA

The United States has long had a two-pronged banking system that consists of both federally-chartered and state-chartered depository institutions. Banks and credit unions can choose to be one or the other. But federal and state financial regulators do not act entirely independently of one another. And state-chartered banks and credit unions are still subject to a significant degree of federal oversight, due to several different laws and regulations.

For example, a depository institution could potentially be liable for criminal penalties for aiding and abetting the illegal distribution of a controlled substance if it assists marijuana-related business by providing banking services to them. *See* 18 U.S.C. § 2. Likewise, a depository institution that provides banking services to a marijuana-related business could arguably be liable for money laundering under the Money Laundering Control Act, which applies to any entity that "knowingly engages or attempts to engage in a monetary transaction in criminally derived property of a value greater than $10,000." 18 U.S.C. § 1957(a). Because marijuana is an "unlawful activity" under the federal law, it comes within the scope of federal money-laundering statute. *See* 18 U.S.C. §§ 1956(a)(1)(B), 1956(c) (2014).

Various federal regulatory schemes also create problems for marijuana-related businesses. Almost all banks and credit unions, for example, regardless of whether they are state or federally charted, desire

FDIC insurance (or in the case of credit unions, NCUA insurance) to back up their depositors' accounts, which means that they have to subject themselves to federal oversight by these agencies. And given the illegal status of marijuana businesses under federal law, these federal agencies have not been favorably inclined to insure marijuana-related businesses.

Similarly, state-chartered banks must subject themselves to federal oversight if they want to be part of the Federal Reserve System (federal banks are required to join the Federal Reserve), and this requires, among other things, that they monitor their depositors' compliance with "applicable laws and regulations." 12 C.F.R. Pt. 208, Appx. D–1 § II.A.5. Furthermore, under regulations enacted pursuant to the Bank Secrecy Act, depository institutions must report illegal and suspicious activities of their customers to the Department of Treasury's Financial Crimes Enforcement Network (FinCEN). 31 C.F.R. § 1020.320(a)(2). And they must also file "Suspicious Activity Reports" (SARs) if they have reason to believe that a transaction involves funds derived from illegal activities, such as the illegal sale of drugs. *Id.*; § 1020(b)(1).

A federal case in Colorado highlights the perils facing depository institutions that try to provide banking services to marijuana-related businesses. In *Fourth Corner Credit Union v. Federal Reserve Bank of Kansas City*, 154 F. Supp. 3d 1185 (D. Colo. 2016), Fourth Corner, a state-chartered credit union, sought to obtain a master account with the Federal Reserve

Bank of Kansas City in order to provide banking services to marijuana-related businesses. The Federal Reserve denied the application, and Fourth Corner filed a lawsuit in federal court, seeking an order compelling the Federal Reserve to open the account. The court ruled for the defendant, holding that it had no authority to grant Fourth Corner's request for relief. "The problem here," the court explained, "is that the Credit Union is asking the Court to exercise its equitable authority to issue a mandatory injunction. But courts cannot use equitable powers to issue an order that would facilitate criminal activity." *Id.* at 1189. Since marijuana-related businesses operate illegally under federal law, it held, then notwithstanding the federal government's decision not to enforce those laws under certain circumstances, a federal court cannot provide equitable relief.

Therefore, because even state-chartered depository institutions are subject to a variety of federal laws and regulations, the illegal status of marijuana under federal law creates a major obstacle for marijuana-related businesses in terms of their being able to obtain banking services. And that in turn creates a major obstacle to the healthy functioning of such businesses. The following sections discuss actions taken by the Treasury Department and by some members of Congress to try to remedy this problem. To date, however, an adequate fix remains elusive.

§ 16–3 THE TREASURY DEPARTMENT'S GUIDANCE POLICY

The Obama administration's approach toward state legalization of marijuana, both for medical and recreational use, was basically to allow the states to experiment with various legislative schemes, but only subject to certain conditions. The administration expressly recognized that both medical and recreational marijuana use are illegal under federal law, notwithstanding state laws to the contrary. It also recognized that the federal government has the constitutional authority (and perhaps also the duty) to enforce these federal laws under the Supremacy Clause of the United States Constitution. But at the same time, the administration chose to exercise discretion with respect to enforcement of these federal laws, and to concentrate only on what it considered to be high priorities. Thus, in August 2013, the Justice Department issued a memorandum, which has come to be called the "Cole Memo" that listed the government's priorities for prosecution, and essentially instructed federal prosecutors to leave state marijuana schemes alone, so long as they comply with the enumerated conditions in the memorandum.

The eight priorities that the Obama administration set out in the Cole Memo are as follows:

- Preventing the distribution of marijuana to minors;

- Preventing revenue from the sale of marijuana from going to criminal enterprises, gangs, and cartels;
- Preventing the diversion of marijuana from states where it is legal under state law to other states;
- Preventing state-authorized marijuana activity from being used as a cover or pretext for the trafficking of other illegal drugs or other illegal activity;
- Preventing violence and the use of firearms in the cultivation and distribution of marijuana;
- Preventing drugged driving and the exacerbation of other adverse public health consequences associated with marijuana use;
- Preventing the growing of marijuana on public lands and the attendant public safety and environmental dangers posed by marijuana production on public lands;
- Preventing marijuana possession or use on federal property.

In February 2014, Deputy Attorney General Cole issued an additional memorandum, re-emphasizing these priorities specifically with respect to the enforcement of federal statutes and regulations governing depository institutions that provide services to marijuana-related businesses. On the same day, the Treasury Department's Financial Crimes Enforcement Network (FinCEN) issued a guidance document (the "Guidance") that laid out the federal government's expectations for financial institutions seeking to provide services to marijuana-related businesses. The FinCEN Guidance clarifies how financial institutions can provide services to marijuana-related businesses, consistent with their obligations under federal law, including the federal Bank Secrecy Act (31 U.S.C. §§ 5311 et seq.).

The Guidance requires depository institutions to conduct due diligence for their marijuana-related business clients, including heightened monitoring for suspicious activity. As part of this due diligence, a depository institution servicing marijuana-related businesses must notify the federal government if one of its marijuana-related business customers has implicated one of the federal government's priorities as laid out in the Cole Memo, or has violated the law of the state(s) in which the institution operates. Furthermore, as noted above, depository institutions must, pursuant to regulations promulgated under the Bank Secrecy Act, submit Suspicious Activity Reports (SARs) if they have reason to know that a transaction involves funds derived from illegal activities, such as the illegal sale of drugs. And since marijuana is illegal under federal law, this means that banks and credit unions servicing marijuana-related businesses must routinely file such reports for marijuana-related business clients.

The Treasury Department's Guidance specifies three different types of reports that the depository institutions servicing marijuana-related businesses must file. Specifically, if the financial institution has no reason to believe that a particular client has implicated the government's expressed priorities, then it should file a "Marijuana Limited" SAR, noting that the institution is filing the SAR solely because the customer is engaged in a marijuana-related business transaction, and that no additional suspicious activity has been identified. Conversely, if the depository institution believes that, based on its due diligence, a marijuana related business customer has engaged in an activity that implicates one or more of the government's priorities, or violates state law, it should file a "Marijuana Priority" SAR, providing details regarding the specific transaction(s) it believes to be suspicious. And if a bank or credit union deems it necessary to terminate a relationship with a marijuana-related business in order to maintain an effective anti-money laundering compliance program, it should file a "Marijuana Termination" SAR, noting the reason for the termination. Finally, a depository institution that terminates a customer account under a Marijuana Termination SAR should notify any subsequent institution of potential illegal activity if it becomes aware that the customer is seeking to open an account with that institution. Through these due diligence requirements, the Treasury Department effectively subcontracts significant oversight responsibilities with respect to marijuana-related businesses to the individual depository institutions.

The Treasury Department's Guidance also sets out a number of "red flags" that depository institutions should look for when monitoring marijuana-related businesses for untoward activity. These red flags include the following:

- A customer appears to be using a state-licensed marijuana-related business as a front or pretext to launder money derived from other criminal activity (i.e., not related to marijuana) or derived from marijuana-related activity not permitted under state law;
- The business is unable to produce satisfactory documentation or evidence to demonstrate that it is duly licensed and operating consistently with state law;
- The business is unable to demonstrate the legitimate source of significant outside investments;
- A customer seeks to conceal or disguise involvement in marijuana-related business activity. For example, the customer may be using a business with a non-descript name (e.g., a "consulting," "holding," or "management" company) that purports to engage in commercial activity unrelated to marijuana, but is depositing cash that has an aroma of marijuana;
- Review of publicly available sources and databases about the business, its owner(s), manager(s), or other related parties, reveals negative information, such as a criminal record, involvement in the illegal purchase or sale of drugs, violence, or other potential connections to illicit activity;
- The business, its owner(s), manager(s), or other related parties are, or have been, subject to an enforcement action by the state or local

authorities responsible for administering or enforcing marijuana-related laws or regulations;

- A marijuana-related business engages in international or interstate activity, including by receiving cash deposits from locations outside the state in which the business operates, making or receiving frequent or large interstate transfers, or otherwise transacting with persons or entities located in different states or countries;
- The owner(s) or manager(s) of a marijuana-related business reside outside the state in which the business is located;
- A marijuana-related business is located on federal property or the marijuana sold by the business was grown on federal property;
- A marijuana-related business's proximity to a school is not compliant with state law;
- A marijuana-related business purporting to be a "non-profit" is engaged in commercial activity inconsistent with that classification, or is making excessive payments to its manager(s) or employee(s).

According to the Guidance, these red flags are not meant to be exhaustive, but they do provide depository institutions with a pretty good idea of what they should be looking for when they do their due diligence. If an institution notices one or more of these red flags with respect to a marijuana-related business customer, it should investigate further as part of its due diligence. The Guidance also notes, however that FinCEN will not prosecute depository institutions for isolated lapses in technical compliance; rather, it will focus on matters of systemic or significant failures in compliance. Thus, if a bank or credit union makes a good faith effort to comply with state law, and to monitor the activities of its marijuana-related business customers for compliance with the government's priorities, looking for the red flags laid out in the Guidance, it should not have to worry about running afoul of federal law enforcement, notwithstanding the federal laws and regulations discussed in § 16–2 above.

In 2016, shortly after the Trump administration took office, Attorney General Sessions withdrew the Cole Memo, replacing it with a memo that empowered local U.S. Attorneys to enforce federal marijuana laws as they thought best. The Treasury Department, however, did not withdraw its FinCen Guidance and continued to follow the policy it had followed under the Obama administration. That policy continues under the Biden administration.

To date, however, relatively few banks and credit unions have ventured into the world of commercial marijuana. Notwithstanding the Treasury Department's assurances regarding the government's prosecutorial priorities, most of the banks and credit unions in states that have legalized marijuana still refuse to provide banking services to marijuana-related businesses. And among those that do, the fees they charge marijuana-related businesses are often quite high, reflecting the risks the depository institutions associate with servicing marijuana-related businesses, as well as the costs that depository institutions incur in connection with their due diligence obligations under the FinCen Guidance. This too has created an obstacle for marijuana-related businesses trying to obtain necessary banking services, particularly for small "mom-and-pop" dispensaries, which cannot easily absorb high banking costs.

Thus, while the quasi-hands-off approach of the Treasury Department has relieved some of the pressure on marijuana-related businesses, it has by no means provided a comprehensive solution to the banking problem marijuana-related businesses face.

§ 16–4 POSSIBLE CONGRESSIONAL REMEDIES

Because the FinCen Guidance does not provide an adequate solution to the problems marijuana-related businesses face in trying to obtain banking services, marijuana-related businesses, banks, and other concerned parties have repeatedly called for federal legislation that would provide a more comprehensive solution. There are several ways this could happen.

One possibility, of course, is for the federal government to legalize (or at least decriminalize) marijuana, e.g., by removing it from the Controlled Substances Act. If marijuana ceased to be unlawful under federal law, then marijuana-related businesses would no longer run afoul of the money laundering statute and other federal statutes that currently prevent banks from dealing with marijuana-related businesses engaged in "unlawful" activities.

Several bills have been introduced in Congress over the past couple of years that would effectively legalize marijuana. The one that currently has the most traction is the MORE Act (Marijuana Opportunity Reinvestment and Expungement Act), which would remove cannabis from the CSA. It would also provide for expungement of criminal records for non-violent persons convicted of possession crimes. And it would implement several other social justice measures, including the Creation of an Opportunity Trust Fund for the benefit of communities that were disproportionately affected by the War on Drugs. The House of Representatives passed the MORE Act in December 2020, but it never reached the Senate floor. The measure was re-introduced as HR 3617 in May 2021, and is now working its way through the legislative process.

A further possible approach to the banking problem would be for Congress to pass a statute that authorizes each state to do as it sees fit with respect to legalization of marijuana, essentially codifying the Obama administration's "hands-off" approach discussed in § 16–3 above. It is likely that states would not be given complete leeway in this respect; instead, Congress would likely set up parameters under which states could legally operate medical marijuana and/or recreational schemes.

Congress has already enacted legislation that indicates its willingness to grant states at least partial autonomy. In December 2014, Congress passed the 2014 Continuing Resolution Omnibus spending bill. Section 538 of that bill (often called the "Rohrabacher-Farr Amendment") prevents the FBI and DEA from spending federal dollars to interfere with the implementation of the state laws authorizing the use of medical marijuana.

Thus far, legislative efforts to go beyond this have not gained too much traction. The bill that stands the best chance would seem to be the STATES Act (Strengthening the Tenth Amendment Through Entrusting States Act), which was originally introduced both the House and the Senate in 2018 and was re-introduced as April 2019 as HR 2093 in the House and S 1028 in the Senate. The STATES Act provides that the CSA would not apply to individuals and entities acing in accordance with legitimate state and tribal marijuana laws; thus it would basically have the effect of de-scheduling marijuana, similar the MORE Act, except that its effect would be limited to legalization states.

Originally, the prospects for the STATES Act looked promising, since it was a bi-partisan initiative, and, according to former Sen. Gardner, one of its original sponsors, it had the likely support of President Trump. More recently, however, enthusiasm for the measure seems to have waned, as Democrats in Congress have expressed a preference for more comprehensive legislation, such as the MORE Act.

Many members of Congress, however, continue to push as well for a more targeted approach to the banking problems currently faced by marijuana-related businesses, introducing legislation that expressly authorizes depository institutions to offer banking services to marijuana-related businesses in states that allow it. Rep. Perlmutter from Colorado, joined by a number of other members of Congress from medical marijuana states, has repeatedly introduced such a bill; the most recent version is called the SAFE Banking Act (Safe and Fair Enforcement Banking Act (HR 2076). This bill provides safe harbor to depository institutions that provide banking services to marijuana-related businesses. Specifically, it provides that federal banking regulators may not penalize Banks solely for providing banking services to legitimate banks that are operating in accordance with state laws. It also provides that proceeds from legitimate marijuana businesses are not "proceeds from unlawful activity" under federal banking laws.

The House of Representatives passed the SAFE Banking Act in 2019, but the Senate did not advance it. The House passed it again last year (in April 2021) with a fair amount of bipartisan support. Whether it will generate similar bipartisan support in the Senate remains to be seen. Of the three bills discussed in this section, the SAFE Banking Act is generally regarded as the one with the best chance of success in the near term.

CHAPTER 17
EMPLOYMENT LAW ISSUES

§ 17-1 INTRODUCTION

One of the more challenging practical issues confronting states that have legalized medical marijuana is how to balance a medical user's legal right to use marijuana for medicinal purposes against an employer's right to keep the workplace drug free. Nearly everyone agrees that an employer should be free to discipline and/or terminate employees who use marijuana while working or are impaired on the job. But similar to the case of impaired driving discussed in Chapter 18, the difficulty arises in determining how to test for such impairment in an accurate way, while at the same time not unduly burdening the medical user's legal right to treat approved medical conditions with marijuana, as recommended by the user's physician. Many employers have traditionally adopted zero-tolerance drug policies, disciplining or terminating employees if they fail a random drug test that detects any amount of an illegal substance (or even a metabolite of the substance) in the employee's body. But as discussed further in Chapter 18 with respect to impaired driving, such tests may not accurately measure impairment at work, but may instead reflect earlier impairment, while the employee is at home, or otherwise off the job site and off the clock.

The issue is further complicated by the fact that medical marijuana use is still illegal under federal law, so that many employers believe that they are duty-bound (morally if not necessarily legally) to not enable an illegal activity on the part of their employees. (In fact, for federal contractors and other companies that receive federal funding, the Drug-Free Workplace Act of 1988 requires employers to maintain drug-free work environments.) Many employers are also concerned that they risk liability themselves if they do not make reasonable efforts to curtail such illegal use, and the resulting impairment causes injury or damage to the employee or to third parties. In fact, some state statutes specifically provide that negligence caused by marijuana use is actionable, notwithstanding the state's legalization of medical marijuana. Thus, balancing the rights of employers and medical marijuana users presents a significant legal challenge for state legislatures and courts.

Section 17–2 below discusses the conflict between federal law and state laws authorizing medical marijuana use, and how this conflict plays out in the employment context. Section 17–3 compares the law's treatment of marijuana with its treatment of prescription drugs that may cause impairment. And § 17–4 discusses alternative approaches to regulating workplace impairment caused by marijuana use, other than the harsh zero-tolerance policies that many employers have traditionally relied upon.

§ 17–2 THE EMPLOYER'S DUTY IN LIGHT OF CONFLICTING FEDERAL AND STATE LAWS

In the absence of specific statutory protections for medical marijuana users in the workplace, courts have generally allowed employers to adopt zero-tolerance policies as regards marijuana use. Thus, most of the early decisions in medical marijuana states uphold the employer's right to make hiring and firing decisions based on the employee's failing a marijuana drug test, even if the employee consumed the marijuana outside of the workplace and was not impaired while at the workplace.

The Colorado Supreme Court addressed this issues in the 2015 case, *Coats v. Dish Network, LLC*, 350 P.3d 849 (Colo. 2015). In *Coats*, the plaintiff was a quadriplegic who had a valid medical marijuana license. He used marijuana to treat painful muscle spasms, at home only, as permitted by Colorado law. Coats was employed as a customer service representative by Dish Network until he failed a random drug test at work one day, at which time he was terminated. Coats argued that his termination was wrongful under a state statute, C.R.S. § 24–34–402.5, which prohibits employers from discharging employees who engage in "lawful activities" off the premises of the employer during nonworking hours. He argued that his medical marijuana use was a "lawful activity" under the meaning of the statute because he was using marijuana pursuant to a valid medical marijuana license. The Colorado Supreme Court, upholding the decisions of the trial court and the court of appeals, rejected Coats' argument that the term "lawful" under the statute was restricted to activities lawful under Colorado law. Rather, it held, an activity must be lawful under both state law and federal law to come within the protection of the statute. Therefore, the court concluded, an activity such as medical marijuana use that is unlawful under federal law is not a "lawful" activity under § 24–34–402.5, and the court accordingly upheld Coats' termination.

A number of other courts have likewise upheld the right of an employer to terminate an employee who tests positive for marijuana use. This is true even though such use took place outside of work hours, and even though the employee had a valid medical marijuana license. In so holding, these courts, like the Colorado Supreme Court in *Coats*, have pointed to the illegal status of medical marijuana use under federal law, which, they hold, takes it out of the protections of the Americans With Disabilities Act, 42 U.S.C. §§ 12101 et seq. (the "ADA"), and its state-law equivalents. *See, e.g., Emerald Steel Fabricators, Inc. v. Bureau of Labor and Industries*, 230 P.3d 518 (Ore. 2010) (holding that, under Oregon's employment discrimination laws, an employer was not required to accommodate an employee's use of medical marijuana, because it constituted an illegal use of drugs under an exclusion to the protections of Oregon's version of the ADA); *Roe v. Teletech Customer Care Management*, LLC, 257 P.3d 586 (Wash. 2011) (holding that Washington's medical marijuana statute did not regulate the conduct of a private employer or protect an employee from being discharged because of authorized medical marijuana use); *Ross v. RagingWire Telecommunications, Inc.*, 174 P.3d 200 (Cal. 2008) (holding that California law allows an employer to require a pre-employment drug test and to take illegal drug use into consideration in making employment decisions because California's version of the ADA does not require employers to accommodate illegal drug use); *Casias v. Walmart Stores, Inc.*, 695 F.3d 428 (6th Cir. 2012) (holding that Michigan's medical marijuana law did not restrict a private employer's ability to discipline an employee for medical marijuana use, and thus, could not support a wrongful discharge claim). *But see Barbuto v. Advantage Sales & Marketing, LLC,* 78 N.E.3d 37 (Mass. 2017) (holding that a medical marijuana user could bring an action under a state statute prohibiting handicap discrimination because the employer failed to agree to a reasonable accommodation).

Increasingly, however. state legislatures have been enacting legislation that provides special protection to medical marijuana users in the workplace. Minnesota, for example, has a statute that prohibits discrimination against an employee on the basis of the employee's registration as a medical marijuana user, and on the basis of the employee's failing a drug test for marijuana. Specifically, Minn. Stat. Ann. § 152.32(3)(c) provides as follows:

> *(c) Unless a failure to do so would violate federal law or regulations or cause an employer to lose a monetary or licensing-related benefit under federal law or regulations, an employer*

> *may not discriminate against a person in hiring, termination, or any term or condition of employment, or otherwise penalize a person, if the discrimination is based upon either of the following:*
>
> *(1) the person's status as a patient enrolled in the registry program under sections* ***152.22*** *to* ***152.37****; or*
>
> *(2) a patient's positive drug test for cannabis components or metabolites, unless the patient used, possessed, or was impaired by medical cannabis on the premises of the place of employment or during the hours of employment.*

Similarly, the State of New York enacted a statute in 2014 that specifically provides that medical marijuana use is protected under the state's version of the ADA, since registered medical marijuana users are considered to be "disabled" under New York's civil rights law. Specifically, McKinney's Public Health Law § 3369 provides as follows:

> *2. Non-discrimination. Being a certified patient shall be deemed to be having a "disability" under article fifteen of the executive law (human rights law), section forty-c of the civil rights law, sections* ***240.00, 485.00,*** *and* ***485.05*** *of the penal law, and section* ***200.50*** *of the criminal procedure law. This subdivision shall not bar the enforcement of a policy prohibiting an employee from performing his or her employment duties while impaired by a controlled substance. This subdivision shall not require any person or entity*

> *to do any act that would put the person or entity in violation of federal law or cause it to lose a federal contract or funding.*

Like the Minnesota statute, the New York statute provides exceptions to the nondiscrimination provision, where the employee is impaired by marijuana on the job, or where the employer is a federal contractor, and therefore subject to conflicting federal law.

Thus far, most of the states that have passed statutes protecting employees who are marijuana users from termination have confined the protections to medical marijuana users, not recreational users. A few have gone further, however, extending at least some protections to recreational users. Nevada, for example, enacted Assembly Bill 132 in 2019, which provides that employers cannot refuse to hire employees based on marijuana use outside of work, whether it is medical or recreational. The statute provides exceptions, however, for certain types of employees, such as firefighters and EMT personnel.

The states that have legalized medical marijuana are pretty evenly divided with respect to an employer's right to terminate an employee for failing a zero-tolerance drug test, even when there is no evidence that the employee used marijuana at work or was impaired while working. The more recent trend appears to be in favor of prohibiting employers from basing adverse employment decisions upon the employee's use of medical marijuana, however, provided the employee does not consume marijuana while at work, and is not impaired at work, and provided the employer is not required by federal law to maintain a drug-free workplace (e.g., federal contractors).

§ 17–3 PRESCRIPTION DRUG USE AND JOB IMPAIRMENT

There are many prescription drugs that can cause impairment if used on the job. The opioids (e.g., OxyContin and Vicodin), for example, are widely used to control chronic pain, and they can certainly cause impairment. Likewise, the benzodiazepines (e.g., Valium, Xanax, and Ambien) are prescribed extensively for anxiety and insomnia, even though they may cause impairment. And there are a number of others.

It seems reasonable to think that the employment laws with respect to medical marijuana use would track laws regulating the use of these drugs in the workplace. But as the cases cited in § 17–2 illustrate, this is often not the reality. Prescription drug use is generally subject to protection under federal and state statutes (e.g., the Americans with Disabilities Act, or ADA) that prohibit discrimination against employees with disabilities and require employers to make reasonable accommodations for such employees (e.g., allowing an employee to start work later if the employee needs to take prescription medicine before bed, and might still be impaired in the morning). Medical marijuana use is, on the other hand, is typically not treated as a disability, and therefore not subject to the same level of protections, even among states that prohibit discrimination on the basis of medical marijuana use. (As noted in the previous section, there are a few states, such as Massachusetts and New York, that do require employers to make reasonable accommodations for medical marijuana users, however.)

Under the federal ADA, an employer cannot lawfully discriminate against an employee by failing to make reasonable accommodations to the known physical or mental limitations of an otherwise qualified "individual with a disability" who is an employee. 42 U.S.C. § 12112(b)(5)(A). The statute thus establishes a cause of action for disabled employees against employers that fail to reasonably accommodate them. But individuals who are currently engaging in the *illegal* use of drugs are subject to different treatment. Users of illegal drugs are specifically excluded from the definition of an "individual with a disability" under the ADA, 42 U.S.C § 12114(a). And of course, under federal law, marijuana, unlike prescription medications, is an illegal drug. Thus, under the federal ADA, medical marijuana users are not afforded the protections given to prescription drug users. *See, e.g., James v. City of Costa Mesa*, 700 F.3d 394 (9th Cir. 2012) (concluding that medical marijuana use is an illegal use of drugs not covered by the ADA's supervised use exception).

Interestingly, the majority of state court decisions that have examined the issue in the context of their state's disability discrimination statutes have similarly distinguished medical marijuana users from prescription drug users, even though medical marijuana use is legal under state law. (Again, however, as noted in the previous section, there are a few states, such as Massachusetts and New York, that do require employers to make reasonable accommodations for medical marijuana users.)

For example, in the California Supreme Court case cited in the previous section, *Ross v. RagingWire Telecommunications, Inc.*, 174 P.3d 200 (Cal. 2008), the plaintiff argued that California's version of the ADA, the California Fair Employment and Housing Act (FEHA), protected his use of medical marijuana in the same way that FEHA protects the employee who uses a prescription drug to treat a disability. In such cases, the plaintiff argued, FEHA would require the employer to try to make a reasonable accommodation for the employee's disability and its treatment. The court, however, disagreed. "Plaintiff's position," it reasoned, "might have merit if the Compassionate Use Act gave marijuana the same status as any legal prescription drug. But the Act's effect is not so broad. No state law could completely legalize marijuana for medical purposes because the drug remains illegal under federal law (21 U.S.C. §§ 812, 844(a)), even for medical users." *Id.* at 204 (citations omitted). Since the California FEHA does not require employers to accommodate the use of illegal drugs, the court held, it does not require the employer to try to work out a reasonable accommodation with the plaintiff employee.

Generally, therefore, medical marijuana users do not receive quite the same level of protection in the employment context as prescription drug users, even in states that have passed legislation prohibiting discrimination in the workplace based on medical marijuana use, because most such state statutes do not require employers to adopt reasonable accommodations for medical marijuana use. Instead, they merely protect medical marijuana use outside of the workplace, *provided* it does not cause any impairment at work.

§ 17-4 ALTERNATIVE APPROACHES TO REGULATING WORKPLACE IMPAIRMENT

Regardless of whether they protect the right of an employee to use medical marijuana outside of the workplace, all states allow employers to prohibit impairment in the workplace. The tricky part is determining reasonably whether employees are in fact impaired at work.

In states that do not protect employees' right to use medical marijuana outside of the workplace, employers are allowed to rely on strict zero-tolerance drug policies for marijuana use and can automatically refuse to hire or terminate all employees (or prospective employees) who show any amount of marijuana in their systems after taking drug tests. However, as discussed in Chapter 18, this is not a very accurate method for testing workplace impairment, since small amounts of THC and other cannabinoids may remain in a medical marijuana user's saliva or blood for some time after the user ceases to be impaired. Thus, employers may find it helpful to rely on alternative means for regulating impairment in the workplace, even in states that don't protect medical use.

In states that do protect medical use, the state anti-discrimination statutes typically provide that an employer may discipline or terminate an employee who uses marijuana at work or is impaired at work. West Virginia's anti-discrimination statute, for example, provides as follows:

> (b) *Employment.—*
>
> (1) No employer may discharge, threaten, refuse to hire or otherwise discriminate or retaliate against an employee regarding an employee's compensation, terms, conditions, location or privileges solely on the basis of such employee's status as an individual who is certified to use medical cannabis.
>
> (2) Nothing in this act shall require an employer to make any accommodation of the use of medical cannabis on the property or premises of any place of employment. This act shall in no way limit an employer's ability to discipline an employee for being under the influence of medical cannabis in the workplace or for working while under the influence of medical cannabis when the employee's conduct falls below the standard of care normally accepted for that position.
>
> (3) Nothing in this act shall require an employer to commit any act that would put the employer or any person acting on its behalf in violation of federal law.

W. Va, Code Ann. § 16A–15–4.

Thus, the West Virginia statute allows an employer to discipline an employee whose workplace impairment causes substandard work. But the statute provides no guidance as to how the employer should make this determination as to impairment. How is the employer to determine whether the substandard work is due to marijuana impairment as opposed to some other cause, e.g., illness?

The failure of state anti-discrimination statutes to address how the employer is to determine whether an employee is impaired creates a void in these statutes that invites litigation. Thus, it is worth considering how states might fill this void.

Here the different approaches states have taken with respect to gauging impairment for purposes of driving under the influence of marijuana are instructive (*see* Chapter 18). One such approach is the zero-tolerance approach, as discussed above with regard to states that do not have anti-discrimination statutes. But there are at least two other major approaches that are perhaps better geared toward gauging impairment in the workplace: (1) the use of *per se* limits rather than zero-tolerance standards in administering employment drug tests; and (2) the use of behavioral evidence, rather than drug tests, in evaluating on-the-job impairment due to marijuana use. Neither of these approaches is free from difficulties, but at least they both put the focus on impairment at the workplace, as opposed to during the employee's free time.

The former approach, relying on *per se* limits, would try to correlate on-the-job impairment with a particular level of THC in the employee's bloodstream at the time of testing. For example, the employer might enact a policy that only those employees whose THC blood content equals or exceeds 5 ng/ml (which is the level used by some states to measure driving impairment) fail the employer's drug test. By measuring active THC content, rather than metabolites that merely indicate past use, the *per se* test would more accurately correlate to actual impairment in the workplace than does a zero-tolerance test.

One problem with this approach, however, is that it would probably need to rely on blood tests rather than urine tests for accuracy, and those are often considered excessively invasive in the employment context. Perhaps, however, the employer could ameliorate this concern somewhat by offering an employee who fails a zero-tolerance test the option to take a blood test to measure actual impairment, if the employee believes that the zero-tolerance test unfairly reflects home use rather than on-the-job impairment. The other problem with *per se* tests, discussed in more depth in Chapter 18, is that, for several technical reasons, they are not as accurate as one might hope for measuring actual impairment at the time of the test. They do not measure current impairment nearly as well as blood-alcohol tests, for example, across groups of users. Thus, while *per se* tests more accurately track actual on-the-job impairment than zero-tolerance tests, they are still far from perfect and may still produce misleading results.

The other principal approach that employers can take is to measure on-the-job impairment via behavioral evidence, rather than through drug tests. In other words, the employee would not be subject to discipline for on-the-job impairment unless, while at work, the employee displays signs of impairment, such as slurred speech, dilated pupils, slowed motor skills, etc. The advantage to this approach is that it strictly correlates on-the-job impairment with discipline; there is no possibility that the employee is being disciplined for something that took place at home. On the other hand, the behavioral evidence approach obviously lacks precision, since it is quite subjective, and the employee may exhibit seemingly impaired behavior for other reasons, such as illness or the use of certain prescription drugs. In the context of impaired driving, law enforcement agencies now employ Drug Recognition Experts to more accurately track drug-induced impairment based on behavioral evidence (*see* Chapter 18). However, it is not clear that employers would want to invest in this kind of training. Nor is it clear that they would want to take the risk of lawsuits for wrongful termination that may result from the inherently subjective nature of behavioral evidence tests.

From a policy perspective, it probably makes most sense in states that allow medical marijuana use is to simply treat medical marijuana users the same as prescription drug users. In other words, if the employee has a disability, and is using medical marijuana pursuant to a valid license to treat this disability, the employer should work with the employee to find a reasonable accommodation, as long as this does not result in undue hardship for the employer. But while this sensible approach has in fact been adopted by a few states, it is not one, as discussed in the previous two sections, that most states that allow medical marijuana use are inclined to follow at the present time.

Finally, with respect to recreational use, employers in states that allow recreational use could treat off-duty recreational marijuana use by employees analogously to how they treat off-duty alcohol use. That is, so long as off-duty use does not affect job performance, employers would refrain from terminating their workers for recreational use. However, while this is in fact the employment policy that many employers have voluntarily adopted in states that allow recreational marijuana use, it again is not a policy that most such states are likely to follow in the near future.

CHAPTER 18

IMPAIRED DRIVING AND MARIJUANA

§ 18–1 INTRODUCTION

One important practical concern that lawmakers have struggled with in states that have legalized medical and/or recreational marijuana is how to discourage impaired driving caused by marijuana consumption. Although there is some evidence that "high" drivers may present less of a hazard overall than drunk drivers (among other things, research has shown that drunk drivers tend to greatly overestimate their ability to drive, whereas high drivers tend to be somewhat more aware of their limitations), there is still a concern among law enforcement officials that increased marijuana use resulting from legalization of marijuana, whether medical or recreational, will lead to an increase in traffic accidents and fatalities. Thus, there is a general agreement, even among marijuana legalization advocates (e.g., NORML) that there needs to be a criminal penalty for impairment caused by high driving. The problem arises in devising an accurate and efficient way to detect and measure such impairment.

Section 18–2 of this chapter looks at how states have attempted to control the corollary problem of driving under the influence of alcohol, and the reasons why this approach is more challenging in the context of "high" driving. Section 18–3 discusses the different approaches states have taken with respect to impairment caused by psychoactive drugs generally. Section 18–4 looks more closely at the approaches different marijuana legalization states have taken to control impaired driving from marijuana intoxication. And § 18–5 discusses prospects going forward for a more satisfactory legal solution to the problem of marijuana-induced impaired driving.

§ 18–2 DRUNK DRIVING VS. HIGH DRIVING

At first blush, the easy solution would appear to be tracking currently existing alcohol policies, modeling "high" driving laws after drunk driving laws. Unfortunately, however, that has not proven to be an easy task. Police agencies are well-equipped to verify whether individuals are driving under the influence of alcohol. The various states have enacted standard *per se* tests for establishing impairment based upon the driver's blood alcohol content (BAC); in most states, a BAC of .08% blood-alcohol will result in a presumption that a driver is under the influence of alcohol. (It is also possible, in most states, to be found guilty of driving under the influence even with a lower BAC, but this takes an additional evidentiary showing.) Some states take a two-tiered approach or even three-tiered approach to drunk driving, establishing harsher penalties for higher BAC levels. In Colorado, for example, the crime of Driving Under the Influence of Alcohol (DUI) is punished more severely than the crime of Driving While Ability Impaired (DWAI); the former is presumed from a BAC of .08%, the latter from a BAC of .05%. In addition, Colorado, like many states, has an enhanced penalty for aggravated drunk driving, which includes driving with a BAC of .2% or higher.

This *per se* approach to punishing marijuana-impaired driving is more problematic than it is for drunk driving, however. First, there is no easily administered field test, comparable to a breathalyzer test, that police officers can use when they make a stop and suspect that the driver is under the influence of marijuana. Instead, police have to rely on a blood test or urine test, which means that the driver must be placed under custodial arrest, taken to the police station, and asked to take a blood or urine test. This cumbersome procedure likely has a chilling effect on testing for impairment, since it takes significantly more time and effort on the part of the police than a breathalyzer test.

Second, the rate of metabolism for marijuana can vary significantly from person-to-person, unlike the metabolism of alcohol, which is quite consistent between individuals. Unlike alcohol, which is water-soluble, THC is fat-soluble, so it moves readily from the blood to fatty tissues, including the brain. As a result, THC is not evenly distributed around the body the way alcohol is. Thus, it is not as easy to determine the amount of THC affecting the brain as it is to determine the amount of alcohol affecting the brain. Additionally, a person's body fat content affects the rate of metabolism, as does the frequency of use. Experts report that regular users (which includes many medical marijuana users) generally have greater amounts of THC in their fat cells on an ongoing basis than occasional users. And this THC gets released into the blood slowly over time, meaning many regular users have constant low levels of THC in their blood, even when they are not impaired. Thus, it is difficult to tell whether a driver who has a certain THC blood level (e.g., 2 ng/ml) was recently using marijuana, and was thus driving while mildly impaired, or alternatively, whether the individual is a regular medical user who consistently has a THC blood level of 2 ng/ml and was not impaired at the time of driving.

Third, impairment caused by marijuana intoxication is less predictable than impairment caused by alcohol intoxication. Persons with a BAC of .08, for example, demonstrate relatively similar levels of driving impairment (as measured by driving performance tests, for example). Conversely, there is evidence that persons with a THC blood level of say 5 ng/ml, which is the cutoff for marijuana impairment in some states, do not demonstrate consistently the same level of driving impairment across groups of individuals. Some individuals with that amount of THC in their blood demonstrate a fairly high level of driving impairment, while others demonstrated a relatively low level of driving impairment. In part this is due to the fact, as noted above, that the amount of THC in the blood does not accurately track the amount of THC affecting the brain, as it does in the case of alcohol. *See generally Field Sobriety Tests and THC Levels Unreliable Indicators of Marijuana Intoxication,* National Institute of Justice (April 5, 2021), www.nij.ojp.gov (research showed "THC levels in bio-fluids were not reliable indicators of marijuana intoxication for the study participants.").

Thus, laws governing impaired driving due to alcohol do not provide a very reliable precedent for regulating impairment due to marijuana. The next section accordingly looks at the various approaches states have taken toward regulating impairment due to other intoxicating drugs.

§ 18-3 DIFFERENT APPROACHES TO THE REGULATION OF DRUGGED DRIVING

The difficulty in controlling impaired driving is not unique to marijuana and alcohol. A number of different drugs, both legal and illegal, can cause driving impairment. Figuring out a way to detect impairment in drivers under the influence of drugs and devising an appropriate punishment scheme to discourage drugged driving without punishing legal use have proven challenging to lawmakers.

The traditional approach to detecting drug-induced impairment in drivers relied heavily on observational evidence about the driver's behavior. Thus, police officer(s) can subject the driver to various physical and cognitive tests (such as walking a straight line, saying the alphabet, etc.) to determine whether the driver is impaired. Similarly, the observations of the police officer at the time the driver was stopped (e.g., the driver had slurred speech, dilated pupils, etc.) can be entered into evidence to show impairment.

The problem with this approach is that it is imprecise and very subjective, relying almost exclusively on the testimony of the police officer(s) making the arrest. In practice, this has made obtaining convictions for drugged driving difficult, particularly in cases where the drug at issue was legally obtained and used, because juries tend to prefer more precise, scientific evidence. In response to this problem, some police departments have begun to employ so-called Drug Recognition Experts, who are police officers specially trained to identify the effects of various drugs on the appearance and behavior of suspected impaired drivers.

A further problem with the traditional observational approach is that is not effective in situations where the driver is injured in an accident and is rendered unconscious or is otherwise unable to be tested observationally. In these situations, a blood test is likely the only way impairment can be established.

A second approach to drugged driving that some states (approximately a third of them) have employed is a so-called *zero-tolerance policy* with respect to the use of controlled substances. Under this approach, a driver is presumed to be impaired if *any* amount of a specified controlled substance is detected in the driver's body, whether or not there is any evidence that the driver was actually impaired at the time the driver was operating the vehicle. The states that have adopted this zero-tolerance approach vary significantly with respect to the drugs that they include in the prohibited category. Most states refer to drugs listed in the CSA to identify prohibited drugs. But some states go beyond this to include a more extensive list of substances, while others limit the prohibited list to Schedule I and Schedule II drugs. And some specifically exclude marijuana.

These zero-tolerance impaired driving statutes do not necessarily apply exclusively to prohibited substances. Even if a particular drug (e.g., an over-the-counter cold medicine) is not on the prohibited list, the driver can still be found to be impaired by virtue of that drug. In those cases, however, the prosecution generally cannot rely on the mere presence of any detectable amount of the drug in the driver's system to establish impairment; rather, the totality of the evidence must be considered to determine whether the driver was actually impaired.

The third principal approach to drugged driving is to set *per se* limits with regard to one or more prohibited substances. This approach is similar to the approach all the states use with respect to driving under the influence of alcohol. (As discussed above in § 18–2, however, such limits have a less significant correlation with impaired driving caused by drugs such as marijuana than they do with respect to alcohol.) Under a *per se* approach, the law presumes (or sometimes just allows a permissive inference) that the driver is operating the vehicle under the influence of a particular drug, such as marijuana, if the driver's blood level contains an amount of the drug that is greater than or equal to the *per se* limit.

This is the approach that Washington and Colorado have taken toward regulation of high driving. Both states impose a *per se* limit of 5 ng/ml of THC to measure impairment from marijuana. The two states differ a bit in how this limit works, however. Washington's *per se* limit establishes a legal presumption; therefore, if a driver with a THC blood level of 5 ng/ml or higher is arrested, the law presumes that the driver is operating the vehicle under the influence of marijuana. *See* Wash. Rev. Stat. § 46.61.502(1)(b). Under the Colorado statute, by contrast, the driver is not presumed to be driving under the influence of marijuana with a THC blood level of 5 ng/ml; rather, the jury is merely allowed to draw an inference of driving under the influence from exceeding this *per se* limit. *See* C.R.S. § 42–4–1301(6)(a)(IV). Several other states also impose *per se* limits for THC blood level, sometimes with lower, and therefore more restrictive, limits of 1 or 2 ng/ml.

§ 18–4 IMPAIRED DRIVING LAWS IN MEDICAL MARIJUANA STATES

Even among states that have legalized marijuana for medical use, there are some significant differences in how they treat evidence of trace amounts of marijuana in a driver's body. And in some cases the state courts have narrowed the reach of particular statutes to make them more driver-friendly.

Arizona's impaired driving statute, A.R.S. § 28–1381, provides a good example. It provides that it is unlawful to drive a vehicle while the driver is:

(1) under the influence of alcohol or any drug and is "impaired to the slightest degree" as a result;

(2) if the person has a BAC of .08%;

(3) if the driver's body contains any trace of a "drug" or metabolite of a drug set out in § 13–3401 of the statute [which lists a host of drugs, including cannabis];or

(4) if the vehicle is a commercial motor vehicle that requires a person to obtain a commercial driver license, the person has a BAL of 0.04 or more.

Section B of the statute provides that it is not a defense under section (1) above that the driver is entitled to use the substance under the laws of the state; however, § D of the statute provides that a driver is not guilty of violating section (3) above if the driver was using the drug pursuant to a valid prescription. Thus, prescription drug users are protected, so long as they are not impaired while driving, even if trace amount of the prescription drug are detected in their systems. But since marijuana can only be *recommended* by physicians, not prescribed, even in legalization states, this provision would not apply to medical marijuana users, who remain subject to a zero-tolerance approach.

In *State ex rel. Montgomery v. Harris*, 346 P.3d 984 (Ariz. 2014), however, the Supreme Court of Arizona narrowed the meaning of the word "metabolite" in the statute, holding that it referred only to those metabolites that actually cause impairment of driving. In that case, the driver (who did not have a medical marijuana license) had smoked marijuana the day before, and his blood test upon arrest revealed no active THC in his blood, but only a trace of an inactive metabolite, formed upon the breakdown of THC in the body. The court looked to, among other things, the Arizona Medical Marijuana Act in holding that the state's interpretation of the statute to include non-impairing metabolites worked an absurd result, since a medical marijuana user may have traces of such metabolites in the user's blood for a month or more following use. Therefore, the court concluded "that the 'metabolite' reference in § 28–1381(A)(3) is limited to any of a proscribed substance's metabolites that are capable of causing impairment. Accordingly, marijuana users violate § 28–1381(A)(1) if they drive while 'impaired to the slightest degree,' and, regardless of impairment, [they] violate § (A)(3) if they are discovered with any amount of THC or an impairing metabolite in their body. Drivers cannot be convicted of the § (A)(3) offense based merely on the presence of a non-impairing metabolite that may reflect the prior usage of marijuana." 346 P.3d at 990.

In a subsequent case a year later, the Arizona Supreme Court again narrowed the reach of the statute. In *Dobson v. McClennen*, 361 P.3d 374 (Ariz. 2015), it held that, as applied to a medical marijuana user, § (A)(3) of the statute, read in conjunction with the Arizona Medical Marijuana Act, allowed liability only where the amount of cannabis or an impairing metabolite of cannabis was in a quantity capable of causing impairment. Thus, there is an affirmative defense available to medical marijuana users in Arizona who are arrested for driving with traces of marijuana in their body. If they can show that the amount of marijuana was not capable of causing impairment, then there is no liability. 361 P.3d at 378.

Minnesota follows a somewhat different zero-tolerance approach to its impaired driving statute, Minn. Stat. § 169A.20. Under the Minnesota statute, the driver is guilty of driving while impaired if *any* of the following apply:

(1) the person is under the influence of alcohol;

(2) the person is under the influence of a controlled substance;

(3) the person is under the influence of an intoxicating substance and the person knows or has reason to know that the substance has the capacity to cause impairment;

(4) the person is under the influence of a combination of any two or more of the elements named in clauses (1) to (3);

(5) the person's alcohol concentration at the time, or as measured within two hours of the time, of driving, operating, or being in physical control of the motor vehicle is 0.08 or more;

(6) the vehicle is a commercial motor vehicle and the person's alcohol concentration at the time, or as measured within two hours of the time, of driving, operating, or being in physical

control of the commercial motor vehicle is 0.04 or more; or

(7) the person's body contains any amount of a controlled substance listed in Schedule I or II, or its metabolite, **other than marijuana or tetrahydrocannabinols**. (emphasis added)

Thus, under § (7), a driver is not guilty of driving while impaired just because the driver's body contains marijuana or a metabolite; rather, the driver must be found to be under the influence of marijuana under § (2).

Among the most lenient of the states that allow medical marijuana use is Maryland. That statute has no marijuana-specific provisions, and it has no *per se* limit for intoxication under its impaired driving statute (Md. Code § 21–902). Rather, liability for drugged driving is found only if either one of two conditions applies:

(1) due to any drugs, the driver is "so far impaired" that the driver could not operate the vehicle safely; *or*

(2) the driver's ability to operate a vehicle is "impaired" by any "controlled dangerous substance," which includes all the controlled substances.

However, § (2) applies only if the driver is not legally entitled to use the substance. And since Maryland allows the medical use of marijuana, this apparently means that medical marijuana users, as well as users of prescription drugs, can be found liable only under the first provision, where they are "so far impaired" that they cannot operate the vehicle safely (and even then, § (c)(1)(iv) provides a defense where the driver was unaware that the drug would cause impairment).

The other states that allow medical marijuana use have similarly varied laws. Some rely on the traditional behavioral test for impairment, some set *per se* limits for THC blood level, and some employ zero-tolerance standards, though generally those in the last category make some exception or qualification for marijuana.

§ 18–5 FUTURE POSSIBILITIES

To date, no state has come up with a fully satisfactory solution to the problem of drugged driving generally, and marijuana-impaired driving in particular. The various approaches that state legislatures have employed all leave something to be desired.

The zero-tolerance approach seems excessively harsh, particularly when applied to drugs that are being used legally. To punish drivers who have only trace amounts of THC (or worse still, inactive metabolites of THC) in their bodies, when a state allows medical marijuana use, arguably creates an undue hardship on medical marijuana users, who essentially cannot legally drive at all, even when they are not at all impaired. The traditional observational approach, by contrast, which looks to objective evidence of impairment in the driver's behavior, seems more fair, but it suffers from subjectivity and imprecision (and with those, the potential for police abuse). And the *per se* approach—which works well for drunk driving regulation—while likely the best option in principle, is not at this time technologically sophisticated enough to accurately correlate *per se* limits with driving impairment.

Researchers continue to work on developing more accurate breath, saliva, and blood tests, looking for chemical markers that can more precisely identify driving impairment. Additionally, police agencies are continuing to expand the use of Drug Recognition Experts, and to improve their ability to accurately detect driving impairment from driver behavior. These efforts have become increasingly important as more states legalize marijuana use, medically or otherwise, and more drivers with THC or its metabolites in their bodies take to the roads.

CHAPTER 19

PROFESSIONAL RESPONSIBILITY ISSUES FOR LAWYERS

§ 19–1 INTRODUCTION

The divergent status of marijuana under federal law and state law, in those states that have legalized medical or recreational marijuana, creates special problems for lawyers. The ABA's Model Rules of Professional Responsibility, which have been adopted by nearly every state, prohibit lawyers from advising clients to engage in criminal conduct, and from assisting clients in conduct the lawyer knows is criminal. They also provide that it is professional misconduct for lawyers themselves to engage in criminal conduct. Because marijuana possession and distribution remain illegal under federal law, lawyers in marijuana-legal states arguably violate the former prohibition when they assist marijuana-related businesses with their legal affairs. And they arguably violate the latter when they themselves partake of marijuana or invest in marijuana-related businesses, even though these activities are legal under state law.

These potential conflicts have caused considerable concern on the part of lawyers in states with legalized marijuana, and as a result, the state bars have been active in weighing the implications of marijuana legalization on their individual rules of professional responsibility. This chapter summarizes these state-level determinations. Section 19–2 discusses the ethical implications involved when lawyers represent marijuana-related businesses, which is the primary issue the state bars have wrestled with in legalization states. The latter two sections discuss subsidiary issues that are still largely unresolved. Section 19–3 discusses the ethical implications involved when lawyers personally use marijuana. And § 19–4 discusses whether lawyers may themselves ethically invest in marijuana-related businesses.

§ 19–2 REPRESENTING MARIJUANA-RELATED BUSINESSES

The most significant ethical issue that marijuana legalization has raised in legalization states is the extent to which lawyers may counsel marijuana-related businesses. That issue arises because the Model Rules prohibit lawyers from (knowingly) assisting clients in the furtherance of criminal and fraudulent conduct. Thus, Rule 1.2 provides as follows:

> *Rule 1.2: Scope of Representation & Allocation of Authority Between Client & Lawyer*
>
> * * *
>
> *(d) A lawyer shall not counsel a client to engage, or assist a client, in conduct that the lawyer knows is criminal or fraudulent, but a lawyer may discuss the legal consequences of any proposed course of conduct with a client and may counsel or assist a client to make a good faith*

effort to determine the validity, scope, meaning or application of the law.

Since marijuana-related businesses are illegal under federal law, providing legal advice to such clients arguably violates Rule 1.2.

Of course, not all such advice would come within the scope of Rule 1.2. Lawyers have always been allowed to provide advice to clients about the meaning of the law and its possible application to the client's situation, even for criminal matters. Accordingly, Rule 1.2 specifically excludes from the prohibition legal advice that helps the client "make a good faith effort to determine the validity, scope, meaning or application of the law." Thus, the rule draws an important distinction between presenting an analysis of legal aspects of questionable conduct, versus recommending the means by which a fraud or crime might be committed with impunity.

With respect to state marijuana laws, therefore, lawyers can definitely advise clients as to the consequences of their actions with respect to state and federal criminal law, particularly their past actions. And they can quite clearly counsel their clients regarding the application of zoning ordinances and other state laws and regulations relating to decisions facing marijuana clients. The trickier issue arises with respect to the lawyers' assistance in the way of drafting documents (such as contracts, leases, and business formation documents), as well as negotiating on behalf of the client, and in providing legal advice to clients regarding the best ways to structure and operate their businesses within the confines of state law.

Early on, some state bar associations raised concerns about lawyers' offering such assistance, consistent with their duties under their Rules of Professional Responsibility. They noted that Rule 1.2 does not make an exception for conduct that is criminal under federal law but not under state law. The Maine Bar Association, for example, issued an opinion on the issue in 2010 that cast significant doubt on a lawyer's ability to ethically represent marijuana-related businesses, though ultimately it declined to take a firm position, noting the fact-intensive nature of the inquiry:

> "Maine and its sister states may well be in the vanguard regarding the medicinal use and effectiveness of marijuana. However, the Rule which governs attorney conduct does not make a distinction between crimes which are enforced and those which are not. So long as both the federal law and the language of the Rule each remain the same, an attorney needs to perform the analysis required by the Rule and determine whether the particular legal service being requested rises to the level of assistance in violating federal law. . . .Where the line is drawn between permitted and forbidden activities needs to be evaluated on a case-by-case basis. Bar Counsel has asked for a general opinion regarding the kind of analysis which must be undertaken. We cannot determine which specific actions would run afoul of the ethical rules. We

> can, however, state that participation in this endeavor by an attorney involves a significant degree of risk which needs to be carefully evaluated."

Maine Board of Overseers of the Bar Opinion 199 (2010).

A few years later, the Connecticut Bar issued a similar opinion, emphasizing the distinction between a lawyer's providing an analysis of the legal implications of certain conduct, versus recommending the means by which a crime or a fraud might be carried out. The committee declined to address particular factual circumstances that might implicate the rule, but nevertheless noted that the rule makes no distinction between crimes which are enforced and those which are not. And it cautioned that "lawyers should carefully assess where the line is between those functions and not cross it." *See* Connecticut Bar Assn. Prof. Ethics Committee, Informal Opinion 2013–02 (2013).

Another opinion along these lines came from the Ohio bar. In August 2016, the Supreme Court of Ohio's Board of Professional Conduct examined the issue and concluded that "a lawyer violates Prof. Cond. R. 1.2(d) when he or she transitions from advising a client regarding the consequences of conduct under federal and state law to counseling or assisting the client to engage in conduct the lawyer knows is prohibited under federal law." Opinion 2016–6. The Board specifically listed tasks such as drafting and negotiating contracts and business formation documents on behalf of marijuana-related businesses as being within the scope of activities prohibited by Rule 1.2(d), along with representation of marijuana-related businesses before state licensing boards.

The Ohio Supreme Court, however, later rejected the Board's position as set out in Opinion 2016–6, adopting an amendment to its Rule 1.2, which made it clear that a lawyer was allowed to counsel or assist a client regarding conduct permitted by Ohio's medical marijuana statute, provided the lawyer advises the client regarding related federal law. *See* Ohio R.P.C. 1.2 (d) (2000).

In keeping with the position of the Ohio Supreme Court, nearly all of the states that have considered the issue in the last several years have been more concerned about denying legal representation of marijuana clients within their states, and they have accordingly created safe harbors for lawyers advising marijuana-related businesses. As the Arizona State Bar put it: "A state law now expressly permits certain conduct. Legal services are necessary or desirable to implement and bring to fruition that conduct expressly permitted under state law." Noting the importance of a strong, independent bar, the Arizona Bar concluded that prohibiting lawyers from assisting clients acting legally under state law would be "depriving [the] clients of the very legal advice and assistance that is needed to engage in the conduct that the state law expressly permits." State Bar of Ariz. Ethics Opinion 11–01 (2011).

Thus, the states that have legalized medical and/or recreational marijuana have almost all now adopted this approach, though they have done so by different means. In 2015, for example, the Oregon Supreme Court adopted an exception to its Rule 1.2(d), specifically exempting marijuana representation from the scope of the rule's prohibition, so long as the lawyer assisting a marijuana-related business advises the client as to conflicting federal laws:

> *(d) Notwithstanding paragraph (c), a lawyer may counsel and assist a client regarding Oregon's marijuana-related laws. In the event Oregon law conflicts with federal or tribal law, the lawyer shall also advise the client regarding related federal and tribal law and policy.*

Other legalization states that have likewise revised their versions of Rule 1.2 include Hawaii (Haw. Ct. R. P. C. 1.2 (2015); California (Cal. R. P. C. 1.2.1 (2018); and New Jersey (N. J. R. P. C. 1.2(d) (2019).

Meanwhile, several other states have issued interpretive comments to their versions of Rule 1.2, making it clear that lawyers are allowed to advise and assist marijuana-related businesses. In 2014, for example, the Washington Supreme Court adopted Comment 18 to its Rule 1.2, which states:

> *[18] At least until there is a change in federal enforcement policy, a lawyer may counsel a client regarding the validity, scope and meaning of Washington Initiative 502 (Laws of 2013, ch. 3) and may assist a client in conduct that the lawyer reasonably believes is permitted by this statute and the other statutes, regulations,*

> *orders, and other state and local provisions implementing them.*

See also New Mexico (N. M. R. P. C. 16–102 (comment 11) (2018); Nevada R. P. C. 1.2, comment 1 (adopted as ADKT 0495, May 7, 2014).

In still other legalization states, the state supreme courts have not changed or added comments to the Rule, but the state bars have issued opinions that are in accord with this interpretation. *See, e.g.*, New York State Bar Ethics Opinion 1024 (2014), aff'd by Ethics Opinion 1177 (2019); Maryland Ethics Docket No. 2016–10 (February 2016); Illinois State Bar Ethics Opinion14–07 (October 2014).

Finally, one state, Minnesota, has legislated this interpretation into law by enacting a statute that provides:

> *An attorney may not be subject to disciplinary action by the Minnesota Supreme Court or professional responsibility board for providing legal assistance to prospective or registered manufacturers or others related to activity that is no longer subject to criminal penalties under state law pursuant to sections 152.22 to 152.37.*

Minn. Stat. § 152.32(2)(i).

Thus, regardless of the manner in which they have gone about doing it, the vast majority of legalization states are now in favor of allowing lawyers to represent marijuana-related businesses, as long as the advice is fully compliant with state law, and (in most states) as long as the lawyer also advises the client regarding conflicting federal law. In fact, even the two contrarian states discussed at the beginning of this section—Connecticut and Maine—have both moved toward the majority view. In January 2015, the Connecticut Superior Court amended Rule 1.2(d) and its official commentary to clarify that lawyers are permitted to assist clients concerning conduct permitted under state law, provided they also counsel clients about the legal consequences of the proposed conduct under other applicable law. And in May 2016, the Maine Professional Ethics Commission issued an opinion (No. 214) recommending that its Rule 1.2 be amended to allow lawyers to provide business services and advice to marijuana-related businesses, so long as the lawyer advises the client on federal law as well.

Thus, the legalization states have now formed a clear consensus with regard to counseling and assisting marijuana clients in accordance with state law, finding that such conduct is permissible under Rule 1.2.

§ 19–3 WHETHER LAWYERS VIOLATE THE RULES OF PROFESSIONAL RESPONSIBILITY IF THEY PERSONALLY USE MARIJUANA

Another issue that arises with respect to a lawyer's ethical duties in marijuana-legalization states is whether a lawyer violates the rules of professional responsibility through the lawyer's personal use of marijuana, even though it is in accordance with state law. The model rule that is arguably implicated by such conduct is Rule 8.4, which states as follows:

Rule 8.4: Misconduct

It is professional misconduct for a lawyer to:

(b) commit a criminal act that reflects adversely on the lawyer's honesty, trustworthiness or fitness as a lawyer in other respects;

At least one state bar has indicated that a lawyer's personal use of marijuana may constitute professional misconduct. In 2014, the Ethics Committee of the North Dakota State Bar was called upon to interpret Rule 8.4 in the case of a North Dakota attorney who wished to move to Minnesota to participate in a medical marijuana treatment program there, while still maintaining his license to practice law in North Dakota. The Committee ruled that this conduct would violate Rule 8.4. Noting the supremacy of federal law that criminalizes marijuana use, and the fact that North Dakota law did not allow the use of medical marijuana, the Committee concluded that "if [the] Attorney purchased, possessed, or ingested marijuana in Minnesota, Attorney would be violating federal law each and every time Attorney did so. In other words, Attorney would be engaging in a 'pattern of repeated offenses' that indicates indifference to legal obligations and constitutes a violation of N.D.R. Prof. Conduct 8.4(b)." State Bar Assn. of N. Dakota Ethics Comm., Opinion 14–02 (August 12, 2014).

The Colorado Bar, on the other hand, took a more tolerant approach to a lawyer's legal (under the laws of the state) use of marijuana. The Colorado state bar addressed this issue in 2012, finding that a lawyer's (medical) marijuana use, by itself, does not implicate Rule 8.4. The opinion stated as follows:

> "[T]he Committee does not see a nexus between the lawyer's conduct and his or her 'honesty' or 'trustworthiness,' within the meaning of Colo. RPC 8.4(b), provided that the lawyer complies with the requirements of Colorado law permitting and regulating his or her medical use of marijuana. The Committee also does not see a nexus between the lawyer's conduct and his or her 'fitness as a lawyer in other respects,' provided that (a) again, the lawyer complies with the requirements of Colorado law permitting his or her medical use of marijuana, and (b) in addition, the lawyer satisfies his or her obligation under Colo. RPC 1.1 to provide competent representation."

C.B.A Formal Opinion 124 (July 2012). The Committee was careful to qualify its conclusion, however, noting in (b) that the lawyer must still satisfy the requirement of Rule 1.1 to provide competent representation.

Rule 1.1 of the A.B.A.'s Model Rules provides as follows:

Rule 1.1: Competence

A lawyer shall provide competent representation to a client. Competent representation requires the legal knowledge, skill, thoroughness and preparation reasonably necessary for the representation.

This provision has been interpreted to apply to mental impairment on the part of the lawyer. Thus, if a lawyer's use of marijuana "materially impairs" the lawyer's ability to represent the client (e.g., the lawyer is high in court), the lawyer's failure to refuse or terminate representation "raises a 'substantial question' about the lawyer's fitness to practice law. . . ." under Rule 8.4. C.B.A Formal Opinion 124 (April 2012). In this respect, the lawyer's use of marijuana is not different from the lawyer's use of legal substances such as alcohol and prescription opiates. If such substances materially impair the lawyer's ability to represent the client, then the lawyer is guilty of professional misconduct, notwithstanding the legal status of the impairing substance.

In 2014, the Standing Committee on the Rules of Professional Conduct in Colorado recommended a change to Rule 8.4 that would have formally adopted the interpretation set out in Formal Opinion 124. The Colorado Supreme Court, however, rejected the proposed rule change without comment, at the same time that it approved the new comment interpreting Rule 1.2 (*see* § 18–2 above) so as to allow lawyers to represent marijuana-related businesses. Thus, the Colorado Supreme Court passed on the opportunity to create a safe harbor for a lawyer's personal use of marijuana. Nevertheless, the Colorado State Bar Ethics Committee has indicated that it will not pursue disciplinary action against lawyers solely on the basis of their using marijuana, as long as that use is in compliance with Colorado law, and it does not result in impairment under Rule 1.1.

The state bar of Washington has followed a similar approach as Colorado's state bar toward a lawyer's personal use of marijuana. In 2015, its state bar issued an opinion stating that a lawyer "may purchase and consume marijuana consistently with I-502 and the CPPA to the same extent that non-lawyers may generally do so. In this context, we again see no substantial public purpose in considering conduct unrelated to the practice of law in which members of the public are free to engage a violation of the RPCs." Washington State Bar Association, Advisory Opinion 201501 (2015). However, in 2018, the Washington Supreme Court added the following comment to its version of Rule 1.2:

> *[18] Under Paragraph (d), a lawyer may counsel a client regarding Washington's marijuana laws and may assist a client in conduct that the lawyer reasonably believes is permitted by those laws. If Washington law conflicts with federal or tribal law, the lawyer shall also advise the client regarding the related federal or tribal law and policy. [Comment [18] adopted effective December 9, 2014; amended effective September 25, 2018.]*

Thus, the Washington Supreme Court, like the Colorado Supreme Court, passed on the opportunity to create affirm the state bar's advisory opinion as to a lawyer's personal use of marijuana, at the same time it affirmed the bar's safe harbor for lawyers assisting and counseling marijuana clients by adding comment 18 to Rule 1.2.

In conclusion, there is some support for the position that a lawyer's personal use of marijuana does not *per se* violate Rule 8.4, as long as such use is in compliance with state law, and the lawyer's use does not materially impair the lawyer's ability to represent the lawyer's clients (i.e., does not violate Rule 1.1). However, the state supreme courts and many bar associations seem to be reluctant to weigh in on the matter, so there remains a fair amount of uncertainty regarding a lawyer's personal use of marijuana.

§ 19-4 WHETHER LAWYERS VIOLATE THE RULES OF PROFESSIONAL RESPONSIBILITY IF THEY INVEST IN MARIJUANA-RELATED BUSINESSES

A related issue that arises under Rule 8.4 is whether lawyers may obtain an ownership interest in marijuana-related businesses. Here again, the authority is too limited to draw any firm conclusions, so lawyers would be wise to exercise caution.

As discussed in the previous section, the possession and distribution of marijuana is a crime under federal law; therefore, the lawyer-owner of a business that possesses or distributes marijuana arguably runs afoul of Rule 8.4's prohibition on criminal behavior that "*reflects adversely on the lawyer's honesty, trustworthiness or fitness as a lawyer*" under the language of Rule 8.4(b).

In some respects, this raises a more difficult ethical issue than a lawyer's personal use of marijuana, since it affects the public and is not a purely personal matter. And thus far, bar ethics committees do not seem eager to render opinions on the topic, probably because the issue is somewhat contentious. In Colorado, for example, a subcommittee of the Colorado Supreme Court Standing Rules Committee that was appointed to address possible rule changes pertaining to the legal use of marijuana recommended a new Rule 8.6 that would have immunized Colorado lawyers from discipline for activities that are legal under Colorado's marijuana laws, even if they are illegal under federal law. But the state's Office of Attorney Regulation Counsel opposed the proposed rule, arguing that "the integrity of the bar is diminished by allowing attorneys to cultivate or distribute significant amounts of marijuana in violation of federal law, even if lawful under the state constitution." The Colorado Supreme Court subsequently declined to adopt the new rule, even though the proposed rule itself did not specifically endorse attorney ownership of marijuana-related interests. Memorandum of Colorado Office of Atty. Regulation Counsel to Colorado Supreme Court Standing Rules Committee (April 26, 2013).

So far, there is still not a lot of authority on this issue. The state bar association that appears to have weighed in most definitively on the matter is the Washington State Bar's Committee on Professional Ethics, which stated that it saw no reason to distinguish lawyers from non-lawyers with respect to the ownership and operation of marijuana-related businesses. In Advisory Opinion 201501 (discussed also in § 18–3 above with respect to a lawyer's personal use), the Committee opined that:

> "[A] lawyer going into a business with a client that complies with [state marijuana laws] would not, without more, constitute either a 'criminal act that reflects adversely on the lawyer's honesty, trustworthiness or fitness as a lawyer in other respects,' RPC 8.4(b), or an 'act involving moral turpitude, or corruption, or any unjustified act of assault or other act which reflects disregard for the rule of law,' RPC 8.4(i)."

Washington State Bar Association, Advisory Opinion 201501 (2015). Thus, the Committee concluded that such conduct was not prohibited under Rule 8.4. (The Committee also noted, however, that a lawyer forming a marijuana-related business with a non-lawyer must comply with the conflict-of-interest requirements of Rule 1.8(a), just as it would with regard to any other type of business.)

Again, however, the Washington Supreme Court passed on the opportunity to validate the existence of a safe harbor for a lawyer's personal investment in marijuana-related businesses, at the same time it validated such a safe harbor for lawyers assisting and counseling marijuana clients by adding comment 18 to Rule 1.2. Thus, the court's silence on this matter creates some uncertainty as to how it would address a future disciplinary matter under Rule 8.4 if called upon to do so.

To date, only a handful of state bar associations and supreme courts have weighed in on the issue of a lawyer's personal investment in marijuana-related businesses. Two state bars have issued advisory opinions. The Maryland State Bar Association's Committee on Ethics issued a non-binding opinion in February 2016, concluding that Maryland attorneys are not prohibited by the Rules of Professional Conduct from owning a business interest in marijuana-related businesses. *See* Ethics Docket 2016–10. Conversely, in August 2016, Ohio's Board of Professional Conduct issued a nonbinding opinion concluding that a lawyer's investment in one or more marijuana-related businesses may implicate Rule 8.4. Opinion 2016–6. As noted in § 18–2, however, the Ohio Supreme Court later rejected the Board's opinion with respect to Rule 1.2, so it is not clear that the Board's opinion with respect to Rule 8.4 is the final word on the issue in Ohio.

Additionally, in 2019, the Nevada Supreme Court added a comment to its Rule 8.4, casting doubt on the propriety of personal ownership: "Because use, possession, and distribution of marijuana in any form still violates federal law, attorneys are advised that engaging in such conduct may result in federal prosecution and trigger discipline proceedings . . . ." Nev. R. P. C. 8.4, comment (2019).

In sum, there is limited authority as to the propriety of a lawyer's personal investment in marijuana-related business, and the limited decisions we have are not in agreement. Thus, in most states, the issue continues to generate significant uncertainty.

CHAPTER 20

TAXATION OF MARIJUANA-RELATED BUSINESSES

§ 20-1 INTRODUCTION

Under federal tax law, the expenses of legal marijuana businesses cannot be deducted. This represents a substantial tax burden on marijuana businesses, not applicable to other genres of businesses, including illegal ones.

Section 280E of the federal tax code denies all deductions incurred in connection with a business trafficking in a Schedule I or II controlled substance, in violation of federal or state law. As marijuana growers, dispensaries, and providers in marijuana legalizing states are the only such businesses operating openly in public view, they are primarily affected by this provision. In addition, tax professionals in those states have to be wary of performing services for marijuana-related businesses, as technically they may be liable for assisting an illegal enterprise under federal law. Although several states allow marijuana businesses to deduct their expenses from state income tax, the effect is relatively negligible compared with that of Internal Revenue Code § 280E.

State taxation of legal marijuana businesses in various forms—sales taxes, excise taxes, licensing fees—is a significant source of revenue. States face complex policy decisions in constructing marijuana tax regimes: what are the bases for taxes, what rates to apply, where on the seedling-to-sale chain to apply the taxes, and from whom to collect the taxes—producers, distributors, or customers.

Sections 20–2 and 20–3 explain the non-deductibility of expenses of marijuana businesses under federal tax law. Section 20–4 describes various challenges to marijuana tax law. Section 20–5 discusses whether tax professionals can service marijuana businesses. And § 20–6 describes state taxation of marijuana-related businesses and providers.

§ 20–2 DEDUCTIBILITY OF ILLEGAL EXPENSES AND LOSSES

The exceptional federal tax treatment now accorded marijuana businesses has its roots in earlier tax policies adverse to illegal commercial activity. Until 1981, Internal Revenue Code (I.R.C.) § 162(c), which disallows deductions for expenditures that are illegal, was the chief provision governing tax treatment of marijuana activity. Although still important, its significance for marijuana law has been overshadowed since 1981 by two developments: first, the enactment of I.R.C. § 280E, applying specifically to Schedule I and II drug businesses; and second, the legalization of marijuana businesses in more than half of the states, highlighting the importance of this provision.

Illegal income is taxable, the same as legal income. *James v. United States,* 366 U.S. 213, 221 (1961). However, as "the federal income tax is a tax on net income, not a sanction against wrongdoing,"

Commissioner v. Tellier, 383 U.S. 687, 691 (1966), the question arises as to how to determine the net income of illegal enterprises. Businesses are allowed to deduct necessary and ordinary expenses and business losses incurred in carrying on trade. I.R.C. § 162(a); § 165(a). However, § 162(c), enacted in 1969, Pub. L. No. 91–172, § 902(b)–(c), 83 Stat. 487, 710, prohibits deductions for illegal bribes, kickbacks, rebates, and other illegal payments. In addition, § 162(f) disallows any deductions for fines and penalties assessed to a taxpayer for violating any law. Deductions under other provisions of the federal tax code, such as business losses otherwise deductible under I.R.C. § 165(a), may also be disallowed under the common law doctrine that disallows deductions for expenses and for losses that would frustrate a sharply defined public policy.

For example, in *Holt v. Commissioner*, 69 T.C. 75, 76 (1977), *aff'd per curiam*, 611 F.2d 1160 (5th Cir. 1980), a taxpayer engaged in the business of selling marijuana was arrested while transporting marijuana from Mexico to Atlanta. Under the federal narcotics asset seizure provision, 21 U.S.C. § 881, assets connected to his drug trafficking were seized, including a pickup truck, a horse trailer, $2000 in cash, and one ton of marijuana. Although the taxpayer was assessed taxes on $780,000 of his marijuana receipts, he was denied deductions for the confiscated assets as either expenses, under § 162(c), or as business losses, as contrary to sharply defined public policy against marijuana use.

That same year, in *Holmes Enterprises, Inc. v. Commissioner*, 69 T.C. 114, 115 (1977), a legal business was denied a deduction after the owner, who was also the president of the corporation, was arrested for transporting 189 pounds of marijuana in a Jaguar car that was used primarily by the corporation. The car was forfeited to the government. The taxpayer argued that as a corporation it was a separate legal entity from the owner, with a strictly legitimate business in selling and servicing of electric motors. Thus it should be permitted a $4,711.42 prorated deduction from its corporate income tax due to the forfeiture of the Jaguar, primarily used for business. However, the Tax Court denied the corporation any deductions under § 165, again citing the doctrine disallowing deductions that would frustrate a sharply defined national policy against possession and sale of marijuana.

In contrast, in *Edmondson v. Commissioner*, 42 T.C.M. (CCH) 1533 (1981), a trafficker in the illegal business of selling amphetamines, cocaine, and marijuana was allowed to deduct the legal expenses of his drug business. The court held that although § 162(c)(2) prohibits the deduction of illegal expenses, it does not prohibit the deduction of legal expenses that are found to be ordinary and necessary under § 162(a), even if the enterprise is illegal. The rationale was apparently that Congress intended § 162(c) to be the exclusive source of denying a deduction for an illegal business expense, subsuming the doctrine of disallowing deductions for business expenses that would frustrate a sharply defined public policy. *See* 26 C.F.R. § 1.162–1(a). Thus, the trafficker was allowed to deduct the expenses of his office rent, scale, packaging, telephone, automobile, and the cost of the illegal drugs, all used in furtherance of selling controlled substances, as ordinary and necessary expenses of his trade.

While the frustration doctrine no longer applies to business expenses, the courts have held that it continues to apply to denying a deduction for business losses which would otherwise be deducted under § 165.

§ 20-3 TAX TREATMENT OF MARIJUANA BUSINESSES UNDER INTERNAL REVENUE CODE § 280E

Congress was outraged by the *Edmondson* decision and in response enacted the most significant tax legislation affecting marijuana businesses, I.R.C. § 280E, included in the Tax Equity and Fiscal Responsibility Act of 1982, Pub. L. No. 97–248, 96 Stat. 324. Section 280E prohibits deduction of all expenses, legal and illegal, of businesses unlawfully selling drugs controlled under Schedule I and II of the Controlled Substances Act:

> No deduction or credit shall be allowed for any amount paid or incurred during the taxable year in carrying on any trade or business if such trade or business (or the activities which comprise such trade or business) consists of trafficking in controlled substances (within the meaning of Schedule I and II of the Controlled Substances Act) which is prohibited by Federal law or the

> law of any State in which such trade or business is conducted.

The Senate Committee on Finance explained the reasoning for this provision:

> There is a sharply defined public policy against drug dealing. To allow drug dealers the benefit of business expense deductions at the same time that the U.S. and its citizens are losing billions of dollars per year to such persons is not compelled by the fact that such deductions are allowed to other legal enterprises. Such deductions should be disallowed on public policy grounds.

S. Rep. No. 97–494, vol. 1, at 309 (1982). As a result of this provision, legal marijuana businesses, unlike other businesses, legal and illegal, are not entitled to deduct their lawful ordinary and necessary expenses. These include such ordinary expenses as rent and utilities, salaries and wages, employee health insurance care and other employee benefits, taxes, fees, and licenses, office and store supplies, depreciation of equipment, professional legal and accounting services, transportation, security services, meals and entertainment, and marketing and advertising. Likewise, they cannot deduct assets seized by the federal government pursuant to the Controlled Substances Act, such as a raid by the Drug Enforcement Administration. *See Beck v. Commissioner*, 110 T.C.M. (CCH) 141 (2015) (denying a California medical marijuana dispensary deductions both for ordinary business and, under

§ 165, for $600,000 of marijuana the DEA seized in a raid).

Under tax regulations, an individual taxpayer cannot deduct the expense of buying medicinal marijuana as a medical deduction, as normally permitted under I.R.C. § 213(a)–(b), (d)(3). The Internal Revenue Service has ruled that the cost of buying marijuana for medical treatment is not deductible even if purchased under a physician's recommendation in a state that has legalized marijuana for medicinal purposes. Rev. Rul. 97–9, 1997–1 C.B. 77. Likewise federal tax-advantaged medical savings accounts, such as health savings accounts (HSAs), health reimbursement arrangements (HRAs), flexible spending arrangements (FSAs), and medical savings accounts (MSAs), cannot be used to purchase medically recommended marijuana.

When § 280E was enacted in 1981, it represented more of a symbolic statement by Congress in support of the War on Drugs than a significant piece of legislation, as illegal drug businesses, like most illegal businesses, do not typically file income taxes. Thus, the provisions of §§ 162(c) and 280E would only come into play when a criminal enterprise was uncovered, prosecuted, and audited by the Internal Revenue Service, whereupon the criminal taxpayer, already flushed into the open, might seek to minimize taxes due. There was little expectation in 1981 that narcotics businesses would be permitted to operate legally in the United States and thus would routinely file tax returns.

This changed in 1996, when California became the first state to legalize marijuana for medicinal purposes. Suddenly there was a business that, while illegal under federal law, openly filed taxes and would be eligible for deductions of legal expenses but for § 280E, which draws no distinction between states that have legalized marijuana and states that have not. As marijuana legalization has proliferated in the United States, many marijuana businesses now find themselves prohibited from taking any deductions for ordinary and necessary expenses deemed legal by the states in which they operate. Commentators have pointed out the anomalous tax situation in which marijuana businesses find themselves in comparison with strictly illegal enterprises. To take a hypothetical, a business which engages in an activity that is illegal under state law, such as gambling, can deduct the cost of its legal business expenses, but a marijuana business deemed legal by the state in which it operates could not deduct the expenses of paying rent for offices or wages to employees. The consequent tax burden on marijuana businesses is significant, for some even overwhelming.

There are further anomalies in § 280E. Although the provision applies to "trafficking" in drugs, "trafficking" has been given the broadest definition, requiring only that the business engage in commercial activity involving a drug, including dispensing medical marijuana. *See, e.g., Californians Helping to Alleviate Medical Problems (CHAMP) v. Commissioner*, 128 T.C. 173, 182 (2007) (defining "trafficking" under the Code as including the supplying of medical marijuana and rejecting any distinction in meaning from "buying and selling"); *Olive v. Commissioner*, 139 T.C. 19, 38 (2012), *aff'd*, 792 F.3d 1146 (9th Cir. 2015) (holding that a California medical marijuana dispensary's provision of medical marijuana pursuant to California law was "trafficking" within the meaning of § 280E).

Although § 280E denies otherwise legal deductions or credits to marijuana businesses, it allows legitimate capital expenditures of a marijuana business to be included in the cost of goods sold (COGS). This cost refers to the aggregate total of costs incurred by a business to produce a product or service, and is deducted from the sales price of the item for taxable income. The Senate Finance Report for the § 280E bill explained that:

> To preclude possible challenges on constitutional grounds, the adjustment to gross receipts with respect to effective costs of goods sold is not affected by this provision of the bill.

S. Rep. No. 97–494, vol. 1, at 309. The "possible challenges" are that the Sixteenth Amendment allows taxes on net income, not gross income. Income has been interpreted as receipts less cost of goods sold; return of capital is not taxed. In contrast, deductions have been interpreted as merely legislative policy; disallowing them does not cause an unconstitutional tax in excess of income. However, unlawful capital expenditures are excluded from the cost of goods sold because of the extension of § 162(c)(2) to capital expenditures by Regulation § 1.471–3(f). That regulation excludes illegal capital expenditures from being utilized in determining gain or losses.

Thus, marijuana businesses can include certain legal expenditures in their cost of goods sold and thereby reduce the profit recognized on the sale. Most taxpayers prefer to maximize categorization of their expenditures as business expenses, to benefit from a current deduction. But because § 280E disallows deductions and credits for ordinary expenses, marijuana businesses have an incentive to categorize as much of their lawful expenditures as possible as capital expenditures, even though the tax benefit is postponed until the time of sale.

The rules governing which cost of goods sold can be capitalized as expenditures and the method for accounting for inventory of marijuana businesses are complex and governed by I.R.C. §§ 471 and 263A, as interpreted by the Internal Revenue Service ruling, C.C.A. 2015–04–011 (Jan. 23, 2015). In a sentence, certain expenses relating to producing or purchasing marijuana, such as the cost of seeds, seedlings, and growing lights (but not those costs relating to marketing or sale of marijuana) can be capitalized depending on which accounting method is employed. Producers can choose a more advantageous method of calculating COGS, but to qualify as a producer, a seller must exercise complete control of the marijuana it cultivates from bud to sale. *Patients Mutual Assistance Collective Corp. (d.b.a. Harborside Health Center) v. Commissioner*, No. 19–73078 (9th Cir. 2021). In addition, marijuana seized from a legal dispensary by the DEA and forfeited cannot be characterized as a cost of goods sold. *See, e.g.*, *Beck v. Commissioner*, 110 T.C.M. (CCH) 141 (2015).

Some recent cases arising from large California dispensaries with various lines of business and substantial revenues have clarified when some deductions are not excluded by § 280E. The general rule is that, although expenses of conducting a marijuana business cannot be deducted, a company may be able to deduct expenses allocated to a different line of services, so long as it constitutes a separate trade or business. For example, deductions by a nonprofit California health provider that supplied legally prescribed marijuana to terminally ill patients were disallowed under § 280E, but the same dispensary could deduct expenses for a second, distinct line of caregiving business substantially independent of its marijuana dispensing. *Californians Helping to Alleviate Medical Problems (CHAMP) v. Commissioner*, 128 T.C. 173 (2007). Expenses are then allocated between the second line of business, with deductions allowed, and the marijuana business, with expenses subject to § 280E and not deductible.

There is an ongoing controversy as to whether another activity of marijuana business qualifies as a separate line of business for purposes of § 280E. Simply labeling caregiving a separate line of business did not qualify a dispensary to deduct caregiving expenses if the caregiving included dispensing marijuana, even as a minimal part of the caregiving activity. *Olive v. Commissioner*, 792 F.3d 1146 (9th Cir. 2015) (holding that a vapor room with amenities and communal activities for AIDS and cancer patients receiving medical marijuana was not a separate line of business for a marijuana dispensary, and confirming the lower court's determination that they share a "close and inseparable organizational and economic relationship"). A business is also precluded under § 280E from taking a deduction for incidental non-marijuana services it provides if dispensing marijuana is its only or primary source of revenue. *Id.* at 1149; *see also Canna Care, Inc. v. Commissioner*, 110 T.C.M. (CCH) 408 (2015).

§ 20–4 CHALLENGES TO MARIJUANA TAX PROVISIONS

The seemingly harsh application of federal tax laws to marijuana businesses has given rise to several legal challenges. The most obvious challenge is that marijuana businesses have been legalized in many states, a situation not contemplated when § 280E was enacted. So, for example, nonprofit Harborside Health, the largest medical marijuana dispensary in the world, contested in Tax Court in 2016 a $2.4 million notice of deficiency for disallowed deductions on the grounds that Congress did not intend for § 280E to apply to legal marijuana businesses, which did not exist at the time of passage. A similar argument was rejected in *Olive v. Commissioner*, 792 F.3d 1146, 1150 (9th Cir. 2015) ("That Congress might not have imagined what some states would do in future years has no bearing on our analysis. It is common for statutes to apply to new situations."). It was again decisively rejected in *Patients Mutual Assistance Collective Corp. (d.b.a.*

Harborside Health Center) v. Commissioner, No. 19–73078 (9th Cir. 2021).

The decision by the Department of Justice not to interfere with state legalization regimes also was held to have no bearing on the application of § 280E. *Canna Care, Inc. v. Commissioner*, 110 T.C.M. (CCH) 408 (2015) (applying the definition of "trafficking" as any buying or selling of marijuana to nonprofit dispensaries, even if in compliance with state nonprofit and medical marijuana laws, and regardless of any change in Department of Justice marijuana enforcement policies). Also unlikely to succeed are current court challenges to § 280E under the theory that Congress has prohibited the Department of Justice from expending funds to prevent states from implementing their medical marijuana laws, or that denying marijuana businesses deductions available to other businesses violates the Equal Protection Clause.

Although the CSA prohibits selling drug paraphernalia, 21 U.S.C. § 863(a), such items do not fall under the definition of a "controlled substance." Thus, a business selling drug paraphernalia is not precluded from deducting necessary and ordinary expenses under § 280E.

A marijuana business cannot refuse to file income taxes under the theory that the Fifth Amendment protects it from incriminating itself as an illegal business under federal law. It has long been established that the constitutional protection against self-incrimination does not excuse a taxpayer engaged in illegal activities from the requirement to file a tax return, even though filing entails certain risks of prosecution. *See United States v. Sullivan*, 274 U.S. 259, 263–64 (1927).

The IRS has ruled that a non-profit entity that distributes medical marijuana in compliance with state law cannot qualify for federal § 501(c)(3) status because it is illegal under federal law. I.R.S. Private Letter Ruling 201224036 (June 15, 2012). Likewise, a proposal that marijuana sellers can avoid the § 280E disallowance of deductions by forming tax-exempt § 501(c)(4) organizations—social welfare charities—is unrealistic. While a nonprofit, medical marijuana business actively involved in community improvement could conceivably satisfy some requirements to be a § 501(c)(4) social welfare organization, it is unlikely that the IRS will find any social benefits of a marijuana business sufficient to override its violation of federal law. However, the IRS has approved tax-exempt status for several marijuana churches, including the Indianapolis First Church of Cannabis and the Colorado Green Faith Ministry.

Because of banking restrictions, most marijuana businesses are conducted on a cash basis. However, they are subject to audit for an apparent widespread failure to file Form 8300, *Report of Cash Payments Over $10,000 Received in a Trade or Business*.

States are not allowed to apply a punitive tax on the possession of marijuana when that possession has been punished under the criminal law. For example, members of the Kurth family had been arrested in 1987 for violating Montana's criminal marijuana laws and forfeited a large number of marijuana plants, harvested marijuana, and paraphernalia. The Kurths were convicted and incarcerated. Montana then applied a $900,000 tax on the Kurths under the Montana Dangerous Tax Act, which imposed a tax on defendants arrested for possession of dangerous drugs. In *Dep't of Revenue of Montana v. Kurth Ranch*, 511 U.S. 767 (1994), the U.S. Supreme Court in a 5 to 4 decision held that taxing the Kurths for actions for which they were criminally punished was punitive in nature and thus violated the Fifth Amendment prohibition against double jeopardy.

§ 20–5 TAX PROFESSIONALS AND THE MARIJUANA BUSINESS

Tax professionals servicing marijuana businesses need to be wary of both state disciplinary rules and federal prosecution, even in marijuana legalizing states. State accounting boards require "good moral character" of accountants practicing in their state. As of now it is a somewhat unresolved question whether providing accounting services to a marijuana business indicates bad moral character as a violation of federal law. Seven state boards of accounting have issued guidelines for certified public accountants servicing marijuana businesses: Colorado, Connecticut, Florida, Maryland, Nevada, Oregon, and Washington. *See* American Institute of Certified Public Accountants (AICPA), "An Issue Brief on State Marijuana Laws and the CPA Profession" (Jan. 8, 2016). All seven states have advised CPAs that servicing marijuana businesses does not indicate bad moral character and thus require disciplinary action against them. Although the accounting boards of the remaining states have not yet issued individual advisories on this matter, it can be presumed that they would take a similar position that regulatory actions not be taken against a CPA who advises a marijuana business in compliance with state law. This is further evidenced by the report, "Providing services to businesses in the marijuana industry: A sample of current board positions," published by the National Association of State Boards of Accountancy (NASBA). In this report, thirteen of fourteen state boards indicated they would not discipline a Certified Public Accountant for providing services to a marijuana business that was in compliance with state law.

Nevertheless, accounting boards have advised CPAs of the uncertainty growing out of the dichotomy between state and federal law. For example, in its November 2015 advisory, the Nevada State Board of Accountancy reminded accountants licensed by the state "that the federal government views such activity as a federal criminal offense. The Board's position does not negate the possibility that disciplinary action may be taken by the Board should a licensee be found guilty of a federal criminal act."

The risk of federal prosecution is real, even though not probable, and shared by all professionals working with marijuana businesses. A person who "aids, abets, [or] counsels" the commission of a federal crime can be found criminally liable for that crime. 18 U.S.C. § 2(a). Providing tax and accounting services to a marijuana business can conceivably be found to be aiding and abetting a federal crime. Tax professionals could conceivably be subject to money laundering and mail fraud offenses as well. Preparing a tax return for a marijuana business assists the taxpayers in fulfilling a legal requirement, although that in itself does not immunize that activity from prosecution. An accountant representing a client on a criminal matter would not seem liable to prosecution. Advising the business on economic and commercial matters, however, could conceivably be characterized as aiding, abetting, or counseling a federal crime.

§ 20-6 STATE TAXATION OF MARIJUANA BUSINESSES

Several states which have legalized marijuana have attempted to ameliorate the adverse effects of § 280E on marijuana businesses operating in their states as it relates to state income taxes. For example, Colorado Tax Form 104 allows marijuana businesses to claim a state tax deduction on expenses that would otherwise be deductible as business expenses on the federal return but for § 280E. California also allows medical marijuana businesses to deduct ordinary and business expenses from corporate income taxes; however it forbids deductions on the personal income tax to individuals found in a court proceeding to be engaged in drug (and marijuana) trafficking. Cal. Rev. & Tax. Code § 17282. In 2010, the legislatures of Arizona, California, Colorado, and Massachusetts petitioned the Internal Revenue Service to stop enforcing

§ 280E in any states that have legalized marijuana. The Internal Revenue Service refused, stating that it was the prerogative of Congress only to amend § 280E.

One of the reasons that states have legalized marijuana has been projections of substantial revenue for state treasuries through taxation. Indeed states have realized substantial revenues for marijuana, although not always as much as projected. For example, Colorado has run marijuana revenue shortfalls due to underestimating the lower revenues derived from taxing medical marijuana as opposed to the higher taxes levied on recreational marijuana sales (although some marijuana revenue projections in Colorado have been exceeded). States earmark marijuana revenues for popular purposes such as school funding, environmental repair, and public health spending. However, as state spending is largely fungible, these earmarks serve mostly a political purpose.

The overall projections for the legal marijuana market in the United States are vast, representing huge tax potentials. The legal marijuana market was estimated to be between $11 billion and $13.7 billion in 2019 and to grow to $39 billion by 2023. The majority of these revenues is represented by recreational marijuana sales, taxed at a higher rate than medical marijuana.

Taxing marijuana at the state level is a complex public policy undertaking, calibrating state goals as to marijuana regulation, and economic forecasts as to revenue enhancement, tax compliance, and the effects on marijuana pricing. Many of the forecasts are based on past experiences and policies relating to the taxation of alcohol and tobacco.

Imposing taxes is only one of the ways that state governments can raise revenues from legalization, but it is the most important means. Revenue can also be raised by applying fees to marijuana businesses, such as application fees for annual licensing and renewal, and various administrative fees governing change of ownership, location, and trade names. Colorado, for example, charges application fees of $5000 for retail marijuana stores, cultivation facilities, and products manufacturers. Initial license fees for retail marijuana stores are $3000, and renewal fees are $3000. Transfer of ownership fees for new owners are $2000. Washington application fees are substantially lower: $250 for marijuana producers, processors, and retailers, and $1381 in annual fees for licensing issuance and renewal. States can also charge licensing fees to consumers. For example, Michigan charges patients $40 to apply to its medical marijuana program. Revenue from such fees is used to cover the costs of administering and regulating marijuana activity.

As to taxes, marijuana is subject to state sales tax but usually at a higher rate. For example, the Colorado general sales tax rate is 2.9%, but 15% for retail marijuana. Washington's general sales tax rate is 6.5%, but 37% for retail-level marijuana (subsuming its state excise tax). In addition, local governments can apply general and special sales taxes to marijuana. Numerous California localities have enacted sales taxes at various rates. And Denver adds a 5.5% sales special tax in addition to its local sales tax of 4.81%.

An excise tax is applied to specific items such as cigarettes or gasoline, and is an indirect tax to consumers. It is in addition to whatever sales tax or value added tax is applied generally to goods sold. Most legalization states impose some kind of excise tax, at least for non-medical marijuana. For example, Washington originally levied its excise tax on marijuana producers, processors, and retailers at 25%. Beginning July 1, 2015, the tax was incorporated into the 37% marijuana sales tax. Colorado imposes a 15% excise tax, and 15% retail tax, although it exempts marijuana purchased for medicinal reasons. There is momentum to levy marijuana taxes as ad valorem excise taxes. For example, in the November 2020 general election, three out of the four marijuana legalization measures that were approved (Arizona, Montana, and South Dakota) also imposed an ad valorem excise tax on retail marijuana.

The question of whether to tax medical marijuana is a thorny one. Most states exempt prescription drugs from general sales tax, but not nonprescription drugs. Marijuana is not a prescription drug, as it is a Schedule I drug that is not approved by the FDA. Excise taxes are usually applied not only to raise revenue but to discourage the use of a harmful substance, such as alcohol or tobacco. But it is not clear that the use of medical marijuana should be discouraged when recommended by a physician. In any event, most recreational states impose lesser sales taxes on medical marijuana than on recreational marijuana. Colorado, for example, subjects medical marijuana to its standard 2.9% sales tax but not to the 15% marijuana retail tax. As a result, medical marijuana cards are valuable, even in states that have legalized marijuana for all purposes.

Taxes can be applied to different bases. There are an almost endless range of possibilities, many of which have already been applied by various California municipalities. The most common bases are to tax marijuana according to its weight or its price (ad valorem tax). In addition marijuana can be taxed by potency, usually calculated by the quantity of THC; by square footage of growing space; or even by an electrical add-on tax that calculates the use of electricity in a home beyond normal use (using excess electricity as a proxy for indoor lighting for marijuana plants).

Taxes can also be levied at multiple stages in the seedling-to-sale delivery chain. States impose taxes on the producers and growers of marijuana, collect additional taxes from the processors and commercial distributors of marijuana, again from the stores and dispensaries that retail marijuana, and finally from the customers who buy and consume marijuana, earning revenue at each level of the industry.

Complex economic calculations contribute to determining the rates at which marijuana is taxed. For example, different rates can affect the price and demand of marijuana, incentives to evade taxes, and aggregate revenue to the state. Of particular concern is the effect of steep taxes that could revive the underground black markets that legalization was intended to eliminate. Public policy considerations usually indicate that medical marijuana is taxed at a lower rate than retail marijuana, if taxed at all. Varying tax rates can be applied to various forms of marijuana—herbal, edibles, and extracts, and can also be applied to marijuana flowers, leaves, and whole plants.

This variety of taxes can be differently named by state and difficult to calculate, making state-by-state comparisons cumbersome. When aggregated, these taxes can represent a substantial percentage of the cost of the marijuana item, referred to as the effective tax rate. For example the total effective tax rate for marijuana sales in Washington State is about 47%. The overall tax rate in Colorado is estimated at about 33%. Colorado collected $387,480,110 in taxes and fees in 2020. From when Colorado began collecting tax revenue on marijuana sales in February 2014, to end of 2020, Colorado reaped almost $1.6 billion in taxes on nearly $9.8 billion in total sales. Washington collected $469 million in taxes in 2020.

CHAPTER 21

ADDITIONAL CIVIL ISSUES

§ 21-1 INTRODUCTION

The previous chapters in this part of the book (i.e., Chapters 16–20) discuss some of the principal practical obstacles that states have had to deal with when they legalize marijuana for medical and/or recreational purposes. These involve: banking issues, employment issues, issues related to impaired driving, ethical issues faced by attorneys representing marijuana-related businesses, and taxation issues. These issues are by no means the only legal issues that arise from legalization efforts, however. The divergence between federal law and state law in states that have legalized marijuana—whether medical or recreational—raises a number of other interesting and challenging legal issues as well. And the law is still in a state of flux with respect to many of these issues.

This chapter briefly discusses five of the issues that seem to be generating the most controversy. Section 21–2 discusses insurance issues that are created by the divergence between state and federal law. Section 21–3 discusses real-estate issues that arise from legalization. Section 21–4 discusses the difficulty marijuana-related businesses have faced when they have tried to obtain bankruptcy protection. Section 21–5 discusses issues that arise in the context of family law, specifically child custody proceedings. And § 21–6 discusses trademark issues.

§ 21-2 INSURANCE ISSUES

The conflict between state and federal law regarding the legal status of marijuana has created problems for marijuana-related businesses in obtaining insurance to cover their operations. Many insurers have been reluctant to enter the market for fear they will be found complicit in the violation of federal criminal laws, similar to the types of fears many in the banking industry have expressed with regard to servicing marijuana-related businesses. And in June 2015, the largest insurer of marijuana-related businesses, Lloyd's of London, announced that it would be leaving the market and originating no new policies. Thus, it is often difficult for marijuana-related businesses in states that legalize marijuana to obtain adequate insurance, and such insurance tends to be more costly than for comparable non-marijuana businesses.

In addition, insurers that do provide coverage to marijuana-related businesses have sometimes taken an aggressive approach toward the payment of claims made under the policies. Insurers have sought to avoid claims by arguing that marijuana-related businesses fall within certain policy exclusions, such as an "illegal acts" exclusion in a commercial liability policy. And some have even tried to avoid paying policy claims based on the argument that the insurance agreement itself is void under the contract doctrine of illegality, notwithstanding the insurer was fully aware of the nature of the company's business when it entered into the agreement.

In *GreenEarth Wellness Center, LLC v. Atain Specialty Insurance Co.*, 163 F. Supp. 3d 821 (D. Colo. 2016), the United States District Court for the District of Colorado heard a case involving a marijuana-related business that was operating a commercial cultivation facility, and had sustained a loss from smoke and ash from a nearby wildfire. GreenEarth made a claim under its policy for damage to its living plants, as well as to its inventory of already harvested marijuana. The insurer denied the claim.

The court sided with the insurer with respect to the living plants, holding that they were not covered by the policy because they fell within the "growing crops" exclusion of the policy. However, the court rejected the insurer's argument that the already harvested marijuana in GreenEarth's inventory fell within an exclusion for "contraband, or property used in the course of illegal transportation or trade," notwithstanding the illegal status of marijuana under federal law. The court found that the "contraband" exclusion was rendered ambiguous by the federal government's policy of limited enforcement of the CSA under the Obama administration, and further found that the parties intended the policy to apply to already harvested marijuana and other inventory. Thus, the court awarded damages to GreenEarth for the value of the harvested marijuana. The court also rejected the insurer's argument that the whole policy was unenforceable as against public policy. The court held that the insurer entered into the policy of its own will, knowingly and intelligently, and was therefore obligated to comply with the terms of the policy.

In so holding, the District Court expressly declined to follow an earlier case from the United States District Court for the District of Hawaii, *Tracy v. USAA Insurance Co.*, No. 11–00487, 2012 WL 928186 (March 16, 2012). In *Tracy,* the plaintiff, an individual who had a valid license to grow marijuana for medical use, submitted a claim to her property insurer after 12 marijuana plants were stolen from her property. The policy covered, among other things, losses caused by the theft of trees, shrubs, and other plants. The insurer denied coverage, and the plaintiff filed an action for breach of contract and bad-faith denial of her claim. The court found that plaintiff likely had a lawful and insurable interest in the marijuana plants under state law, since the plaintiff's use was in accordance with Hawaii's medical-marijuana statute. Nevertheless, the court denied the plaintiff's claim under the policy, finding that enforcement of the insurance policy in this circumstance would be contrary to federal law and federal public policy. The court held that, under the doctrine of contract illegality, courts may decline to enforce contracts that are illegal or contrary to public policy, and that this rule applies where the enforcement of the contract would violate federal law as well, including the CSA.

Thus, the courts appear to be somewhat divided with respect to the enforceability of insurance contracts pertaining to marijuana. One solution to the uncertainty would be for state legislatures to clarify this issue. Oregon, for example, passed a statute in 2016 that provides that contracts are not unenforceable by virtue of their being contrary to federal law. Or. Rev. Stat. Ann. § 475B.535. There is no guarantee, however, that federal courts will defer to such statutes, given that the illegality arises under federal law, not state law.

Thus, at present, the enforceability of insurance contracts covering marijuana-related businesses remains a somewhat murky issue. As a result, marijuana-related businesses continue to have a difficult time obtaining adequate insurance coverage. *See generally*, Francis J. Mootz, III and Jason Horst, *Cannabis and Insurance*, 23 Lewis & Clark L. Rev. 893 (2019).

§ 21-3 REAL ESTATE ISSUES

Another area of law that has been affected by legalization efforts at the state level is real-estate law. For example, marijuana-related businesses have faced some unique issues in dealing with landlords who may not be favorably disposed to leasing business spaces to businesses trafficking in marijuana, even though the businesses are operating legally under state law. Likewise, landlords may not like the idea of tenants smoking marijuana or cultivating marijuana plants in apartments and rented houses.

Furthermore, beyond personal objections to such use, landlords can potentially face significant problems with renting space to marijuana-related businesses and individual users. For one thing, the neighbors of marijuana-related businesses and individuals using or cultivating marijuana in rental units may object. As a result, landlords may find it more difficult to rent adjacent properties. And they may even face the prospects of nuisance lawsuits. Additionally, there is an issue with potential property damage. Smoking, for example, may cause damage to the premises, and in the case of cultivation, the high humidity created by grow operations may lead to mold issues or other property damage. In the case of marijuana dispensaries, which generally operate on a cash only basis, there is also the danger of crimes such as burglaries and robberies.

Most significantly, landlords that lease spaces to marijuana-related businesses may legitimately fear that they will subject themselves to potential criminal liability, since marijuana trafficking remains illegal under federal law. This raises the possibility that landlords could be subject to aiding and abetting the commission of a felony under 21 U.S.C. § 846. It also raises the possibility that the property could be subject to the civil forfeiture penalty under 21 U.S.C. § 881(a), which can apply to real property as well as personal property. (For more on these issues, *see* Chapter 6.)

As a result of these types of concerns, some landlords have taken an aggressive posture toward tenants that traffic in marijuana. The landlord can include a lease provision that prohibits marijuana use or distribution, and make the violation of such a provision a material default under the lease, entitling the landlord to take possession. Often, however, the landlord does not know of the planned marijuana use, or does not take a proactive step to include such language in the lease. In those cases landlords have tried several arguments to avoid their obligations under the lease, once they discover that a tenant is involved with marijuana.

One approach has been to seek an equitable remedy under the illegality doctrine in contract law, which allows courts to refuse to enforce contracts if they pursue illegal ends or otherwise act against public policy interests. Landlords have argued that, since marijuana is illegal under federal law, a lease made for the purpose of running a marijuana-related business is an illegal contract. Since the illegality doctrine is an equitable doctrine, however, this remedy requires that the landlord have "clean hands" itself, which can be problematic if the landlord knew of the intended use at the time the lease was entered into. Furthermore, since illegality is an equitable doctrine, it requires courts to balance the public policy rationale for not enforcing the contract not only against the contrary public policy concern, but also against the injustice that may result in an individual case from not enforcing the contract. *See, e.g., Green Cross Medical, Inc. v. Gally,* 395 P.3d 302 (Ariz. Ct. App. 2017) (holding that prospective marijuana dispensary could bring action against landlord for cancellation of lease notwithstanding federal law criminalizing marijuana because, among other things, "refusing to enforce such contracts would undermine the medical marijuana program the voters approved").

Aside from the legal doctrine of illegality, a related argument landlords have raised is that marijuana-related businesses that rent spaces may be in violation of a common prohibition in leases for "illegal activity." Such clauses allow the landlord to terminate its lease obligation if the tenant engages in illegal activities. Again, since marijuana is illegal under federal law, a colorable argument can be made that this provision applies, even if marijuana is legal under state law.

Another possible provision that landlords may try to avail themselves of is the "no smoking" clause found in many leases. On its face, this clause is ambiguous because it is not clear that smoking includes both tobacco and marijuana, and some leases may even refer specifically to tobacco use, which would seem to preclude its applicability to marijuana smoking. Extreme smoke and odors may even be sufficient to create a legal nuisance, justifying the landlord in terminating the lease.

One possible defense that some individual renters have relied on is the "reasonable accommodation" defense under the Americans with Disabilities Act and comparable state laws, similar to the type of defense discussed in Chapter 17 concerning employment issues. As discussed in that chapter, employees have sometimes argued that medical use of marijuana constitutes a disability, and that employers are required to make reasonable accommodations to allow such use. As discussed in that chapter, however, the courts have generally rejected that argument in the employment context.

And while there is less case law in the area of real-estate law, what law there is seems to indicate that courts will likely reject the reasonable accommodation argument in the real-estate context as well.

In *Forest City Residential Management, Inc. v. Beasley*, 71 F. Supp. 3d 715 (2014), for example, the United States District Court for the Eastern District of Michigan held that the tenant in that case was not entitled to use medical marijuana to treat her multiple sclerosis under her HUD lease. The court followed the memorandum of HUD General Counsel in holding that neither the Fair Housing Act nor the Rehabilitation Act of 1973 required the landlord to grant the defendant a reasonable accommodation to use marijuana in violation of federal law. Such a requirement, it noted, would go against Congress' mission to provide drug-free, federally assisted housing. The tenant is not a qualified individual with a disability, the court held, because marijuana is a drug that is illegal under federal law and therefore is not entitled to the protections of federal anti-discrimination laws. Notably, however, the court went on to hold that it would not issue a declaration as requested by the landlord, which would declare that the use, possession, or distribution of marijuana was cause for the plaintiff to evict tenants and was not in violation of the Michigan Medical Marihuana Act. Thus, there are still issues to be resolved with respect to what protections, if any, are provided to tenants by state laws legalizing medical marijuana.

In addition to landlord-tenant issues, marijuana legalization has raised other important issues of real estate law as well, most notably state and local zoning laws. *See generally* Lisa L. Mead and Adam J. Costa, *Zoning for Medical Marijuana: Approaches and Considerations*, 60 Bos. B. J. 26 (Spring 2016). For example, local laws may restrict where marijuana-related businesses are allowed to operate (e.g., not within 1000 feet of a school), and state laws may allow individual municipalities to opt out of the legalization scheme, insofar as they do not have to allow medical marijuana-related businesses within their jurisdictions. (For more on zoning issues, *see* Chapter 13, § 13–4.)

§ 21–4 BANKRUPTCY ISSUES

One of the most difficult challenges facing marijuana-related businesses is their inability to obtain relief from creditor claims in United States Bankruptcy Court. While the number of reported decisions on this issue is limited, to date it appears that the federal bankruptcy courts have consistently refused to allow relief to marijuana-related businesses under the bankruptcy code. These courts have relied upon various theories, including the equitable doctrine of unclean hands, as well as the statutory requirement of good faith, to justify dismissing the petitions of marijuana-related businesses.

Most notably, a United States bankruptcy appellate panel of the Tenth Circuit upheld the dismissal of a bankruptcy petition by the United

States Bankruptcy Court for the District of Colorado in the case *In re Arenas*, 535 B.R. 845, B.A.P (10th Cir., Aug. 21, 2015). The petitioner in that matter, Frank Arenas, obtained a license to grow and dispense medical marijuana in Colorado. He leased a building that he owned to third parties, who dispensed medical marijuana from it. The petitioner filed a Chapter 7 bankruptcy petition after the tenants obtained a judgment against him in state-court litigation. The petitioner later attempted to convert the Chapter 7 case to a Chapter 13 case, and the United States trustee objected, asking the bankruptcy court to dismiss the case. The bankruptcy court found that, even though petitioner's business was legal under state law, it violated the CSA, and was therefore illegal under federal law. The court accordingly denied the motion to convert the petition to a Chapter 13 case, but also concluded the debtors could not receive Chapter 7 relief, because engaging in federal criminal conduct demonstrated a lack of good faith that would bar confirmation of their Chapter 13 plan, and also constituted cause to dismiss their Chapter 7 case. The appellate panel upheld the bankruptcy court's decision, finding that the bankruptcy trustee would not be able to administer the petitioner's estate because doing so would constitute a federal crime. Thus, administering the bankruptcy would require the trustee to either violate federal law or abandon the petitioner's assets, both of which created good cause to dismiss the bankruptcy petition under § 707(a) of the Bankruptcy Code.

The appellate panel's decision in *Arenas* is consistent with the decisions of other bankruptcy courts that have considered the applicability of federal bankruptcy laws to marijuana-related businesses. For example, in a 2015 case before the U.S. Bankruptcy Court for the District of Arizona, *In re Medpoint Management, LLC*, 528 B.R. 178 (Bkrtcy. Ariz. 2015), a group of creditors filed an involuntary Chapter 7 petition against Medpoint, a licensed marijuana dispensary, seeking to put Medpoint in bankruptcy proceedings. The court, however, granted Medpoint's motion to dismiss the petition, finding that the unclean hands defense prevented the creditors from bringing their action, since they had voluntarily entered into business transactions with Medpoint, knowing that Medpoint derived its revenues from activities that were illegal under federal law. The court held that it would not enter an order for relief that would result in the bankruptcy trustee's necessarily having to violate federal law in carrying out the trustee's duties under the bankruptcy code.

Likewise, in *Rent-Rite Super Kegs West, Ltd.*, 484 B.R. 799 (Bkrtcy. Colo. 2012), the U.S. Bankruptcy Court for the District of Colorado refused to sustain the Chapter 11 bankruptcy petition filed by a debtor that derived 25% of its revenues from leasing warehouse space to tenants who were engaged in the business of growing marijuana, even though the activities were legal under state law. The court noted that even if Rent-Rite was never prosecuted under the CSA, its business operations violated federal criminal law. Therefore, it held, unless Congress changes federal law, a federal bankruptcy court cannot enforce protections of the Bankruptcy Code in support of a debtor whose activities constituted a continuing federal crime. *See also In re Malul*, 614 B.R. 699 (Bkrtcy. Colo. 2020) (denying petitioner's attempt to re-open case to include assets relating to marijuana business and observing that "participants in the marijuana industry will continue to experience difficulty and uncertainty in predicting the outcome of any particular marijuana-related bankruptcy case unless and until Congress provides a legislative solution to the divergent federal and state drug laws").

Thus, it appears that, barring legislative action by Congress, federal bankruptcy courts will not allow marijuana-related businesses to avail themselves of the protections of the Bankruptcy Code. As a result, marijuana-related businesses that are unable to pay their debtors will not be able to restructure their obligations and continue operating the way that other businesses are allowed to do, adding to the difficulty of owning and operating a marijuana-related business in states that have legalized marijuana.

§ 21-5 CHILD CUSTODY ISSUES

Another area of the law where marijuana has caused some confusion is child custody. Like alcohol use, a parent's marijuana use can play a factor in a court's determination as to the best interests of the children, particularly if it rises to the level of drug abuse. The uncertain legal status of marijuana, and the conflict between federal and state law in marijuana legalization states, have added to the potential for confusion.

Traditionally, a parent's use of marijuana, even if illegal under state law, has not served as an absolute bar to custodial rights. In *Barton v. Hirshberg*, 767 A.2d 874 (Ct. Spec. App. Md. 2001), for example, the parties entered into a custody agreement, whereby the wife had principal physical custody, while they shared joint legal custody. Subsequent the husband, unhappy with the agreement, filed a complaint seeking custody. The wife filed a counter-petition, seeking full custody herself. After hearing testimony on a variety of issues pertaining to parental fitness, the trial court awarded joint legal custody, and it gave the wife primary physical custody. As part of the proceeding, the issue of the husband's marijuana use came up, but the trial court ruled that it did not render him unfit as a parent. The Court of Appeals upheld this finding, holding that while it could not condone the husband's illegal use of marijuana, such use did not operate to automatically disqualify him as a fit parent. In making this determination, the Court of Appeals noted that the husband's marijuana use never occurred in the presence of the son, that it had been infrequent, and that there was no evidence that the husband had been under the influence of marijuana while caring for the son. Thus, it held that the trial court did not err in its evaluation of the best interests of the child.

To say that the parent's marijuana use does not automatically disqualify the parent, however, is not to say that marijuana use is irrelevant. Even in states that allow marijuana use legally, substance abuse is a factor that courts will generally take into account in determining the best interests of the child, particularly if there is evidence that it affects the emotional or physical well-being of the child. In *Co v. Matson*, 313 P.3d 521 (Alaska 2013), for example, the Alaska Supreme Court upheld an order of the trial court awarding sole custody to the mother. During the divorce trial, one of the factors the trial court had relied upon was the father's use of marijuana. The trial court noted that evidence of substance abuse affecting the well-being of the child was one of the statutory factors courts were required to consider in determining the best interests of the child. And it found that the father's regular marijuana use and the role of marijuana in his life weighed against awarding custody to the father. The Supreme Court upheld the trial court's order, holding that the trial court did not err in finding that the father's admitted marijuana use had a negative effect on the emotional well-being of the children, in light of evidence presented at trial of how his marijuana use had adversely affected the children in the past.

Thus, courts tend to analyze a parent's marijuana use on a case-by-case basis in custody matters. If there is evidence that the marijuana use adversely affects the child's physical or emotional well-being, then a court will likely take that factor into account in determining custody, just as it would if evidence that a parent's abuse of alcohol was adversely affecting the child's well-being. The effect on custodial rights therefore depends less on the legal status of marijuana in a given state than on the effect on the child in the particular circumstances at issue. However, the law is still uncertain as to what extent the legal status of marijuana should have a bearing on the best-interests determination. And the answer in any given state turns in part on the precise wording of that state's law.

In some states, statutory law provides protection for parents who use medical marijuana legally in accordance with state law. In Michigan, for example, s state statute requires a clear evidentiary showing of potential harm to the child in order to deny custody or visitations:

> "(c) A person shall not be denied custody or visitation of a minor for acting in accordance with this act, unless the person's behavior is such that it creates an unreasonable danger to the minor that can be *clearly articulated and substantiated*." (emphasis added)

M.C.L 333.26424, § 4(c).

Likewise, in Pennsylvania, a state statute provides that the court cannot base custody determinations solely on the basis of medical marijuana use:

> "(c) Custody determination—
>
> The fact that an individual is certified to use medical **marijuana** and acting in accordance with this act shall not by itself be considered by a court in a custody proceeding. In determining the best interest of a child with respect to

> custody, the provisions of 23 Pa.C.S. Ch. 53 (relating to child custody) shall apply."

35 Pa. Stat. Ann. 10231.21039(c).

In *H.R. v. C.P.*, 224 A.3d 729 (Pa. Super. Ct. 2019), the court interpreted this provision in a custody case in which the father sought increased visitation time. The trial judge found that the father's abuse of marijuana posed a danger to the child, based on credible testimony from the mother, including testimony that the father had fed a marijuana-laced snack to the child. The Superior Court rejected the father's argument that the trial court's determination violated the provision in the state's medical marijuana act quoted above. "While that act prohibits the fact-finder from penalizing a parent **simply** for utilizing medical marijuana," it held, "the trial court did not deny Father's motion to modify custody simply because Father sought to utilize a medical marijuana card." *Id.* at 736. Rather, the court held, the trial court correctly looked to the best interests of the child. And under the very statute cited in the state's medical marijuana act, the finder of fact in a best-interests determination is required to consider, among other things, a parent's history of drug and alcohol use. *Id.* Accordingly, the court affirmed the trial court's order.

Thus, it seems doubtful, particularly in light of the very circumstance-specific nature of custody determinations involving medical marijuana use, that the courts will adopt any kind of blanket protection of medical marijuana use, even in states that have statutes protecting parents in custody disputes that use medical marijuana. The fact that a parent may have a legal right to use marijuana—even one recognized under both federal and state law—would not preclude courts from taking marijuana use into consideration in determining best interests, just as the courts may take alcohol use or smoking in the home into consideration. The determinative question, regardless of the legal status of marijuana, is whether such use adversely affects the child. *See In re Alexis E v. Patrick E*, 171 Cal. App. 4th 438 (2009) (even legal use of medical marijuana can be grounds for modifying custody if the use presents a risk of harm to minor children).

§ 21-6 TRADEMARK ISSUES

Trademarks are important tools for protecting a business's intellectual property rights. They consist of words, phrases, symbols, or designs that are unique to a company and distinguish its product from those of other companies. While trademark owners have some protections under state law and common law, the best way for a company to protect its trademark is for the company to register its trademark with the United States Patent and Trademark Office (USPTO).

The problem that arises for marijuana-related businesses is that under the Lanham Act, goods protected by a federally registered trademark must be "used in commerce." 15 U.S.C. § 1051(d). And the USPTO has interpreted this language such that only goods used "lawfully" in commerce can receive federal copyright protection. Thus, illegal goods and services cannot receive federal trademark protection. And since marijuana is illegal under federal law, the USPTO refuses to approve trademark applications for marijuana and related products. *See generally* Sam Kamin & Viva R. Moffat, *Trademark Laundering, Useless Patents, and Other IP Challenges for the Marijuana Industry*, 73 Wash. & Lee L. Rev. 217, 241–250 (2016).

Intellectual property lawyers have attempted to help marijuana-related businesses work around this problem through various mechanisms. As noted above, common-law trademark rights provide some intellectual property protection, as does state law in legalization states. Additionally, some marijuana-related businesses have applied for federal trademarks for ancillary products, such as clothing, and then used the same trademarks in connection with their marijuana products as well, even though technically the protection only applies to the ancillary products. *Id.* at 250–256.

Still, these types of workarounds provide only a partial fix, and thus marijuana-related businesses continue to be disadvantaged with respect to trademark and other intellectual property rights, relative to other businesses.

PART 5

SOCIAL AND POLICY ISSUES

CHAPTER 22

MARIJUANA AND OTHER DRUGS

§ 22-1 INTRODUCTION

Since 1970, marijuana has been included as a Schedule I drug under the Controlled Substances Act, meaning that, under federal law, it has an unproven safety profile, with no accepted medical use, and a high potential for abuse. Perhaps the main theme of this book has been the rejection of that view in recent years by a large portion of American society, and corresponding efforts on the part of many states and municipalities to work around federal law and to allow the local use of marijuana as a medicine, and sometimes also as an adult-use "recreational" intoxicant. In our view, this increasingly glaring divergence between federal and state/local laws argues for a re-assessment as to how marijuana should be treated under the law.

In undertaking such a re-assessment, it would seem helpful to consider how relevantly similar substances are treated under the law, and to examine the rationale, if any, for treating marijuana differently from these substances. Of course, as discussed in Chapter 2, there really are no drugs that are all that similar to marijuana. It is a relatively unique substance, and it is this uniqueness that has, to a large extent, made a rational regulatory scheme for the drug challenging. Nevertheless, there is value in thinking about the way substances that are at least somewhat similar to marijuana are regulated, as these provide at least partial precedents for marijuana regulation, even if there are no direct corollaries. And thus they may shed some light on the best way for governments to regulate (or not) marijuana.

This chapter accordingly looks at four types of substances that share some characteristics in common with marijuana, and at their status under federal law. Section 22–2 discusses over-the-counter analgesics and other over-the-counter (i.e., non-prescription) drugs. Section 22–3 discusses alcohol and tobacco. Section 22–4 looks at some of the principal illegal recreational drugs. And § 22–5 discusses prescription drugs with the potential for abuse, such as opiates, barbiturates, and benzodiazepines.

§ 22–2 OTC DRUGS

Over-the-counter (i.e., "OTC") drugs provide the most lenient possible precedent for marijuana regulation. One of the principal medical uses marijuana is reputed to have is the ability to treat pain. The principal drugs currently used to treat pain in the United States are (1) OTC analgesics, including the NSAID's (e.g., ibuprofen and aspirin) and acetaminophen (a.k.a. paracetamol, Tylenol), and (2) prescription opiates. The latter are discussed below in § 22–5; this section considers whether it makes sense to treat marijuana the same as the OTC analgesics or other OTC drugs.

If marijuana were to be treated in a manner similar to the OTC analgesics, it could potentially be sold in drugstores, just as it was a century or so ago.

However, almost everyone agrees that marijuana should not be sold to minors, given its intoxicating and addictive potential, as well as some evidence that it may be harmful to developing brains. Thus, if it were sold in drugstores, it would have to be treated more like alcohol and tobacco (discussed in § 22–3 below) insofar as store personnel would have to require identification of persons who are not clearly adults. Or perhaps marijuana sales could be limited to dispensaries (similar to liquor stores) that are restricted to adults, as is the case in most legalization states now. Either way, the arrangement would basically look the same as the scheme in recreational marijuana states such as Colorado and Washington, whereby any adult who wanted to do so could legally obtain the drug.

In assessing how marijuana compares to any other drug, safety concerns are paramount. So the starting point in terms of whether it makes sense to treat marijuana the same as the OTC drugs, such as analgesics, is whether marijuana is potentially more harmful. To a large extent, as discussed in Chapter 2, this question remains unresolved due to the lack of comprehensive research on the effects of marijuana. Based on the limited research that is available, however, it does appear that marijuana has some potentially deleterious effects. As discussed further in Chapters 2 and 23, for example, there is evidence that chronic marijuana use may hurt long-term memory and even slightly diminish IQ. There is also some evidence that it may affect the brain in such a way as to diminish ambition in the user. And there is evidence that it can trigger acute psychotic episodes in susceptible individuals, and trigger a worsening of psychotic symptoms in persons with schizophrenia.

On the other hand, the OTC analgesics are certainly not themselves wholly benign. The NSAID's can cause serious gastrointestinal bleeding. And acetaminophen can cause serious liver damage; in fact, in the United States, it is the leading cause of acute liver failure. In terms of the potential for fatalities, the OTC analgesics are decidedly more dangerous than marijuana. Thus, looking at safety alone would probably not provide a strong reason to treat marijuana more stringently than these readily available drugs.

Another way to compare marijuana to other drugs for public policy purposes is to look at the potential for impairment, e.g., while driving a car. Automobile accidents are among the leading causes of death, and impaired drivers certainly contribute significantly to that problem. And on this metric, the OTC analgesics clearly fare better than marijuana, since they do not cause impairment, and marijuana can. (For more on the issue of impaired driving in marijuana use, *see* Chapter 18.) On the other hand, the potential for impairment does not automatically disqualify a drug from being dispensed over-the-counter. There are a number of OTC drugs, such as Dramamine and certain decongestants, that can cause significant drowsiness and interfere with the user's ability to operate a vehicle. It is likely, however, that the potential is greater in the case of marijuana, particularly when it is used recreationally, and that alone could arguably justify moving it to the prescription drug category (*see* § 22–5 below).

Another important metric when comparing marijuana to other drugs is the potential for dependency and abuse. On this metric, marijuana is potentially more harmful than the OTC analgesics. It is estimated that approximately 10% of regular marijuana users become dependent, which is not the case with the OTC analgesics. And while those drugs can be abused in the sense that some people take amounts in excess of the recommended amount in an effort to control severe pain, they do not lead to problems at home, at work, or in interpersonal relationships, nor do they lead to legal problems. Thus, the potential for abuse seems to be greater with marijuana, though not nearly as great as some other drugs discussed below, such as the opioids and alcohol.

Finally, one could look to the potential for intoxicating effects as a deleterious consequence, independent of the potential for impairment. In other words, policy makers may decide that it is simply wrong for people to use drugs recreationally for their intoxicating effect, and to prohibit them on that basis alone, or in conjunction with other factors. This of course raises significant libertarian objections, since many individuals feel that intoxication *per se* is a person's private business and not something to be subject to regulation. This topic is discussed further in § 22–3 below in connection with alcohol and tobacco. For present purposes it is sufficient to note that marijuana has intoxicating effects, and the OTC analgesics do not. (There is some recent evidence, however, that acetaminophen, in particular, can affect mood adversely.)

In sum, a fairly persuasive argument can be made for treating marijuana more restrictively than OTC drugs, such as analgesics. Marijuana's potential for causing driving impairment, as well as its potential for dependence and abuse, distinguish it from OTC analgesics, even setting aside the issue of intoxication.

§ 22-3 ALCOHOL AND TOBACCO

Alcohol and tobacco provide another obvious point of comparison for marijuana. Indeed, one of the most commonly advanced arguments in favor of marijuana legalization is that the drug is less dangerous and otherwise problematic than either alcohol or tobacco. Proponents of marijuana legalization compare the Controlled Substances Act to the Volstead Act, which prohibited the production and distribution of alcohol in the United States pursuant to the Eighteenth Amendment during the prohibition era of the 1920s. (Tobacco, on the other hand, has always been legal in the United States, though subject to some significant regulation.)

Today, with the exception of a few "dry" counties, alcohol and tobacco are freely available to adults in the United States over the age of 21. They are, in essence, America's officially sanctioned "recreational" drugs. In other words, both are readily available substances sought after almost exclusively for their psychoactive effect and the pleasure users derive from them. For that reason, they arguably provide a good precedent for legalizing marijuana for recreational use.

If marijuana were to be treated similarly to alcohol and tobacco, it would therefore be regulated under federal law quite similarly to the way it is now regulated under the laws of recreational marijuana states. Perhaps it would even be added to the purview of the Bureau of Alcohol, Tobacco, Firearms and Explosives (ATF). It would continue to be restricted from minors, and it would be subject to significant governmental oversight. But it would nevertheless be freely available for purchase by adults.

In terms of health comparisons, marijuana appears to be a somewhat less dangerous drug than either alcohol or tobacco. The excessive use of alcohol is renowned for a host of health problems. According to the CDC, excessive alcohol use accounts for approximately 88,000 deaths in the United States annually, shortening the lives of those afflicted by an average of 30 years. For adults between the ages of 20 and 64, excessive drinking is responsible for one in 10 deaths. The most widely known danger from drinking excessive amounts of alcohol is liver disease, but there are a host of other health problems associated with alcohol as well. These include short-term risks, such as alcohol poisoning and accidental deaths, as well as long-term risks, such as heart disease and strokes, certain cancers, memory problems and dementia, mental health problems, and various other conditions.

Tobacco may have an even worse health profile than alcohol. Lung cancer and Chronic Obstructive Pulmonary Disease (i.e., "COPD") are probably the best-known smoking-related conditions. But ever since the United States Surgeon General's Office issued its first health advisory for tobacco smoking in 1964, the evidence of tobacco's damaging effects has continued to accumulate. According to the CDC, cigarette smoking harms nearly every organ of the body and causes many diseases. It causes nearly one-half million deaths each year in the United. Smoking causes more deaths per year than all of the following causes combined: HIV, illegal drug use, alcohol use, motor vehicle accidents, and firearm-related accidents. In addition to causing lung cancer and COPD, smoking significantly increases the risk of heart disease and strokes, and it causes a number of other types of cancer, including oral cancer, colon cancer, pancreatic cancer, cancer of the esophagus, liver cancer, stomach cancer, and several other cancers. Overall, it accounts for one in three cancer deaths in the United States. In addition, cigarette smoking contributes to a number of other health problems, including pregnancy complications and prenatal injuries, problems with teeth and gums, eye problems, rheumatoid arthritis, and adverse systemic effects to the body, including inflammation and decreased immune defense. Furthermore, many of these adverse health consequences are not limited to the user, but are inflicted as well on non-smokers via secondhand smoke. Overall, tobacco use is the leading preventable cause of death in the United States.

Thus, while marijuana is certainly not devoid of deleterious effects to the health, as discussed in Chapter 2 above, marijuana appears to create less of a danger for public health than the recreational drugs that are already legal throughout the United States: alcohol and tobacco.

In terms of the potential for dependency and abuse, all three substances can cause addiction, though withdrawal from alcohol produces the most serious symptoms. Withdrawal symptoms from alcohol begin within days or even hours of stopping alcohol, depending on the level of addiction. They include restlessness, shakiness, nausea and vomiting, anxiety, fast heart rate, headache, insomnia, and in severe cases, delusions, hallucinations, and seizures that can be life-threatening in the absence of treatment.

Withdrawal from tobacco is less traumatic, though still challenging. According to the National Institute on Drug Abuse, withdrawal symptoms from nicotine (the principal addicting substance in tobacco) include irritability, craving, depression, anxiety, cognitive and attention deficits, sleep disturbances, and increased appetite. These symptoms may begin within a few hours after the last cigarette. Symptoms peak within the first few days of smoking cessation and usually subside within a few weeks, although they can persist for months. Withdrawal from marijuana appears to be more similar to tobacco; the symptoms are not traumatic or medically dangerous like alcohol withdrawal symptoms. Marijuana withdrawal symptoms include anger, anxiety, irritability, depression, insomnia, gastrointestinal symptoms, and decreased appetite. Generally these symptoms resolve within a few weeks.

As for the potential for abuse, marijuana probably falls somewhere between the other two drugs. On the one hand, tobacco is not generally associated with social abuse. It does not usually lead to significant problems at home, at work, or in interpersonal relationships (unless the smoker exposes others to secondhand smoke), nor does it lead to significant legal problems.

Alcohol, on the other hand, has a high potential for social abuse. The principal reason it was outlawed during prohibition was due to its potentially devastating effect on families and on the ability of the alcoholics to maintain employment and lead normal lives. Rehab centers, groups such as Alcoholics Anonymous, and "rescue missions" all testify to alcohol's devastating potential for abuse. And while marijuana can reputedly hinder ambition, which is not good for the user's career prospects, it has not shown itself to be a destroyer of lives and families the way alcohol can be. Marijuana can also cause impairment, of course, as discussed further below. And to that extent it may interfere with the user's employment if the user is unable to abstain during work hours, or if it keeps the worker from getting to work. That level of addiction, however, seems to be less common with marijuana than with alcohol. Similarly, family and interpersonal relationships seem less affected by marijuana than alcohol. For one thing, marijuana, unlike alcohol, does not generally aggravate aggression in the user.

Finally with respect to the potential for intoxication and impairment, alcohol and marijuana have similar profiles. Unlike tobacco, which causes minimal impairment, both marijuana and alcohol are capable of significant impairment of the user's faculties and can make activities such as driving dangerous. The limited data that is available, however, seems to indicate that alcohol is somewhat more impairing than marijuana with respect to operating a vehicle.

On balance, therefore, marijuana does not present a significantly greater harm profile than alcohol or tobacco. All three substances are addictive, though alcohol has the most serious withdrawal symptoms. Both alcohol and marijuana are intoxicants with the potential for abuse, and both cause impairment. Tobacco causes minimal abuse and impairment, but it probably has the most significant adverse effect on public health. Alcohol is a close second, and marijuana a distant third. In fact, marijuana is the only one of the three that has a demonstrated medical use. Thus, setting aside the historical context and focusing just on the drugs' impact, it would be difficult to build a rational case for continuing to criminalize marijuana while keeping these other two drugs legal. Society's regulation of alcohol and tobacco accordingly makes a good precedent for regulating marijuana, rather than criminalizing it.

§ 22-4 ILLEGAL RECREATIONAL DRUGS

Recreational drugs are those taken for pleasure or their psychoactive effects. The previous section compared marijuana to the recreational drugs that are currently legal in the United States: tobacco and alcohol. This section compares marijuana to some other common recreational drugs that, like marijuana, have traditionally been illegal throughout the United States.

There are numerous substances that various persons use for purposes of intoxication. This section will not attempt to cover them all here; rather, the point is just to consider whether there appears to be a rationale for distinguishing marijuana as a recreational drug from other recreational drugs that are currently illegal. If so, then it may make sense to legalize marijuana while keeping these other recreational drugs illegal. If not, then it makes sense for policy makers to either keep the recreational use of marijuana illegal, or conversely, legalize at least some other recreational drugs, which is a position rapidly gaining traction among a number of municipalities and even some states.

Some of the drugs that are used for recreational purposes are legal as prescription drugs; others are on Schedule I of the CSA, and are therefore illegal for all purposes, just as marijuana is under federal law. Drugs in the former (i.e., prescription) category include certain opiates (e.g., Oxycontin, Vicodin), the benzodiazepines (e.g., Valium, Ambien), most amphetamines (e.g., Adderall), and barbiturates. These are discussed further in the following section.

Drugs in the latter category include LSD, MDMA (i.e. "Ecstasy"), cocaine, methamphetamine's, heroin, psilocybin, and mescaline.

All of these drugs, of course, cause intoxication of some sort; if they did not, they would not be sought after as recreational drugs. Thus, in comparing them to marijuana, the focus should be primarily on safety and the potential for addiction and abuse, as well as any potential for medical use.

Looking first at the prescription drugs that are used recreationally, a pretty strong case can be made for keeping these drugs controlled (though not necessarily criminalized), even if marijuana is legalized for recreational use. Prescription opiates, in particular, have demonstrated a devastating potential for harm and abuse. In recent years, tens of thousands of users per year have died from opiates, and more than half of them are from prescription opiates (heroin is the other main culprit). It is thus reasonably clear that prescription opiates are more dangerous and have greater potential for abuse than marijuana. They are also more addicting.

The same is true to a somewhat lesser extent of prescription benzodiazepines (e.g., Xanax) and barbiturates. While they do not kill as many persons as prescription opiates, they still cause thousands of deaths per year in the United States, whereas marijuana kills no one directly (though it may lead to fatal car accidents and other accidental deaths). These prescription drugs can also be highly addictive, and their potential for abuse is significant.

As for the Schedule I substances, the issue gets a little more complicated. Heroin, for example, while effective as an analgesic, has a demonstrated potential for causing abuse, addiction, and harm that is equal to or greater than the prescription opiates. Thus, it does not serve as a reasonable precedent for marijuana: in other words, it is reasonable to continue criminalizing heroin (or at least treating it as a controlled substance), even if marijuana is legalized for recreational use.

Cocaine is a little harder case. It is actually a Schedule II drug, since at one time physicians believed that it might have some therapeutic value, primarily as a topical analgesic. Today, however, it is not used in the medical context. And it certainly appears to be a more dangerous drug than marijuana, with the significant potential to cause heart attacks and strokes, in addition to other adverse health effects. It also has significant potential for addiction and abuse. So a reasonable argument can be made for continuing to criminalize (or at least control the distribution of) cocaine as well, even if marijuana is legalized.

The so-called "hallucinogenic" drugs (also known as entheogens), however, such as MDMA (i.e., Ecstasy), psilocybin, mescaline, and LSD, cannot so easily be distinguished from marijuana in terms of their fitness for recreational use. While there are adverse health effects associated with these drugs, and they do cause impairment for purposes of driving, their effects pale somewhat in comparison to the opioids' potential for causing addiction, abuse, and death. And like marijuana, they appear to be safer in this regard than benzodiazepines, barbiturates, or cocaine.

Some of the hallucinogens may also have some medical efficacy (e.g., for treating conditions such as PTSD and depression), and several major academic medical centers are currently undertaking research to bear this out. These drugs are also not highly addictive, and they have not been shown to have a high potential for abuse. Accordingly, policymakers might have a more difficult time making the case that drugs such as psilocybin and MDMA should continue to be criminalized, if marijuana is legalized for recreational use.

And in fact, over the past several years, there has been a growing movement to legalize, or at least decriminalize, these drugs. In November 2020, Oregon voters passed Ballot Measure 109, which legalized psilocybin for therapeutic use and also decriminalized it for general use. Psilocybin is a naturally occurring drug derived from certain types of mushrooms. This followed decriminalization of psilocybin in a handful of municipalities, beginning with Denver in 2019. Some of these municipalities have decriminalized other hallucinogens as well. Oakland, for example, decriminalized peyote (a cactus that contains the hallucinogen mescaline) as well as psilocybin in June 2019. And Ann Arbor passed a resolution in September 2020 that effectively decriminalized the possession of entheogenic plants and plant compounds, making them the city's lowest enforcement priority. So it will be interesting to watch over the next several years whether hallucinogens become the "new marijuana" in terms of legalization efforts.

§ 22-5 PRESCRIPTION DRUGS WITH INTOXICATING EFFECTS

The final point of comparison for marijuana is society's treatment of the prescription narcotics (viz., opiates, benzodiazepines, barbiturates). Here we are focusing not on illegal recreational use, but on their uses as prescription medications. As the previous section discussed, a good argument can be made for keeping these drugs illegal for recreational use, even if marijuana is legalized for recreational use. The remaining question is whether a reasonable case can be made for keeping marijuana illegal for medical use, given that these other drugs are legal for such use.

In making this determination, the principal focus needs to be on the efficacy of marijuana as a medicine, since, as discussed in the previous section, it is reasonably clear, given the present state of medical knowledge, that the prescription narcotics are overall more dangerous than marijuana, and that they have a greater potential for dependence and abuse. Thus, using the federal government's treatment of these prescription narcotics as a legal precedent, it would seem that opponents of medical marijuana would have a difficult time arguing against affording marijuana the same status as these prescription narcotics, unless marijuana has no significant medical value. To be sure, the safety of marijuana has not been extensively proven in the types of clinical trials the FDA requires; however, the evidence that is out there, and it is substantial, indicates that marijuana is safer and less prone to addiction and abuse than many prescription narcotics.

The medicinal uses of marijuana are extensively discussed in Chapter 2 and Chapter 23. By way of summary, marijuana has been touted by proponents for numerous ailments, but it seems demonstrably helpful, based on the existing evidence, for seizure and related disorders, pain relief, treatment of insomnia and anxiety, appetite stimulation, and treatment of nausea. It is important to keep in mind that marijuana need not be the *most* efficacious drug for any such condition in order for legalization of its medicinal use to make sense. Some drugs work better for some persons than others do, and sometimes an individual cannot take a drug for a certain reason, meaning that alternatives—even if somewhat less efficacious—are still valuable. Furthermore, since the safety profile of marijuana, though not yet conclusively determined, appears to be better than that of the opiates, the benzodiazepines, and the barbiturates, as noted above, there may well be a place in medicine for marijuana to treat conditions such as pain, anxiety, and insomnia, even though it may not do so quite as effectively as these other drugs. One study by researchers at the University of Michigan, for example, concluded that patients taking opiates for chronic pain were able to reduce their consumption of opiates by some 80% by using marijuana to treat their pain. The authors of the study commended this substitution in light of marijuana's better safety profile and lower potential for abuse.

Therefore, in terms of balancing efficacy and safety, the narcotic prescription drugs provide a good precedent for regulating marijuana. Marijuana may not be as powerful as these drugs, but it is likely safer, and that would seem to commend its medical use in at least certain circumstances, in the absence of any new evidence of significant adverse health effects.

CHAPTER 23

MEDICAL ARGUMENTS FOR AND AGAINST LEGALIZATION

§ 23–1 INTRODUCTION

Arguments for and against legalization underlie the evolving marijuana law in the United States. These arguments draw both on medical and scientific research and also on economic, political, and social factors. This chapter first introduces the overarching arguments regarding legalization, and then focuses on the medical and scientific research. This research has been summarized in two comprehensive reports by the National Academies of Sciences, Engineering, and Medicine, one in 1999 and one in 2017. The following chapter (Chapter 24) considers public policy considerations as to legalization.

The debate over marijuana is long-standing and complex. Both sides draw from the same data but produce opposing conclusions. Most arguments reflect legitimate differences in perspectives and beliefs; some reflect entrenched biases and self-interest.

The pro-legalization side argues the relative harmlessness of marijuana consumption; the evidence of its medical benefits; and the onerous social costs of enforcing prohibitions against this widely-used substance, which could be regulated and taxed instead. The anti-legalization side focuses on the lack of studies definitively showing the effectiveness of marijuana as medicine; the dangers of its psychotropic capacities; and the greater harms to society in increased marijuana consumption. The debate is complicated by the open-ended meaning of "legalization" as used in the debate. It can refer to decriminalization (replacing criminal penalties with civil sanctions); removing marijuana from Schedule I or from the CSA schedules entirely; or allowing medical or recreational use, at either the federal, state, or local level.

Section 23–2 summarizes the arguments for and against legalization. Section 23–3 discusses the scientific research into the health effects of marijuana.

§ 23–2 SUMMARY OF ARGUMENTS

Both pro and con arguments rely on similar medical data but draw different conclusions. In the summary of arguments that follows, both sides address similar policies, often relying on the same literature and studies, but from opposing perspectives. To some extent, both sides are hampered by a lack of data due to the limited research studies that have been conducted on marijuana in the United States.

§ 23–2.1 ARGUMENT IN FAVOR OF LEGALIZATION

The fundamental argument in favor of legalization is that marijuana is not dangerous to consumers and has benefits for treating certain medical disorders. Numerous scientific studies, supported by decades of anecdotal evidence, and by centuries of use by non-

Western cultures, indicate its effectiveness in relieving anxiety, nausea, and pain and in producing a mild euphoria. Synthetic derivatives of cannabis, such as FDA-approved Marinol, Cesamet, and Syndros, lack the full "entourage effect" of marijuana, and are thus inadequate substitutes. Epidiolex, which was approved by the U.S. Food and Drug Administration in 2018 for the treatment of two rare seizure disorders in children, demonstrates that a highly purified cannabidiol extracted from the cannabis plant can have safe and effective therapeutic uses. The side effects associated with marijuana are within the range of tolerated medications. Marijuana does create dependence in certain individuals, but withdrawal symptoms are relatively mild. Studies have found marijuana to be less dangerous than alcohol or tobacco, as well as painkillers such as opioids.

If marijuana is legalized, it can be regulated for product safety and quality control standards, including additives, contaminants, consistency, and potency. Physicians will be able to monitor prescriptions for dosage, ingredients, and ratio of THC to CBD.

If marijuana does not represent a danger to the consumer, then the extensive law enforcement apparatus to suppress marijuana activity is a colossal waste of resources and a burden on society, which falls especially on minorities and the disadvantaged. Millions of Americans have been arrested for marijuana consumption and possession; billions of dollars wasted in police, court, and prison expenditures; and young people diverted into the prison system because of relatively harmless recreational use. Income that goes to criminal and underground suppliers of cannabis could go to more productive uses. In addition, governments would realize a large portion of this money in taxes, a boon to deficit ridden budgets. The overwrought campaign against marijuana has also led to a problematic prohibition against hemp, an undeniably valuable agricultural and industrial resource. This ban was only removed in 2018. Canadian and Chinese farmers produce large quantities of hemp; American farmers were largely shut out.

U.S. social and legal culture has increasingly valued individual autonomy and rights; adults should be allowed to make their own decision as to marijuana use. The half-century war on marijuana has been a monumental failure. It has not deterred marijuana consumption. A majority of American states have legalized marijuana for certain purposes, and there is no turning back. If the United States wants to create a rational, consistent national policy on marijuana, it can only do so through a legalized, regulatory framework.

§ 23–2.2 ARGUMENT OPPOSED TO LEGALIZATION

As with the arguments in favor of legalization, arguments opposed to legalization of marijuana depend fundamentally on assessing its effect on health—but conclude that its dangers potentially outweigh its benefits. Although there is evidence that marijuana can provide some health benefits, at least four factors militate against legalizing medical marijuana for that reason. First, no large-scale, FDA-approved scientific study has definitively shown that marijuana has significant health benefits for the wider population, and the FDA has not approved whole plant marijuana as a safe and effective drug. The 1999 and 2017 comprehensive reports by the National Academies of Sciences, Engineering, and Medicine did not definitively show that the health benefits of marijuana outweighed its risks. Second, if the evidence is inconclusive, it weighs against a mind-altering drug, rather than in its favor—the FDA process of approval is rigorous for good reason. Third, any medical benefits that marijuana might have are more palliative than curative. Other medicines provide similar benefits but with fewer risks. The FDA has approved three man-made forms of cannabis and undoubtedly will approve others as clinical trials are completed. Epidiolex, the only cannabis extract approved by the U.S. Food and Drug Administration, has only a limited application. Fourth, regardless of any benefits that may be found, marijuana remains a potentially dangerous drug. For example, studies indicate that marijuana can impair the memory function of users, especially in young people whose neurological development is not complete.

Regulation for marijuana safety is elusive. As a whole plant drug, marijuana is inherently inconsistent as to various strains, quantities of THC, potency, and method of delivery. Over a hundred class action lawsuits have already been filed against marijuana companies, as to labeling, marketing, disclosures, and contaminant product liability.

Criminalization is important to prevent people from engaging in harmful activities, whether these activities harm themselves or others. Psychoactive drugs are addictive and have been subject to significant abuse in modern society, especially hurting the poor and minority neighborhoods. As marijuana potency has increased manifold over the last decades, the threat is even greater. Studies of a range of marijuana products found potency to have increased from about 4% THC in 1995 to about 12% in 2014, to about 17% in 2017. Higher potency THC confers a greater risk for adverse outcomes. Although arrests for marijuana use are a necessary deterrent, in fact few people are sentenced to prison terms for marijuana consumption—mostly just for large-scale drug trafficking. The criminal justice system routes most users to substance abuse treatment.

Opponents of legalization also argue that revenue projections from taxing marijuana are both inflated and misguided. Experience with alcohol and tobacco suggests that whatever tax revenues the government will gain are more than offset by social costs connected to increased marijuana consumption, such as drug treatment programs, impaired driving, and lost productivity.

§ 23–2.3 DECRIMINALIZATION

Decriminalization represents a compromise between legalization and prohibition. With decriminalization, possession (and rarely, cultivation) of small amounts of marijuana for personal use remains prohibited but subject only to civil sanctions, such as a small fine, rather than to criminal penalties, such as incarceration. Decriminalization allows society to express its disfavor of marijuana consumption while reserving criminal penalties for large-scale traffickers. However, those who favor legalization complain that users are still stigmatized and subjected to the criminal justice system, even if in the end they receive only fines. For those who favor retaining full criminal prohibition, decriminalization lacks sufficient deterrence, offers treatments that are already a major component of the criminal justice system, and would seem to violate U.S. obligations under international treaties to retain criminal sanctions against marijuana use (*see* Chapter 10). Decriminalization also leaves unaddressed the important problem of allowing a black market to meet demand, since large-scale, if not all, domestic cultivation and distribution of marijuana would remain illegal.

§ 23-3 MARIJUANA IN SCIENCE

The most important questions in deciding the legal status of marijuana would seem to be scientific ones. Plants have been used for medicines in every culture; over 40% of medicines prescribed in the United States contain chemicals derived from plants. But drugs can also be addictive, debilitating, and subject to abuse. Advocates of cannabis cite the healthful effects of marijuana on both the body and mind, backed up by centuries of anecdotal evidence. On the other hand, Congress and the DEA have declared as a matter of law that cannabis is in the most dangerous category of drugs, with no accepted medical use. What do the scientific studies say?

A definitive study of the health effects of cannabis is hard to obtain. Research on marijuana has been hampered by its prohibited status, although the international drug regime makes provision for its scientific study. Marijuana use varies by plant strain, gender, dosage and potency; its effect on individuals varies with the genetic profile of the user and interplay with the hundreds of chemical compounds in cannabis. Anecdotal evidence of its medical capacities abounds and should not be discounted, but the scientific community demands controlled experiments, and preferably those that are peer-reviewed and double-blind tested. Even if a study shows association of certain health factors with marijuana, it does not necessarily prove causation.

The most referenced studies are by the federally chartered National Academies of Sciences, Engineering, and Medicine (NASEM). The original study by the medical division of NASEM, then named the Institute of Medicine (IOM), was commissioned by the White House Office of National Drug Control Policy ("the Drug Czar") in 1997 and published in 1999 in a 257 page report. Institute of Medicine, *Marijuana and Medicine: Assessing the Science Base*. The second NASEM report, *The Health Effects of Cannabis and Cannabinoids: The Current State of Evidence and Recommendations for Research*, was published in 2017 and can be characterized as the gold standard study on this topic. In addition, ProCon.org., a non-profit which operates a reputable online resource for debating controversial issues, identified 60 peer-reviewed articles on medical marijuana from 1990 to 2014. And certain states that have legalized marijuana, such as Colorado and Massachusetts, have produced their own comprehensive government reports surveying the medical literature.

§ 23–3.1 PHYSICAL HEALTH

Medical studies have found health benefits to marijuana for an assortment of conditions, but especially in palliative care. However, it is disputed whether marijuana is the most effective treatment for these conditions, given possible adverse effects, and the other medical treatments available.

As with many studies of the health effects of marijuana, the original IOM Report in 1999, although comprehensive, was neither clearly positive nor negative. The Report found marijuana similar to other medications in having some benefits for certain conditions, although for more of a palliative than healing nature. Marijuana also has adverse side effects, but "except for the harm associated with smoking," not beyond those tolerated for other medicines. Thus, the Report's strongest conclusion was that smoking marijuana is a "crude" method of delivering helpful components of THC and "delivers harmful substances."

The IOM Report found medical benefits of marijuana as an antiemetic to alleviate vomiting and nausea and also as a palliative, mitigating pain and stimulating appetite. The report found some evidence of beneficial effects for muscle spasticity for movement disorders, and to reduce high intraocular pressure in glaucoma patients for short intervals. As to side effects, marijuana could tend to suppress the immune system, and when smoked contains many of the same chemical elements as tobacco smoke, including carcinogens, that are "important risk factors for developing respiratory disease," including bronchitis and respiratory cancer.

The IOM Report was criticized for not recognizing that the mix of chemicals found in the cannabis plant may be more effective ("the entourage effect") than assessing a component chemical in isolation. For example, the FDA approved synthetics of THC, dronabinol (sold under the tradenames Marinol and Syndros) and nabilone (sold under the tradename Cesamet), lack the flavonoids and terpenoids that contribute to the overall health effects of the plant. Their effectiveness is also constrained by the oral route of administration, which accounts for slow and diminished absorption into the system, in contrast to inhaled marijuana, which is rapidly absorbed. Although the IOM Report offered strong criticism of smoked marijuana, there are other ways of ingesting marijuana without accompanying carcinogenic effects, such as vaporization and edibles. As with other medical studies about marijuana, the results of the IOM were employed by both sides of the debate.

A concurrence by Ninth Circuit Judge Alex Kozinski in *Conant v. Walters*, 309 F.3d 629, 641 (9th

Cir. 2002) stated that "the IOM Report cautiously endorsed the medical use of marijuana." In contrast, the DEA stated that the IOM study was inconclusive, in that it found only limited anecdotal information on the medical benefits of smoked marijuana for some ailments.

ProCon.org has identified numerous U.S. peer-reviewed articles on medical marijuana that have addressed studies of medical marijuana as it relates to ALS, bipolar disorder, cancer, glaucoma, HIV, Huntington's disease, Crohn's disease, multiple sclerosis, nausea, pain, Parkinson's disease, posttraumatic stress syndrome, schizophrenia, rheumatoid arthritis, and Tourette syndrome. Of these studies, the majority showed marijuana had at least some benefit for the medical condition in question. For example, six studies found marijuana as beneficial for treating pain. The only study on marijuana as it relates to nausea found it to be an effective medicine.

A systematic review and meta-analysis of "Cannabinoids for Medical Use," published in the June 2015 *Journal of American Medicine* (vol. 313, No. 24) surveyed 79 clinical studies of cannabinoid drugs. This rigorous and comprehensive survey found good evidence that marijuana was beneficial for the treatment of chronic neuropathic or cancer pain, and some evidence that it improved nausea and vomiting due to chemotherapy. It also assisted weight gain for HIV patients and alleviated sleep disorders and Tourette syndrome. An open-label trial published in the March 2016 *Lancet Neurology* found evidence that treatment with an oral cannabidiol (CBD)—a non-psychoactive element of cannabis—could reduce seizure frequency in epileptics without major adverse consequences and recommended randomized controlled trials. And a European study in Scientific Reports 5 (Article number: 8126, 2015) found marijuana to have a lower risk of toxicity than alcohol or tobacco, and other illicit drugs as well.

In its most recent denial of a petition to initiate proceedings to reschedule marijuana in August 2016, the DEA relied on a June 25, 2015 evaluation by the Department of Health and Human Services and the FDA of the scientific and medical properties of marijuana. Surveying a wide range of literature, this report concluded that marijuana has harmful psychoactive effects, including behavioral impairment but not psychotic episodes. Physiologically, marijuana smoking can harm the cardiovascular, autonomic, respiratory, and possibly the immunological systems. In contrast, the report found that "no published studies" met FDA criteria for "proving marijuana's efficacy."

Individual states are also publishing their own studies of the health benefits and risks of marijuana. For example, in February 2015, the Colorado Department of Public Health and Environment Review, as mandated by the Colorado legislature, published a 188 page report reviewing existing studies. Although the report found marijuana to have some health benefits, it also found that marijuana use can result in memory loss, birth defects, and impaired driving, and most significantly development of mental disorders in adolescents and young adults.

In January 2017, the National Academies of Sciences, Engineering, and Medicine (NASEM) published a 395-page review of the current state of evidence as to the health effects of cannabis use, updating the original 1999 IOM report. This new study, titled *The Health Effects of Cannabis and Cannabinoids: The Current State of Evidence and Recommendations for Research*, was praised by both sides of the debate for its rigor, thoroughness, and balance, and is the most comprehensive study of the medical status of marijuana, synthesizing over 10,000 studies, written and overseen by panels of impartial and leading scientific experts. As such it may be the gold standard study of marijuana health effects for the near future.

The aim of the 2017 NASEM Report was to develop a consensus, scientific-based report summarizing evidence for the therapeutic benefits and medical risks arising from use of cannabis and cannabinoids. In addition, the Report aimed to identify significant areas requiring additional research, and in particular, as to the therapeutic effects relating to epilepsy. The Report relied on a large set of clinical trials published in the medical literature.

As to health benefits, the Report found evidence of the effectiveness of cannabis and cannabinoids in treating or alleviating nausea, anxiety, and chronic pain. In particular strong evidence indicated benefits in treating chronic pain and nausea related to undergoing chemotherapy. Some evidence supported effectiveness in treating sleep disorders and other anxiety-related conditions. Although the Report found no evidence of therapeutic benefit in treating epilepsy with cannabis and cannabinoids, the researchers acknowledged that there were ongoing clinical trials studying the possibilities of pharmaceutical-grade cannabidiol for refractory seizures. In fact, after publication of the 2017 Report, the FDA approved Epidiolex, a cannabidiol ([CBD) oral solution for the treatment of seizures associated with two rare and severe forms of epilepsy, Lennox-Gastaut syndrome and Dravet syndrome, and tuberous sclerosis complex. Epidiolex is the first FDA-approved drug that contains a purified drug substance derived from cannabis and was placed on Schedule V of the CSA. In addition, Epidiolex is the first FDA approval of a drug for the treatment of patients with Dravet syndrome.

As to the negative aspects of cannabis use, the NASEM report found evidence of a connection between cannabis use and the development of psychotic disorders such as schizophrenia. Additional evidence demonstrated a likely link between cannabis use and increased incidence of anxiety disorders. Long-term smoking of cannabis could worsen respiratory problems and cause bronchitis episodes. Maternal cannabis smoking was associated with premature or underweight babies and pregnancy complications. The Report also showed a connection between cannabis use and impairments in cognitive learning and in increased incidence of anxiety disorders and anti-motivational syndrome.

A 2021 study aimed to update the NASEM Report by reviewing 198 recent studies: "A Mapping Literature Review of Medical Cannabis Clinical Outcomes and Quality of Evidence in Approved Conditions in the USA from 2016 to 2019" (*Medical Cannabis and Cannabinoids* 2021, 4:21–42). This review found that a paucity of randomized controlled trials remains, but significant evidence suggests favorable risk-benefit ratios for select dosage forms and routes of administration of cannabis in treating epilepsy and chronic noncancer pain.

Other studies since publication of the NASEM report have found increasing dangers from cannabis. For example, a July 2021 study from University of Michigan researchers found that adolescents who vape cannabis are at greater risk for respiratory symptoms indicative of lung injury (EVALI, "e-cigarette, or vaping, product use associated lung injury") than adolescents who smoke cigarettes or marijuana or vape nicotine. (Vaping is a method of inhaling intoxicating cannabis vapors.) Recent studies have highlighted the proemetic effects of cannabinoids, known as Cannabinoid Hyperemesis Syndrome (CHS). The proemetic effects following prolonged, high-dose marijuana use manifest as cyclical episodes of nausea and vomiting, accompanied by abdominal pain.

§ 23–3.2 PSYCHOACTIVE EFFECTS

The psychogenic effects of marijuana are as controversial as their physiological effects. Studies have found both pros and cons as to the mood altering effects of cannabis. It produces positive effects of anxiety reduction, sedation, and euphoria in most users, but negative psychological effects in others. Some patients, especially the elderly, report feelings of dysphoria, that is discomfort and disorientation, but also panic attacks. Also the euphoric effect can exaggerate belief in the therapeutic effectiveness of marijuana, to the neglect of other more helpful medicines.

Some studies have found that the harmful effects of marijuana use may be most pronounced in adolescents and youths, whose neurological development is incomplete. For example, it has been found to cause memory loss and amotivational syndrome (apathy towards social activities and lethargy) in minors. It also affects psychomotor performance and impairs driving, as well as skilled mechanical activities.

Again, the array of studies provides support for arguments on both sides of the question as to whether marijuana produces dependence. A 1994 study found that one in 11 adult users and one in six adolescent users report becoming addicted to marijuana. The 1999 IOM Report made a more nuanced conclusion, identifying a distinctive marijuana withdrawal syndrome, but describing it as "mild and subtle." The withdrawal syndrome has both physiological and psychiatric effects, resulting in restlessness, irritability, mild agitation, insomnia, sleep EEG disturbance, nausea, and cramping. These symptoms, however, were short-lived, usually lasting less than a week. Other studies have indicated that in some patients, heavy use of marijuana can create a dependence that can result in antisocial personality and behavioral disorders.

Aspects that are hard to evaluate are questions of euphoria and dysphoria, reported by many marijuana users, and varying widely due to the idiosyncratic effect of cannabinoid receptors in individuals. Although rarely mentioned in studies as a concrete health effect, there is an argument that the feelings of relaxation and pleasantness many users of marijuana feel, can itself be considered of therapeutic value, absent other physiological change. On the other hand, the feelings of anxiety, fear, distrust, experienced by some users can be considered a significant health detriment.

In summary, the medical studies have reached some conflicting conclusions about marijuana use, and this argues in favor of additional clinical research. It seems well-established that marijuana has some medical benefits (such as relieving pain, controlling nausea and stimulating appetite for certain patients), and for certain forms of childhood epilepsy. But there are also health risks associated with marijuana (such as respiratory illness if marijuana is smoked), as there are for most medications. The psychogenic risks of marijuana for young users, such as increased incidence of schizophrenia, anxiety disorders and anti-motivational syndrome, are alarming and should not be discounted. Striking the appropriate balance will provide a continuing challenge for policymakers and medical researchers going forward.

CHAPTER 24

POLICY ARGUMENTS FOR AND AGAINST LEGALIZATION

§ 24–1 INTRODUCTION

The issues of marijuana legalization go beyond the question of the medical effects of marijuana, however important those considerations weigh. This chapter focuses on the public policy considerations bearing on the legalization debate. Section 24–2 considers economic arguments. Section 24–3 explores marijuana in politics. Section 24–4 examines marijuana in society. Section 24–5 examines the role of marijuana in criminal justice. Section 24–6 looks at environmental arguments for and against marijuana legalization. Section 24–7 adds questions of social justice to the controversy. And § 24–8 summarizes the changing terms of the legalization debate.

§ 24–2 MARIJUANA AND THE ECONOMY

Some of the most important policy considerations are economic, as lawmakers assess the revenue and expenditure consequences of legalizing marijuana and hemp.

Revenues and Expenditures. The tax-and-revenue argument in favor of legalization is twofold. Governments would 1) reap revenues from licensing and taxing marijuana sales and 2) reduce the expense of enforcing marijuana prohibitions and incarcerating offenders. The illicit U.S. market in marijuana is valued at about $60 billion per year, most of the revenues going to underground dealers and suppliers, as well as foreign drug cartels. If legalized, legitimate businesses could reap the profits, and governments would collect a large share of the revenue in taxes. Likewise, there would be tremendous savings to state treasuries as police, prosecutors, and courts concentrate on more serious offenses. Even more importantly, the cost of incarcerating everyday users would be ameliorated. The American Civil Liberties Union estimated the costs of enforcing marijuana laws in 2010 at $3.6 billion, a dollar figure that remained fairly level over subsequent years. For these reasons 500 distinguished economists called for legalization in a 2005 open letter to the U.S. Senate.

However, many of the projections of revenues that would accrue to states were overly optimistic. For example, California lowered its budget forecast of $355 million and $514 million in cannabis excise tax revenues for fiscal years 2019 and 2020, to $288 million in 2019 and $359 million in 2020, respectively. Nevertheless, in 2020, Colorado collected $362,027,103 in State Tax Revenue from adult-use Cannabis. Since 2014, when Colorado became the first state to legalize adult-use marijuana, states have collected a combined total of $7.9 billion in tax revenue from legal, adult-use marijuana sales. In first years of legalization, marijuana tax revenues for Colorado and Washington came in under most projections. Even if governments gain in tax receipts, it is not clear that the net costs to society would be reduced, as increased marijuana consumption could lead to more extensive substance abuse treatment, more visits to the emergency room, and an increase in impaired driving and accidents. As to industry, legalization could lead to loss of productivity, impaired psychomotor skills in workers, and increased industrial accidents and business liability. Grassroots activists have expressed concern that medical conglomerates and providers would reap the benefits of any savings, with regulations designed to keep small growers and producers out of competition, creating "big weed" in the model of "big tobacco" and "big pharma."

Marijuana as a Commodity. Most economists agree that legalizing marijuana will lower its cost, but this may result in a benefit or detriment. It saves money for consumers but could increase the number of abusers. Legalized marijuana could lead to a safer and higher quality product, with more variety and higher standards. However, grassroots activists have expressed concern that legalization will add a layer of bureaucratic interference and FDA red tape that will complicate what is otherwise an easily cultivated plant. Viewing marijuana as a commodity more akin to an herbal supplement than a dangerous substance, many activists hope to preserve economic rights in the plant, such as the right to individual cultivation ("home grow") and small-scale transfer.

Hemp. The U.S. hemp industry was for decades collateral damage on the War on Drugs, and it is not clear that even with recent legalization it can fully recover. Hemp is bred to increase its value as a commodity, has only trace amounts of THC and is therefore non-psychoactive. In 1943, for example, when the United States lost access to raw materials in Asian markets, U.S. farmers produced more than 150 million pounds of hemp on 146,200 harvested acres. Although it is an important agricultural crop, it was largely prohibited under U.S. law because it is made from the cannabis plant. The DEA argued, for example, that marijuana can be hidden in hemp fields, although cross-pollination would reduce the desired qualities of both plants. Although the United States is the largest consumer of hemp products, industrial hemp was not allowed to be grown commercially in the United States (although it could be imported under certain conditions). In contrast, about 30 other countries grow hemp, of which China is the largest producer. As several agricultural groups supported changing the prohibition of hemp cultivation, Congress enacted the 2014 Agricultural Act Section 7606, codified as 7 U.S.C. § 5940, which allows pilot programs to grow hemp. The 2018 Farm Bill deleted hemp and derivatives of cannabis with extremely low THC content, under 0.3% on a dry weight basis, from the definition of marijuana in the Controlled Substances Act. As a result, certain CBD products, produced in compliance with the Farm Bill, are no longer classified as marijuana. The FDA retains regulatory jurisdiction over both hemp and CBD products, although states are given primary responsibility to oversee production of hemp upon obtaining federal approval for plans to monitor and control production. As hemp can be cultivated easily and can be used in the production of fibers, paper, construction materials, and FDA-regulated products such as foods, nutritional supplements, and cosmetics, there has always been commercial support to legalize hemp, unlike with other marijuana products. The movement to legalize hemp picked up steam quickly when conservative politicians such as Senate Majority Leader Mitch McConnell also provided support. Policy arguments against hemp legalization in the only major industrialized nation to have prohibited it, were never strong and seem to have dissipated. (For more on hemp, *see* Chapter 11.)

§ 24–3 MARIJUANA AND POLITICS

A remarkable aspect of the political debate over marijuana is how much has taken place at the ground level rather than in legislatures, especially in Congress. Although the classification of marijuana as a Schedule I drug is the dominant factor in U.S. marijuana law, few bills that have addressed this issue have made it out of Congressional committee or have been debated on the floors of Congress. Likewise, most state legalization of marijuana has been the result of voter initiatives and referendums rather than bills initiated by legislators. Politicians apparently see great risks from being on either side of the marijuana debate. However, with Democrats gaining control of Congress in 2020, several marijuana reform bills have made more progress, such as the MORE Act and the Cannabis Administration and Opportunity Act, introduced in the Senate in 2021. These reform bills reflect a determination by Democratic party leaders to work together to advance comprehensive cannabis reform legislation.

The policy debate has seen an unusual alignment between political activists on the left and right—that is, marijuana activists and libertarians. Both groups emphasize marijuana as a victimless offense, if an offense at all, and one that should be left to the discretion of the adult consumer. This position has found support in state courts, such as Alaska, which found a constitutional privacy right for its residents to grow and ingest marijuana in their homes. *Ravin v. State*, 537 P.2d 494 (Alaska 1975). Likewise, some commentators have suggested that Supreme Court cases such as *Washington v. Glucksberg*, 521 U.S. 702 (1997) and *Lawrence v. Texas*, 539 U.S. 558 (2003) lay the foundation for a U.S. constitutional right to use medical marijuana for palliative care. So far, federal courts have not proved amenable to this argument but it remains a significant backdrop for legalization advocacy.

§ 24–4 MARIJUANA AND SOCIAL LIFE

In the socialization of young people, is marijuana a gateway to more dangerous drug use, such as heroin and LSD? Some studies suggest that marijuana use is correlated with the use of other illegal drugs. Columbia and University of Oviedo researchers in 2015 estimated that 44.7% of individuals with lifetime marijuana use progressed to other illicit drug use at some time in their lives. Other researchers have found little or no evidence that marijuana use leads to subsequent abuse of illicit drugs. And if such a link exists, the mechanism of causation could still be in dispute. For example, does marijuana use create a craving for more intense euphoria and hence more dangerous narcotics? Or is marijuana correlated with hard drug use precisely because it is illegal, in that adolescent users are forced into contact with underground traffickers who then push more dangerous narcotics? Empirical evidence is difficult to come by, given the difficulty of controlling for all possible factors. 2013 and 2015 studies by the Colorado Department of Public Health and Environment found that marijuana consumption by Colorado high school students stayed steady or declined slightly after legalization. Another issue with legalization is whether or not recreational marijuana use is addictive. The National Institute on Drug Abuse claims, supported with a good deal of evidence, that marijuana use can lead to the development of problem use, known as marijuana use disorder, which takes the form of addiction in severe cases. Marijuana use disorders are often associated with dependence, in which a person feels withdrawal symptoms, including irritability, mood and sleep difficulties, decreased appetite, and cravings.

Mexican drug cartels (DTO's—drug trafficking organizations) were estimated by drug enforcement agents to derive 30 percent of their revenue from marijuana sales in 2014. Legalizing marijuana could reduce these DTO revenues and consequently the trafficking violence that has plagued Mexican and U.S. societies (assuming legalization schemes do not impose such high taxes that the illegal alternative continues to flourish). The Congressional Research

Service in a 2020 report projected a continued decline in U.S. demand for Mexican marijuana because drugs other than marijuana would predominate. This is due perhaps to legalized marijuana in U.S. states and Canada reducing its value as part of Mexican trafficking organizations' distribution. However, DTO's may find new ways of profiting from the loss of the marijuana trade, e.g., by promoting more dangerous drugs such as heroin, to fill the void.

Finally, designer drugs known as "synthetic marijuana," or "synthetic cannabinoids," a mix of man-made chemicals that mimic the effects of THC, such as Spice and K2, have become popular with young users, despite their harmful properties. Legalization and increased availability of marijuana may decrease the popularity of these synthetic drugs that appear to carry substantially greater dangers than marijuana itself.

§ 24–5 MARIJUANA AND THE CRIMINAL JUSTICE SYSTEM

As to the criminal justice system, proponents of legalization can point to the high number of arrests for marijuana activity, averaging about 700,000 arrests per year. Opponents of legalization point out that few of these arrests result in incarceration, except for large-scale traffickers; most users are routed to court supervision and drug treatment.

The United States has the highest incarceration rate in the world. With some 5% of the world's population, it houses about 25% of the world's prison inmates. 2014 statistics indicate that of 700,993 arrests in the U.S. for marijuana activity, 619,809 were for possession only (88%). The statistics are similar for the decade 2001 to 2010 with 8,244,943 arrests for marijuana, of which 7,295,880 (88%) were for possession alone. In 2018, there were more than 663,000 marijuana-related arrests made in the United States; more than 608,000 (91.7%) were for marijuana possession only. In 2019, there were 545,602 marijuana-related arrests, 500,395 of which for possession; in 2020, 350,150 marijuana-related arrests, 317,793 of which for possession. In addition, there is evidence of racial bias in marijuana arrests. Although studies show marijuana use by black and white populations to be roughly similar, the arrest ratio of blacks for marijuana use is higher. For example, in 2010 blacks were arrested for marijuana use at the rate of 716 per 100,000 of the black population, while whites were arrested at a rate of 192 per 100,000 of the white population, an arrest ratio 3.73 times higher.

Opponents of legalization point to the low incarceration rate for everyday users. It is estimated that about 40,000 federal and state inmates are incarcerated for marijuana offenses, less than 3% of the total prison population. The Bureau of Justice counted only 0.1% of people in state prisons in 2004 as serving sentences for first-time marijuana possession and only 1.4% of inmates were for offenses involving only marijuana crimes. Of the inmates who were convicted of marijuana offenses alone, the vast majority were sentenced for large-scale production or distribution, not for everyday possession or consumption.

Nevertheless, the collateral consequences of even minor marijuana violations can be life-changing, resulting in loss of a driving license, a professional license, or license to do business with the government; federal housing; government food and cash assistance; college loans; and parental rights; denial of a firearms permit; and deportation. Although a conviction for marijuana possession may not result in immediate incarceration, it may be counted in a habitual offender or recidivism sentence, contributing to lengthy incarceration.

An argument for legalization involves an apparent police practice of pretextual stops. Because marijuana is widely used and capable of detection by sight and odor, it can serve as the pretext for a police stop. These stops can be pretextual if used by police not to find marijuana but to allow searches for other evidence. At least one court suspected that police commonly fabricate testimony of detecting marijuana as a pretext for further police activity. *United States v. Nielsen*, 9 F.3d 1487, 1489 (10th Cir. 1993). Pretextual stops seem to correlate to racial disparities. Numerous studies have found that black Americans are more likely to be stopped by police than white Americans. In some states, legalization has removed suspicion of marijuana possession alone as providing probable cause for a police stop, thereby reducing the probability of pretextual stops.

Under an "expressivist" theory of law, that is, that law sends social messages, the spectacle of mass arrests for what seems to many the use of a relatively harmless substance—legal in some jurisdictions but a felony in others—could diminish respect for the system of criminal justice. On the other hand, some argue that in an American culture which has long cited the dangers of mind-altering substances and has devoted large resources to eradicating their abuse, the sight of numerous people intoxicated from marijuana could undermine the belief in the capacity of law to uphold common values.

§ 24–6 MARIJUANA AND THE ENVIRONMENT

The Office of National Drug Control Policy and other opponents argue that marijuana cultivation has an adverse effect on the environment due, for example, to deforestation and use of pesticides, herbicides, and fungicides. The National Park Service estimates that it costs from $14,900–$17,700 per acre to restore parkland after illegal marijuana growth is eradicated. Indoor grow operations using high intensity light bulbs consume large amounts of electricity and water. Like other agricultural operations, marijuana cultivation releases fertilizer greenhouse gases and chemicals. However, advocates of legalization argue that legalizing marijuana would alleviate the environmental strain caused by surreptitious cultivation and cross-border smuggling. For example, legalization encourages open, outdoor cultivation, which benefits from solar energy and rainfall. Regulations could be enacted to encourage environmental friendly practices, such as labeling low greenhouse gas marijuana, taxing peak hour electrical use, and licensing energy efficient production.

Marijuana cultivation can strain the water supply of certain states. In California, marijuana is often grown in remote, forested watersheds and may require almost 22 liters of water per plant a day during the growing season. A particular problem in the state are "trespass" growers: cultivators operating unlicensed farms on public lands. There is some evidence that appropriation of water by these cultivators is having detrimental impacts on California populations of Coho salmon and steelhead trout. Moreover, trespass growers use high amounts of pesticides and rodenticides, which has been linked to the deaths of fish, birds, and mammals. Large-scale outdoor cultivation can cause soil erosion and deforestation.

§ 24–7 MARIJUANA AND SOCIAL JUSTICE

In many ways, the decades long war on drugs became a war on marijuana in the 1990s. Several studies have found that since 1990, the primary focus of the war on drugs shifted to low-level marijuana offenses. For example, from 1990 to 2002, 82% of the increase in drug arrests nationally was for marijuana offenses, and virtually all that increase was in possession offenses. The total number of marijuana arrests more than doubled in that period, from 327,000 in 1990 to 697,000 in 2002, an increase of 113%. All non-marijuana drug arrests increased by only 10%. By 2002, marijuana arrests constituted nearly half (45%) of the 1.5 million drug arrests annually; marijuana arrests in New York City grew from 774 in 1991 to 18,000 in 1997 to 50,000 by 2000.

As a result of the damage inflicted on minority communities, cannabis reform legislation usually includes a social justice element. The most recent and significant cannabis reform bill illustrates this well. When U.S. Senators Cory Booker, Ron Wyden, and Chuck Schumer, introduced their comprehensive cannabis reform legislation in summer, 2021, they framed the new bill explicitly in terms of social justice.

> The War on Drugs has been a war on people—particularly people of color. The Cannabis Administration and Opportunity Act aims to end the decades of harm inflicted on communities of color by removing cannabis from the federal list of controlled substances and empowering states to implement their own cannabis laws. . . . By ending the failed federal prohibition of cannabis, the Cannabis Administration and Opportunity Act will ensure that Americans—especially Black and Brown Americans—no longer have to fear arrest or be barred from public housing or federal financial aid for higher education for using cannabis in states where it's legal. State-compliant cannabis businesses will finally be treated like other businesses and allowed access to essential financial services, like bank accounts and loans. . . . The Cannabis Administration and Opportunity Act includes restorative measures to lift up people and communities who were unfairly targeted in the War on Drugs. The bill automatically expunges federal non-violent marijuana crimes and allows an individual currently serving time in federal

> prison for non-violent marijuana crimes to petition a court for resentencing. The legislation also creates an "Opportunity Trust Fund" funded by federal cannabis tax revenue to reinvest in the communities most impacted by the failed War on Drugs, as well as helping to level the playing field for entrepreneurs of color who continue to face barriers of access to the industry. Importantly, the legislation also ends discrimination in federal public benefits for medical marijuana patients and adult use consumers.

As expressed in the above quote, social justice has become an essential component of the debate over cannabis. Cannabis reform thus includes ameliorating penalties and collateral consequences that have an outsized impact on minority populations; expunging the records of those convicted of cannabis crimes; and providing reparations for the impact of the War on Drugs. As a further example, the MORE act, perhaps the most significant marijuana reform bill introduced into the 116th Congress (2019–2020), proposed removing marijuana from the Controlled Substances Act and eliminating criminal penalties for individuals who manufacture, distribute, or possesses marijuana. The MORE Act was reintroduced into Congress in early 2021 and passed the House Judiciary Committee in a 26–15 vote on September 30, 2021, The bill would provide social justice initiatives including the following:

- establish a trust fund to support various programs and services for individuals and businesses in communities impacted by the war on drugs,

- prohibit the denial of federal public benefits for certain marijuana-related conduct or convictions,
- prohibit the denial of benefits and protections under immigration laws on the basis of marijuana-related conduct or a conviction,
- establish a process to expunge convictions and conduct sentencing review hearings related to federal marijuana offenses, and
- direct the Government Accountability Office to study the societal impact of marijuana legalization.

The interplay between cannabis law and racial issues is topical given the ferment over racial divisions, especially as it relates to police enforcement, that erupted in the United States in spring and summer of 2020. Studies have indicated the existence of racial disparity in arrests for marijuana possession. However, several commentators have warned that legalization of cannabis could perpetuate racial disparities in both enforcement and legal commercial use, for example, by disqualifying individuals with criminal records from operating marijuana businesses, or by allowing established, white-owned businesses to monopolize the cannabis market. A January 2021 study estimates that Black Americans constitute merely 1.2% to 1.7% of marijuana business owners.

To a large extent because of racial disparities, the New York County District Attorney's Office (Manhattan) in August 2018, announced it would no longer prosecute minor marijuana crimes. In addition, numerous prosecutors' offices throughout the country have stopped prosecuting minor marijuana crimes. These prosecutors' offices include those in Nashville, in Baltimore, in two Northern Virginia counties, in Marion County, Indiana, in Livingston County, Missouri, in Douglas County, Kansas, in Jefferson County, Kentucky, in the Ohio cities of Columbus and Cleveland, in Gwinnett, Cobb and Richmond Counties, Georgia, in Kalamazoo, Michigan, and throughout Florida, Delaware, and Texas.

Recognizing the toll that the war on drugs has taken on minority communities, several jurisdictions are considering reparations through marijuana revenues. For example, Evanston, Illinois voted in November 2019 to divert adult use cannabis funds to a separate fund for reparations to African American residents and entrepreneurs. Social equity licensing programs aim to increase minority-owned cannabis businesses. Likewise, several commentators have called for abolition of "collateral consequences" for drug offenses, including deportation for non-citizens, as these collateral sanctions make re-entry into society for those convicted of drug offenses extremely difficult and may contribute to recidivism.

§ 24-8 THE CHANGING TERMS OF LEGALIZATION

Arguments for legalization depend in part on a more precise understanding of how controlled substances are regulated. These arguments will also be affected by empirical studies of marijuana use in states that have now legalized.

§ 24-8.1 LEGALIZATION AND CONTROLLED SUBSTANCES

Although the marijuana debate is usually presented as "for" or "against" legalization, it depends more precisely on an understanding of the nature of controlled substances regulation. In a sense, controlled substances are neither uniformly legal nor illegal. Rather they are "controlled"—that is, legal only if FDA-approved and prescribed by a physician, or otherwise permitted by the DEA. Marijuana is only "illegal" because as a Schedule I drug it cannot be legally prescribed and is not FDA-approved. However, in certain circumstances the DEA has permitted marijuana consumption as well as scientific research into its properties.

Therefore, arguments as to legalization of marijuana are actually arguments over how (and whether) it should be classified as a controlled substance. If reclassified as a Schedule II substance, it would remain highly regulated but could be prescribed by a physician if it received FDA approval. If it is reclassified to Schedule III, some of the laws that the federal government has enacted in its "War on Drugs" would no longer apply—such as Internal

Revenue Code section 280E, which forbids deductions for businesses that trade in Schedule I or II drugs. (*See* Chapter 20.)

Nevertheless there seems to be little prospect that DEA would remove marijuana products from schedule I if not approved by the FDA. And there are tremendous hurdles to the FDA approving whole plant marijuana, as opposed to single molecule synthetic cannabinoids, which are easier to test and quantify. For example, it is difficult to deliver a consistent dose via inhalation of marijuana, which limits FDA's ability to approve research. Existing regulatory structure in place under the DEA and FDA impose barriers that hamper research into marijuana's risks and benefits. Even if marijuana were removed from the Controlled Substances Act altogether, the FDA, due to the United States Federal Food, Drug, and Cosmetic Act, would still play the dominant role in approving the distribution and marketing of marijuana products for human ingestion. FDA approval is necessary to satisfy the United States Federal Food, Drug, and Cosmetic Act (FDCA), 21 U.S.C. ch. 9 § 301 et seq., without which dietary and health products are precluded from the stream of commerce.

If marijuana remains in any of the five federal schedules, it would remain illegal for recreational use. If marijuana were removed from the schedules altogether, it would no longer be a federally controlled substance. It would then no longer require FDA approval and could be used without medical prescription—much like herbal supplements. But even in that case it could still be highly regulated by law, as alcohol is. For example, almost every proposal for legalization would still restrict the use of marijuana by minors or by those required to exercise psychomotor skills safely, such as in driving a vehicle or operating machinery.

As the legal systems of the United States overlap geographical areas, the most important legal question concerning marijuana reform is jurisdictional. Most of the discussion above involves legalizing marijuana at the federal level. But it may be sufficient for marijuana advocates if voters legalize marijuana in the vast majority of states, for both medical and recreational purposes, without changing federal law. This would have the benefit (or danger) of allowing marijuana to bypass the expensive FDA approval process. If so, it would seem necessary to codify the DOJ's recent policy of conditional non-enforcement, for example, with legislation that allowed states to opt out of the CSA. A step in that direction has already been taken with Congressional defunding of DEA crackdowns on state medical marijuana and hemp cultivation programs.

This also raises the fundamental question as to whether marijuana law should be nationalized. States can be permitted to have different legal regimes as to marijuana, reflecting the notion that states are a laboratory for social policy. But as marijuana is easily portable and easily trafficked, there is an inevitable tension with marijuana being legal in some jurisdictions and not others. (*See*

Chapter 14 for discussion of interstate legal disputes over conflicting state regimes.)

§ 24–8.2 EMPIRICAL EVIDENCE

Much of the debate over legalization of marijuana has been conducted on a theoretical level. With the legalization of recreational marijuana in such states as Washington and Colorado, more empirical data is available to answer some of the pro and con arguments. However, the conclusions from statistical studies themselves can be contested, in part because they are distorted by the presence of a majority of states which still criminalize marijuana, and the federal restrictions as to marijuana use and research.

With legalization, these states have an even stronger interest in resolving the details of the marijuana debate. For example, the Colorado legislature has established the Retail Marijuana Public Health Advisory to develop a systematic, unbiased view of scientific evidence for marijuana health effects. This commission has already issued reports on eight specific health topics as to marijuana use (during pregnancy and breastfeeding; unintentional exposures in children; use among youth; drug interactions; neurological effects; respiratory effects; extrapulmonary effects; marijuana use and injury), with more to follow. It is likely that additional studies of this nature will inform the public policy debate going forward. A particularly contentious issue is whether legalization leads to more motor vehicle accidents. Studies on this are mixed. A 2017 study published in the American

Journal of Public Health found that three years after recreational marijuana legalization, incidents of motor vehicle crash fatality rates for Washington and Colorado did not differ statistically from those in similar states without recreational marijuana legalization. Other studies, however, have found that crashes increased as much as 6% in Washington, Oregon, and Colorado, compared to neighboring states that have not legalized marijuana.

A 2016 comprehensive study from the Cato Institute found that states' legalization of marijuana had only a modest effect on marijuana use and very little effect on the price of marijuana. Studying evidence from some of the earliest states to legalize recreational marijuana, Colorado, Washington, Oregon, and Alaska, the study found increasing marijuana use is correlated with lowered opposition to legalization and a lessened perception of the riskiness of using marijuana. Legalization also had very little effect on overall suicide rates, crime statistics, traffic fatalities, or standardized test scores in each state. However, state tax revenue rose sharply in Colorado, Oregon, and Washington after legalization. Thus the study found there is, overall, little support for extreme statements by either supporters of marijuana legalization or its detractors.

CHAPTER 25

FOREIGN LAW APPROACHES

§ 25-1 INTRODUCTION

The regulation of cannabis is a global phenomenon, as is marijuana consumption. Reflective of its worldwide prevalence, cannabis goes by distinctive names such as weed, marijuana, hashish, ganja, hierba, bhang, kief, maconha, charas, and the like. (This chapter generally refers to marijuana as "cannabis" to reflect international law usage.) The U.N. Office on Drugs and Crime 2020 World Drug Report estimated that 192 million people used cannabis in 2018, corresponding to 3.9 percent of the global population. Historically, cannabis consumption has had many purposes, including medicinal. On the Indian subcontinent, cannabis is part of the traditional Ayurvedic systems of medicine, a use that was accommodated in the first international anti-drug regimes. Cannabis was significant in ancient Chinese medicine and agricultural production as well; manufactured hemp fibers dating back 12,000 years have been excavated from an archaeological site in what is now Taipei, Taiwan. Cannabis, including its psychoactive component THC, has also been excavated from a 2,700-year-old temple in the Negev Desert. Cannabis has traditionally been smoked, as well as consumed it in various other manifestations, e.g., as a beverage mixed with foods such as curry.

Over the last hundred years, nations have coordinated efforts to prohibit cannabis cultivation, possession, consumption, and trade. They have signed treaties, including the 1961 Single Convention on Narcotic Drugs, the 1971 Convention on Psychotropic Substances, and the 1988 United Nations Convention Against Illicit Traffic in Narcotic Drugs and Psychotropic Substances. Under these treaties, member nations are obligated to enact and enforce laws to restrict cannabis activity and to cooperate in combating international cannabis trafficking. As explained further in Chapter 10, these treaties permit "production, manufacture, export, import, distribution of, trade in, [and] use and possession" of cannabis in medical and scientific contexts only.

In the last few years, however, nations such as the United States, the Netherlands, Portugal, Spain, Uruguay, and Canada have experimented with decriminalization or legalization of recreational cannabis in various manifestations. Many nations are bound by the anti-cannabis provisions of the global drug treaties, so there has been little actual legalization of cannabis. And yet, several countries have de facto allowed for cannabis to be sold and consumed by individuals in limited amounts through decriminalization and non-enforcement. Their experiences have been closely examined for insights as to the future of cannabis regulation, as well as to gauge international reaction to their efforts.

Few countries have challenged the treaties directly. However, since the treaties by and large do not mandate specific penalties for violation, countries may claim compliance even if they impose light sentences on cannabis use or, more controversially, permit remedial measures (e.g., entering a substance abuse program) rather than criminal sanctions. These mitigating practices have come under sharp criticism by the U.N. agencies tasked with monitoring compliance with the drug treaties. Nevertheless, there are now calls for modifying or amending the international agreements. Given the complexity of treaty amendment, and the apparent opposition of most of the world's nations, such modifications would be arduous.

This chapter summarizes the law of cannabis outside of the United States and surveys trends in international enforcement. Section 25–2 takes a broad view, surveying the world's most populous nations, as well as those in the forefront of cannabis reform. And § 25–3 summarizes trends in foreign cannabis law and the reaction of U.N. monitoring agencies.

§ 25–2 CANNABIS REGULATION IN OTHER COUNTRIES

The 21st century has seen a new era in the international law of cannabis. In the last two decades of the 20th century, the Netherlands pioneered non-enforcement of "soft" drugs like cannabis. And in the first two decades of the 21st century, several nations have decided to decriminalize and even legalize cannabis. This section looks first at the laws regulating cannabis in the 10 most populous countries in the world (excluding the United States, the subject of other chapters of this book). It then looks at some additional countries that are unique players on the international cannabis scene.

§ 25–2.1 CANNABIS REGULATION IN THE 10 MOST POPULOUS COUNTRIES

Almost every country in the world has enacted laws regulating the manufacturer, sale, possession, and consumption of drugs, and has applied criminal penalties to cannabis activity, in conformance with Article 36(1)(a) of the Single Convention and Article 3 of the 1988 United Nations Convention Against Illicit Traffic in Narcotic Drugs and Psychotropic Substances. Several countries allow for medical use of cannabis, in conformity with its classification in Schedule I of the Single Convention; other countries, such as the United States, have enacted more restrictive frameworks, consistent with its parallel listing under Schedule IV of the Convention.

In December 2020, the Commission for Narcotic Drugs, a United Nations commission with 53 member states, voted to remove cannabis from Schedule IV of the 1961 Single Convention on Narcotic Drugs. Although the vote is largely of symbolic significance, many countries look to global conventions for guidance on writing their drug policies.

Surveying the cannabis laws of the ten most populous nations in the world shows the wide range and extent of cannabis prohibition throughout the world.

China—Cannabis use is illegal in China and carries severe criminal penalties, especially for trafficking. Given its traumatic history with the Opium Wars of the 19th century, China reacts harshly to both domestic drug use and direction from the international community as to its drug laws. Execution of drug offenders was common until 2014.

As to international trade in cannabis, however, China is a leading cultivator and exporter of hemp, which is legal. In recent years, Chinese industrial farms have entered the global market for cannabidiol (CBD). In addition, China will undoubtedly play a large role in trade with countries that legalize cannabis because Chinese firms have filed many cannabis patents.

India—India has a long tradition of cannabis, which is reflected in the use of the term "India hemp" in the earliest international treaties and in the accommodations for cultural use. *Bhang, charas,* and *ganga,* as cannabis in several varieties is known in India, have been used in Hindu rituals and medicine. The 1961 Single Convention on Narcotic Drugs exempted cannabis leaves from control to accommodate India's bhang culture of mixing cannabis leaves with various drinks. Even though cannabis is currently illegal in India, the law is not fully enforced in some states, and in other states, cannabis is dispensed for certain purposes in government shops.

Indonesia—Cannabis is illegal for all purposes in Indonesia, as it is classified under the 2009 Narcotics Act as a Group I drug. Similar to Schedule I of the

U.S. Controlled Substances Act, Group I drugs have a high potential for abuse and addiction, and no medical benefits. Possession of cannabis in any amount is subject to lengthy imprisonment; in addition, trafficking is subject to lengthy imprisonment, heavy fines, and in sufficient quantities, capital punishment.

A highly publicized case is that of the Australian Schapelle Corby, who in 2004 was arrested at the Ngurah Rai International Airport in Indonesia with 4.2 kilograms of cannabis in a bag of which she disclaimed knowledge. She was sentenced to 20 years in prison, and was released after serving nine years. In 2015, Indonesia executed several international prisoners convicted of heroin-smuggling offenses (the "Bali 9"), including nationals of Brazil, the Netherlands, Australia, Nigeria, and the Philippines. This caused Australia, Brazil, and the Netherlands to recall their ambassadors.

Brazil—Possession and cultivation of cannabis in Brazil have been partially decriminalized, with civil penalties applied for small amounts. A 2006 drug law decriminalized cannabis consumption and personal cultivation, replaced strict sentences with warnings, community service, and educational measures, and helped alleviate Brazil's notoriously overcrowded prison system. Trafficking, however, is severely punished, as the 2006 law increased the minimum sentence for trafficking cannabis from 3 to 5 years (with a maximum of 15 years plus a fine). In December 2019, the National Health Surveillance Agency, or "ANVISA," granted regulatory approval for firms to produce medicinal cannabis-based products but maintained prohibitions on domestic cultivation of medical cannabis.

Pakistan—Located in the Indian subcontinent, Pakistan also has a long tradition of ritual and medical cannabis use. Pakistan is one of the world's largest producers of hashish, which is trafficked to other countries. Possession and consumption of cannabis are criminal offenses, and trafficking cannabis is subject to severe penalties, including capital punishment for large amounts. In September 2020, however, Pakistan approved domestication and commercialization of medicinal and industrial cannabis and hemp. Pakistan's Minister for Science and Technology tweeted that the reform positions Pakistan to enter the CBD industry.

Nigeria—Cannabis is strictly illegal in Nigeria, with no exemption for religious or medical use. Nevertheless, it is widely cultivated and trafficked throughout West Africa. Eradication of cannabis cultivation waxes and wanes with successive governments. The primary statute restricting cannabis use and cultivation is the 1966 Indian Hemp Decree (amended 1975 and 1984), which is enforced by the National Drug Law Enforcement Agency. Possession of cannabis can result in a prison term as lengthy as 12 years, while trafficking cannabis can result in life imprisonment.

Bangladesh—Although cannabis is illegal in Bangladesh, the prohibitions often go unenforced because of its traditional use on the Indian subcontinent. An annual festival in honor of a Shah

Sultan Balkh, a Sufi saint, that is held in Bogra is known for its use of cannabis by celebrants.

Russia—Cannabis is not historically prevalent in Russia. Although cannabis laws are strict, possession of small quantities has been partially decriminalized.

In 2018, Russia's World Cup Organizing Committee announced that it would permit visiting soccer fans to bring cannabis (and other drugs, including cocaine and heroin) into the country, so long as attendees have supporting medical documentations.

Japan—Hemp has long been manufactured in Japan. Hemp fibers have been found in archaeological sites dating back 10,000 years. In 1948, there were 25,000 cannabis farms in Japan. (A cannabis museum opened in 2001 in Tochigi Prefecture, the longtime center for cannabis farming.) However, in 1948, during the U.S. military occupation, Japan enacted the Cannabis Control Act, which applied strict criminal penalties for possession and required licenses for cultivating hemp. According to a 2018 report, only 34 cannabis cultivators remain in Japan.

Japanese cannabis laws are strict. The police eradicate about one to two million cannabis plants annually, wild-growing descendants of Japan's hemp legacy. Possession can result in five years' incarceration; illicit growing, seven years. Japan has one of the lowest rates of cannabis consumption at 0.1% of the population—about 2000 Japanese are sentenced yearly for these crimes. When seven ounces of cannabis were found in Beatle Paul McCartney's luggage in 1980, Japan jailed him for ten days and then deported him. Research into medical cannabis is also prohibited. Just hours after New York legalized recreational marijuana, the Consulate General of Japan in New York warned Japanese citizens and tourists not to use marijuana while in the state, as they could be punished under Japan's anti-cannabis law. The number of individuals involved in cannabis offenses has increased in recent years. According to a 2020 police report, 2019 saw a record-high of 4,321 cannabis involved individuals.

European Union—All of the nations belonging to the European Union are also signatories of the international drug treaties. Although the EU has no independent drug laws, it adopted a Resolution on Cannabis in 2004 urging member states to discourage personal use of cannabis through educational and training programs, and to act against internet sites that promote use of cannabis. In February 2019, the European Parliament adopted a resolution urging the European Commission and members state to develop a legal framework governing the use of cannabis for medical purposes. No EU-wide policy for medical cannabis has been enacted, as each member state has authority to decide whether the cultivation and use of medical cannabis is legal. The Council of The European Union, Council Resolution on Cannabis, Brussels, 7 July 2004, 11267/04 CORDROGUE 59.

§ 25–2.2 SIGNIFICANT COUNTRIES FOR RECENT CANNABIS REGULATION

The Netherlands—The Netherlands is the country most famous for allowing cannabis consumption. In fact, it is a popular misconception that the Netherlands has legalized cannabis. Because of the international treaties to which it is party, cannabis activity in the Netherlands remains officially illegal. However, the Netherlands adopted a non-enforcement policy for consumption of cannabis in "coffee shops," attracting an international tourist trade, which the Netherlands has recently tried to combat.

In 1972, the Netherlands reduced the offense of personal possession of cannabis from a felony to a misdemeanor. The amended Dutch Opium Act on Illicit Drugs of 1976, as part of a broader relaxation of its drug laws, allowed consumption of under five grams of cannabis to go unpunished. Likewise illegal but not punished is cultivation of small amounts of cannabis (five plants). However, the Netherlands continues to prosecute large-scale cannabis trafficking. Possession in excess of 30 grams can carry a two-year prison sentence and a substantial fine.

The Netherlands' notoriety as a cannabis destination is due to its "coffee shops," where sale and consumption of small amounts of cannabis are not penalized, both as to Dutch citizens and, until recently, to tourists. To mitigate its reputation for drug tourism, the Netherlands in the last few years has imposed stringent regulations on coffee shops.

For example, it has banned foreigners from buying cannabis, closed coffee shops located near schools, and forbidden coffee shops from advertising. As a result, the number of coffee shops has declined from a peak of 1,179 in 1997 to about 570 in 2019. There is disagreement as to whether these revisions reflect a failure of the Netherlands' lenient cannabis policy or external pressure from the International Narcotics Control Board and neighboring countries.

Although the Netherlands has signed all three international drug treaties, it has retained some flexibility by making a reservation to certain provisions, such as Article 3 of the 1988 United Nations Convention Against Illicit Traffic in Narcotic Drugs and Psychotropic Substances, which required drug use to be "specifically a criminal offense."

Spain—Although possession and use of cannabis is illegal in Spain, courts have ruled that consumption in limited quantities does not represent a punishable crime, spurring the growth of Spain's "cannabis social clubs." Cannabis clubs are private establishments and thus granted an exception from public prohibition. The clubs provide an allocation of cannabis to each member for strictly private use. The allocation includes both growing and distributing cannabis for the members, somewhat similar to a food cooperative. Members of the club pay dues for the cost of growing cannabis (but not for buying cannabis directly) and upkeep of the clubs. Organized as a federal union, the clubs also provide premises and paraphernalia for consuming cannabis. Although vaguely reminiscent of the infamous opium dens of the 19th century, the clubs may be luxuriously appointed and are secure and discreet. The clubs are required to carefully police their membership, and cannabis cannot be distributed outside of the club or consumed in public. Although membership rolls were originally limited to Spanish residents, the laws governing club membership are ambiguous. In recent years, clubs have increasingly catered to tourists.

Barcelona is home to between 200 and 350 clubs, an estimated 70 percent of clubs in Spain. However, the city's cannabis industry has recently faced a number of legal setbacks. In 2017, the Superior Court of Justice of Catalonia overruled a Catalan law stating that the private consumption of cannabis by adults is part of the fundamental right to free personal development and freedom of conscience. Although the Barcelona clubs still operated under a city law, the Court overturned it in in 2021, holding that city regulators were not competent to legislate on cannabis policy, as it is a matter governed by the state.

Despite the existence of these clubs, Spain plays a major role in fighting cannabis trafficking. Most cannabis and cannabis resin trafficked into Europe originates in Morocco and passes through Spain. According to the European Drug Report of 2021 the European Union countries reported that in 2019, law enforcement made 326,019 individual seizures of cannabis resin (465,404 kg) and 313,272 seizures of cannabis herb (147,650 kg). Authorities made 187,328 cannabis resin seizures in Spain, and

143,922 cannabis herb seizures. Most of the supply originates in Morocco, and smaller quantities arriving from Afghanistan, Lebanon, and Pakistan.

Portugal—Although many nations have decriminalized cannabis, Portugal is the first nation to do so in the context of openly and systematically decriminalizing drug use. In 2001, Portugal enacted statute 30.2000 decriminalizing all drugs, including heroin, cocaine, and cannabis. Decreto-Lei 30/2000 [Decree Law 30/2000], DIÁRIO DA REPÚBLICA de 29.11.2000 (Port.). Portugal claims to be in compliance with the Single Convention because it did not legalize cannabis and other drugs, but subjected cannabis users to administrative, although not criminal, sanctions. These administrative remedies include fines, classes, community service and mandated treatment. A 2009 report by the Cato Institute (Glenn Greenwald, "Drug Decriminalization in Portugal: Lessons for Creating Fair and Successful Drug Policies") found that drug usage in Portugal has since declined in comparison with other European Union nations. Moreover, the number of Portuguese adults (age 15 to 64) who report experimenting with cannabis in their lifetime is a good bit lower than the share of Europeans who report the same: 11 percent of Portuguese adults compared to 27.2 percent of EU residents.

Uruguay—Uruguay can perhaps be considered the first country to officially legalize cannabis, with a law that took effect in 2014. Uruguay admitted that it was abrogating its formal duties under the international treaties and deciding to legalize cannabis, reasoning that its commitment to human rights overrides its treaty obligations. Specifically, Uruguay claimed that legalization was necessary to (1) reduce exposure to more harmful drugs; (2) synchronize the legal framework to enable users to grow, as well as to consume, cannabis; and (3) increase public access to medicinal cannabis. In place of penalties, Uruguay introduced an extensive regulatory scheme, governing cannabis from "seed-to-sale." A newly formed governmental agency, the Institute for Regulation and Control of Cannabis, oversees cultivation, sale, use, import and export of cannabis. Pharmacies employ biometric fingerprint scanners to identify authorized buyers. Adults are permitted to register to buy cannabis in limited quantities and to grow up to six plants. They also can join private cannabis clubs, which consist of with up to 45 members, and each member is entitled to 480 grams of cannabis annually. However, to avoid drug tourism or conflict with neighboring countries, cannabis can be sold only to Uruguayan citizens and residents, not to foreign visitors or for export.

The government taxes cannabis production and sales and tightly controls cannabis dispensaries and prices. Although the Uruguay legalization statute, 19,172, was enacted by the General Assembly and signed by the president, a survey by America's Barometer estimated that as many as 60% of the general population disagreed with legalization. The U.N. International Narcotics Control Board (INCB) attempted to meet with Uruguayan legislators to halt the legislation, but was rebuffed. Although the INCB has described Uruguayan legalization as a direct violation of international law, it has not imposed any sanctions. In January 2021, the INCB issued a press release publicizing its continued engagement with the Government of Uruguay on drug control matters.

Morocco—Morocco is a major producer and exporter of cannabis. Most of this cannabis is processed into hashish resin or oil and trafficked to Europe, where it is estimated to provide about 60 to 70% of European supply. In Morocco itself, cannabis is illegal. Nevertheless, consumption of cannabis and hashish, known as *kief*, has long been part of Morocco's religious rituals and culture, smoked in a pipe or mixed into food. The Moroccan government has taken successful steps to reduce the cultivation of cannabis. In 2018, the United Nations Office on Drugs and Crime reported that Morocco was a source of cannabis resin to a large share of countries in North Africa (80 percent of cannabis seized) and Western and Central Europe (41 percent of cannabis seized).

Jamaica—Jamaica's approach to cannabis is significant because Jamaica has legalized Rastafari ritual cannabis use, and because of the popularity of cannabis-laced lyrics in reggae music. Additionally, in 2015, the Jamaican Parliament legalized medical cannabis and industrial hemp. It decriminalized possession of 2 ounces (56 grams) of cannabis and cultivation of five or fewer plants per household. The law also established the Cannabis Licensing Authority, which ensures the lawful regulation of the cannabis industry for medical, therapeutic, and scientific purposes.

U.S. Neighbors—As the United States' North American neighbors, the cannabis regimes of Mexico and Canada are of particular import to the study of international cannabis law and policy by American law students. Mexico has always been a leading source of cannabis consumed in the U.S., and for that reason U.S. drug enforcement has been active at both the border with Mexico and in working with Mexico's law enforcement to suppress the Mexican cannabis supply. Although Canada also shares a long border with the U.S., there is no large-scale cannabis trafficking between the two nations. Like the United States, Canada is attempting federal cannabis prohibitions with provincial and municipal legalization. In particular, Canada is considered to have one of the most successful medical cannabis systems in the world. Each nation will be discussed separately, below.

Mexico—Mexico may raise the most complex questions about cannabis of any nation. Mexico, is one of two nations (along with Morocco) that traditionally supplies cannabis to other nations. Mexico supplies the United States, almost exclusively. Mexico's battle against cannabis trafficking is thus intertwined with the interests, attitudes, and influence of its powerful northern neighbor. The connection between the United States' "War on Drugs" and the Mexican drug cartels, which have become increasingly violent in the last few decades, has been much debated.

Mexico must also take into account the views of its own citizens as to domestic legalization; Mexico has a relatively low rate of cannabis consumption, and polls indicate that a majority of Mexicans oppose legalization. Although cannabis is illegal in Mexico, possession of up to 5 grams of cannabis is permitted under the national health code.

Mexico may decline as a major source of American cannabis, as cultivation is legalized in American states. In 2011, the United States border patrol seized 2.5 million pounds of cannabis crossing the border from Mexico. In 2015, the figure had fallen to 1.5 million pounds. In addition, under the *Merida* initiative, paid for by the United States, the Mexican army confiscates and burns large quantities of cannabis crops.

In recent years, Mexico has made strides toward cannabis legalization. In November 2015, the Mexico Supreme Court held that prohibition of personal production, possession, or consumption of cannabis infringes the constitutional right of the "free development of personality," although it is not clear how extensively this judicial rule will be applied. In June of 2017, President Enrique Peña Nieto signed a decree legalizing medical cannabis with broad support from Mexico's Senate and Lower House of Congress. In November 2018, Mexico's Supreme Court struck down laws prohibiting the recreational use of cannabis, finding that such laws infringe a person's fundamental right. In March 2021, Mexico's Chamber of Deputies, the lower chamber, passed a bill to legalize production of cannabis for industrial, medical, and recreational purposes. It provides that anyone in Mexico over the age over the age of 18 will be able to purchase and possess less than 28 grams of cannabis, though possession of a higher amount is still prohibited. The bill was expected to pass the Senate and to be signed by President Andrés Manuel López Obrador but expired at the end of the legislative session. On June 28, 2021, the Supreme Court voted 8–3 to legalize adult use marijuana.

Canada—Canada has made steady progress toward legalization in recent decades. Although the 1996 Controlled Drugs and Substances Act, S.C. 1996, c. 19 (Can.). outlawed cannabis, access to medical cannabis was formalized in the 2001 Marihuana Medical Access Regulations (MMAR), which permitted cannabis for end-of-life patients and patients with debilitating symptoms resulting from medical conditions. The MMAR was replaced by the Marihuana for Medical Purposes Regulations (MMPR) on April 1, 2014.

In response to the Canadian Federal Court of Appeals decision in *Allard v. Canada*, FC 236 (2016), invalidating the MMAR, the Canadian Minister of Health instituted new regulations effective August 24, 2016—the Access to Cannabis for Medical Purposes Regulations (ACMPR). Under the ACMPR, Canadians can grow a limited quantity of cannabis for their own medical purposes, if authorized by a health care practitioner, or purchase cannabis from one of 34 producers licensed by the Canadian health department. "Dispensaries" and "compassion clubs" remain illegal.

In 2018, the Cannabis Act, S.C. 2018 c. 16 (Can.) legalized recreational cannabis. Adults are now permitted to possess, carry and share with other adults up to 30 grams of dried cannabis, Moreover, Canadian are permitted to grow a maximum of four homegrown cannabis plants per household in most provinces.

As with the United States, individual provinces and municipalities in Canada have taken the lead in decriminalizing and even legalizing cannabis by local law. In 2015, Canada's newly elected liberal government promised wide-ranging legalization of cannabis. By April 2016, Canada's Minster of Health stated at the United Nations General Assembly Special Session on Drugs (UNGASS) that legislation to legalize cannabis will be introduced in 2017. Then, in 2018, Canada passed legislation legalizing cannabis.

§ 25–3 FOREIGN LAW TRENDS

The recent trends towards liberalization of cannabis laws should not obscure the fact that most of the world's governments, at least officially, stand solidly behind the anti-cannabis strictures of the international treaties with no indication of imminent change. In fact, many nations, particularly in Africa and Asia, have cannabis prohibitions, especially as to trafficking, that exceed what is required by international law. Some 32 countries retain capital punishment for at least some form of cannabis trafficking; for example, Singapore permits capital punishment for trafficking as little as 500 grams of cannabis. (Mandatory capital punishment was eliminated in 2013.) Whether these strict penalties are causal or not, Singapore has perhaps the lowest cannabis consumption rate in the world, estimated at about .004% of the population. In the Philippines, anger towards illicit trafficking, drug gangs, and drug-fueled government corruption erupted in 2016, spurred on by President Rodrigo Duterte, with the vigilante killing of thousands of accused drug dealers.

International drug treaties allow use of cannabis for "medical purposes." Art. 2(5) and Art. 4(c) of the 1961 Single Convention on Narcotic Drugs. Prominent jurisdictions that have legalized cannabis for medical and scientific purposes include Canada, Israel, Chile, the Czech Republic, France, Germany, Switzerland, the Netherlands, the United Kingdom, and a majority of the states of the United States, although not the federal government itself. In November 2016, Denmark announced a four-year trial to allow citizens with certain illnesses to consume cannabis, and Australia amended its laws to allow cultivation to provide a domestic supply of medicinal cannabis.

Nations have taken different approaches to defining medical purposes, as contemplated by the inclusion of cannabis in both Schedule I and the more restrictive Schedule IV of the 1961 Single Convention. For illegal drugs in general, the Convention focuses less on medicinal benefits than on the regulation of consumption of narcotics necessary to alleviate withdrawal by addicts—a criterion less relevant to cannabis consumption.

In January 2019, the Expert Committee on Drug Dependence of the WHO made a series of recommendations to the United Nations to update the scope of control of cannabis and cannabis-related substances to reflect the emerging therapeutic role of cannabis-based medicine. In December 2020, the WHO's Commission on Narcotic Drugs voted narrowly (27 in favor, 25 against, one in absentia) to remove cannabis from Schedule IV of the 1961 Single Convention on Narcotic Drugs—where it was listed alongside dangerous, addictive opioids, including heroin, recognized as having little to no therapeutic purposes. The United States voted to remove cannabis from Schedule IV of the Single Convention while retaining them in Schedule I, stating that it is "consistent with the science demonstrating that while a safe and effective cannabis-derived therapeutic has been developed, cannabis itself continues to pose significant risks to public health and should continue to be controlled under the international drug control conventions".

Rather than openly flouting their international treaty obligations, nations have devised ways to allow possession and consumption of limited amounts of cannabis, usually less than 5 grams, under the theory that this makes a distinction between everyday street users and large-scale sellers and traffickers. Italy, for example, decriminalized small amounts of cannabis as far back as 1973, and this trend has accelerated in recent years. For example, starting in 1987, four Australian jurisdictions decriminalized growing a limited number of plants, imposing only a small fine. And cannabis clubs, which allow for pooling of resources to grow and consume cannabis, have proliferated in such countries as Spain, Belgium, and Germany, despite questionable legal status.

Although few governments have expressed open opposition to the international cannabis regime, it is possible that a desire to liberalize cannabis laws may lead to more open confrontations with treaty obligations. This might take several forms. As noted above, the 53 Member States of the CND, the UN's central drug policy-making body, voted to remove cannabis from Schedule IV, the most restrictive category under the Single Convention, and could recommend that cannabis be removed from the schedules altogether. This rescheduling required only a majority vote, whereas amending U.N. drug treaty requires unanimity. The CND could vote to remove cannabis from Schedule I, but given consistent WHO reports as to the dangers of cannabis, this seems unlikely. The signatory nations might also vote to amend the treaties by their own authority in order to mitigate cannabis prohibitions. But given continued opposition by the majority of governments to relaxing cannabis restrictions, especially as relating to trafficking, this seems even more unlikely.

Under international law, nations when ratifying treaties can also make reservations, which exclude the legal application of enumerated provisions to that nation. *See, e.g.*, Single Convention, Art. 4, §§ 11–12. Because of fears that broad cannabis prohibition would interfere with traditional health practices,

India and Pakistan made such reservations to clauses in the Single Convention forbidding nonmedical use of cannabis. Likewise, the Netherlands made a reservation to Article 3 of the 1988 Convention, which required signatories to include personal consumption of cannabis as specifically a criminal offense under domestic law. Thus, the Convention allowed that "the Kingdom of the Netherlands accepts what is stipulated only insofar that the resulting obligations comply with the national criminal law and the national criminal policy."

However, reservations cannot be made after accession to the treaty. Single Convention, Art. 50(1). As almost all nations have already signed or acceded to the treaties, this would require a nation to denounce the treaties ("denouncing" being the technical term for withdrawing from a treaty), and then re-accede to the cannabis provisions with reservations. Denunciation is procedurally a simple process, requiring only a written statement addressed to the Secretary-General of the United Nations; re-accession, however, is complicated.

In order to protect indigenous tribes' consumption of the coca leaf, Bolivia, for example, denounced the Single Convention. In fact, it submitted its re-accession instrument on Dec. 29, 2011, before its denunciation even went into effect (Jan. 1, 2012), and the U.N. recognized the re-accession on January 11, 2013. However, this is a very cumbersome and disruptive process, and therefore it is unlikely that most countries will go through it. In addition, such an action is likely to bring major repercussions to the denouncing nation, if not formal sanctions, such as ostracization from the world drug regime and intense pressure from neighboring countries.

For these reasons, challenges to the international treaties so far have largely been in the area of technical compliance. In other words, states have maintained that by decriminalizing cannabis, or selectively not enforcing its punishments, they are still in broad compliance with the treaty obligations. Uruguay has taken this argument to its furthest limit by claiming a human rights necessity to legalize and regulate cannabis.

The U.N. officials charged with implementing the international treaties have responded with alarm to cannabis liberalization, seeing a threat to their carefully and well-established international drug regime. For example, in a 2008 report, the executive director of the U.N. Office on Drugs and Crime, Antonio Maria Costa, wrote:

> Cannabis is the most vulnerable point in the whole multilateral edifice. In the Single Convention, it is supposed to be controlled with the same degree of severity as cocaine and the opiates. In practice, this is seldom the case, and many countries vacillate in the degree of control they exercise over cannabis. Even worse is the persistent habit in too many countries to change cannabis-related policies as coalitions alternate in power: this leads to confusion in public opinion, leaving it with the false impression that this drug is not dangerous for health. As a

> consequence, cannabis remains the most widely produced and the most openly used illicit drug in the world. Unless we face this issue squarely, and rebuild an international consensus on how to tackle cannabis multilaterally, we risk ruining the whole system.

United Nations, Commission on Narcotic Drugs, 51st Session "Making Drug Control Fit for Purpose: Building on the UNGASS Decade": Report by the Executive Director of the United Nations Office on Drugs and Crime as a Contribution to the Review of the 20th Special Session of the General Assembly (March 7, 2008). The UN Commission on Narcotic Drugs' 2020 decision to remove cannabis from Schedule IV of the 1961 Single Convention on Narcotic Drugs, however, shows that liberalization efforts have considerable momentum and may well alter international treaty obligations.

In summary, disagreements as to whether and how to maintain the international regime against cannabis are surfacing. The United States was foundational to enforcing the worldwide ban on cannabis. In fact, the United States went beyond its international obligations in outlawing medical cannabis, and in influencing an ally like Japan to do the same. As of 2021, eighteen states in the United States, along with Canada and several countries in Latin America and Western Europe, are pioneers in legalizing adult recreational cannabis. Nevertheless, two important facts must be kept in mind. First, the international treaties prohibiting cannabis are difficult to modify without United Nations approval, which requires the support of a majority of signatory nations. Second, that majority seems nowhere on the horizon, due to the determination of the INCB and many nations in Asia and Africa to maintain strict prohibitions.

CHAPTER 26

MARIJUANA IN AMERICAN CULTURE

§ 26–1 INTRODUCTION

This chapter describes marijuana in American culture, while noting ramifications for its evolving legal status. Section 26–2 looks at cultural perceptions of marijuana. Section 26–3 looks at marijuana in American arts and entertainment and sports. Section 26–4 looks at marijuana in the counterculture. And § 26–5 looks at changed attitudes towards marijuana in recent years.

§ 26–2 CULTURAL PERCEPTIONS

Cultural views of marijuana have played an important role in its legal status. Initial perceptions of marijuana as a foreign, poisonous weed contributed to its prohibition as a dangerous drug. Its alien status was seemingly confirmed by its adoption—often under colorful nicknames—by jazz musicians and beat poets. Federal campaigns against marijuana in the 1930s and 1940s were associated with salacious movies that depicted marijuana as a narcotic of the lascivious, the crazed, and seducers of American youth. Public intellectuals by contrast praised marijuana for expanding consciousness and transgressing norms. When embraced by the 1960s counterculture, and associated with the hippie and antiwar movement, marijuana became a proxy for protest—and the Nixon administration struck back.

Nixon's domestic policy advisor John Ehrlichman later told a journalist that criminalizing marijuana allowed the administration to disrupt the anti-war movement. Marijuana was classified under Schedule I of the newly enacted CSA in 1970, with the most dangerous narcotics. As drug use proliferated with middle class youth, law enforcement proclaimed marijuana prohibition as a lynchpin of the War on Drugs, linking marijuana trafficking to the international drug cartels. More liberalizing social mores in recent decades explain in part the growing acceptance of legalized marijuana in modern America.

At least three reasons help explain the close linkage of perceptions of marijuana to its legal status. First, marijuana is an ancient herb that grows easily—"weed"—and has been cultivated and consumed in cultures throughout the world. In 2020, archaeologists determined that cannabis, including its psychoactive component THC, had been used in a 2,700-year-old temple in the Negev Desert. This constitutes the first evidence of psychotropic drugs being used in early Hebrew worship. The Hindu *Atharva Veda* invokes cannabis as one of five sacred plants. Cannabis was cited for its healing properties in the ancient Chinese medical book, the *Shennong Bencaojing*, and written recordings to marijuana's healing properties in Chinese literature date to at least the 15th century BC and perhaps a thousand years earlier. The warriors of the 12th century Islamic Assassin sect were rumored to be inflamed by hashish, from which their name may derive. With this long cultural history, cannabis has been subject to a multiplicity of images and associations.

Secondly, cannabis is a complex plant, with approximately 525 identified chemical constituents, including at least 144 cannabinoid compounds, producing a variety of psychoactive effects. THC is the most prevalent cannabinoid in marijuana followed by CBD (cannabidiol). Two cannabinoids growing in popularity are CBN (cannabinol) and CBG (Cannabigerol). Research on cannabis has been varied and inconclusive. In the absence of scientific consensus, cultural attitudes fill the void. Third, because of its variety of cannabinoids, flavonoids, terpenes, and terpenoids (the interaction of which is referred to as an "entourage effect"), marijuana is an idiosyncratic intoxicant. It induces different reactions in individuals. Perhaps for this reason celebrities such as Louis Armstrong, Alice Toklas, Margaret Mead, Allen Ginsberg, and Willie Nelson have expressed their affection for marijuana.

Perceptions of marijuana as an alien and destructive agent contributed to its prohibition in the early 20th century. The armies of the bandit-general Pancho Villa, who raided New Mexico in 1916, were reputed to be emboldened by smoking cannabis. One version of the famous *corrido* song *La Cucaracha* bemoans a soldier who is bereft his customary dose of marijuana ("La cucaracha ya no puede caminar, porque no tiene, marihuana que fumar.") In the western states, where marijuana was first prohibited, it was linked to Mexican culture and Mexican immigrants. The word "marihuana" is itself derived from Mexican usage, as are such nicknames as oregano, marimba, Rosa Maria, Mary Jane (*María Juana*), toke (*toque*), Acapulco Gold, porro, mota, bacha, and sinsemilla. The association between Mexico and marijuana contributed to racist sentiments and hence its prohibition. For example, a Texas state senator justified the passage of Texas's first anti-marijuana law in 1919 because "all Mexicans are crazy, and this stuff is what makes them crazy."

§ 26–3 MARIJUANA IN THE ARTS AND ENTERTAINMENT

Marijuana's status as a forbidden drug enabled it to attain cult status in 20th century American entertainment. In music, it signified that jazz, blues, and rock defied convention. In imaginative literature, it stood for altered consciousness and a rebellious lifestyle. In movies it became a pervasive and even comic element of modern American life.

§ 26–3.1 MARIJUANA IN AMERICAN MUSIC

Marijuana found a natural home in American jazz, pop and rock music. Marijuana was forbidden but friendly; it was underground, defying convention but not debilitating. Musicians claimed that it boosted their creativity, although it also led to some notable troubles with the law.

Jazz originated in turn-of-the-century New Orleans, in Storyville, the legalized red light district. Sailors and immigrants from the Caribbean brought marijuana into the thriving and cosmopolitan port of turn-of-century New Orleans. Jazz musicians gathered in Storyville bordellos to play music all night, many smoking cannabis because they thought it did not have the somnolent effects of alcohol, and might even enhance their ability to perform into the night. When the prostitution houses of Storyville were closed in 1917 by order of the U.S. Navy, jazz musicians spread across the country, with marijuana hitching a ride. Moving to New York City, the great jazz trumpeter and pop singer Louis Armstrong encountered Mezz Mezzrow, a clarinetist who supplied high quality Mexican marijuana to musicians in Harlem, as Mezzrow recounts in *Really the Blues* (1947). His nickname "Mezz" became a code word for marijuana, surfacing in numerous jazz songs. Louis Armstrong was also a steady client. Armstrong smoked marijuana, which he called "muggles," every day of his adult life, praising its relaxing qualities, unlike heroin which afflicted other jazz musicians.

The 1930s saw a sub-genre of jazz music celebrating marijuana—"viper songs." Marijuana laws were still relaxed and viper songs celebrated marijuana under transparent lingo and double entendres, such as "tea" and "muggles." Armstrong recorded "Muggles" (1928) and "Song Of The Vipers" (1934). The great jazz pianist and showman Fats Waller recorded "A Viper's Drag" (1934) and "If You're a Viper" (1943) ("Dreamed about a reefer five foot long/A mighty mezz, but not too strong/You'll be high/But not for too long/If you're a viper"). "Chant of the Weed" (1931) was the Don Redman Orchestra theme song; the orchestra also recorded "The Reefer

Man" (1932). Blues singer Bessie Smith, another daily marijuana smoker, recorded "Gimme a Reefer" (1933); Benny Goodman, "Texas Tea Party" (1933); Mezz Mezzrow, "Sendin' the Vipers" (1934); Ella Fitzgerald, "When I Get Low I Get High" (1936); Sidney Bechet, "Viper Mad" (1938); Duke Ellington, "Smoke a Little Tea" (1938); Barney Bigard, "Sweet Marijuana Brown" (1945); Julia Lee, "One Lotus Blossom" (1947); and Lalo Guerrero, "Marihuana Boogie" (1949).

The most flamboyant of viper singers was Cab Calloway, who recorded "The Man from Harlem" in 1932 ("I've got just what you need/Come on, sisters, light up on these weeds/and get high and forget about everything.") In the 1933 film "International House," Calloway and his orchestra perform "Reefer Man," a song about the hallucinogenic effects of marijuana, with Cab and band members writhing to the lyrics.

Armstrong commented in 1953 about the connection between marijuana and race. "It relaxes you, makes you forget all the bad things that happen to a Negro." He also decried a false connection between marijuana and harder drugs. "It pains me to see marijuana connected with narcotics," he wrote in his 1968 memoirs. "It's really a shame." In the 1930s, marijuana was not yet widely prohibited, but when Armstrong travelled to Los Angeles in 1931, he was arrested for marijuana possession and faced a six-month jail sentence. The judge, aware of his fame, suspended the sentence. Armstrong was only one of the first of many entertainers to be arrested for possessing marijuana. Gene Krupa was arrested in

1943; Anita O'Day in 1947; Robert Mitchum in 1948; Ray Charles in 1961.

By the advent of 1960s rock 'n roll, more potent drugs had become a mainstay of musicians, but marijuana was not displaced. Smoke-ins and smoke-fests of the 1960s combined rock music and marijuana consumption, often tolerated by the police. In the 1970s, Jamaican reggae musicians Bob Marley, Bunny Wailer, and Peter Tosh celebrated "ganja," their music attaining great popularity in the U.S. They were adherents of the Rastafari religion, which promotes the spiritual use of cannabis. Shortly after their formation as a band, the Grateful Dead played an "End Marijuana Prohibition" concert in San Francisco on May 29, 1966. The Grateful Dead continued to play to packed houses throughout the 70s and 80s, with occasional paeans to "Sweet Jane," the smell of marijuana wafting through the audience. Their most loyal fans were known as "deadheads," a term akin to "potheads." Jack Herer, author of the pro-marijuana manifesto, *The Emperor Wears No Clothes* (1985), proselytized for cannabis and hemp at Grateful Dead concerts. The Grateful Dead also helped popularize "4/20" as a signature for marijuana.

The British invasion of the 1960s revealed that marijuana laws were nearly as strict in the United Kingdom as they had become in the United States. British Detective Sgt. Norm Pilcher—a British Harry Anslinger of sorts—made high level marijuana arrests of the Rolling Stones Keith Richards and Mick Jagger in 1967 and the Beatles John Lennon in

1968 and George Harrison in 1969. Beatle Paul McCartney was arrested for marijuana possession in Sweden in 1972, in Scotland in 1973, in Los Angeles in 1975, in Japan in 1980, and in Barbados in 1984.

A British marijuana conviction almost got John Lennon and his wife Yoko Ono deported from the United States. Under § 212(a)(23) of the Immigration and Nationality Act (INA), an alien who has been convicted of marijuana possession is "excludable" from the United States. In 1968, the Scotland Yard Drug Squad found one-half ounce of hashish secreted in Lennon's London apartment. Although Lennon denied knowledge of the presence of the marijuana, he was convicted of possession and fined $150. Based on this conviction, U.S. deportation proceedings were launched in 1972 against Lennon and Ono, then residing in New York City. After several hearings, the Immigration Court on March 23, 1972 ordered Lennon deported (but not Ono, who had permanent resident status). Their fans responded with a "Let them Stay in the USA" campaign; the 1972 Lennon-Ono album "Sometime in New York City" included a petition to the INS. Numerous celebrities and artists, including Bob Dylan, Joan Baez, John Updike, Jasper Johns, Leonard Bernstein, Joseph Heller, and New York Mayor John Lindsay rallied to the cause. The "Let them Stay" campaign complained that the Nixon administration had chosen to deport Lennon because of his political views and protests of the Vietnam War.

The deportation order was appealed to the Second Circuit, which reversed it. In a highly technical opinion, *Lennon v. Immigration and Naturalization Service*, 527 F.2d 187 (2d. Cir. 1975), Judge Irving Kaufman found the British conviction insufficient to render Lennon an excludable alien. The British marijuana law lacked a mental requirement, imposing strict liability on any person found in possession of marijuana, regardless of knowledge. However the language of § 212(a)(23)—"any alien who has been convicted of a violation of . . . any law or regulation relating to the illicit possession of . . . marihuana" implied a requirement of *knowing* possession of marijuana. In addition, Judge Kaufman suggested that Lennon was being selectively deported due to "his political activities and beliefs." A vigorous dissent claimed that § 212(a)(23) should apply to all persons equally regardless of "whether he be John Lennon, John Doe or Johann Sebastian Bach." The dissent also disputed Kaufman's constricted reading of British precedents.

Reading past the obscurities of British *mens rea* law, it is fair to say that in the end the courts, perhaps bowing to public pressure, decided that the United States should not lose an internationally famous figure over a trifling conviction for marijuana possession.

Perhaps no genre of music has celebrated marijuana to the same degree as rap music. Rapper Snoop Dogg popularized "chronic" as slang for high-grade marijuana, as well as its status in hip-hop lifestyle. Snoop Dogg even claimed that he smoked marijuana in a bathroom in the White House, a claim that reflects both the historical association between cannabis and social protest, as well as the growing acceptance of marijuana in popular culture. Marijuana in hip-hop was more than a recreational drug—it had become a status symbol, like money and mansions that proved the rise from street life to the promised land of leisure, freedom, and sensual pleasure in an otherwise oppressive American society. Even the commercialization of marijuana has inspired rock musicians. In October 2016, the heavy metal band Testament recorded "Canna-Business," which celebrated the growing legal marijuana industry.

§ 26–3.2 MARIJUANA AND THE BEAT POETS

The black jazz counterculture of the 1930s and 1940s prefigured the Beat generation of the 1950s and the hippie culture of the 1960s. Marijuana traversed the same paths. Norman Mailer in his famous 1957 essay, "the White Negro," called marijuana the "wedding ring" of the union of black jazz and white bohemian culture. The great jazz tenor saxophonist Lester Young pioneered the phraseology and attitude of the 1950s hipsters, and so it is perhaps fitting that he links jazz marijuana culture and that of the Beat poets: he is reputed to have given Jack Kerouac his first taste of marijuana in 1941.

The Beat writers Allen Ginsberg, William S. Burroughs, Neal Cassady, Jack Kerouac, and Ken Kesey became marijuana adepts. Ginsberg was the most forceful advocate for cannabis legalization. In the November 1966 issue of *The Atlantic* magazine, he wrote a paean to marijuana, "The Great Marijuana Hoax." In this essay, Ginsberg hopes to cross the cultural divide between the Beat generation and the general public by effusing about the effects of marijuana. The public has been bamboozled by the Federal Bureau of Narcotics, he writes; marijuana expands consciousness and increases creativity, with no harm to the individual. Ginsberg rhapsodizes about smoking *ganja* in India, *kif* in the Arab world, marijuana in Mexico. If this essay were intended to proselytize for the pleasures of marijuana, it could not have been more ill-conceived: Ginsberg mocks Western medicine, police and judges, puritanical attitudes and patriotism in a rush of words that is meant to simulate a marijuana high. Although it is unlikely that Ginsberg made many converts among the establishment, these themes would become staples of the marijuana culture of subsequent decades.

§ 26–3.3 MARIJUANA IN AMERICAN FILM

Marijuana began as a villain in the movies and ended as a comedic hero.

In the late 1930s, anti-marijuana movies came to screen. Ostensibly intended to educate parents as to the dangers of marijuana, these films appealed to the prurient interests of viewers, with scenes of cavorting couples and lurid seductions. In *Marihuana* (1935), a young girl smokes marijuana and ends up having sex with her boyfriend and becoming pregnant. She moves on to heroin and becomes a hardened criminal. In *Assassin of Youth* (1937), based on the article of the same name by Federal Bureau of Narcotics Chief Harry Anslinger, a journalist investigates a marijuana gang trying to rob a young heiress of her fortune. In *She Shoulda Said No* (1949), also released as *The Devil's Weed*, a young woman falls in with a drug dealer. After smoking marijuana, she becomes sexually promiscuous. Only a 50-day jail sentence brings her to her senses, and she helps the police nab the drug dealer.

The most notorious of these marijuana exploitation movies is *Reefer Madness*, originally released as *Tell Your Children* in 1936 and re-released in 1939 as *The Burning Question*. In 1947, it gained wider release under the title *Reefer Madness*. In *Reefer Madness*, high schoolers are enticed into smoking marijuana. They are quickly hooked and engage in all-night parties, sex, and homicide. Several characters laugh maniacally as they descend into madness. In the 1970s *Reefer Madness* became a cult classic. Ironically it was featured in numerous marijuana decriminalization campaigns of the period, as audiences mocked its hysterical warnings and campy moralizing. A satirical musical version of *Reefer Madness* debuted on stage in 1998 with a televised adaptation in 2005.

By the 1970s, however, marijuana had become a movie punchline. A new genre of movies emerged—"stoner films"—in which protagonists navigate life in comedic fashion, enjoying marijuana euphoria. In their best known movie, *Up in Smoke* (1978), Cheech and Chong (Richard Marin and Tommy Chong) played comical "stoners," traversing the United

States and Mexico in search of high-grade marijuana, in the process getting friends and police officers high, often unwittingly. Decades later the *Harold and Kumar* movies from 2004 to 2011 continued the tradition of multi-ethnic "stoners" traversing a confused and hypocritical America.

§ 26–3.4 MARIJUANA IN AMERICAN SPORTS

Use of marijuana by professional athletes has long been banned. This ban was the result both of the illegality of marijuana and the general ban on performance-enhancing drugs. Drug testing of American athletes has been the norm from about the year 2000. Numerous athletes have been suspended or otherwise disciplined for marijuana use—some of these suspensions lasted for as long as a season, dislocating both collegiate and professional athletic careers. Perhaps the most famous athletes disciplined for marijuana include football receiver Randy Moss in 1995, football running back Ricky Williams in 2003, 2004, and 2006, and swimmer and Olympic Champion Michael Phelps in 2009.

However, the strict ban on marijuana in professional sports has been eroding over recent years for two reasons. Numerous studies have found that marijuana does not enhance athletic performance. And the rapid legalization of marijuana has removed the stigma, as well as legal repercussions, for its use. In 2020, Major League Baseball removed marijuana from its list of banned substances and the National Football League eliminated suspensions for positive marijuana tests.

In 2021, the National Football League mostly eliminated testing for THC. The National Basketball Association extended its policy of not randomly drug testing players for marijuana to the 2020–2021 season. However growing acceptance of marijuana use in American professional sports is not necessarily echoed on the international level. American sprinter Sha'Carri Richardson was given a one-month ban for testing positive for cannabis, preventing her from competing in the Tokyo Olympics held in summer 2021.

§ 26–4 MARIJUANA AND THE COUNTERCULTURE

Marijuana was an integral part of the 1960s counterculture. Rock musicians sang about it and audiences smoked it. It was said to enhance the sensations of free love. As with other illicit drugs, it symbolized protest against the establishment, repressed society, segregation and racial inequality, and the Vietnam War. "Turn on, Tune in, Drop out," a phrase popularized by Timothy Leary, captured the mood. As noted in chapter two, Leary was arrested in 1965 for possession of marijuana. This conviction, along with another conviction for possession in 1968, was reversed in *Leary v. United States*, which also held the Marihuana Tax Act unconstitutional.

The legal system took note in various ways of the bond over marijuana use formed between hippies and radical activists, of the growing use by middle class youth, and of the prevalence of marijuana in counterculture music. This is exemplified by the saga of John Sinclair. In an interweaving fashion, rock music, mass protests, pamphleteering, activism, and pressure on the courts influenced the course of marijuana law.

As recounted in Chapter 4, Sinclair was an activist and community organizer in Detroit, who in 1968 cofounded the White Panther Party to support the Black Panther Party in an "assault on the culture." (The White Panther Party later coalesced into the Rainbow People's Party.) During his imprisonment for possession of two marijuana cigarettes, he wrote *The Marijuana Revolution* to elicit support both for marijuana reform and for his freedom. *The Marijuana Revolution*, Pamphlet One of the Rainbow People's Party, aims to unite cultural hippies and radical activists through their common affection for marijuana.

Protests to free Sinclair had a direct impact on the law. At the oral argument of his appeal on November 2, 1971, his supporters raucously jammed the court room. After the hearing, his wife Leni stood outside the court house, bound and gagged, as political advocates made speeches on his behalf. Shortly thereafter, the Michigan Supreme Court ordered Sinclair discharged from prison. The court also found the Michigan Controlled Substances Act unconstitutional in classifying marijuana as a narcotic. After a lengthy review of the "true state of facts" as to marijuana, including its own scientific assessment, the Michigan Supreme Court declared the "relative harmlessness" of marijuana. *People v. Sinclair*, 194 N.W.2d 878 (1972). In celebration, the first Ann Arbor Hash Bash was held in April 1972; still going strong, the 50th annual Hash Bash held in April 2021.

In September 1972, the Ann Arbor city council decriminalized marijuana, the first city to do so. On September 29, 1972, Michigan District Court Judge S.J. Elden invalidated this ordinance as an unconstitutional "intrusion of the legislative body of Ann Arbor in the judicial functions of the state of Michigan." Nevertheless, the entire saga was a milestone and helped spur 11 states and several municipalities to decriminalize marijuana over the course of the 1970s.

§ 26–5 CHANGED ATTITUDES TOWARDS MARIJUANA

The cultural manifestations of marijuana reviewed so far represent depictions by those on the margins of society who relished the opprobrium of mainstream culture. As a result much of their descriptions of marijuana are celebratory. Even the anti-marijuana propaganda movies of the 1930s and 1940s were later embraced by the cannabis movement as reflecting the hypocrisy of the United States establishment. This favorable depiction of marijuana was counteracted not so much by cultural influences as by law enforcement, especially the DEA, which has been vocal in opposition. Certainly mainstream attitudes towards marijuana during this period were more in line with those of law enforcement, which saw psychoactive drugs, including marijuana, as a great danger to society. In other words there was wide popular support for maintaining marijuana as an illegal drug.

By the 1970s however marijuana had begun to migrate from groups on the fringes of society to the mainstream. A publication like *High Times*, published in 1974 as a one-time parody, flourished, and is still circulating. As the 1960s and 1970s generations aged, cultural perceptions of marijuana changed. By the 21st century many Americans saw marijuana not as foreign, subversive, and dangerous, but as a milestone of their experimental youth, which had not left lasting damage. In commerce, for example, the original trefoil logo of the Adidas sportswear company had been noted for its similarity to the cannabis plant, although coincidental. In April 2016, Adidas came out with a special edition "Happy 420" sneakers, made from natural hemp, with cannabis designs. The depiction of marijuana on the movie screen had progressed from sensationalist anti-marijuana movies of the 1930s through the outrageous but favorable *Cheech and Chong* movies of the 1980s, and later to the *Harold and Kumar* movies, and Ice Cube's *Friday* movies, where marijuana is mostly a comedic plot device. On television, the hit series, *Weeds*, revolved around a suburban family selling marijuana to make ends meet. In the film *Pineapple Express* (2008), a process server and a marijuana dealer flee from hitmen and a corrupt police officer who observed them commit a murder. Marijuana use is frequently portrayed as humorous throughout the film. *Workaholics* is an American television comedy originally broadcast from 2011 to 2017, Marijuana use is frequently an object of humor in *Workaholics*.

According to the Gallup poll, in the early 1970s about 83% of Americans thought that marijuana should remain illegal. But by 2011, a slight majority of Americans surveyed favored the legalization of marijuana. And by 2016, over 60% of Americans favored legalization. In 2020, the percentage of Americans favoring legalization reached 68%,

The change in cultural perceptions is well-illustrated in the travails of politicians who admitted to smoking marijuana. In earlier decades, exposure as consuming a Schedule I controlled substance would have ended any political career. After all, it is politicians and judges who made and maintained the harsh marijuana laws. But with the changing perceptions of marijuana, not only did admission of early experimentation with marijuana not curtail the careers of politicians, but some used it in an effort to obtain votes—a tactic unthinkable with other Schedule I drugs.

The list of politicians who have admitted to experimenting with marijuana is long. In 1987, federal judge Douglas Ginsburg withdrew his nomination to the Supreme Court in large part because of allegations that he smoked marijuana on several occasions. In recent years, however, such allegations have caused little damage to the careers of elected officials. Among the hundreds of politicians who have admitted to using marijuana with no apparent political repercussions are Vice President Kamala Harris, Arizona Governor Bruce Babbitt,

New York City Mayor Michael Bloomberg, New Jersey Senator Bill Bradley, New York Governors Andrew Cuomo, George Pataki and David Paterson, Vermont Governor Howard Dean, vice presidential candidate John Edwards (although he fell in disgrace for an extramarital affair), Speaker of the House Newt Gingrich, New Mexico Governor Gary Johnson, Ohio Governor John Kasich, Secretary of State John Kerry, New York City Mayor Ed Koch, Alaska Governor Sarah Palin, Rhode Island Senators Lincoln Chafee and Claiborne Pell (although students with marijuana convictions could be denied Pell grants to attend college), Vermont Senator Bernie Sanders, Pennsylvania Senator Rick Santorum, Texas Senator Ted Cruz, California Governor Arnold Schwarzenegger, and Minnesota Governor Jesse Ventura.

In the 2016 presidential primaries, many of the candidates had already admitted to experimenting with marijuana in their youth. In the September 16, 2016 debate among Republican presidential candidates, Jeb Bush announced that he had smoked marijuana twenty years before. Remarkably enough, reflecting the enormous change that had come about as to American perceptions of marijuana use, Bush apparently made the announcement to loosen his staid image and gain votes. As for the presidency, President Bill Clinton admitted to smoking marijuana as a student, although he "did not inhale." Both presidential candidates in 2000, Al Gore and George W. Bush, admitted they had smoked marijuana. Bush explained that he had recovered from his alcohol problem—no one seemed to care about his smoking marijuana. President Barack Obama also admitted to smoking marijuana. In fact, he is said to have belonged to the "Choom Gang," a group of high school friends who "choomed," that is, smoked marijuana. However, marijuana use is not disregarded for federal employees, especially at higher echelons. As recently as March 2021, the Biden Administration terminated five White House staffers over marijuana use.

CHAPTER 27
LOOKING FORWARD

§ 27-1 INTRODUCTION

At present, marijuana law in the United States is unstable and divisive. Looking forward, it is likely to change, although the contours of the change are uncertain. The trend towards liberalization of marijuana laws at the state level will likely continue, as evidenced by the November 2020 election cycle. In the last few years, the federal government has relaxed its prohibitions against marijuana to some degree, in the form of Department of Justice discretionary policy and Congressional budgetary legislation, although the federal government can easily reverse course here as well.

Change is likely to come in areas where there is a broad alliance in support and where inconsistencies in the law seem most evident. As to federal law, these areas include: 1) transferring marijuana from Schedule I to a less restrictive schedule, either by congressional amendment or Drug Enforcement Administration decision; 2) obtaining FDA approval of additional synthetic drugs derived from cannabis and the occasional drug comprised of an active marijuana derivative, such as Epidiolex; 3) streamlining regulations on cultivating hemp; 4) restricting the ability of the government to seize property under asset forfeiture laws; and 5) loosening restrictions on marijuana-related businesses in areas such as tax, banking, and federal bankruptcy law. The best indications of further change in these areas of law are the recent incremental changes that have already occurred. As to state law, more states are likely to legalize marijuana, for medical and perhaps recreational purposes also. If so, the United States may soon reach a tipping point where state legalization overwhelms the strictures of the Controlled Substances Act.

Section 27–2 of this chapter reviews the current state of uncertainty and flux in the law. Section 27–3 previews possible changes to federal marijuana law. And § 27–4 previews possible changes to state marijuana laws.

§ 27–2 LOOKING BACKWARDS

The uncertain situation over marijuana law is the result of the increasing disconnect between popular belief as to the relative lack of danger of marijuana consumption and the inertia of a drug regime that was consolidated in the 1970s with a view of marijuana as among the most dangerous of narcotics. The prospects of marijuana law reform reflect a reversal of how this regime was assembled. The drug regime is in a certain sense top-down. International agreements among nations, most importantly the 1961 Single Convention on Narcotic Drugs, require each signatory to outlaw production, possession, and distribution of cannabis, except for scientific and medical purposes. To comply, major nations have enacted laws prohibiting marijuana to a greater or lesser extent. The United States consolidated its variety of federal marijuana laws into one strict prohibition—classification of cannabis as a Schedule

I drug under the CSA, which permitted no exceptions for medical use and little for scientific research. The states followed suit, enacting their own versions of the Uniform Controlled Substances Act, which tracked federal law and enrolled marijuana as a Schedule I drug. State laws by definition applied to cities and localities.

Looking forward, it seems that the marijuana law regime will likely be reformed in reverse order. The pressure for reform is from the bottom up, from local activists, agricultural and commercial groups, and from marijuana consumers. This has translated into citizen-initiated ballot referenda, the main force driving medical and recreational legalization in states. That voters in many states can bypass their own legislatures (but not the U.S. Congress) through referenda explains in part why states are taking the lead in legalizing marijuana, and probably will continue to do so.

Although the federal government resisted state legalization to some extent, this resistance had become murky under the Obama administration, as the Department of Justice declared a more or less hands-off approach to state law. With the proliferation of state legalization, pressure is now on the federal government to reform its own marijuana laws, especially as to the scheduling of marijuana. The United States, a long time staunch opponent of relaxation of marijuana laws, is now at the forefront of marijuana reform, along with several nations in Western Europe and Latin America.

The international drug regime, under the custody of the United Nations, will perhaps be the last to change, if it changes at all. The majority of nations, especially those in Eastern Europe, the Middle East, Africa, and East Asia, remain committed to strong measures prohibiting marijuana, and the United Nations drug agencies remain committed as well. Nevertheless, if enough countries opt out of marijuana prohibition—openly, discreetly, or otherwise—international cannabis prohibition, at least in its present form, may eventually topple. A step in that direction was the United Nations vote to remove cannabis from Schedule IV of the 1961 Single Convention on Narcotic Drugs.

§ 27-3 LOOKING FORWARD—FEDERAL LAW

Although federal law has been consistent in maintaining a near absolute prohibition against marijuana activity since 1970, change may be forthcoming. If the federal law changes, it is likely to do so as a result of state legalization and dwindling popular support for strong measures against marijuana users. Specifically, the most significant ways in which federal marijuana law might change in the near future are 1) changes in the DOJ non-enforcement policy; 2) rescheduling of marijuana either by congressional amendment or DEA administrative action; 3) regularization of recent legislation that legalizes hemp production; 4) reform of the civil asset forfeiture laws; and 5) relaxing restrictions on marijuana-related businesses in areas such as taxation and banking. For the last few years

Congress has enacted incremental legislation in these areas, and these are likely to continue.

§ 27–3.1 DOJ NON-ENFORCEMENT

The DOJ non-enforcement policy as to state legalization is a matter of prosecutorial discretion. It is not enacted into law and can be changed by a new administration without the involvement of any other branch of government. It is hard to gauge what will be the position of any new administration. The Democratic Party platform calls for wide-ranging reform of marijuana law to allow legal marijuana businesses to operate without uncertainty and individuals to consume marijuana without fear of punishment. The Republican party has certainly been more ambivalent, with some party leaders asking to resume federal prosecution of marijuana dispensaries and businesses, regardless of state law.

However, it is unlikely that even the most law-and-order administration would reignite a total war on marijuana where it has been legalized by states, and resume all-out raids on medical dispensaries. A reversal of the DOJ non-enforcement policy would likely frustrate popular opinion. A survey, conducted by Pew Research Center from April 5–11, 2021, polled 91% of U.S. adults in favor of legal marijuana for medical and recreational use (60% support legal for medical use only and 31% support also for recreational use.). Reversal also may be inconsistent with the cooperative federalism envisioned by the CSA, especially if individual users are targeted. Traditionally, the federal government has prosecuted large-scale traffickers and drug cartels and left prosecution of everyday, street level marijuana activity to the states, with state enforcement accounting for 99% of the nation's marijuana arrests.

However, a Republican party return to congressional control in 2022 would probably slow efforts to codify recent DOJ policy, such as proposed Democratic bills to allow a state to opt out of the CSA's marijuana provisions.

§ 27–3.2 RESCHEDULING MARIJUANA UNDER THE CSA

The prospect of rescheduling marijuana from Schedule I is probably the most significant issue looking forward. The most controversial aspect of marijuana law has always been its placement under Schedule I, with Congress declaring marijuana to be equivalent to the most dangerous narcotic, that has no recognized medical value. If marijuana is rescheduled to any of the less restrictive four schedules, it will no longer be illegal for medical purposes. However a patient would still need a physician's prescription, and any marijuana products would first need FDA approval before they could become available by prescription.

Rescheduling at the federal level can happen in two ways. First, Congress, which placed marijuana in Schedule I, can amend the CSA to reschedule marijuana. Second, the DEA, the agency charged with administrative oversight of scheduling, can reschedule marijuana, after assessing data from other federal agencies as required by federal law. In either case, rescheduling would constitute the beginning of a new era in federal marijuana law—but one with its own set of questions and complexities as marijuana would remain a controlled and highly regulated substance. Even if classified in a less restrictive schedule, marijuana products would need to obtain FDA approval, itself an arduous procedure. In a sense, rescheduling can be thought of as transferring marijuana regulation from the DEA as a criminal enforcement matter, to the FDA, as a question of health evaluation and product approval.

Congressional Rescheduling

It is possible that Congress will reschedule marijuana in the near future. Since 1981 numerous bills have been introduced to Congress, mostly in the House of Representatives, to reschedule marijuana; all died quietly in committee. Recently, however, rescheduling bills have passed the House of Representatives and have been introduced into the Senate, a significant step.

With 36 states and the District of Columbia legalizing marijuana for medical use and 18 states and the District of Columbia legalizing marijuana for recreational use, the public attitude towards marijuana is shifting. Similarly, a number of recent bills, though largely unsuccessful to date, indicate that momentum for marijuana may be shifting at the federal level, as well.

Some bills aim to change the banking incentives around the marijuana industry. For example, the SAFE Banking Act (Secure and Fair Enforcement

Banking Act) seeks to prohibit banking regulators from sanctioning financial institutions that provide services to marijuana related businesses. H.R. 1595, 116th Cong. (2019). Other bills have focused on the tensions between state legalization of marijuana and federal criminalization. The STATES Act (Strengthen the Tenth Amendment Through Entrusting States Act) seeks to remove the prosecution of individuals for marijuana if they are in compliance with state law. S. 3032, 116th Cong. (2019).

Other bills target the social justice implications of the criminalization of marijuana. For example, the Marijuana Justice Act (S. 597, 116th Cong. (2019)) and the reintroduced MORE Act (Marijuana Opportunity Reinvestment and Expungement Act, H.R. 3617, 117th Cong. (2021) both seek to not only legalize marijuana, but also to expunge criminal records and create community reinvestment funds for communities that have historically been harmed by marijuana prohibition.

Finally, even some bills primarily related to COVID relief contained marijuana support. Although the 2020 CARES Act (Coronavirus Aid, Relief, and Economic Security Act, H.R. 748, 116th Cong. (2019)) excluded marijuana businesses from eligibility, the HEROES Act (H.R. 6800, 116th Cong. (2019)) in 2020 supported the SAFE Banking Act around marijuana banking reform.

The Compassionate Access, Research Expansion, and Respect States Act (CARERS Act), S. 683; H.R. 1538 was originally introduced in Congress in 2015 as S. 683; H.R. 1538 and has been reintroduced into the 116th Congress as H.R.127. It is one of the most important pieces of marijuana reform legislation introduced in Congress. Besides its strong bipartisan support, it emphasized the therapeutic value of marijuana—clearly the most popular tack and the most likely area of reform: legitimating state legalization of medical marijuana.

The aim of the CARERS Act is to "extend the principle of federalism to State drug policy, provide access to medical marijuana, and enable research into the medicinal properties of marijuana." It transfers marijuana from Schedule I to Schedule II status. It codifies the Obama Administration Department of Justice non-enforcement memoranda, in that it forbids enforcement of the CSA against persons who act in compliance with state marijuana laws. It prohibits regulators from punishing federally chartered banks for conducting marijuana-related business. It expands research opportunities and allows VA physicians to provide access to marijuana for veterans.

The Democratically-controlled House of Representatives passed the Blumenauer-McClintock Amendment in June 2019. Since 2014 the various Rohrabacher Farr amendments have prohibited the Justice Department from expending federal funds to prevent states from implementing medical marijuana programs. The Blumenauer-McClintock Amendment would extend that ban to protecting state recreational marijuana laws from federal prosecution as well. The Blumenauer-McClintock

Amendment was not taken up by the Senate however and faces an unlikely future to obtain the needed 60 votes needed for passage in the near future. The Marijuana 1-to-3 Act of 2021, H.R.365, proposes reclassifying marijuana to the less restrictive Schedule III, which would not only remove federal criminalization, but would exempt marijuana from IRS code § 280E, thereby allowing marijuana businesses to deduct ordinary business expenses from federal taxation.

On July 14, 2021, Senate majority Leader Chuck Schumer and Senators, Cory Booker and Ron Wyden introduced a proposed legalization bill titled "The Cannabis Administration and Opportunity Act." This extensive bill would remove marijuana and THC from the Controlled Substances Act. As such marijuana use would no longer be a federal crime, but the Food and Drug Administration would still be responsible for determining if it is safe to use. The bill would also impose a federal excise on marijuana sales, joining the number of states that already raise substantial revenue by taxing marijuana. As with many such bills being introduced, there is a social justice component, using a substantial portion of the revenue raised to support marijuana businesses owned by women and historically socially and economically disadvantaged populations. In addition, funding would be provided to states to expunge the records of persons convicted of state level marijuana crimes.

Whatever the fate of these various bills, they indicate the manner in which Congress is most likely to reform marijuana law: by allowing the states to serve as "laboratories of social change" as to medical and recreational marijuana, removing onerous federal restrictions on legal marijuana businesses, expanding access to marijuana by researchers, allowing veterans with post-traumatic stress disorder access to medical marijuana options in the Veterans Administration health system, and providing reparative relief and other social justice measures to disadvantaged populations.

DEA Rescheduling

The second pathway for rescheduling marijuana would be through the executive branch, that is, as an administrative decision of the DEA. However, in August 2016 the DEA formally denied a petition to reschedule marijuana for the fifth time since enactment of the CSA.

Rescheduling marijuana through this process is quite complex, as it involves the coordination of several administrative agencies, none of which so far has shown an inclination to approve rescheduling. (The DEA has taken in the past, 5 to 16 years to dispose of Petitions to Reschedule, and even then only when prompted by court orders.) The decision to reschedule is made by the Office of the Attorney General, which has delegated the decision to the DEA. 21 U.S.C. § 871(a); 28 C.F.R. § 0.100(b). After the DEA receives a petition to reschedule marijuana, it obtains medical input from the Health and Human Services Department, which is in turn delegated to the FDA.

When the medical report is received from HHS and FDA, the DEA evaluates the report and all other relevant data and makes an independent decision as to whether to reschedule marijuana.

However, there is some reason to think that the DEA may reschedule in response to a future petition for two reasons. First, the DEA loosened its restrictions significantly for the first time, even while denying the most recent petition. Notably, the DEA announced that it would "foster research" by expanding the number of DEA-registered marijuana manufacturers beyond the University of Mississippi, currently the only approved manufacturer of research marijuana, under a contract with NIDA (National Institute on Drug Abuse). As the DEA denied the petitions on the grounds that there are no rigorous, double-blind studies proving the efficacy of marijuana as medicine, additional research may induce the DEA to reverse this conclusion.

The second reason is that for the first time since its creation in 1973, the DEA is under pressure from the federal government itself to relax strict prohibitions against marijuana. This pressure is being exerted from the executive, congressional, and judicial branches. From the executive branch, this pressure is clear in the DOJ's acquiescing in state legalization of marijuana, a policy shift resisted by the DEA. It is also evident in the restrictions to the DEA budget imposed by Congress to limit DEA enforcement—the first laws enacted by Congress that relax marijuana laws even to a small degree. These restrictions include the 2014 Rohrabacher-Farr Medical

Marijuana Amendment which prohibits the DEA from employing its budget to combat state legalization of medical marijuana. Similar language in the 2015 through 2020 appropriations acts prohibit the DEA from employing funds to interfere with state legalization of hemp production and research.

A similar change can be seen in the federal judiciary, which in the past has upheld a strict interpretation of federal marijuana law. Decisions sympathetic to a more relaxed interpretation of federal marijuana law can be seen in cases such as *United States v. Marin Alliance for Medical Marijuana,* 139 F. Supp. 3d 1039 (N.D. Cal 2015) and *United States v. McIntosh*, 833 F.3d 1163 (9th Cir. 2016) (holding that the Rohrabacher-Farr Amendment prohibits the DOJ from prosecuting businesses or individuals acting in accord with state medical marijuana laws); and *United States v. Pickard*, 100 F. Supp. 3d 981 (E.D. Cal. 2015) (employing a "rational basis test" in ultimately upholding the CSA prohibition of marijuana).

The FDA and Rescheduling

Even if marijuana is rescheduled either by congressional or executive action, many questions remain. If marijuana were reclassified to Schedule II, marijuana would still be considered a drug with "a high potential for abuse," that "could lead to severe psychological or physical dependence," but has "currently accepted medical use in treatment in the United States." Marijuana products would still need to go through a rigorous process of clinical trials to be approved by the FDA and available for prescription. This might entail separate approval for edibles, tinctures, oils, and for various plant strains. However, research into marijuana would likely expand, and the pharmaceutical industry would be more likely to invest in research to obtain approval of cannabis products.

If marijuana were reclassified to Schedule III or lower, a significant change would arise in federal taxation of marijuana businesses. Currently, § 280E of the Internal Revenue Code denies a deduction for all expenses paid or incurred in connection with the trade or business of trafficking in controlled substances listed in Schedules I and II of the Controlled Substances Act. This provision falls especially hard on marijuana businesses legally operating according to state law, as they cannot deduct their ordinary business expenses, unlike other businesses. If marijuana were reclassified to Schedule III, this provision would no longer apply, although marijuana businesses might still have to contend with §§ 162(c) and 165 of the Internal Revenue Code, which prohibit deductions for certain illegal business expenses and losses. (*See* Chapter 20.)

It is important to note that rescheduling or removing marijuana from the CSA entirely would not remove marijuana from the FDA's purview. The Federal Food, Drug, and Cosmetic Act (FDCA) and the FDA would still factor into the distribution and use of marijuana products. Nevertheless, marijuana could be more widely marketed in herbal dietary supplements, which are subject to less FDA scrutiny.

Even if marijuana is not rescheduled, synthetic cannabinoids will continue to pass through the FDA pipeline. The FDA granted approval to Marinol (synthetic pill version of Delta-9-THC) in 1985, Cesamet (synthetic pill cannabinoid) in 1985 and 2006, and Syndros (liquid formulation of cannabinoid) in July 2016. Epidiolex is a cannabinoid pill, derived from the cannabis plant. It was approved by the FDA for treating epilepsy in 2018. Sativex is a cannabis-based oral spray that is approved in much of Europe for treating multiple sclerosis spasticity. It is currently in Phase III, the final phase of FDA clinical trials.

Although the DEA has argued that legalization of marijuana is unnecessary, given that the FDA has approved these synthetic products, many medical patients are unlikely to agree. Although the THC and cannabinoids in synthetic pills have a therapeutic benefit, they have shown themselves not to be fully effective in that they are expensive, slow acting, difficult to swallow if the patient has nausea, and compared with the marijuana plant, lacking the full "entourage effect" (*see* Chapter 2). In that sense they are unlikely to quench the demand for inhaled or edible marijuana.

§ 27–3.3 HEMP

It is almost certain that the steps that Congress has taken to legalize, regularize, and revive hemp cultivation will continue. Most states which have land suitable for hemp cultivation have legalized it under state law. Congress in the 2014 Agricultural Act § 7606, 7 U.S.C. § 5940, allowed pilot programs to grow hemp. In addition, Congress prohibited the DEA from expending funds to interfere with hemp cultivation in states where it is legal. A broad coalition of marijuana activists and agricultural and commercial concerns supported legalization of hemp. There was little substantive opposition to hemp cultivation, as hemp is not intoxicating, containing less than 0.3% of THC, and marijuana plants are unlikely to be hidden in hemp fields, given the adverse effects of cross-pollination. The long-standing opposition of law enforcement associations to hemp cultivation as undermining marijuana prohibitions did not prevail, and hemp was legalized in 2018.

Rules for full implementation of hemp legalization have not been finalized. States have been given primary responsibility to fashion their own hemp laws, consistent with federal strictures. As the states do so, there will be a need for more consistency of regulations on the federal and state level.

§ 27–3.4 ASSET FORFEITURE LAWS

Under federal and state civil forfeiture laws, assets can be seized and retained by law enforcement if there is evidence that they are being used in connection with illegal activities such as marijuana or drug trafficking, even if no criminal prosecution is brought against individuals. The DOJ estimates that in 2012, federal law enforcement seized $4.2 billion of assets. Asset forfeiture laws have been described by critics as rife with abuse and as "legal plunder." Like other marijuana-related issues highlighted in this chapter, there is a broad coalition lobbying to reform these laws, including civil libertarians, drug reform activists, and conservatives concerned about property rights. However, this issue extends beyond marijuana activity, and relates to all drugs and illegal activities in general.

Numerous bills have been introduced to reform civil asset forfeiture. Most commonly, they change the standard of evidence required for the government to retain seized assets. For example, under current federal law, assets are forfeited if there is a preponderance of evidence that the assets were used in connection with illegal drug transactions. Several bills propose changing the standard to require clear and convincing evidence. In addition, in January 2015 the Department of Justice announced temporary restrictions to federal-state equitable sharing of asset seizures.

Several states have reformed their forfeiture laws. For example, in 2015 New Mexico banned civil asset forfeiture, while Nebraska did so in 2016. Michigan limited civil forfeiture of assets in suspected drug cases in 2019.

§ 27-4 LOOKING FORWARD—STATE LAW

The main factor in the evolving landscape of U.S. marijuana law is legalization by the states, and by all indications, this trend will continue if not accelerate. There are numerous bills sitting in state legislatures to legalize marijuana, but future legalization in states is likely to be the result of voter initiatives rather than legislative action. This is how legalization has happened in the majority of states so far, and there is no reason to expect that to change—an example of direct democracy where politicians fear to tread.

In the November 2020 election cycle, voters in four states—Arizona, Montana, New Jersey, and South Dakota—approved statewide ballot measures to legalize marijuana for adult, recreational use. Voters in Mississippi and South Dakota, states that previously had stern across the board marijuana prohibitions, approved statewide ballot measures to legalize marijuana for medical use. With these initiatives, well over half of the states have medical marijuana, and 43% of Americans live in states with recreational marijuana. The results in California alone, constituting one-tenth of the nation's population and the world's sixth largest economy, may represent a sea change in American marijuana law.

The more states that continue to legalize marijuana, for either medical or recreational purposes or both, the more likely that the United States will reach a tipping point, where national legalization of marijuana is inevitable, either in fact or law. First, as more states legalize, pressure is put on other states to do so. Marijuana is a highly portable and profitable item. If it is legalized in one state, it is difficult to prevent marijuana from pouring over the border into a traditional criminalization state. States which attempt to retain marijuana prohibition can find themselves fighting a losing battle, with no compensating tax revenues to show for it. This was in large measure the message of the lawsuit that Nebraska and Oklahoma brought against Colorado in 2014, which was quashed by the U.S. Supreme Court. Although the Court found no justiciable issue, there is no denying that a patchwork quilt of some states legalizing marijuana and other states not, is inherently divisive and unstable. When the tipping point is reached, few states may be able to hold out.

Second, as more states legalize, pressure is put on the federal government to relax its strict prohibitions against marijuana. If the vast majority of states find medical and recreational benefits to marijuana, it would seem perverse for federal administrative agencies to declare otherwise. In addition, doing so would seem a pointless exercise, as almost all persons in the United States would have access to marijuana. Finally, the federal government lacks the resources to fight everyday crime without the cooperation of state enforcement. At the very least, if the federal government wanted to retain enforcement powers against large-scale trafficking and international drug cartels, it would be pressured to craft more narrow laws to do so.

The trend in states legalizing adult recreational use is to include provisions expunging criminal records of those convicted of minor marijuana crimes. Expungement means that those who apply and qualify can have their misdemeanor or felony convictions either reduced or totally erased from their record. For example, three states to recently legalize recreational, adult use—Vermont, Michigan, and Illinois—include expungement provisions for those who qualify. Expungement would eliminate many of the collateral consequences of a marijuana conviction.

Most of the reform marijuana legislation refers to marijuana substances with the term "cannabis" instead. This is in large part because of racist overtones perceived to be connected to the word "marijuana." As states reform their marijuana laws, and especially if the federal government joins the effort, it is likely that "cannabis" will replace "marijuana" in legal codes across the nation.

Finally, as more states enact a legalized regulatory scheme of marijuana, the current compromise between federal and state marijuana laws, which portrays itself as a form of federalism, would be undermined. The current theory is that states can legalize marijuana, in the face of federal prohibition, which is the supreme law of the land, because legalization does not present affirmative impediments to federal enforcement of the marijuana laws. As state regulatory schemes are expanded into positive assistance by the state, this view of federal preemption and federal-state cooperation would be threatened. For example, if states owned or operated marijuana production facilities, supplied medical marijuana to needy citizens, or to researchers, as the federal government does with the NIDA Program, or established employment and disability accommodation rights for medical marijuana users, courts might well find state officials in violation of the Controlled Substances Act, as creating a positive conflict between state action and enforcement of federal law.

APPENDIX

LEGALITY OF MARIJUANA BY UNITED STATES JURISDICTION AS OF SEPTEMBER 2021

Jurisdiction	Marijuana for Medical Use[1]	Marijuana for Adult Use[2]	High CBD, Low-THC[3]
United States			
Federal	No	No	Restricted[4]
Washington, DC	Yes	Yes	Yes

---

[1] Thirty-six states, D.C., and four territories have legalized medical use of marijuana purposes, including for pediatric patients. This column indicates states that have comprehensive medical marijuana programs for broadly defined health issues, but not states that limit medical use to High CBD, Low-THC (0.3%) products.

[2] Eighteen states, D.C., and four territories have legalized adult (recreational) use of marijuana, in varying amounts, for 21 years of age and older; these states retain medical marijuana programs as well.

[3] Forty-seven states allow High CBD, Low-THC products, although some states, marked restricted, impose limits to sone extent, which might include: only medical use, with physician recommendation; prohibit smokable CBD flower or the ingestion of low THC oil through vapor; prohibit sale of food or beverage infused with low THC oil, or as dietary supplements.

[4] At the federal level, there are no FDA-approved medical products (required under the FD&C Act) that contain CBD, other than prescription-only Epidiolex to inhibit certain childhood seizures. The FDA also prohibits sale of CBD products as dietary supplements or any food (including animal food) to which CBD has been added.

Jurisdiction	Marijuana for Medical Use	Marijuana for Adult Use	High CBD, Low-THC
<u>**State**</u>			
Alabama	Yes	No	Yes
Alaska	Yes	Yes	Yes
Arizona	Yes	Yes	Yes
Arkansas	Yes	No	Yes
California	Yes	Yes	Yes
Colorado	Yes	Yes	Yes
Connecticut	Yes	Yes	Yes
Delaware	Yes	No	Yes
Florida	Yes	No	Yes
Georgia	No	No	Restricted
Hawaii	Yes	No	Yes
Idaho	No	No	No
Illinois	Yes	Yes	Yes
Indiana	No	No	Restricted
Iowa	No	No	Restricted
Kansas	No	No	No
Kentucky	No	No	Yes
Louisiana	Yes	No	Restricted
Maine	Yes	Yes	Yes
Maryland	Yes	No	Yes

Jurisdiction	Marijuana for Medical Use	Marijuana for Adult Use	High CBD, Low-THC
Massachusetts	Yes	Yes	Yes
Michigan	Yes	Yes	Yes
Minnesota	Yes	No	Yes
Mississippi	No[5]	No	Restricted
Missouri	Yes	No	Yes
Montana	Yes	Yes	Yes
Nebraska	No	No	No
Nevada	Yes	Yes	Yes
New Hampshire	Yes	No	Yes
New Jersey	Yes	Yes	Yes
New Mexico	Yes	Yes	Yes
New York	Yes	Yes	Yes
North Carolina	No	No	Yes
North Dakota	Yes	No	Restricted
Ohio	Yes	No	Yes
Oklahoma	Yes	No	Yes
Oregon	Yes	Yes	Yes
Pennsylvania	Yes	No	Yes
Rhode Island	Yes	No	Yes
South Carolina	No	No	Restricted

[5] Ballot measure passed but invalidated by state supreme court, 5/21.

Jurisdiction	Marijuana for Medical Use	Marijuana for Adult Use	High CBD, Low-THC
South Dakota	Yes	No[6]	Yes
Tennessee	No	No	Yes
Texas	No	No	Restricted
Utah	Yes	No	Yes
Vermont	Yes	Yes	Yes
Virginia	Yes	Yes	Yes
Washington	Yes	Yes	Yes
West Virginia	Yes	No	Yes
Wisconsin	No	No	Restricted
Wyoming	No	No	Restricted
Territories			
American Samoa	No	No	No
Guam	Yes	Yes	Yes
Northern Mariana Islands	Yes	Yes	Yes
Puerto Rico	Yes	No	Yes
US Virgin Islands	Yes	No	Yes

6 Ballot measure passed but invalidated by state supreme court, 11/21.

INDEX

References are to Pages